Low-Carbing Among

By (alphabeti
Kent Altena (Aι
Judy Barnes Baker ⟨
Jennifer Eloff (Author and Editor)
Kyndra Holley (Author)
Carolyn Ketchum (Author and Editor)
Vanessa Romero (Author)
Low-Carb Friends

With contributions from
Tom Nikkola, Dr. Parker and Dr. Su

Canadian Cataloguing in Publication Data
Low-Carbing Among Friends (vol-3)
First Printing ~ December, 2012

Includes Index.
1. Low-carb diet recipes. 2. Sugarless recipes.
3. Gluten-free 4. Desserts, cooking and baking low-carb recipes.
5. Title 6. Low-Carbing Among Friends

Dedication: This cookbook is dedicated with love and grateful, humble thanks to God, to our family, friends and colleagues. Thank you also to all our fellow low-carbers who enjoy, participate in and buy these cookbooks. And we would also like to commemorate Dr. Atkins' lifetime commitment to the low-carb way of life; where would we all be without him?

Photography: Kent Altena, Judy Barnes Baker, Jennifer Eloff, Kyndra Holley, Carolyn Ketchum and Vanessa Romero
Amongfriends.us and Front and Back Cover Design: Jonathan Eloff
Printed by: A&A Printing, (http://printshopcentral.com/)

Pictured on front cover: Whoopie Pies (Kent Altena), Sour Cream Smothered Chicken (Kyndra Holley), Almond Flour French Toast (Carolyn Ketchum), Dairy-Free Sour Cream (Vanessa Romero), Creamy Strawberry Pie (Judy Barnes Baker), Peanut Butter Cups (Jennifer Eloff)

Published by **Eureka Publishing**

1

CONTENTS

INTRODUCTION

Low-Carbing Among Friends Vol-3 is the 3rd cookbook of a new collaborative, low-carb, team-based cookbook series, whose recipes are 100% low-carb, wheat-free, sugar-free AND also Gluten-free! The 1,111 innovative recipes are designed by professionals to help you get your figure and health back, whilst enhancing your enjoyment of food – and returning some of your old favorite treats to you! *Low-Carbing AmongFriends is a most unique cookbook series.* Since all of the cookbooks in this series can only be purchased online at: www.AmongFriends.us or: www.Amazon.com/shops/eureka_publishing, we've designed these books as hybrids, printing them as perfect-bound paperbacks (or as coil-bound). Since color photos would raise the price too much (top 20, LC books on Amazon have none), we instead showcase some 450 beautiful color photos for Vol-1, 2 & 3 online at: www.AmongFriends.us (click the "RECIPES" button) and many more in blogs and at: www.facebook.com/LowCarbingAmongFriends where you also can meet our authors and interact with them – and all this in a $20 cookbook. *That's truly unique!* The team Facebook page is unique in many ways. All of our authors post there regularly and are accessible to you. In addition, though Facebook has no easy-to-use INDEX of posts with a text SEARCH feature to find previous posts that have disappeared off of the main page, we do. On our main page, below the photos of the team, is a graphic blue "F" which links to: amongfriends.us/FBindex.php and there you will find a full index of all our team's historic Facebook posts, with a familiar text SEARCH capability, from GOOGLE, as well as a well-organized INDEX (like in a book) with FB posts sorted into categories to make life easy. And to the LHS of that link is a PHOTOS link which hosts several ALBUMS of well-categorized photos, so it's easy to SEARCH our FB page graphically. amongfriends.us/addendum.php lists PDF's of the Indexes of all these books for easy searching (use FIND feature). If you are beginning to get the sense that these cookbooks are awesome low-carb resources, you're right ... but there's more! Each team member makes it easy to navigate from our team Facebook page directly to their BLOGS or Facebook pages, opening up an even larger treasure chest of knowledge and recipes. Our website www.amongfriends.us has a list of *Common Supplies* as well as a *Bios* button with links to all the past and current contributors. All in all, you get a truly awesome package deal when you buy our team's books and become a low-carb friend. That brings me to a very important feature of these cookbooks - the Friends' section! We have set aside a section of each book for you to share your favorite recipes, if you like, with this team and its circle of low-carb friends. You see, we all understand that it's not just us that have all the best ideas – sometimes our low-carb friends truly amaze us with their innovative ideas, but they cannot write a whole cookbook. We remedy that, by giving them space in a book, full credit and a free cookbook. With Vol-4, we will switch formats to organize all recipes by category only rather than by author and by category. We are constantly adapting to meet the needs of you ... our Low-Carbing Friends.

ACKNOWLEDGMENTS

I, the publisher, want to take this opportunity to personally thank the team, to tell them how proud we all are of them for all they have done for the low-carb world! We want to acknowledge and warmly thank our low-carbing friends and family members for their support in helping this cookbook become a reality. We want to remember Dr. Atkins who left us with an amazing low-carb diet legacy.

Tiki Byrd at Low Carb Tiki (http://lowcarbtiki.blogspot.com/)

Ivonne Carlo at (http://www.ivonnecarlo.com/) – photography)

Char Cunningham (Charski) at (http://lowcarb4life.proboards.com)

Dottie, Administrator at Low Carb Friends (http://lowcarbfriends.com)

Christine F at (http://www.lowcarbcrock.com/)

Linda Sue Genaw at Linda's Low-Carb Menus & Recipes (http://www.genaw.com/lowcarb)

Susie T. Gibbs at Fluffy Chix Cook (fluffychixcook.blogspot.com)

Barbara (Barbo) Goldstein at (http://barboslowcarbkitchen.proboards.com/index.cgi)

Tamara Jones at Low Carb Layla (http://www.lowcarblayla.blogspot.com/) Georgene Harkness at (http://georgeneharkness.com/)

Birgit Kerr at Birgit's Daily Bytes (http://birgitkerr.blogspot.com/)

Carol Lovett at (http://ditchthewheat.com)

Darryll Reid at (http://lowcarbboy.com/)

Sandy Rodriguez at Sandy's Simple Recipes and More (http://www.facebook.com/SandysSimpleRecipes)

Kelly Schumann at (http://happytexans.blogspot.com/)

Karen Sorenson at Living Low Carb…One Day at a Time (http://lconeday.blogspot.com)

A special thank you to: *Anita Kinsella, Cathy Lawrence and Joyce Vennum.*

Kent Altena: I would first like to show my appreciation to my brother, Tim Altena, for proving weight loss success is possible. He set the bar further and further ahead and I simply had to follow. I would like to thank my relatives as much of my inspiration came from their Sunday dinners and eating in their restaurant. I would also like to thank the viewers of my YouTube channel and members of Atkins Diet Bulletin board and other low-carb message boards, many of whom I consider friends in every sense of the word. I would also like to thank the many low-carb cooks who have shared their work. Without them I might have fallen into the same trap many others did believing the diet was boring and lacking in variety. People like Linda Genaw, Jennifer Eloff, Dana Carpender and Jimmy Akin, all taught me to look at food in a different way.

Finally and most of all, I would like to thank my family for putting up with my experiments in the kitchen, hours of filming my cooking mistakes and successes, enabling me to help other people starting the diet, and finally allowing me to pursue my dreams in reenlisting in the Iowa National Guard and the local Fire Department. Without their constant loving support, none of this... even my weight loss, my marathon running, my videos and my support of others...would have been possible.

Judy Barnes Baker: It has been a privilege to work with Jennifer and Ian Eloff and I am grateful for their vision, expertise, hard work, and especially for their generosity for inviting me and others to be part of the LCAF's team. I'd also like to thank Jonathon Eloff for designing the beautiful covers and the supporting Website for the *Low Carbing Among Friends'* series and Carolyn Ketchum for stepping up to help with the editing. Her gentle corrections and helpful advice were invaluable. I am thrilled to be part of this talented group of friends who share a common mission to spread the message about good nutrition and to make food for health that tastes like food for pleasure.

Jennifer Eloff: I give humble thanks to my heavenly Father and my dearest family; husband, Ian, and sons, Daniel and Jonathan. Thank you, Ian, for your support, for believing in all of us and for all your computer and business expertise. Thank you, Daniel, for always being ready to assist with your computer programming expertise. Thank you, Jonathan, for your expertise helping with the inside of the cookbook, creating the cookbook covers and for the cookbook website. Congratulations on your new novel, the third in the series of Africa's Snow White, your two successful, science fiction novels and for being promoted to Director of Eureka Publishing and last, but not least, for your upcoming marriage! A special thanks to the amazing, talented team of authors and contributors and to all of you, our gifted low-carb friends. Many thanks go to Carolyn Ketchum for being an editor of this cookbook alongside me.

Acknowledgments

Kyndra Holley: First and foremost, I would like to thank my husband, Jon. Without his constant love, support, and nurturing, none of this would have been possible. A special thank you to my loving family and incredible friends. I love you all more than you know. Last but certainly not least, thank you to all of the wonderful people that follow my site and Facebook. I may not have met all of you in person, but I feel like I have gotten to know you and that we have become one big, low-carb family.

Carolyn Ketchum: My thanks go out to all my family: to Dad and Chris for their love and support, to Mum and Amanda for reading my blog and caring about what I have to say, and to my three darling children, Austin, Celia and Maggie, for putting up with Mummy's low-carb shenanigans. I must also thank the many friends who have been willing and even eager taste-testers, Susan and Ted in particular. And to the readers of my blog, whose comments and encouragement have kept me going on my low-carb journey. But without question, my biggest thanks are to my husband, Tim, for his unfailing patience and support in all aspects of our lives together. We make a great team.

Vanessa Romero: First and foremost, I give glory to God. I am richly blessed. All I am and have done is because of what I have been given. I would like to thank Jennifer and Ian Eloff for giving me the opportunity to be part of this collaborative project. Thank you to my husband Tom, my two boys, Jacob and Brodrick and my dad, Ray, for always being willing to taste test my low-carb recipes. Finally I want to thank my blog readers and Facebook fans, because of you, I get to do what I am passionate about doing each and every day.

I'M EATING LOW-CARB, WHY AM I NOT LOSING WEIGHT?

By Tom Nikkola
Senior Director of
Nutrition and Weight Management for Life Time Fitness
www.lifetime-weightloss.com/blog

If you purchased this cookbook, you're among a small, but growing number of people who realize the benefits of a reduced-carbohydrate diet. With the overwhelming amount of research showing the benefits of low-carb diets compared to conventional diet advice, it still surprises me more people haven't changed their dietary lifestyle. Reducing carbohydrates has been shown to improve lipid levels, reduce visceral fat and overall body fat, and help maintain lean body mass, lower blood sugar and insulin levels and even slow the growth of some forms of cancer. It's pretty remarkable.

As beneficial as low-carbohydrate diets appear to be in a research setting, the success rates in the real world may not be as impressive as we'd hope they would be. There are several reasons for this, which I'll briefly address. This topic could cover the span of several books, so by no means will I be able to provide all the answers. I do hope that if you're not seeing the results you expect, you'll have an idea of where to look or what questions you should ask to achieve better results.

1. Too much low-carb, processed food instead of low-carb, real food.

As much as we'd love to have firm rules for what "low-carb" means, there aren't any. Low-carb for some could mean limiting carbohydrate intake to 30-50 grams per day and staying in ketosis. For others, it's dropping from 400 grams of carbs a day to a more moderate 150 grams. It's easy to get fixated on the number of carbs an individual eats, believing that it is the only thing that matters when it comes to weight loss on a low-carb diet. However, just like weight loss is more than calories in versus calories out, the same goes for carbohydrates. The quality of carbohydrates matters just like the quality of calories matters.

On many occasions, over the years, I've spoken with people who experience lackluster results with their low-carb nutrition plan, only to find out they were eating a lot of either processed low-carb foods made with artificial sweeteners or homemade, low-carb versions of their favorite sweets and treats.

At Life Time, our approach is to steer people toward the right foods first, including a variety of non-starchy vegetables, animal-based protein sources, nuts, seeds and some starchy vegetables when activity levels deem it appropriate. In doing so, we automatically increase micronutrient intake and lower carbohydrate intake without much effort. If progress slows, we start tweaking things. That said, we've seen over and over, when people fall into the trap of eating low-carb versions of their favorite junk food each day, they may not gain weight, but they often stop losing weight and stop seeing improvements in their metabolic health markers.

As a user of this cookbook, if your goal is weight loss, I strongly recommend you use the meat and vegetable recipes on a daily basis and save the dessert foods for once a week or special occasions.

2. Lack of exercise, especially weight training.

I know you've heard many times you don't have to exercise in order to lose weight. While that's true, the type of weight you lose when you include exercise can be significantly different than if you don't exercise. Resistance training plays a very important role in the maintenance of lean body mass, or muscle, as people lose weight. Your body was designed to squat, lunge, pull, press and twist. It was designed to lift heavy things. It was also designed to move around.

Exercise, especially strength training, has a significant effect on our ability to manage glucose levels, which is at the heart of the low-carb approach to nutrition. It often surprises me the conviction people have for living a low-carb lifestyle, yet they ignore the importance of regular, intense strength training. Resistance training helps to reduce insulin resistance, increases or maintains bone density, improves posture, function and range of motion and changes the shape of an individual's physique.

To get the maximum benefit from strength training, you have to stress your muscular system beyond what it has been exposed to in the past. In the beginning, a few body weight exercises and light dumbbells may be all that you need. Over time, you get stronger. As you get stronger, you have to lift heavier weight or expose your muscles to greater stress. There are a variety of ways to do this, but it has to be done if you're looking to improve your level of health, fitness and to maintain your weight loss long-term. It's amazing how much of a difference a few days of resistance training makes when it's done consistently.

3. Too little movement.

As I mentioned above, our bodies are built to lift and they're also built to move. Some movement can be considered exercise, like climbing stairs, using the elliptical or taking part in a group fitness class. Other movement is simply lifestyle related. There was a time when we didn't have cars. People walked to the store. They walked to school. They walked to visit friends. They walked to work. We don't do that today. But we should.

I believe in the near future, we're going to see more published research that shows how bad our sedentary lives are for our health and metabolism. I'm not talking about the fact that we watch too much television. The time people spend watching television, though it's significant, pales in comparison to the time people spend sitting at work. One of the best tools people can use is a pedometer or activity monitor which monitors the number of steps taken per day.

If you've never worn one, you may be surprised by how little you actually move during the day. You may be busy, and your mind may be active, but your body may not be getting nearly the activity you think it is. I know I was shocked when I began tracking my daily movement. I exercise for an hour five to six days a week, four of which are pretty intense strength training days. Outside of exercise, my days are filled with meetings, phone calls and other work, and it includes very little activity and a lot of time spent sitting. At least it did until I became aware. Now I try to make a point of doing some of my laptop work from a standing position as well as taking a short morning and afternoon walk through the three levels of our corporate office. I call it GOYA time, for get off your...well, you know.

At Life Time we recommend individuals get 10,000 steps a day. With this as a goal, after work, I often need to walk on our treadmill or go outside for a walk before the day is over to finish up my steps. None of this is about calorie-burning per se, but about moving the body the way it was designed. If you spend too much time sitting, it can have profound effects on your health and metabolism which in turn impacts your weight loss success.

4. Insufficient sleep and excessive stress.

Chances are this isn't the first time you've seen a recommendation to get more sleep or better manage stress. The mental demands for most of us are extraordinary. Too much stress and lack of sleep easily creates a downward spiral. Chronic stress disrupts our ability to relax and fall asleep, or stay asleep. A lack of sleep disrupts our natural rhythm of stress hormones, specifically cortisol. It's far easier to design a personalized strength and cardio program for someone than it is to help them redesign their life to better manage stress and get adequate sleep.

A single night of insufficient sleep can make an individual insulin resistant that day. Again, one of the biggest goals of carbohydrate reduction is managing blood sugar and insulin. If someone only reduces carbohydrate intake but doesn't exercise or get enough sleep, they change the hormonal environment in the body, which affects how it manages blood sugar, insulin and ultimately fat burning. That's why you can't overlook the importance of consistent 7 to 8 hours of sleep every night.

Taking it a step further, the stress hormone cortisol can cause the body to rely on glucose for fuel more than fat. When we're under chronic levels of stress, cortisol rhythms get disrupted. Ideally, cortisol secretion is at its highest levels in the morning and falls as the day goes on. With chronic stress, levels can be elevated all day long. The result is difficulty sleeping at night, constant cravings for sugary foods and breakdown of muscle tissue. Eventually, as a protective mechanism, the body stops producing cortisol. When cortisol levels plummet, doing even the simplest chores becomes laborious and chronic fatigue sets in.

We offer a variety of lab tests at Life Time, but the most popular by far is called our Stress and Resilience test, which uses saliva to determine one's cortisol levels throughout the day. This test resonates with people because so many know they're under more stress than they should be. The test confirms that, but it also helps us identify when and how people should be exercising to best address their issues. It also allows our dietitians to determine which nutritional supplements, beyond the basics, would best support that person's stress patterns and sleep needs.

5. Metabolic dysfunction.

The four points above are pretty easy to identify. They may require some work in order to properly address them, but they can be identified with some tracking or in the case of stress, an easy-to-do saliva test. As significant as stress, sleep, lack of movement and exercise, or the quality of our food choices may be there can be a lot going on inside us that we're unaware of.

A quarter of men over 30 years old have low levels of testosterone. A growing number of women are dealing with polycystic ovary syndrome which at its core is a problem with the levels of various hormones inside the body. Other people have excessively high levels of inflammation they're unaware of. Chances are, if you're a female and you haven't been diagnosed as being hypothyroid, you know someone who has.

Your metabolism is the sum of all the processes going on inside your body to maintain your health, not just simply the number of calories you can eat or burn. Many of these processes impact your ability to maintain a healthy weight, *even if* your lifestyle, nutrition and exercise program are appropriate. The environment, food and lifestyles our bodies are exposed to are dramatically different than even a hundred years ago. We're not just seeing a growing number of overweight and obese individuals; we're also seeing a growing number of diseases related to a dysfunctional metabolism.

Unfortunately, many individuals spend months pursuing better health, performance or weight loss and become frustrated, as even though they're doing things right, they don't see results. Some become frustrated and give up. Others keep seeking answers and find their way to a knowledgeable health and fitness professional.

We recommend those over 30 years old get a comprehensive blood test each year. Our health and fitness professionals are fortunate because Life Time offers lab testing. It's a huge advantage for our members and even non-members to be able to order a variety of lab tests through our online site **www.lifetime-labtesting.com**.

The most informative test we recommend is our Longevity and Vitality panel, which includes a complete lipid profile (NMR), inflammatory markers, sex hormones, vitamin D, complete blood count, glucose, full thyroid panel and a number of other metabolic markers. The data itself is interesting, but the key to using the information is understanding it. With a good lab interpretation, you should learn how to optimize your metabolism through nutrition, supplementation, exercise and lifestyle changes. Our lab tests include a lab interpretation session with one of our dietitians, which is a powerful experience.

The bottom line is, take the time and make the investment to understand if your metabolism is functioning optimally. If it isn't, you can take appropriate action. Then your nutrition and exercise program is much more likely to succeed.

6. Weight loss and weight management is more than just eating low-carb food.

I hope this cookbook helps you to adhere to your low-carb nutrition plan. At the same time, I hope I've given you a glimpse into the fact that long-term health and optimal weight management isn't just about eating low-carb food. Exercise, movement, your lifestyle and your metabolism all play critical roles as well.

You've likely already realized that if you want to live a healthier way of life, you can't eat the way everyone else does. One final piece of advice is to continue learning. The more you learn, the more conviction you'll feel in the decisions you make. I encourage you to check out our blog where we post at least three new educational articles each week on the topics above and more. Check it out at **www.lifetime-weightloss.com/blog**.

Good luck on your journey toward a healthier way of life.

Tom Nikkola
Senior Director of Nutrition and Weight Management for Life Time Fitness

LOW-CARB RESEARCH UPDATE
By Steve Parker, M.D.

http://SteveParkerMD.com
http://DiabeticMediterraneanDiet.com
http://PaleoDiabetic.com
http://AdvancedMediterranean.com

As much as possible, I base my nutrition and medical recommendations on science-based research published in the medical literature. In the early 2000s, a flurry of research reports demonstrated that very-low-carb eating (as in the style of Dr. Robert Atkins) was safe and effective for short-term weight management and control of diabetes. Eighty hours of literature review in 2009 allowed me to embrace low-carbohydrate eating as a logical and viable option for many of my patients. The evidence convinced me that the relatively high fat content of many low-carb diets was nothing to worry about long-term.

By the way, have you noticed some of the celebrities jumping on the low-carb weight-management bandwagon lately? Sharon Osbourne, Drew Carey and Alec Baldwin, to name a few.

My primary nutrition interests are low-carb eating, the Mediterranean diet, and the Paleo diet. I'm careful to stay up-to-date with the pertinent scientific research. I'd like to share with you some of the pertinent research findings of the last few years.

Low-Carb Diets

- Low-carb diets reduce weight, reduce blood pressure, lower triglyceride levels (a healthy move) and raise HDL cholesterol (another good trend). These improvements should help reduce your risk of heart disease. (In the journal *Obesity Reviews*, 2012.)

- Dietary fat, including saturated fat, is not a cause of vascular disease such as heart attacks and atherosclerosis (hardening of the arteries). (Multiple research reports.)

- If you're overweight and replace two sugary drinks a day with diet soda or water, you'll lose about four pounds over the next six months. (*American Journal of Clinical Nutrition*, 2012.)

- United States citizens obtain 40% of total calories from grains and added sugars. Most developed countries are similar. Dr. Stephan Guyenet notes that U.S. sugar consumption increased steadily "...from 6.3 pounds [2.9 kg] per person per year in 1822 to 107.7 pounds [50 kg] per person in 1999. Wrap your brain around this: in 1822 we ate the amount of added sugar in one 12-ounce can of soda every five days, while today we eat that much sugar every seven hours."

- A very-low-carb diet improves the memory of those with age-related mild cognitive impairment. Mild cognitive impairment is a precursor to dementia. (University of Cincinnati, 2012.)

- High-carbohydrate and sugar-rich diets greatly raise the risk of mild cognitive impairment in the elderly. (Mayo Clinic study published in the *Journal of Alzheimers' Disease*, 2012.)

- Compared to obese low-fat dieters, low-carb dieters lose twice as much fat weight. (University of Cincinnati, 2011.)

- Diets low in sugar and refined starches are linked to lower risk of age-related macular degeneration in women. Macular degeneration is a major cause of blindness. (University of Wisconsin, 2011.)

- A ketogenic (very low-carb) Mediterranean diet cures metabolic syndrome (*Journal of Medicinal Food*, 2011.)

- For type 2 diabetics, replacing a daily muffin (high-carb) with two ounces (60 g) of nuts (low-carb) improves blood sugar control and reduces LDL cholesterol (the "bad" cholesterol). (*Diabetes Care*, 2011.)

- For those afflicted with fatty liver, a low-carb diet beats a low-fat diet for management. (*American Journal of Clinical Nutrition*, 2011.)

- For weight loss, the American Diabetes Association has endorsed low-carb (under 130 g/day) and Mediterranean diets, for use up to two years. (*Diabetes Care*, 2011.)

- High-carbohydrate eating doubles the risk of heart disease (coronary artery disease) in women. (*Archives of Internal Medicine*, 2010.)

- One criticism of low-carb diets is that they may be high in protein, which in turn may cause bone thinning (osteoporosis). A 2010 study shows this is not a problem, at least in women. Men were not studied. (*American Journal of Clinical Nutrition*.)

Dr. Parker

- High-carbohydrate eating increases the risk of developing type 2 diabetes (*American Journal of Clinical Nutrition*, 2010.)

- Obesity in U.S. children tripled from 1980 to 2000, rising to 17% of all children. A low-carb, high-protein diet is safe and effective for obese adolescents. (*American Journal of Clinical Nutrition*, 2010.)

Mediterranean Diet

The traditional Mediterranean diet is well established as a healthy way of eating despite being relatively high in carbohydrate: 50 to 60% of total calories. It's known to prolong life span while reducing rates of heart disease, cancer, strokes, diabetes, and dementia. The Mediterranean diet is rich in fresh fruits, vegetables, nuts and seeds, olive oil, whole grain bread, fish, and judicious amounts of wine, while incorporating relatively little meat. It deserves your serious consideration. I keep abreast of the latest scientific literature on this diet.

- Olive oil is linked to longer life span and reduced heart disease. (*American Journal of Clinical Nutrition*, 2012.)

- Olive oil is associated with reduced stroke risk. (*Neurology*, 2012).

- The Mediterranean diet reduces risk of sudden cardiac death in women. (*Journal of the American Medical Association*, 2011.)

- The Mediterranean diet is linked to fewer strokes visible by MRI scanning. (*Annals of Neurology*, 2011.)

- It reduces the symptoms of asthma in children. (*Journal of the American Dietetic Association*, 2011.)

- Compared to low-fat eating, it reduces the incidence of type 2 diabetes by 50% in middle-aged and older folks. (*Diabetes Care*, 2010.)

- A review of all available well-done studies on the Mediterranean diet confirms that it reduces risk of death, decreases heart disease, and reduces rates of cancer, dementia, Parkinson's disease, stroke, and mild cognitive impairment. (*American Journal of Clinical Nutrition*, 2010.)

- It reduces the risk of breast cancer. (*American Journal of Clinical Nutrition*, 2010.)

- The Mediterranean diet reduces Alzheimer's disease. (New York residents, *Archives of Neurology*, 2010).

- It slows the rate of age-related mental decline. (Chicago residents, *American Journal of Clinical Nutrition*, 2010.)

- In patients already diagnosed with heart disease, the Mediterranean diet prevents future heart-related events and preserves heart function. (*American Journal of Clinical Nutrition*, 2010.)

Clearly, low-carb and Mediterranean-style eating have much to recommend them. Low-carb eating is particularly useful for weight loss and management, and control of diabetes, prediabetes, and metabolic syndrome. Long-term health effects of low-carb eating are less well established. That's where the Mediterranean diet shines. That's why I ask many of my patients to combine both approaches: low-carb and Mediterranean. Note that several components of the Mediterranean diet are inherently low-carb: olive oil, nuts and seeds, fish, some wines, and many fruits and vegetables. These items easily fit into a low-carb lifestyle and may yield the long-term health benefits of the Mediterranean diet. I've posted on the Internet a Low-Carb Mediterranean Diet that will get you started, if interested. It's at http://diabeticmediterraneandiet.com/low-carb-mediterranean-diet/

*Steve Parker, M.D., is a leading medical expert on the **Mediterranean diet** and creator of the world's first low-carb Mediterranean diet. He has three decades' experience practicing Internal Medicine and counseling on effective weight-loss strategies. Dr. Parker is the author of "**The Advanced Mediterranean Diet: Lose Weight, Feel Better, Live Longer** (2nd Edition)," "**Conquer Diabetes and Prediabetes: The Low-Carb Mediterranean Diet**," and "**KMD: Ketogenic Mediterranean Diet**."*

*Dr. Parker is an active blogger at Advanced Mediterranean Life (**http://AdvancedMediterranean.com**), Diabetic Mediterranean Diet (**http://DiabeticMediterraneanDiet.com**), and Paleo Diabetic (**http://PaleoDiabetic.com**).*

Why Can Carbohydrates Kill
By
Robert Su, Pharm.B., M.D.
www.carbohydratescankill.com

Since I published my book, *Carbohydrates Can Kill*, in the spring of 2009, I have had a handful of people who had not read my book, but challenged me with questions or statements, such as "Can carbohydrates really kill?" or, "I have been eating lots of carbohydrates, and am still healthy!"

On the other hand, almost all the readers of my book greatly appreciated the information that I provided with my personal life experiments, volumes of medical and nutritional literature, my analysis on the ill health impacts of carbohydrates, and dietary advice. With that information in hand, they restricted carbohydrate foods, and were able to improve or recover from diabetes mellitus and cardiovascular diseases, among other diseases, and to enjoy their renewed lives.

As the number of overweight and obese individuals continues to rise, we have found dieting is the indispensable key to losing weight. Limiting the caloric intake to an amount smaller than the individual's daily caloric output certainly helps lose weight. Thus, theoretically, the most effective dieting for weight loss is starvation. However, starvation or severe caloric restriction is unsustainable and impractical, although starvation or severe caloric restriction was reportedly helpful in reversing some diseases such as atherosclerosis and cancer, among other diseases, which are a result of nutritional imbalance.

Besides starvation or dieting with severe caloric restriction, the carbohydrate-rich, fat-restricted diet and the carbohydrate-restricted, fat-rich diet are also available in weight loss programs.

Since the mid-1900s, medical and nutritional professionals have vigorously promoted the carbohydrate-rich, fat-restricted diet for weight loss and preventing diseases. However, this diet is effective for weight loss only if it is practiced in combination with caloric restriction. With this diet, many experienced the lack of satiety and struggled with constant hunger pangs because of caloric restriction. Others who adopted this diet without caloric restriction failed to lose weight, or even worse, they gained more weight and developed diseases, such as diabetes mellitus, atherosclerosis, and many more.

Carbohydrate restriction for weight loss has become a popular diet program since the early 1970s, thanks to late Dr. Robert C. Atkins, a cardiologist, for his staunch stance on promoting a low carbohydrate diet to his patients despite continued criticism from the medical establishment of his unconventional approach. In fact, Dr. Atkins did not invent the low-carbohydrate diet. Carbohydrate restriction for weight loss and restoring health had already been practiced in the 1800s.

With the restriction on carbohydrates, individuals can gain satiety with foods rich in both fat and protein. Consequently, they are able to effortlessly reduce the daily amount of caloric intake and lose weight, without hunger. Thus, although caloric reduction is an indispensable key to weight loss, restricting calories from carbohydrate-rich foods is apparently the best approach for weight loss. Conversely, consuming an excess of carbohydrate-rich foods raises the blood glucose level and traps the individual in a vicious cycle between postprandial hyperglycemia, followed by a surge of insulin in the body, and hypoglycemia, with the need of more carbohydrate-rich foods for raising the blood glucose level. I named this vicious cycle "Sweet Rollercoaster." With this vicious cycle, diseases begin to develop.

In the meantime, more studies have found that restricting carbohydrate intake improves biomarkers for many diseases including morbid obesity, diabetes mellitus, coronary artery disease, Alzheimer's disease, inflammatory diseases, and more. Contrary to the belief commonly held by medical and nutritional professionals, fat restriction does not reduce the risks of diseases. Ironically, replacing carbohydrate with saturated fat in diets reduces the risk of coronary artery disease. Likely this is true for other diseases, because the findings in my literature research have consistently supported the statement that Carbohydrates Can *Really* Kill!" In order to share my findings with you, I included in my book synopses of 35 out of more than 1,100 articles that I had reviewed at the time I published the book.

Equipped with a large volume of information from my book that includes essential advice on how to develop a carbohydrate-restricted, fat-rich diet, you will understand why "Carbohydrates Can Kill". You do not need another diet book. You just need a series of cookbooks such as "Low-carbing Among Friends" to help you build a roster of low-carb menus and then see how your diet restores and maintains good health.

For your reference, I have reprinted comments from some of my readers below.

"Excellent reference for low-carb dieters." ----- *J. Elwell "mokipal" (Amazon.com)*

"Wow that's a STRONG implicating title for a book! Here is a medical doctor pouring out his soul about his battle with health, and..." ----- *Blue's Blog (www.sparkpeople.com)*

Dr. Su

"..........While most people erroneously think that your body somehow needs carbs to function, Dr. Su outlines brilliantly in his book that this is a bald-faced lie. The body actually needs fat and some protein, but there is absolutely no dietary requirement for the body to consume carbs. CARBOHYDRATES CAN KILL is an eye-opening book for anyone who is still caught up in decades-old thinking that fat is the enemy and carbs are your friend. Flip those two around and you'll see what Dr. Su sees - low-carb will work for you, too!" ----- *Jimmy Moore, Podcast Host. (Amazon.com)*

"........Dr. Su uncovers the science behind carbohydrate restriction and its effects on health by clearly and concisely explaining it in a way that is easy to digest. The information contained in the myriad of scientific journals is overwhelming and many times incomprehensible for those of us without an MD or PhD. Dr. Su explains much of the literature for us in a way that makes sense while also providing the reader with the reference information to access the research directly. The abundance of research on the benefits of carbohydrate restriction Dr. Su points out may shock you!" ----- *Laurie Cagnassola, former Director, Metabolic and Nutrition Society. (Amazon.com)*

"We've heard that carbohydrates can cause myriad problems in the body, but rarely is that sentiment laid out this boldly. Rarer yet is when it is penned and asserted by a physician..." ----- *Jamie J. Van Eaton, Low Carb Blogger. (Amazon.com)*

"Before reading Dr. Robert K. Su's Carbohydrates Can Kill, I had flashbacks of the myriad books I'd read about carbohydrates in the past. Many were boring and told of the wonders of carbohydrates, wonders I had not discovered after following their respective advice. However, I plunged into the book because I'm an avid learner, and after speaking with Dr. Su personally, I grew fond of him and his ideologies regarding a healthy lifestyle. Carbohydrates Can Kill is an amazing book, the way it was written, the information and research it contains, and the personal experiment conducted by Dr. Su brought to mind Jeff Goldblum's performance in The Fly......." ----- *Michelle Bush, English Professor (www.carbohydratescankill.com)*

"I just finished reading the book by Dr. Robert K. Su "Carbohydrates can kill". It goes into a lot of details on how carbs cause different diseases. He also chronicles his life on low carb for several years and how things improved - even his skin! I really recommend it and especially if you know someone you are trying to covert to the low-carb lifestyle!" ----- *steflou* (www.livinlowcarbdiscussion.com)

"Dr Su, thanks for making such good information available........." ----- *Ernie (www.carbohydratescankill.com)*
"I am enjoying reading your book. I would be interested in seeing an occasional personal update by you on your health developments, similar to the reports in your book....." ----- *John Dawson (www.carbohydratescankill.com)*

"Anyone who is serious about achieving or maintaining good health must read this book. Dr. Su has provided information that you cannot find elsewhere, with charts, facts, figures, and illustrations to back up his research. Along with a friendly writing style, the author shares his personal health journey that is sure to inspire you. Don't believe all the misinformation that is so rampant regarding what we should eat! Get a copy of *Carbohydrates Can Kill* and see for yourself how to control blood sugar (whether you have diabetes or not) for better health and a longer life." -----*Autumn Rose (Amazon.com)*

Robert Su, Pharm. B., M.D. is an anesthesiologist and a specialist in pain management and acupuncture. He is a believer of the saying "Physician Heal Thyself." Dr. Su is the author of a mini medical book for the lay public, **Carbohydrates Can Kill**, *and host of* **The Carbohydrates Can Kill Podcast Show**. *He is also the author of a chapter, Nutrition and Cancer of a book,* **Dieta Dunka Y Salud (Low-carb Diet and Health)**, *published in Spanish, in October 2012. He writes blogs and commentary for his website at* **www.carbohydratescankill.com**, *on which he interacts with his fans and book readers in the forums. He has also spoken at meetings on the subject of diet and health. An autographed copy of his book is available for purchase both on his website* **www.carbohydratescankill.com** *and at Amazon.com. He can be reached at* **carbohydratescankill@verizon.net**. *This article is published on Dr. Su's website, www.carbohydratescankill.com, which also has links to related articles and sites for reference.*

~~~ooOoo~~~

KENT ALTENA
APPETIZERS

FRIED PICKLES
Extended Induction Friendly – This recipe was highly requested
by many viewers and is similar to those found in many bars.

$^{1}/_{4}$ cup oil, coconut, OR olive oil (60 mL)
  preferred
2 large eggs
$^{1}/_{2}$ cup heavy cream (125 mL)
2 tbsp water (60 mL)
$^{1}/_{2}$ cup grated Parmesan cheese (125 mL)
$^{1}/_{4}$ cup coconut flour (60 mL)
1 tsp Taco Seasoning, page 50 (5 mL)
$1^{1}/_{2}$ cups dill pickles, OR sugar-free (375 mL)
  Bread and Butter pickles
$^{1}/_{8}$ tsp salt (0.5 mL)
$^{1}/_{8}$ tsp black pepper (0.5 mL)

Yield: 6 servings
8 pickles per serving
72.0 calories
2.7 g protein
6.2 g fat
0.6 g fiber
1.2 g net carbs

Add oil to small frying pan, and heat to 350°F (180°C).

In baking dish, add eggs, cream, and water. Beat the ingredients together.

In second baking dish, add Parmesan cheese, coconut flour, and Low-Carb Taco Seasoning, page 50.

On a plate, spread out the pickles. Lightly season with salt and pepper. Dredge pickle chips in grated cheese mixture, dunk in egg wash, and return to grated cheese dish. Shake until well covered.

Freeze covered chips for 10 minutes. Add breaded chips to hot oil in frying pan. Flip to second side after 30 seconds or when the breading is golden brown. Cook another 30 seconds and remove to paper towels on a plate. Serve warm with choice of condiments.

~~Atkins Tips & Tricks~~
Print out the Atkins Diet Induction Acceptable Foods list and place it on your fridge and carry it with you in the store. Forgetting how much cream or olives you can consume in one day will no longer be an excuse.

BEDEVILED EGGS

*Induction Friendly – This recipe is a unique look at a common
Atkins Induction recipe. You won't want normal Deviled eggs again.*

10 eggs, hard-boiled
4 slices bacon
$^1/_2$ cup mayonnaise (125 mL)
1 oz Cheddar cheese, shredded (30 g)
1 tsp hot sauce (5 mL)
$^1/_8$ tsp cayenne pepper (0.5 mL)

Yield: 10 servings
2 halves per serving
186.0 calories
9.0 g protein
16.4 g fat
0.0 g fiber
1.0 g net carbs

Place eggs in saucepan, and cover with cold water. Bring water to a boil and immediately remove from heat. Cover, and let eggs stand in hot water for 10 to 12 minutes. Remove from hot water and cool. To cool more quickly, rinse eggs under cold running water.

Place bacon in skillet. Cook over medium high heat until evenly brown. Crumble and set aside.

Peel the hard-cooked eggs, and cut in half lengthwise. Remove yolks to a small bowl. Mash egg yolks with mayonnaise, crumbled bacon, Cheddar cheese, hot sauce and cayenne pepper. Stir in mustard. Fill egg white halves with the yolk mixture and refrigerate until serving.

~~Atkins Tips & Tricks~~
If you are feeling bored with your diet, you might need to liven up your spice cabinet. On all phases of the Atkins diet, you are allowed to consume spices, and while most people think of the common ones like salt and black pepper, there are other spices that are allowed like cinnamon, cumin, and even cocoa powder. Herbs represent another way to bring new flavors from across the globe into your cooking whether it be Italian with oregano and basil to Southwestern with cilantro leaves. Here are some carb counts for a few spices, per tbsp (15 mL):
- *Salt – 0 g*
- *Black Pepper – 4 g (2 g Fiber)*
- *Garlic Powder – 6 g (1 g Fiber)*
- *Cinnamon – 6 g (4 g Fiber)*
- *Chile Powder – 4 g (3 g Fiber)*
- *Cocoa Powder – 3 g (1g Fiber)*
- *Onion Powder – 5 g (0 g Fiber)*
- *Cumin – 3 g (minus 1 g Fiber)*

HOT VOCADO

Extended Induction Friendly – This recipe could be a dip or served as an entree. Avocados are a delicious way to add fat into one's diet.

1 tbsp butter (15 mL)
2 tbsp coconut flour (30 mL)
1 tsp Low-Carb Taco Seasoning, (5 mL)
  page 50
$^1/_4$ cup heavy cream (60 mL)
$^1/_4$ cup water (60 mL)
1 tsp grated Parmesan cheese (5 mL)
1 tsp chipotle-flavored hot sauce (5 mL)
2, 5 oz cans tuna (300 g)
2 avocados
2 oz Cheddar cheese, shredded (60 g)

> **Yield:** 4 servings
> $^1/_2$ avocado per serving
> 366.0 calories
> 25.7 g protein
> 26.5 g fat
> 6.0 g fiber
> **2.8 g net carbs**

Preheat oven to 375°F (190°C).

In large skillet on medium heat, melt butter. Once melted, stir in coconut flour and Low-Carb Taco Seasoning, page 50. Stir until mixture becomes a dark tan color. Add cream, water and Parmesan cheese to mixture. Whisk in the liquids, and let moisture evaporate until it reaches a thick consistency. Remove mixture from heat, and drain the cans of tuna. Add and stir the tuna and hot sauce into mixture.

Cut avocados in half, remove the pits, and scrape out interiors into the skillet. (Retain the shells). Using a fork, mash the avocado and stir into the mixture. Once combined, add the mixture into the emptied avocado shells. Place filled shells in 2-quart (2 L) glass baking dish, and top with shredded Cheddar cheese. Place baking dish in oven for 10 to 15 minutes until cheese is browned.

Remove from oven and serve with low-carb nacho chips.

~~Atkins Tips & Tricks~~
Be careful of the amount of protein one consumes. Many people think Atkins is a high-protein diet, but when in actuality it is a high-fat diet. The general percentages of caloric intake during the Induction phase should be 65% from Fat, 30% from Protein, and 5% from Carbohydrates. Excess protein consumed is either excreted as waste or converted into glucose by the process of gluconeogenesis, which can, of course, affect your blood glucose level.

BREAKFASTS

CINNAMON ROLL PANCAKES

Extended Induction Friendly – A new way to combine two former high-carb favorites into a new low-carb treat

Pancake Batter:
8 oz cream cheese, softened (250 g)
1 cup almond flour (250 mL)
3 large eggs
$^1/_3$ cup heavy cream (75 mL)
$^1/_2$ tsp vanilla extract (2 mL)
$^1/_2$ tsp baking powder (2 mL)
$^1/_3$ cup water (75 mL), PLUS
  $^1/_3$ cup more, if needed (75 mL)

Cinnamon Swirl Icing:
$^1/_4$ cup butter, melted (60 mL)
Liquid sucralose to equal $^2/_3$ cup (150 mL)
  SPLENDA® Granular
1 tbsp almond flour (15 mL)
3 tbsp cinnamon (45 mL)
1 tablespoon vanilla extract (15 mL)
$^1/_2$ tsp blackstrap molasses, optional (2 mL)

Yield: 6 servings
2 pancakes per serving
371.0 calories
11.9 g protein
33.0 g fat
4.0 g fiber
4.5 g net carbs

Pancake Batter: In large bowl, whisk together cream cheese, almond flour, eggs, cream, vanilla extract and baking powder until smooth. Add water until it reaches the right consistency. Set aside.

Preheat a griddle to medium heat.

Cinnamon Swirl Icing: In small bowl, combine butter, liquid sucralose, almond flour, cinnamon, and vanilla extract. Add molasses if desired. Whisk together until smooth. Add water if necessary to reach icing consistency.

Transfer the cinnamon mixture into a large plastic bag. Snip a small corner from the bag.

Spray frying pan with nonstick cooking spray. Pour about $^1/_4$ cup (60 mL) to $^1/_3$ cup (75 mL) of batter into the pan, and pipe a swirl of cinnamon around the pancake, so that it looks like a cinnamon roll. Flip pancake as the edges become dry and browned. Serve bottom side up.

LOW-CARB WAFFLES

*Extended Induction Friendly – The epitome of a low-carb breakfast are
Low-carb waffles. You can serve them with whipped cream or syrup.*

8 oz regular cream cheese, softened (250 g)
4 large eggs
$^1/_2$ cup almond flour (125 mL)
$^1/_4$ cup coconut flour, homemade (60 mL)
  ground coconut flour
$^1/_2$ tsp vanilla extract (2 mL)
Liquid sucralose to equal 1 tbsp (15 mL)
  SPLENDA® Granular (optional)
1 tsp baking powder (5 mL)
$^1/_2$ tsp baking soda (2 mL)
$^1/_8$ tsp salt (0.5 mL)

> *Yield:* 6 servings
> 1 waffle per serving
> 220.0 calories
> 10.0 g protein
> 18.3 g fat
> 1.7 g fiber
> *2.5 g net carbs*

Preheat waffle iron 5 to 10 minutes until iron is ready.

In food processor or stand mixer, add cream cheese, eggs, almond flour, coconut flour, vanilla extract, liquid sucralose, baking powder, baking soda, and salt. Process until thoroughly combined.

Using a $^1/_2$ cup (125 mL) measuring cup, pour ingredients into hot waffle iron as directed by product instructions. Cook until done and serve with butter and pancake syrup.

~~Atkins Tips & Tricks~~
When starting the diet, keep a food journal of everything you are eating and drinking. This simple level of accountability will oftentimes prevent bad behavior from happening. If you are accountable to write down what you ate, knowing you have to record you ate that sugary treat or slice of pizza may make it less tempting. A food journal also becomes immeasurably helpful too when plateaus occur as you can see what potentially changed in your diet in the last couple weeks or perhaps which area needs to change – for instance, have you increased the amount of carbs per day or added a new food in the last week?

Helpful Hints: I have found Fitday.com and Fatsecret.com to be among the best websites for tracking food intake. They have most foods or ingredients that I use and also feature fast food items for easy additions. There are also many smartphone applications that track one's intake and, in particular, the carbohydrates consumed.

DENVER MUFFINS

Induction Friendly – A great breakfast and proves once again a great low-carb meal does not need to be bland or expensive.

1 tbsp butter (15 mL)
$^1/_2$ medium onion, diced
$^1/_2$ green pepper, diced
$^1/_2$ red pepper, diced
$^1/_2$ tsp salt (2 mL)
$^1/_4$ tsp black pepper (1 mL)
4 oz ham, diced (125 g)
8 large eggs
$^1/_2$ cup cream (125 mL)
4 oz Cheddar cheese, shredded (125 g)
$^1/_3$ cup almond flour (75 mL)
  (omit on Induction)
1 tsp dried parsley (5 mL)

Yield: 12 servings
1 muffin per serving
146.0 calories
8.8 g protein
11.2 g fat
0.6 g fiber
2.5 g net carbs

Preheat oven to 350°F (180°C).

In large skillet over medium heat, melt butter. Add onion, green pepper, red pepper, salt, and black pepper. Cook until tender. Reduce heat once veggies are tender, and add ham.

In large bowl, add eggs. Beat lightly. Add cream, Cheddar cheese, almond flour, and parsley. Beat the ingredients together.

Spray 12 muffin tins well with cooking spray. Pour egg mixture into each muffin cup, and then add ham/veggie mixture over the egg mixture. Push ham mixture under the surface.

Bake 12 to 15 minutes until the eggs are set. Serve warm, or chill in refrigerator.

~~Atkins Tips & Tricks~~
Make sure you are measuring yourself as routinely as you are weighing yourself. The scale only tells half the story, and the real story of one's weight loss is where the weight is coming from – lean body mass or fat. Measuring yourself will give you the complete picture as one is able to determine an approximate body fat percentage (similar to the military tape test) from one's measurements.

BACON DONUTS

OWL Friendly – This recipe is a unique look at an old recipe. It can be served either as sweet or savory donuts.

3 slices thick bacon, diced
2 tbsp oil, coconut or olive preferred (30 mL)
$^1/_4$ cup butter (60 mL)
2 mini peppers, diced
$^1/_3$ cup vanilla whey protein powder (75 mL)
1 large egg
1 oz sharp Cheddar cheese, shredded (30 g)

Yield: 2 servings
3 mini donuts per serving
320.0 calories
21.3 g protein
26.0 g fat
0.3 g fiber
2.1 g net carbs

In 8-inch (20-cm) frying pan, cook bacon until done, but not crispy. Remove bacon from frying pan, but leave oil in pan. Add additional oil and heat to 350°F (180°C).

In medium bowl, melt butter in microwave. Add diced bacon, mini peppers, whey protein powder, egg, and Cheddar cheese. Stir together.

Using a tablespoon, place dollop of donut mixture in hot oil. Fry 30 to 60 seconds per side. Flip when necessary, and if donuts become too brown, lower your oil temp. After the first one is finished, you can fry two or three donuts at a time. Optionally, serve with either pancake syrup or salsa and sour cream to provide additional flavors.

~~Atkins Tips & Tricks~~

Be sure to keep the amount of healthy fats in your diet high. Roughly two thirds of your daily calories should be from grams of fat. Fat is the only substance we eat that will not affect your blood sugar levels. It also promotes feelings of satiety through ketosis and naturally limits the amount of food that you eat. I personally found my hunger switch for the first time on Atkins. Prior to Atkins, I could eat and eat without feeling full. The high-fat diet of Atkins for the first gave me the ability to say "No, I'm full."

The high fat also helps prevent the feelings of deprivation while on the diet. It is extremely hard to feel deprived or that you can't eat your favorite foods if you are satiated on acceptable foods, like ribeye steaks, double cheeseburgers or even cheesecake.

MAIN COURSES AND SIDES

BACON-WRAPPED CHICKEN

Induction Friendly – This dish combines the two flavors of my two favorite restaurants – El Pollo Loco and a Brazilian Steakhouse.

Marinade:
$^1/_4$ cup olive oil (60 mL)
$^1/_4$ cup onion, finely diced (60 mL)
$^1/_4$ cup lemon juice (60 mL)
2 tbsp butter, melted (30 mL)
2 tbsp minced garlic (30 mL)
1 tsp oregano (5 mL)
1 tsp orange extract (5 mL)
$^1/_4$ tsp cumin (1 mL)

Chicken:
4 large boneless, skinless chicken breasts
12 slices bacon
4 oz cream cheese, softened (125 g)
2 tbsp green chilies (30 mL)
1 tsp minced garlic (5 mL)

Yield: 6 servings
2 pieces
376.0 calories
44.5 g protein
20.2 g fat
0.0 g fiber
1.2 g net carbs

Marinade: In medium bowl, add oil, onion, lemon juice, butter, minced garlic, oregano, orange extract and cumin. Whisk to combine.

Chicken: Cut up chicken breasts into 1-inch (2.5 cm) cubes. Add chicken breasts to a large plastic bag and pour marinade over top. Place bag in refrigerator for 45 to 60 minutes. Cut each slice of bacon into two even pieces.

In small bowl, add cream cheese, green chilies, and minced garlic. Combine together with a fork.

Take chicken cube and spread cream cheese mixture over it. Wrap cube with two half slices of bacon in both directions, and insert a tooth pick to hold bacon in place. Heat grill to medium heat. Place each wrapped chicken piece on the grill. Rotate the chicken every 3 minutes until all sides are cooked. If bacon starts to burn, move the chicken pieces to indirect heat.

Helpful Hint: You can also bake these in the oven. Preheat oven to 375°F (190°C). Place chicken cubes on a foil-lined baking sheet. Bake 30 to 40 minutes until the center reaches 170°F (77°C).

WIENER SCHNITZEL

Induction Friendly – An international treat dedicated to an Austrian viewer. It is true the original recipe featured veal, but many contemporary Austrian cooks prefer to use pork for the recipe.

$1\,^1/_4$ lbs tenderized pork cutlets (0.57 kg)
$^1/_8$ tsp salt (0.5 mL)
$^1/_8$ tsp ground black pepper (0.5 mL)
1 cup Parmesan cheese (250 mL)
$^1/_2$ tsp paprika (2 mL)
$^1/_4$ tsp cayenne pepper (1 mL)
1 large egg
$^1/_2$ cup heavy cream (125 mL)
$^1/_4$ cup water (60 mL)
1 cup pork rinds, crushed (250 mL)

Yield: 4 servings
1 pork cutlet per serving
543.0 calories
52.0 g protein
31.0 g fat
0.0 g fiber
0.8 g net carbs

If pork tenderloins have not been mechanically tenderized, tenderize them until they are flattened and muscle tissue is broken up. Season tenderloins with salt and ground black pepper.

In glass baking dish, add Parmesan cheese, paprika, and cayenne pepper. Stir ingredients into each other. In flat-bottomed bowl, crack one egg, and add heavy cream and water. Beat together. In another bowl, add crushed pork rinds.

Place pork cutlet in Parmesan cheese mixture and flip over. Ensure the tenderloin is well-covered. Dunk it into the egg-cream bath. Shake off any excess liquid.

Finally, place in the crushed pork rinds and flip to coat both sides. Place on a holding plate, and repeat for remaining tenderloins.

Preheat oil in a deep fryer to 375°F (190°C). Put breaded tenderloins in freezer for at least 15 minutes while the oil heats up.

Cook 2 wiener schnitzel at a time, and flip cutlets after 4 minutes. After another 2 minutes (6 minutes total cooking time), the wiener schnitzel should be cooked. Remove from oil, and place on paper towel until all schnitzel are cooked.

CHICKEN SALAD
Induction Friendly – Only takes minutes to make!

4 thick slices bacon
2$^1/_2$ cups cooked chicken, diced (625 mL)
$^1/_2$ cup celery, finely chopped (125 mL)
1 tbsp sugar-free, sweet pickle relish (15 mL)
$^1/_2$ tsp black pepper (2 mL)
$^1/_2$ cup mayonnaise (125 mL)

Yield: 8 servings
3 oz (90 g) serving
213.0 calories
16.0 g protein
15.6 g fat
0.1 g fiber
0.9 g net carbs

In large skillet, fry bacon until crisp. Pat cooked bacon with paper towel and chop into small pieces. In large bowl, combine bacon, cooked chicken, celery, sugar-free sweet pickle relish, black pepper and mayonnaise. Chill for 30 minutes before serving. Serve chilled with romaine lettuce.

Helpful Hint: Rotisserie chicken from a grocery store makes this an extremely fast meal. Dill relish can be used instead of the sugar-free relish with no change in carb count. Both Vlasic® and Mt Olive® make readily-available sugar-free sweet pickle relishes.

PIZZA BURGER
Induction Friendly –A quick, pizza-flavored lunch ready in minutes.

1 pound ground beef (0.45 kg)
1 pound Italian sausage (0.45 kg)
4 oz Mozzarella cheese (125 g)
$^1/_4$ cup no-sugar added pizza sauce (60 mL)

Yield: 8 servings
4 oz (125 g) patty
382.0 calories
25.5 g protein
28.7 g fat
0.3 g fiber
4.2 g net carbs

In large bowl, add ground beef and Italian sausage. Mix together by hand, but be careful not to overwork the meat. Preheat large skillet to medium high heat.

Measure out the meat mixture to 4 oz (125 g) balls. Press down the balls into patty form and add to the large skillet. Cook 3 to 4 minutes. Flip the burger. Add 1$^1/_2$ tsp (7 mL) pizza sauce to top of each burger and $^1/_2$ oz (15 g) of Mozzarella cheese as well. Cook another 2 minutes covered; remove to serve.

PASTA CARBONARA

*Induction Friendly – Inspired by my daughter's birthday dinner at
Olive Garden, this recipe has a rich low-carb Italian sauce.*

1 spaghetti squash
8 slices bacon
$^1/_2$ small onion, diced
2 cloves garlic
$^1/_4$ cup white wine, (60 mL)
  (omit on Induction)
4 large eggs, beaten
$^1/_2$ cup Parmesan cheese, grated (125 mL)
$^1/_4$ cup heavy cream (60 mL)
$^1/_8$ tsp salt (0.5 mL)
$^1/_8$ tsp black pepper (0.5 mL)
$^1/_4$ cup water, as needed (60 mL)
$^1/_8$ tsp dried parsley (0.5 mL)
1 oz shredded Parmesan cheese (30 g)

Yield: 6 servings
1 cup (250 mL) per serving
197.0 calories
11.2 g protein
12.1 g fat
1.5 g fiber
5.9 g net carbs

Slice the spaghetti squash in half. Scrape out the interior stringy mass and seeds. Cut pieces in half again. In large pot, place spaghetti squash in boiling water for 20 minutes. Remove the stringy insides and set aside.

Chop the bacon into $^1/_2$-inch (1.3 cm) pieces. In frying pan, cook bacon until crispy. Remove bacon from frying pan. Remove all but 2 tbsp (30 mL) of bacon fat from pan. Add onions and cook until translucent. Add garlic and cook one more minute. Add white wine if desired, and reduce to desired consistency.

Add chopped bacon and spaghetti squash back to frying pan. Add beaten eggs, continuously stirring until beginning to set. Add grated Parmesan cheese, cream, salt, black pepper, and water. Stir until well incorporated and "noodles" are covered.

Serve with Parmesan cheese and a sprinkle of parsley.

~~Atkins Tips & Tricks~~
When I first started Atkins, I thought I knew what it was all about before reading the book, and ate things like low-carb yogurt on Day 1. I discovered my mistake when others suggested I read the book. I read the book and purged my pantry of all the low-carb convenience foods not appropriate for Phase 1.

JAMAICAN JERK CHICKEN

Induction Friendly – After a trip to Jamaica on the Low-Carb Cruise,
I wanted to recreate the flavors of the Caribbean at home.

8 to 10 pieces of chicken, brined
Dry Rub:
1 tbsp Splenda® Granular (15 mL)
2 tsp allspice (10 mL)
2 tsp salt (10 mL)
1 tsp thyme, ground (5 mL)
1 tsp black pepper (5 mL)
$^1/_2$ tsp garlic powder (2 mL)
$^1/_2$ tsp cinnamon (2 mL)
$^1/_2$ tsp ground ginger (2 mL)
Jamaican Jerk Sauce:
2 tbsp Jamaican Jerk dry rub (30 mL)
$^1/_4$ cup diced onion (60 mL)
1 jalapeno, diced
2 sweet mini peppers
$^1/_4$ cup soy sauce (60 mL)
2 tbsp olive oil (30 mL)
1 tbsp vinegar (15 mL)
1 tsp garlic, minced (5 mL)

Yield: 6 servings
1 to 2 pieces of chicken
447.0 calories
24.6 g protein
36.5 g fat
0.3 g fiber
4.3 g net carbs

Dry Rub: In small bowl, combine Splenda® Granular, allspice, salt, thyme, black pepper, garlic, cinnamon, and ginger.

Remove chicken from brine, pat dry with paper towels, and sprinkle half of dry rub on top of chicken skin.

Jamaican Jerk Sauce: In blender or food processor, add remaining dry rub, onion, jalapeno, sweet mini peppers, soy sauce, olive oil, vinegar, and minced garlic. Process until smooth.

Preheat grill to medium heat. Place chicken on grill skin side down. Rotate chicken every 5 minutes and flip after 10 minutes. When chicken is almost done, add jerk sauce to the top of the chicken. Cook another 3 minutes to heat up the sauce.

Helpful Hint: To brine chicken, combine $^1/_2$ gallon water (2 L), $^1/_2$ cup (125 mL) salt and seasonings of choice in a large container. Add chicken, cover and refrigerate at least 2 hours.

"BIG MAC" PIE

Induction Friendly – A great takeoff of Linda Genaw's famous White Castle Pie recipe. It combines all the flavors of a Big Mac® in a unique way.

1¹/₂ lbs ground beef (680 g)
2 tbsp dried onion flakes (30 mL)
1 tbsp (heaping) of chicken bouillon (20 mL)
1 tbsp dried parsley (15 mL)
2 tsp onion powder (10 mL)
1 tsp garlic powder (5 mL)
8 oz Cheddar cheese, shredded (250 g)
¹/₂ cup Low-Carb Thousand Island (125 mL)
   Salad dressing, page 47
3 large eggs
¹/₄ cup sour cream (60 mL)
¹/₄ cup chopped dill pickles (60 mL)

Yield: 8 servings
1 slice
401 calories
19.5 g protein
34.5 g fat
0 g fiber
2.9 g net carbs

Preheat oven to 375°F (190°C).

In large skillet, brown ground beef over medium heat. Season with dried onion flakes, chicken bouillon, parsley, onion powder and garlic powder. Transfer seasoned ground beef to large bowl.

In medium bowl, combine Cheddar cheese, Low-Carb Thousand Island salad dressing, page 47, eggs, sour cream, and dill pickles. Mix together thoroughly.

Add ground beef mixture to 8 x 11-inch (20 cm x 28 cm) baking dish and spread to corners. Add cheese mixture on top of the ground beef mixture. Ensure complete coverage to the corners. Bake 30 minutes.

~~Atkins Tips & Tricks~~
My number one suggestion for those starting any diet is to read the book. Often times, I find people typically have the best of intentions, but lack the knowledge of how to actually do the diet. They do what they believe the diet is or what their friends did rather than what the expert said. There are many plans, which could lead you to success, but in order to have the best chance possible, pick a plan, learn the rules of the plan, and then give it 2 to 4 weeks to evaluate the response.

HONEY MUSTARD CHICKEN

Induction Friendly – This recipe uses the paillard method of cooking, which is very cathartic. The chicken is really juicy and full of flavor.

4 large boneless, skinless chicken breasts
$^3/_4$ cup Honey Mustard, page 47 (175 mL)
2 tbsp coconut oil (30 mL)
$^1/_8$ tsp paprika (0.5 mL)
2 oz cheese (60 g)

Yield: 8 servings
1 slice
267.0 calories
32.0 g protein
14.3 g fat
0.1 g fiber
0.9 g net carbs

Preheat the oven to 350°F (180°C).

Slice chicken breasts in half. Place each half of chicken in a plastic bag. Pound each to $^1/_4$ to $^1/_3$-inch (0.6 to 0.8 cm) even thickness. In large bowl, place chicken pieces and $^2/_3$ cup (150 mL) of Honey Mustard Sauce, page 47. Ensure complete coverage in between slices of chicken. Refrigerate 30 to 60 minutes.

In large skillet, heat coconut oil. Sauté each side of the chicken 3 minutes on medium high heat. The goal is not to cook the chicken entirely. It may be slightly pink in the middle.

Place chicken in 9 x 13-inch (2 L) glass baking dish. Sprinkle chicken with paprika and drizzle 2 to 3 tbsp (30 to 45 mL) of sauce over all the chicken and add cheese. Bake 20 minutes until the cheese on top is browned. Broil final minute if needed.

~~Atkins Tips & Tricks~~

If starting the diet, prepare your household. Get rid of the off-plan foods to minimize the temptation while you are weakest. Go to the grocery store and stock up on acceptable snack foods, like olives, cheese, summer sausage or deli meats (without sugar in the ingredients), hardboiled or deviled eggs, and, of course, bacon.

Hunger is not your friend on Induction. If you are hungry, you should find something acceptable to eat. Plan ahead of time what your snacks will be for the day or week. It is when we are hungry that our decision making is at its weakest. By planning ahead of time, you have already made the wise decisions for yourself. Finally, be sure to keep your snacks varied and interesting. If you always have the same snack, it's time to start looking at new options before old temptations take hold.

BUFFALO "CRACK SLAW"

Induction Friendly – "Crack slaw" got its name from its supposed addictive taste on many low-carb forums. This one takes that flavor and adds Buffalo sauce kick.

1 lb ground beef (0.45 kg)
$^1/_2$ tsp onion powder (2 mL)
$^1/_2$ tsp garlic powder (2 mL)
$^1/_4$ tsp salt (1 mL)
$^1/_4$ tsp black pepper (1 mL)
$1^1/_2$ lbs cabbage (0.68 kg)
1 tsp garlic, minced (5 mL)
2 tbsp sesame oil (30 mL)
2 tbsp soy sauce (30 mL)
2 tbsp Frank's® hot sauce (30 mL)
1 tsp apple cider vinegar (5 mL)
Liquid sucralose to equal 2 tsp SPLENDA® Granular (10 mL)
$^1/_2$ tsp crushed red pepper, optional (2 mL)

> **Yield:** 6 servings
> 1 serving
> 267.0 calories
> 15.0 g protein
> 19.8 g fat
> 3.0 g fiber
> **4.7 g net carbs**

In large frying pan, brown ground beef on medium heat. Season with onion powder, garlic powder, salt and black pepper. Remove ground beef from pan, and set aside.

Leave grease in the pan. Add cabbage, sesame oil and garlic to pan. Cook until cabbage mixture begins to brown.

Add soy sauce, Frank's® hot sauce, apple cider vinegar, liquid sucralose and red pepper to frying pan. Return ground beef to pan and heat for two minutes. Serve hot.

~~Atkins Tips & Tricks~~

Trying to do Atkins without including exercise is like driving down the road with a flat tire. You may eventually get to your destination, but you will certainly not look as good doing it. The food lifestyle of Atkins is extremely effective in getting you to lose weight, but one key component of maintenance is being able to do the things you only dreamed of in your former life. Exercise is also a vital component to improve one's level of fitness where food alone cannot improve it. "Exercise is non-negotiable," said the late Dr. Robert Atkins.

PIZZA QUICHE

Induction Friendly – Looking for a crustless pizza? This entree has all the flavor and serves as a great breakfast or lunch meal.

1 1/2 lbs ground beef (680 g)
1/2 small onion, diced
1 red bell pepper, diced
4 oz pepperoni, diced (125 g)
1/4 cup no-sugar-added pizza sauce (60 mL)
1/4 tsp salt (1 mL)
3/4 tsp black pepper, divided (3 mL)
6 large eggs
1 cup heavy cream (250 mL)
8 oz Swiss cheese, shredded (250 g)

Yield: 8 servings
1 slice per serving
509.0 calories
26.5 g protein
42.0 g fat
0.5 g fiber
4.9 g net carbs

Preheat the oven to 350°F (180°C).

In large frying pan over medium heat, brown ground beef. Remove browned ground beef, and cook onions and peppers until translucent. Drain any excess fat.

To the onions and peppers in the pan, add ground beef, diced pepperoni, pizza sauce, salt and add 1/4 tsp (1 mL) of black pepper.

In large mixing bowl, beat eggs. Add cream and remaining black pepper, and beat together. Add shredded cheese to egg and cream mixture.

Grease a large casserole dish well. Layer the ground beef mixture on the bottom, and then pour the egg-cream mixture over top. Bake 30 minutes covered, and then another 15 minutes uncovered.

~~*Atkins Tips & Tricks*~~
Many people in the first few days of starting a ketogenic diet experience what is commonly referred to as "Induction Flu." Common symptoms are extreme fatigue, muscle or joint pain, mental fogginess, nausea, and most commonly headaches. Here are some suggestions to alleviate these symptoms:

- *Drink adequate amounts of water*
- *Consume enough sodium, potassium, and other electrolytes to replace those that are lost; cup of chicken broth or bouillon cubes help*
- *Ensure you are eating the 3 cups (750 mL) of vegetables*
- *Finally, take solace. The discomfort is only temporary.*

PULLED CHICKEN
*Induction Friendly – Pulled chicken is great by itself
or even served on a salad.*

Brine:
$^{1}/_{2}$ cup salt (125 mL)
8 cups water (2 L)
$^{1}/_{4}$ cup Dry Rib Rub, page 50 (60 mL)
2 tbsp liquid smoke (30 mL)
Chicken:
4 to 5 lbs chicken, thighs, (1.8 to 2.2 kg)
  OR breasts
$^{1}/_{4}$ cup Dry Rib Rub, page 50 (60 mL)
$^{1}/_{2}$ small onion

Yield: 10 servings
4 oz (125 g) per serving
356 calories
35.9 g protein
22.1 g fat
0.1 g fiber
0.7 g net carbs

In medium pot over medium heat, dissolve salt in the water. Add Dry Rib Rub, page 50 and liquid smoke. Remove from heat, and add ice as needed to cool the brine. In a cooler, place the chicken parts. Pour the brine over the chicken and ensure it is covered. Refrigerate for an hour.

Preheat oven to 300°F (150°C).

Remove chicken from brine, and pat dry with paper towels. Sprinkle the Dry Rib Rub, page 50 over skin of the chicken. Slice onion into rings.

Place chicken parts into an aluminum foil pouch. Add onion slices to the top of chicken. Seal aluminum pouch, and place on top of a roasting pan. Place roasting pan in oven for approximately 2 hours.

Once chicken thighs, OR breasts reach an internal temperature of 180°F (82°C) near the bone, open aluminum pouch to expose chicken and onions to the heat directly. Increase the oven temperature to 375°F (190°C).

Return to oven for another 30 to 45 minutes. The internal temperature of the chicken should reach at least 200°F (93°C) to be able to be flaked with a fork.

Serve with a good Barbecue Sauce, such as the one on page 49.

REUBEN CASSEROLE

Induction Friendly – Great low-carb entree for those looking to recover the flavor of an awesome sandwich

2 Flax Breads, page 51
16 oz can sauerkraut, drained (500 g)
1 cup Low-Carb Thousand Island (250 mL)
   Salad Dressing, page 47
10 oz corned beef (300 g)
1 cup Swiss cheese, shredded (250 mL)

Yield: 8 servings
1 piece per serving
422.0 calories
14.3 g protein
38.0 g fat
3.2 g fiber
2.8 g net carbs

Preheat the oven to 375°F (190°C).

Prepare the Flax bread, page 51 in the microwave. Chop the flax bread into small pieces. Allow to dry out on the counter top or toast in the oven.

Grease a 9 x 13-inch (23 x 33 cm) baking pan. Add the stale or toasted flax bread to the baking pan. Drain the sauerkraut, and place on top the flax bread crumbles.

Add $^1/_2$ cup (125 mL) of Low-Carb Thousand Island Dressing, page 47. Chop corned beef into small pieces and sprinkle over. Place Swiss cheese on the corned beef. Add remaining Thousand Island Dressing, page 47 on top of the casserole. Cover baking dish with glass cover or tinfoil.

Bake casserole for 20 minutes covered, and 10 to 15 minutes uncovered.

~~Atkins Tips & Tricks~~

I am often asked by new Atkins followers, "Should I count calories while on Induction?" For me, counting calories was one of the reasons for failure in all past dieting attempts. The daily accounting and tracking of the calories for everything that entered my mouth was time consuming and not very productive on the scale.

For most people, I recommend simply counting one's carbohydrate intake per day and ensure that you are eating according to the acceptable foods list. The only time I counted calories was to ensure I ate enough of them - not to limit them on the diet. The natural appetite suppression of ketosis was more than sufficient to ensure I did not overeat on the diet.

Kent Altena

"SMOKED" PULLED PORK

Induction Friendly – I made this recipe for my daughter's graduation, and it was regarded by many as better than some legendary, local BBQ places.

Brine:
8 cups water (2 L)
$^1/_2$ cup salt (125 mL)
$^1/_4$ cup Dry Rib Rub, page 50 (60 mL)
2 tbsp liquid smoke (30 mL)
Pork:
8 to10 lb pork roast picnic, OR (4 kg)
 Boston butt
$^1/_4$ cup Dry Rib Rub, page 50 (60 mL)

Yield: 10 to 20 servings
6 oz (180 g) serving
476 calories
34.0 g protein
36.0 g fat
0.1 g fiber
0.2 g net carbs

Butterfly the pork roast along the bone to increase the surface area.

In medium pot, pour water and over medium heat dissolve salt in the water. Add the dry rib rub and liquid smoke. Remove from heat, and add ice as needed to cool the brine. In a cooler, place the rib roast. Pour the brine over the roast and ensure it is covered. Refrigerate 4 hours.

Preheat oven to 275°F (135°C).

Remove roast from brine, and pat dry with paper towels. Add dry rub to the inside of roast and the top. Wrap with two sheets of aluminum foil in opposite directions to hold in moisture, and place roast in oven for 6 hours.

Once the roast reaches an internal temp 180°F (82°C), remove the the aluminum foil from top of roast. Increase oven temperature to 375°F (190°C). Bake in oven for another hour or two to develop a good "bark" or crust on the outside of the roast.

The internal temperature of the roast should reach at least 200°F (93°C). Remove roast from the oven, and flake with a fork.

Serve with a good Barbecue Sauce, such as the one on page 49.

BARBECUE BAKE

Induction Friendly – Another great make-ahead dish for that busy weeknight dinner.

4 large eggs
$^3/_4$ cup heavy cream (175 mL)
2 tbsp Dry Rib Rub, page 50, (30 mL)
  divided
10 oz Cheddar cheese, shredded and (300 g)
  divided
$1^1/_2$ lbs ground beef (680 g)
$^1/_2$ small onion, chopped
$^1/_4$ cup low-carb ketchup (60 mL)
1 tbsp mustard (15 mL)
1 tsp liquid smoke (5 mL)

Yield: 8 servings
1 slice
447.0 calories
24.6 g protein
36.5 g fat
0.3 g fiber
4.3 g net carbs

Preheat the oven to 375°F (190°C).

Into large bowl, crack the 4 eggs. Add heavy cream and whisk eggs and cream together. Add 1 tsp (5 mL) of Low-Carb Dry Rib Rub, page 50 to mixture and mix together.

Grease a 9 x 13-inch (23 x 33 cm) baking pan. Add 6 oz (180 g) of the shredded cheese to baking dish. Pour cream and egg mixture over top. Shake pan to even out the mixture and spread until smooth. Place in oven 20 minutes until golden brown. Pop any bubble that may form in the crust.

In large skillet, brown ground beef with onion and remaining Dry Rib Rub, page 50. Add ketchup, mustard, and liquid smoke to the ground beef.

Add meat mixture on top of crust. Top with remaining cheese, and return dish to the oven for another 10 to 15 minutes.

~~Atkins Tips & Tricks~~

Exercise is a key component of the Atkins Diet lifestyle and a requirement to be fit once the weight is lost. However, it is my opinion that one should forego exercising in the first 2 to 3 weeks of the diet. The body is acclimating during this period to burning fat almost exclusively for fuel. If you are already exercising when you started Induction and feel compelled to continue, take it slow and make sure you stay hydrated and that electrolytes, like sodium and potassium, are replenished. Otherwise, dizziness and excessive fatigue can occur and you really want to avoid that.

BUFFALO STUFFED CHICKEN

Induction Friendly – I love Buffalo chicken and this recipe gives chicken burgers a ton of flavor which plain ground chicken is often missing.

1$^1/_2$ lbs boneless, skinless chicken (680 g) breasts
4 slices bacon
$^1/_2$ small onion
$^1/_3$ cup Buffalo, OR Louisiana Sauce (75 mL)
$^1/_2$ tsp salt (2 mL)
$^1/_2$ tsp black pepper (2 mL)
$^1/_8$ tsp cayenne pepper (0.5 mL)
4 oz Cheddar cheese (125 g)
1 egg, beaten

Yield: 6 servings
2 patties
218.0 calories
24.7 g protein
11.5 g fat
0.2 g fiber
2.5 g net carbs

Preheat grill to medium high heat.

In food processor, place chicken breasts and bacon. Process the chicken and bacon until thoroughly chopped. Add onion, Buffalo, OR Louisiana hot sauce, salt, black pepper and cayenne pepper; process again for 30 to 60 seconds.

In large bowl, remove chicken mixture from food processor. Add cheese and egg. Mix thoroughly by hand. Using $^1/_3$ cup (75 mL) of mixture at a time, form into individual patties.

Place patties on the grill. Rotate after 3 minutes and flip after 5 to 6 minutes. Cook until done.

Serve with ranch dressing.

~~Atkins Tips & Tricks~~

How often one should weigh oneself really depends on one's personality. If weighing yourself each day and the daily bounces (up and down) discourages you and leads to making choices where you cheat or question your diet then weighing every day is not for you. Weighing infrequently can also lead to "cramming", i.e. eating dramatically less or starving the day before a weigh-in and lax behavior in between weigh-ins.

My suggestion would be to figure out which traits match your personality and to measure your body to ensure you are losing (fat vs. lean body mass).

TUNA CAKES

*Induction Friendly – A nice budget-conscious meal that is great
for breakfast or lunch.*

3, 5 oz cans tuna, drained (450 g)
2 green onions, chopped
1 large egg, beaten
1 tbsp mayonnaise (15 mL)
1 tsp Worcestershire sauce (5 mL)
1 tsp Dijon mustard (5 mL)
1 tsp Cajun, OR salt-free seasoning (5 mL)
$^1/_4$ cup Parmesan cheese, grated (60 mL)
1 to 2 oz pork rinds, crushed (30 to 60 g)
$^1/_4$ cup coconut, OR olive oil (60 mL)

Yield: 6 servings
2 cakes per serving
182.0 calories
25.5 g protein
7.8 g fat
0.2 g fiber
0.8 g net carbs

In large bowl, add tuna, green onions, egg, mayonnaise, Worcestershire sauce, mustard, Cajun, OR salt-free seasoning and Parmesan cheese. Combine mixture.

In another container, add crushed pork rinds. Take 1 tbsp (15 mL) of tuna mixture, form a ball, and roll in the pork rinds until coated.

In a frying pan, heat coconut, OR olive oil until it shimmers, at approximately 375°F (190°C). Place 3 to 4 tuna cakes in the oil and roll them around to reach a golden brown color on all sides. Remove from oil and place on paper towel. Continue until all cakes are done. Serve warm with Low-Carb Tartar Sauce, page 48.

~~Atkins Tips & Tricks~~

Another way to stay motivated is find a weight-loss buddy or a good support group (online or in person), who understands what you are going through and preferably one on the same plan as what you are. Many times friends and family will give bad advice out of ignorance or bias and will not be able to support you. Well-meaning suggestions that "one time will not hurt" or "you need to confuse your system and cycle low-carb with high-carb" (both suggestions I received at one time) will only breed hard feelings between both parties. Learning from others who have dealt with things like Induction Flu or the holidays while low-carbing was extremely important for my success.

*The good news is between online forums, like **Atkins Diet Bulletin Board** or **Low Carb Friends**, and Facebook groups, there is no shortage of people willing to help you be as successful as they were or are. The experts in the field, like **Dr. Eric Westman (Duke)** and **Dr. Jeff Volek (University of Connecticut)** are also more approachable than ever before as well.*

CHICKEN NUGGETS

Extended Induction Friendly – This recipe proves low-carbing is perfect for all ages, and a low-carb parent does not necessarily have to make two meals – one for them and one for the kids.

1½ cups Parmesan cheese, grated (375 mL)
½ cup coconut flour (125 mL)
  (omit on induction)
1 tbsp onion powder (15 mL)
1 tsp garlic powder (5 mL)
1 tsp black pepper (5 mL)
1 tsp baking powder (5 mL)
1 large egg
½ cup heavy cream (125 mL)
½ cup water (125 mL)
2 lbs boneless, skinless chicken breasts (0.9 kg)
1 tsp favorite seasoning, OR salt (5 mL)

Yield: 6 servings
6 pieces
313.0 calories
37.0 g protein
16.2 g fat
0.5 g fiber
2.9 g net carbs

In plastic, sealable container, add Parmesan cheese, coconut flour, onion powder, garlic powder, black pepper, and baking powder. Place lid on container and shake to combine. In medium bowl, crack one egg and add heavy cream and water. Beat together.

Remove excess fat off chicken, and slice chicken breast into 1-inch (2.5 cm) strips on the bias against grain of chicken. Season chicken with favorite seasoning, OR simply use salt.

In large container, add ¾ cup (175 mL) of cheese and flour mixture. Add a handful of chicken. Shake to coat. Dunk chicken strips in egg-cream bath, and shake off excess liquid. Return chicken to large container for second breading. Place chicken on a plate, and repeat for remaining chicken. Add remaining cheese-flour mixture as needed.

Heat deep fryer oil to 375°F (190°C). Place breaded chicken in freezer for 10 minutes while oil heats. When oil is hot enough, remove chicken from freezer and place roughly a third of the pieces in the oil. Cook chicken for 5 minutes until done. Place chicken on cooking sheet in preheated oven, and repeat cooking process with remaining chicken.

HOLUBETS CABBAGE ROLLS

Induction Friendly – An Eastern European favorite, these Cabbage Rolls feature a creamy tomato sauce.

1 head cabbage
$^1/_2$ head cauliflower
$^1/_2$ small onion
$1^1/_4$ lbs ground beef (0.57 kg)
1, 14-oz can diced tomatoes (398 mL)
$^1/_2$ cup chicken broth (125 mL)
$^1/_4$ cup heavy cream (60 mL)
1 tsp Italian seasoning (5 mL)
1 tsp salt (5 mL)
$^1/_2$ tsp black pepper (2 mL)
6 slices bacon

Yield: 8 servings
2 rolls per serving
270.0 calories
7.0 g protein
27.0 g fat
1.0 g fiber
2.0 g net carbs

Preheat oven to 375°F (190°C).

Core the head of cabbage. In large pot of boiling water, cook cabbage until leaves are tender but not falling apart, roughly 10 to 15 minutes. Set aside the cabbage leaves to cool.

In food processor, rice one half head of cauliflower using the grating bed. Finely dice onion.

In large frying pan over medium heat, brown ground beef. When beef is about half done, add cauliflower and onion. Stir occasionally to prevent cauliflower from burning. Cook beef mixture until ground beef is completely cooked and cauliflower is tender. Set aside to cool.

In second pot, add diced tomatoes, chicken broth, heavy cream, Italian seasoning, salt, and pepper. Using an immersion blender, puree the contents into a thin soup. Cook until sauce reduces by roughly a third.

Take cabbage leaves, and place about 2 to 3 tbsp (30 to 45 mL) of ground beef mixture into each leaf. Roll the leaf like a burrito, and place lengthwise into a large casserole dish. Pour the creamy tomato sauce over top. Lay bacon across the rolls.

Bake for 30 minutes.

CHEESY BACON SPINACH

Induction Friendly – One of my LCHF Swedish friends and fellow success story, Tommy Runesson, turned me on to this excellent side dish.

4 thick slices bacon
4 cups Spinach, raw (1 L)
2 oz sharp Cheddar cheese (60 g)

Yield: 2 servings
$^1/_2$ cup (125 mL) per serving
245.0 calories
16.5 g protein
18.3 g fat
1.3 g fiber
2.6 g net carbs

In large frying pan, cook the thick slices of bacon over medium heat. When almost fully cooked, remove bacon from frying pan, and chop into small pieces.

Leave leftover bacon grease in pan and add spinach. Stir spinach into bacon grease to coat it well. Cook until spinach is well wilted.

Add Cheddar cheese and chopped bacon to frying pan. Continue to heat until the cheese is melted and stirred into the spinach. Serve warm.

CABBAGE WITH BACON

Induction Friendly – This recipe proves that not all delicious recipes need to be involved or difficult to prepare.

2 tbsp coconut oil (30 mL)
$^1/_2$ head of cabbage
3 slices thick bacon
$^1/_4$ cup onion (60 mL)
$^1/_2$ tsp salt (2 mL)
$^1/_2$ tsp black pepper (2 mL)

Yield: 4 servings
$^1/_2$ cup (125 mL) per serving
103.0 calories
4.0 g protein
7.5 g fat
3.0 g fiber
4.5 g net carbs

In a large frying pan, add coconut oil and heat to medium heat.

Finely shred cabbage, and chop bacon and onion. Add cabbage, bacon and onion to frying pan. Sprinkle salt and pepper over the top. Cook mixture until onions are tender, and cabbage is slightly browned.

Serve warm.

POPCORN CAULIFLOWER

Induction Friendly – This is a great appetizer or side dish. By roasting the cauliflower, you bring out the sweetness and flavor.

$1^1/_2$ heads (6 cups) cauliflower (1.5 L)
$^1/_4$ cup oil, coconut preferred (60 mL)
1 tbsp salt (15 mL)
1 tsp salt-free seasoning, optional (5 mL)

> **Yield:** 4 servings
> 1 cup (250 mL) per serving
> 96.0 calories
> 3.0 g protein
> 7.0 g fat
> 3.8 g fiber
> **4.2 g net carbs**

Preheat oven to 425°F (220°C).

Chop cauliflower into florets. Discard stems and cores. In large bowl, add oil, salt and salt-free seasoning, and mix. Add cauliflower. Toss until it is well-coated in oil and spices.

Line an 18 x 13-inch (46 x 33 cm) half sheet pan with parchment paper. Spread cauliflower on sheet pan and try to minimize pieces touching. Place sheet pan in oven. Bake 60 minutes. Flip or rotate the cauliflower every 20 minutes until the cauliflower is golden brown. They can be slightly blackened but do not burn too many.

~~Atkins Tips & Tricks~~

Many people are reluctant or scared to migrate on to the Ongoing Weight Loss (OWL) phase of the diet. They believe their weight loss will be slower or stop. In actuality, some people actually see their weight loss increase by moving on to the next phase. Here are the rules for the OWL phase:

- *Keep fats and proteins as the mainstays of your diet.*

- *Increase your daily carbohydrate intake by no more than 5 additional grams per week. For instance in the first week of OWL, you can eat up to 25 g net carbs per day.*

- *Stop adding additional carbs when your weight loss stops or you experience weight gains in consecutive weeks.*

- *Add new foods, one new group (dairy, nuts/seeds, berries/melon, alcohol, starchy vegetables, etc.) at a time to capture any food sensitivities. Eat the new food group daily for the first week.*

- *Monitor yourself for any negative impacts, like greater cravings or weight gain.*
Continue doing OWL phase until you have 5 to 10 pounds left to lose

AWESOME BROCCOLI CASSEROLE

Induction Friendly – A perfect side dish for potlucks or simply dinners at home.

1 cup mayonnaise (250 mL)
4 oz cream cheese, softened (125 g)
$1/_2$ cup heavy cream (125 mL)
$1/_2$ small onion, chopped
1 large egg, beaten
2 bunches broccoli, chopped
8 oz Cheddar cheese, shredded (250 g)
$1/_2$ tsp salt (2 mL)
$1/_2$ tsp black pepper (2 mL)
$1/_4$ tsp paprika (1 mL)

> **Yield:** 8 servings
> $1/_2$ cup (125 mL) per serving
> 295.0 calories
> 7.3 g protein
> 27.3 g fat
> 1.5 g fiber
> **4.5 g net carbs**

Preheat oven to 350°F (180°C).

In a large bowl, combine mayonnaise, cream cheese, heavy cream, onion, and egg. Add broccoli florets, cheese, salt, black pepper, and paprika to mayonnaise mixture. Mix together well.

Grease 9 x 13-inch (2 L) glass baking dish. In baking dish, pour broccoli mixture. Spread the mixture, and eliminate any air pockets by dropping it lightly on the counter. Bake 40 minutes until the cheese is browned on top.

Variation: To make this casserole a main dish, add 4 oz (125 g) of cooked bacon or ham to the broccoli mixture.

~~Atkins Tips & Tricks~~

I get asked quite often for how long one should do the Induction phase of the diet. The answer often is it depends upon the person, their situation, and their tastes. Some people can eat the same general food items and are not bothered by the more limited food selection of the Induction phase. Others, however, are chomping at the bit to add more vegetables, dairy or to be able to cook with items like almond flour. Here is my checklist for deciding when to move on to the Ongoing Weight Loss (OWL) phase:

☐ *Am I satisfied with the current food choices on the diet?*

☐ *Has my blood work come back deficient in any categories?*

☐ *Do I still have a significant amount of weight to lose?*

☐ *Am I having any prolonged fatigue or poor exercise performance after the first few weeks?*

MISCELLANEOUS

HONEY MUSTARD SALAD DRESSING

Induction Friendly – A versatile salad dressing with many uses both as a salad dressing and as a sauce in other recipes

1 cup mayonnaise (250 mL)
$^1/_4$ cup mustard, yellow, OR Dijon (60 mL)
Liquid sucralose to equal 2 tbsp (30 mL)
 SPLENDA® Granular
1 tsp apple cider vinegar (5 mL)
1 tsp blackstrap molasses, optional (5 mL)
$^1/_8$ tsp onion powder (0.5 mL)
$^1/_8$ tsp garlic powder (0.5 mL)

Yield: 10 servings
2 tbsp (30 mL) per serving
166.0 calories
0.5 g protein
17.6 g fat
0.2 g fiber
1.2 g net carbs

In large bowl, combine mayonnaise, mustard, liquid sucralose, vinegar, molasses (omit if on Induction), onion powder, and garlic powder. Stir until well combined and chill 30 minutes before serving.

THOUSAND ISLAND SALAD DRESSING

Induction Friendly – This is my wife's favorite salad dressing, and one of the items that made the low-carb lifestyle palatable for her.

1 cup mayonnaise (250 mL)
$^1/_3$ cup low-carb ketchup (75 mL)
2 tbsp sugar-free, sweet pickle relish (30 mL)
$^1/_2$ tsp onion powder (2 mL)
$^1/_8$ tsp salt (0.5 mL)
$^1/_8$ tsp garlic powder (0.5 mL)

Yield: 12 servings
2 tbsp (30 mL) per serving
133.0 calories
0.4 g protein
14.0 g fat
0.0 g fiber
1.2 g net carbs

In large bowl, combine mayonnaise, low carb ketchup, sugar-free, sweet pickle relish, onion powder, salt, and garlic powder. Stir until well combined and chill 30 minutes before serving.

Helpful Hints: Heinz® Reduced-Sugar Ketchup, formerly called Heinz® One-Carb Ketchup, is the most popular low-carb ketchup and is Induction Friendly. Both Vlasic® and Mt. Olive® brands sell sugar-free, sweet pickle relish. If either one is not available, you can use dill pickle relish instead.

RANCH SALAD DRESSING

Induction Friendly – A favorite salad dressing for many low carbers, and by making your own, you can eliminate any added sugars.

1 cup mayonnaise (250 mL)
$^1/_2$ cup sour cream (125 mL)
1 tsp minced garlic (5 mL)
$^1/_2$ tsp parsley, dried (2 mL)
$^1/_2$ tsp onion powder (2 mL)
$^1/_2$ tsp dill weed (2 mL)
$^1/_8$ tsp salt (0.5 mL)
$^1/_8$ tsp black pepper (0.5 mL)

Yield: 10 servings
2 tbsp (30 mL) per serving
160.0 calories
0.5 g protein
17.5 g fat
0.0 g fiber
0.8 g net carbs

In large bowl, combine mayonnaise, sour cream, minced garlic, parsley, onion powder, dill weed, salt and pepper. Stir until well combined and chill 30 minutes before serving.

Variation: **Post-Induction Atkins version:** Replace $^1/_2$ cup (125 mL) sour cream with 1 tbsp (15 mL) dry buttermilk powder and $^1/_4$ cup (60 mL) water. *Nutritional analysis:* 162 Calories, 0.5 g Protein, 17.5 g fat, 17 g fat, 0 g fiber, *1.0 g net carbs.*

TARTAR SAUCE

Induction Friendly – Perfect condiment to go with Tuna Cakes, page 41 or low-carb fish entrees.

1 cup mayonnaise (250 mL)
1 tbsp sugar-free pickle relish (15 mL)
2 tbsp lemon juice (30 mL)
1 tbsp minced onion (15 mL)

Yield: 16 servings
1 tbsp (15 mL) per serving
100.0 calories
0.2 g protein
10.8 g fat
0.0 g fiber
0.8 g net carbs

In large bowl, combine mayonnaise, sugar-free pickle relish, lemon juice, and minced onion. Stir until well combined and chill 30 minutes before serving.

BEST LOW-CARB BARBECUE SAUCE

Induction Friendly – With the loss of commercial low-carb barbecue sauces, this sauce fills a huge hole in my diet.

1 cup low-carb ketchup (250 mL)
1 cup tomato sauce (250 mL)
Liquid sucralose to equal $^1/_2$ cup (125 mL)
 SPLENDA® Granular
$^1/_2$ cup white vinegar (125 mL)
$^1/_4$ cup blackstrap molasses, (60 mL)
 (optional)
1 tbsp butter (15 mL)
2 tsp liquid smoke (10 mL)
$^1/_2$ tsp paprika (2 mL)
$^1/_2$ tsp salt (2 mL)
$^1/_2$ tsp ground black pepper (2 mL)
$^1/_4$ tsp garlic powder (1 mL)
$^1/_4$ tsp onion powder (1 mL)
$^1/_4$ tsp cayenne pepper (1 mL)
$^1/_8$ tsp chili powder (0.5 mL)
$^1/_8$ tsp cinnamon (0.5 mL)

> *Yield:* 48 servings
> 1 tbsp (15 mL) per serving
> 10.0 calories
> 0.2 g protein
> 0.1 g fat
> 0.0 g fiber
> *2.0 g net carbs*

In large saucepan over medium heat, mix together ketchup, tomato sauce, liquid sucralose, white vinegar, molasses, butter and liquid smoke. Season with paprika, salt, black pepper, garlic powder, onion powder, cayenne pepper, chili powder and cinnamon.

Reduce heat to low, and simmer for up to 20 minutes. For thicker sauce, simmer longer, and for thinner, less time is needed. Sauce can also be thinned using a bit of water if necessary.

Helpful Hint: Heinz® is probably the most readily-availably, low-carb ketchup on the market. It has changed its name a few times since being released. It has been known as both Heinz® One Carb Ketchup and Heinz® Reduced-Sugar Ketchup. The ingredients have remained the same with no added sugars.

You can, however, make your own as well, and there are a number of recipes in the low-carb community.

LOW-CARB TACO SEASONING

*Induction Friendly – Before Atkins, one of my favorite meals
was taco pizza and I love this recipe for the seasoning.*

2 tbsp chili powder (30 mL)
2 tbsp paprika (30 mL)
4 tsp cumin (20 mL)
1 tbsp ground black pepper (15 mL)
1 tbsp salt (15 mL)
1 tbsp garlic powder (15 mL)
1 tbsp onion powder (15 mL)
1 tsp cayenne pepper (5 mL)

Yield: 24 servings
1 tsp (5 mL) per serving
6.2 calories
0.3 g protein
0.2 g fat
0.5 g fiber
0.9 g net carbs

In small bowl, combine chili powder, paprika, cumin, black pepper, salt, garlic powder, onion powder and cayenne pepper. Store in airtight container.

LOW-CARB DRY RIB RUB

*Induction Friendly – The source of any good rib recipe
has to begin with a great rub.*

$^3/_4$ cup SPLENDA® Granular (175 mL)
$^3/_4$ cup paprika (175 mL)
$^1/_2$ cup chili powder (125 mL)
$^1/_2$ cup salt (125 mL)
$^1/_4$ cup garlic powder (60 mL)
2 tbsp onion powder (30 mL)
1 tbsp black pepper (15 mL)
2 tsp cayenne pepper (10 mL)
1 tsp thyme (5 mL)

Yield: 24 servings
2 tbsp (30 mL) per serving
20 calories
0.8 g protein
1.0 g fat
1.5 g fiber
2.5 g net carbs

In large bowl, combine SPLENDA® Granular, paprika, chili powder, salt, garlic powder, onion powder, black pepper, cayenne pepper and thyme together. Store in airtight container.

BREADS, MUFFINS AND MORE

FLAX BREAD

*Induction Friendly – Atkins followers are allowed flax meal for
regularity, and here is an awesome way to get your flax.*

1 tbsp butter (15 mL)
2 tbsp flax meal, golden flax (30 mL)
  preferred
1 large egg
$^1/_2$ tsp baking powder (2 mL)

> **Yield:**
> 1 serving
> 249.0 calories
> 9.0 g protein
> 22.5 g fat
> 3.9 g fiber
> *0.6 g net carbs*

In microwave-safe bowl, soften butter. Add flax meal, egg, and baking powder
to butter. Mix until smooth. Microwave 2 minutes.

Variation: **Cinnamon Toast Bread:** Add $^1/_2$ tsp (2 mL) cinnamon to batter. If
desired, you can toast the bread after microwaving it. *Nutritional analysis:* 249
calories, 9 g protein, 22.5 g fat, 4.0 g fiber, *0.6 g net carbs*.

PUMPKIN MUFFIN IN A MINUTE

*Induction Friendly – Muffin in a minute recipes are very popular
on the Atkins Diet Facebook page, and here is my favorite version.*

1 oz cream cheese (30 g)
$^1/_4$ cup flax meal, golden flax (60 mL)
  preferred
$^1/_4$ cup pumpkin, canned (60 mL)
1 large egg
Liquid sucralose to equal 2 tsp (10 mL)
  SPLENDA® Granular
$^1/_2$ tsp cinnamon (2 mL)
$^1/_2$ tsp baking powder (2 mL)

> **Yield:** 2 servings
> 1 serving
> 175.0 calories
> 7.0 g protein
> 13.5 g fat
> 4.5 g fiber
> *3.5 g net carbs*

In microwave-safe bowl, soften cream cheese, about 10 to 15 seconds. Add flax
meal, pumpkin, egg, liquid sucralose, cinnamon, and baking powder. Mix until
smooth. Microwave 2 to 3 minutes until the center is cooked. Serve warm.

BANANA NUT BREAD

Extended Induction Friendly – The ultimate in low-carb snack breads, and it works equally well as a muffin or as a quick bread.

$^1/_2$ cup butter (125 mL)
4 oz cream cheese (125 g)
Liquid sucralose to equal 1 cup (250 mL)
SPLENDA® Granular
1 tbsp banana extract (15 mL)
1 tsp vanilla extract (5 mL)
5 large eggs
1 cup almond flour (250 mL)
$^1/_2$ cup coconut flour, home-ground (125 mL)
1 tsp baking powder (5 mL)
$^1/_3$ cup walnuts, chopped (75 mL)

Yield: 10 servings	

Yield: 10 servings
1 slice per serving
254.0 calories
7.8 g protein
23.6 g fat
2.0 g fiber
2.1 g net carbs

Preheat the oven to 350°F (180°C).

In microwave-safe bowl, soften butter by microwaving for 10 seconds. In stand mixer, add butter and cream cheese, and cream the ingredients together. Add liquid sucralose, banana extract and vanilla extract to the mixing bowl. Turn mixer on to low medium speed. Slowly add eggs individually until well combined. Scrape the sides to ensure everything is combined. Mix 30 seconds on medium speed.

Reduce mixer speed to low and add almond flour, coconut flour and baking powder. Mix 60 seconds. Mix walnuts into the batter. Pour into two well-greased mini loaf pans. Bake 25 to 35 minutes until an inserted knife returns clean or with a few crumbs.

~~Atkins Tips & Tricks~~

Utilize weight milestones or mini goals along the way towards your ultimate goal to keep you motivated. Perhaps every 10 or 25 pounds lost or perhaps crossing the 200 pound barrier would be a good milestone to reward and celebrate. These goals are like first downs in American Football. They give you the opportunity to see how far you have come and evaluate perhaps new things to do to reach the next milestone. "Is it time to progress to the next Phase (OWL or Pre-Maintenance)?" "Is it time to add a new rung or a new recipe to keep interested?"

These incremental mini goals are lines in the sand against recidivism as well. If something takes you off plan or away from goal, the milestones represent mental barriers to throwing in the towel or letting the derailment go unchecked.

CHEWY GARLIC CHEESE BISCUITS

Extended Induction Friendly – Want a gluten-free biscuit similar to the Cheddar Biscuits at Red Lobster, then this recipe is it.

2 oz butter, chilled (60 g)
2 cups almond flour (500 mL)
2 oz sharp Cheddar cheese, shredded (60 g)
$^1/_2$ tsp garlic powder (2 mL)
$^1/_2$ tsp dried parsley flakes (2 mL)
$^1/_2$ tsp baking soda (2 mL)
$^1/_8$ tsp salt (0.5 mL)
$^1/_2$ cup heavy cream (125 mL)
$^1/_2$ cup water (125 mL)

Yield: 10 servings
1 biscuit per serving
230.0 calories
6.3 g protein
21.8 g fat
2.4 g fiber
3.0 g net carbs

Preheat oven to 450°F (230°C).

In large bowl, cut the cold butter into the almond flour. Incorporate until the flour forms a coarse meal. Add cheese, garlic powder, parsley flakes, baking soda, and salt. Mix together.

Add heavy cream and just enough water to incorporate all the meal into a heavy dough ball. You can either make biscuits or breadsticks at this point. Line a sheet pan with parchment paper. Using a tablespoon, form into 10 small dough balls, and place lightly onto the parchment paper.

Bake 10 to 12 minutes until tops and bottoms are brown.

~~Atkins Tips & Tricks~~
When eating out on Atkins, do not be afraid of asking questions of your server. Remember you are the customer in this situation, and a good server wants a happy customer with their meal, and to be of service to them to presumably earn a good tip. Be willing to ask for substitutions or alterations if necessary. If you receive poor service or unwillingness to change to meet your needs, spend your entertainment and food dollars elsewhere.

The same forthrightness applies at the deli counter as well when dealing with unknown deli meats and finding out their carb counts.

LEMON POPPY SEED MUFFINS

Extended Induction Friendly – The ultimate in low-carb snack breads, and it works equally well as a muffin or as a quick bread.

$^1/_2$ cup butter (125 mL)
4 oz cream cheese (125 g)
Liquid sucralose to equal 1 cup (250 mL)
 SPLENDA® Granular
2 tsp lemon extract (30 mL)
1 tsp poppy seeds (5 mL)
5 large eggs
1 cup almond flour (250 mL)
$^1/_2$ cup coconut flour, home-ground (125 mL)
1 tsp baking powder (5 mL)

Yield: 12 muffins
1 muffin per serving
212.0 calories
6.5 g protein
20.0 g fat
1.7 g fiber
1.8 g net carbs

Preheat the oven to 350°F (180°C).

In microwave-safe bowl, soften butter. In stand mixer, add butter and cream cheese, and cream the ingredients together. Add liquid sucralose, lemon extract, and poppy seeds to the mixing bowl. Turn mixer on to low medium speed. Slowly add eggs individually until well combined. Scrape the sides to ensure everything is combined. Mix for 30 seconds on medium speed.

Reduce mixer speed to low, and add almond flour, coconut flour, and baking powder. Mix for 60 seconds. Place muffin liners into twelve muffin tins. Pour mixture into each muffin tin. Bake for 20 to 25 minutes until an inserted toothpick returns clean.

~~Atkins Tips & Tricks~~

Maintenance is a scary topic for many Atkins followers still losing weight. They hear all the stories from those who have regained all the weight after they reached goal. My trick for remaining at goal is:

- *Keep the same images in your head of why you wanted to lose the weight in the first place.*
- *Find a new goal to shoot for to keep motivated. Exercise-related goals are great ones to develop as they kill two birds with one stone.*
- *Finally, help others achieve the same success you did. It is much harder to give up the lessons you learned if you are teaching and helping others.*

"CHICKEN IN A BISKIT" CRACKERS

OWL Friendly – One of the things missing for most low-carbers is a chip or cracker replacement to use with dips or salsa. This recipe fills that need.

$^1/_2$ cup almond flour (125 mL)
$^1/_4$ cup coconut flour (60 mL)
$^1/_4$ cup Parmesan cheese, grated (60 mL)
1 tbsp ground chia seeds, heaping (15 mL)
1 tsp chicken bouillon (5 mL)
$^1/_4$ tsp garlic powder (1 mL)
$^1/_4$ tsp dried parsley (1 mL)
1 large egg
1 tbsp coconut oil (15 mL)
1 tbsp water (15 mL)

Yield: 6 servings
6-8 crackers per serving
120.0 calories
5.0 g protein
10.4 g fat
1.8 g fiber
1.5 g net carbs

Preheat the oven to 350°F (180°C).

In large bowl, combine the almond flour, coconut flour, Parmesan cheese, chia seeds, chicken bouillon, garlic powder and parsley.

In separate bowl, beat one egg and mix in the coconut oil. Combine with the dry ingredients. Add 1 tbsp (15 mL) or enough water to allow the dough ball to hold together.

Place dough ball on a cookie sheet, cover with plastic wrap, and roll out to roughly $^1/_4$-inch (0.6 cm) or less thickness. The thinner you roll the crackers out, the crispier the crackers will be. Use a fork to puncture the crackers in a row to help with the crispness. Bake 20 to 25 minutes or until crackers reach the desired level of doneness.

Helpful Hint: Chia seeds are great ingredients to add to recipes to hold moisture within the food. They hold more than ten times their weight in moisture.

~~Atkins Tips & Tricks~~

I am often asked how I stayed motivated to lose over two hundred pounds over fifteen months. My recommendation for everyone is to visualize why you want to lose the weight or said differently what does goal weight look like to you. I had a powerful vision for why I wanted to lose the weight – rejoin the National Guard, never having to be embarrassed by asking for an extender belt on an airplane, or being able to ride amusement park theme rides with my kids. Just being healthy or thin might not be clear enough motivation. By having this concrete vision of what goal looks like, you can use that as a shield against temptation. Do you want to be working towards that vision of success or away from it?

LOW-CARB DONUTS

OWL Friendly – A fast, quick snack with all the flavor of past,
unhealthy treats but with none of the negative consequences.

$^1/_4$ cup oil, coconut preferred (60 mL)
$^1/_4$ cup butter, melted (60 mL)
$^1/_4$ cup vanilla whey protein powder (60 mL)
$^1/_4$ cup almond flour (60 mL)
1 large egg
Liquid sucralose to equal 1 tbsp (15 mL)
 SPLENDA® Granular
$^1/_2$ tsp vanilla extract (2 mL)
1 tsp SPLENDA® Granular, (5 mL)
 powdered

Yield: 3 servings
2 mini donuts per serving
248.3 calories
12.2 g protein
22.0 g fat
1.0 g fiber
1.9 g net carbs

In a small omelet frying pan, add coconut oil and heat to 350°F (180°C).

In small bowl, add butter, vanilla whey protein powder, almond flour, and egg.
Beat together until well combined. Add liquid sucralose and vanilla extract; stir.

Using metal tablespoon, spoon out approximately 1 tbsp (15 mL) of mixture into
hot oil. Flip donuts when the outside is set, and the bottom of the donut is brown.
Cook approximately 45 to 60 seconds per side. Remove from oil, and place on a
paper towel. In coffee grinder or small blender, place SPLENDA® Granular and
process until the crystals are powdered. Sprinkle powdered SPLENDA® on top
of donuts. Serve warm.

~~Atkins Tips & Tricks~~

One of the misconceptions I often have to address with skeptics is how expensive
the diet is to do. I have personally found it to be the opposite as the only
required cost of the diet is the price of the book, which I found for less than a
dollar in a used book store. Here are my tips to keep food costs low:

- *Pay attention to what is on sale at the time. Items like meat and cheese,*
  even cream cheese, can be frozen to take advantage of sales.

- *Buy fresh vegetables in season and canned vegetables outside of the*
  season. Both are acceptable.

- *Instead of buying expensive ingredients like almond or coconut flour,*
  grind your own with a cheap coffee grinder or buy in bulk. The
  difference can be dramatic - $4 per lb of raw almonds vs. $9 to $14 per
  lb for almond flour.

- *Limit purchases of low-carb convenience or snack foods. They often add*
  greatly to the expense of the diet

SWEET ENDINGS

SCOTCHAROOS

OWL Friendly – Rice Krispie® treats were always a treat when growing up, and these are a definite hit at any party.

Peanut Butter Layer:
Liquid sucralose to equal 1 cup (250 mL)
 SPLENDA® Granular
²/₃ cup vanilla whey protein powder (150 mL)
¹/₂ cup butter, melted (125 mL)
¹/₂ cup peanut butter, sugar free (125 mL)
3 cups coconut, toasted, (750 mL)
 page 60

Chocolate Layer:
¹/₂ cup coconut oil, melted (125 mL)
Liquid sucralose to equal 3 tbsp (45 mL)
 SPLENDA® Granular
2 tsp (heaping) cocoa powder (12 mL)

Yield: 24 servings
1 inch square per serving
152.0 calories
4.3 g protein
14.3 g fat
1.3 g fiber
1.6 g net carbs

Peanut Butter Layer: In large bowl, add liquid sucralose, whey protein powder, butter, and peanut butter. Stir thoroughly. Add toasted coconut and combine thoroughly. Pour into metal loaf pan, and press flat with a piece of plastic wrap. Chill for 1 hour.

Chocolate Layer: In small bowl, combine coconut oil, liquid sucralose and cocoa powder. Remove peanut butter layer from refrigerator. Pour chocolate layer on top and press down any high areas. Chill 5 to 10 minutes in the freezer.

Helpful Hint: After the initial freeze, the Scotcharoos can be stored in the fridge or on a counter up to 3 or 4 hours without the chocolate layer melting.

~~Atkins Tips & Tricks~~

Seeing the changes in one's measurements is often a powerful voice against one's self doubt as well. It is difficult to discount the changes between when you started and today when the tape measure tells you that you have lost man yinches or centimeters. Your family may lie, your mirror may deceive you, but the tape measure changes are hard to ignore. If you are in a weight loss stall, capturing these changes can mean the difference between depression and motivation to continue dieting.

BANANA FLIP

*Extended Induction Friendly – Another portable snack cake perfect
for eating while on the go.*

Cakes:
$1\frac{1}{2}$ cups almond flour (375 mL)
$\frac{1}{2}$ cup coconut flour (125 mL)
1 tsp baking soda (5 mL)
$\frac{1}{3}$ cup butter (75 mL)
Liquid sucralose to equal $\frac{1}{2}$ cup (125 mL)
  SPLENDA® Granular
1 large egg
1 tsp vanilla extract (5 mL)
$\frac{1}{3}$ cup vanilla whey protein powder (75 mL)
$\frac{1}{3}$ cup heavy cream (75 mL)
$\frac{1}{3}$ cup water (75 mL)

Filling:
4 oz cream cheese (125 g)
Liquid sucralose to equal $\frac{1}{3}$ cup SPLENDA® Granular (75 mL)
3 tbsp butter (45 mL)
1 tbsp heavy cream (15 mL)
1 tsp vanilla extract (5 mL)
1 to 2 tsp banana extract (5 - 10 mL)
2 drops yellow food color

Yield: 10 servings
1 Banana Flip per serving
268.0 calories
9.4 g protein
25.5 g fat
2.1 g fiber
2.2 g net carbs

Preheat oven to 375°F (190°C).

Cakes: In large bowl, combine almond flour, coconut flour and baking soda. In bowl of a stand mixer, add butter, liquid sucralose, egg and vanilla extract. Start mixer and slowly add whey protein powder. Beat batter together until well combined. In small bowl, add cream and water and stir. Turn on stand mixer to low speed, and alternate adding a portion of flour mixture and cream mixture until all are combined. Scrape down sides of mixer and mix for another 20 seconds on medium.

Line a baking sheet pan with parchment paper, and using a tablespoon, portion out dollops on the sheet pan. Only do one pan at a time, and refrigerate the batter in between batches. Bake 8 to 9 minutes. Transfer finished cakes to cooling rack to cool for 30 minutes. Repeat process for remaining batter.

Filling: In second stand mixer bowl, add cream cheese, liquid sucralose, butter, cream, vanilla, banana extract and yellow food coloring. Whip the ingredients together. Match the banana flip cakes with similarly-sized cakes. Take the bottom and spread with filling. Place top cake on filling and press down.

PEANUT BUTTER COOKIES

OWL Friendly – Great portable snack for those low carbers on the go.

1 cup peanut butter, natural and (250 mL) sugar-free
$^1/_2$ cup almond flour (125 mL)
3 tbsp SPLENDA® Granular (45 mL)
1 tsp vanilla extract (5 mL)
1 large egg
$^1/_2$ tsp baking soda (2 mL)

Yield: 12 servings
1 cookie per serving
160.0 calories
7.0 g protein
13.5 g fat
2.0 g fiber
3.2 g net carbs

Preheat oven to 325°F (160°C).

In mixing bowl, add peanut butter, almond flour, Splenda® Granular, vanilla extract, egg, and baking soda. (**Note:** if your peanut butter does not include salt, add $^1/_2$ tsp (2 mL) salt to the mixing bowl.) Turn mixer on to medium speed for 2 minutes to combine ingredients. Mix until all dry ingredients have been combined. Line a cookie sheet with parchment paper. Using a tablespoon, portion out 1-inch (2.5 cm) balls of cookie dough onto the cookie sheet. Press cookie balls flat with a fork. Place cookie sheet in oven, and bake for 10 to 12 minutes. Remove from oven and place cookies to cool on cooling rack.

CHOCOLATE CHIA PUDDING

Extended Induction Friendly – This recipe is a quick, single-serving treat for people wanting a chocolate fix.

1 tbsp chia seeds (15 mL)
$^1/_2$ cup almond milk (125 mL)
1 tbsp (heaping) cocoa powder (20 mL)
Liquid sucralose to equal 2 tsp (10 mL)
  SPLENDA® Granular
$^1/_2$ tsp vanilla extract (2 mL)

Yield: 1 serving
116.0 calories
3.7 g protein
10.5 g fat
6.8 g fiber
3.7 g net carbs

To a Magic® or Ninja® blender cup, add chia seeds, and grind until powdered. To the blender cup, add almond milk, cocoa powder, liquid sucralose and vanilla extract. Process another 30 seconds until well combined. Chill 10 to 15 minutes until thickened.

Variation: **Banana Chia Pudding:** Replace cocoa powder with $^1/_2$ tsp (2 mL) banana extract. Optionally, add 2 drops of yellow food coloring for aesthetic purposes. *Nutritional analysis:* 108 calories; 3.7 g protein; 10.5 g fat; 4.2 g fiber; **3.5 g net carbs.**

MAGIC PEANUT BUTTER PUDDING

OWL Friendly – One oft-requested recipe is a snack one can prepare quickly.
This dish gets its name from the Magic Bullet® blender many use to mix it.

2 tbsp peanut butter (30 mL)
1 tbsp heavy cream (15 mL)
Liquid sucralose to equal 2 tsp (10 mL)
 SPLENDA® Granular
1 tbsp raw coconut, unsweetened (15 mL)

Yield: 1 serving
$^1/_2$ cup (125 mL) per serving
290.0 calories
9.0 g protein
26.4 g fat
3.2 g fiber
4.8 g net carbs

To the blender cup, add peanut butter, heavy cream, liquid sucralose, and coconut. Process the ingredients in the blender (Ninja® or Magic Bullet® blender recommended) for 30 to 60 seconds. The blender will beat air into the mixture and stiffen the heavy whipping cream to form a pudding-like consistency.

TOASTED COCONUT

Extended Induction Friendly – This recipe proves that not all delicious recipes
need to be involved or difficult to prepare.

3 cups raw coconut flakes (750 mL)
2 tbsp coconut oil, melted (30 mL)
2 tsp SPLENDA® Granular (10 mL)

Yield: 30 plus servings
1 tbsp (15 mL) per serving
27.0 calories
0.5 g protein
2.7 g fat
0.5 g fiber
0.7 g net carbs

Preheat oven to 350°F (180°C).

In large bowl, add the raw coconut and melted coconut oil. Mix the two ingredients together, and spread on a foil-lined quarter sheet pan.

Place sheet pan in oven for 4 minutes. Stir the coconut. Bake for another 4 minutes. Remove from oven and add Splenda® Granular and mix together.

WHOOPIE PIES

Extended Induction Friendly – Great snack or dessert reminiscent of Suzy Q® or HoHo® snack cakes.

Cakes:
5 tbsp butter (75 mL)
$^1/_2$ cup SPLENDA® Granular (125 mL)
1 tsp blackstrap molasses, optional (5 mL)
$^1/_3$ cup cocoa powder (75 mL)
1 large egg
1 tsp vanilla extract (5 mL)
1 tsp baking soda (5 mL)
$1^1/_2$ cups almond flour (375 mL)
$^1/_2$ cup coconut flour (125 mL)
$^1/_3$ cup heavy cream (75 mL)
$^1/_3$ cup water (75 mL)

Filling:
4 oz cream cheese (125 g)
3 tbsp butter (45 mL)
1 tsp vanilla extract (5 mL)
Liquid sucralose to equal $^1/_2$ cup (125 mL)
  SPLENDA® Granular
$^1/_3$ cup powdered sweetener (75 mL)
1 tbsp heavy cream (15 mL)

Yield: 8 servings
1 Whoopie Pie per serving
343.0 calories
7.8 g protein
32.4 g fat
3.3 g fiber
5.7 g net carbs

Preheat oven to 375°F (190°C).

Cakes: To stand mixer bowl, add butter, SPLENDA® Granular and molasses, if using. Cream ingredients together. Add cocoa powder, egg, vanilla extract and baking soda to the mixing bowl. In large bowl, add almond and coconut flour, and mix together. In small bowl, add cream and water; stir. Turn on stand mixer to low speed, and alternate adding a portion of flour mixture and wet ingredients until all are combined. Scrape down sides of mixer and mix for another 20 seconds on medium. Line a baking sheet pan with parchment paper, and using a tablespoon, portion out dollops on the sheet pan. Only do one pan at a time, and refrigerate the batter in between batches. Bake for 8 to 9 minutes. Move the finished cakes to a cooling rack to cool for 30 minutes. Repeat process for remaining batter.

Filling: In a second stand mixer bowl, add cream cheese, butter and vanilla. Cream the ingredients together and reduce mixer to slow speed. Slowly add liquid sucralose, powdered sweetener and heavy cream. Mix another 60 seconds on medium. Match cakes with similarly-sized cakes. Take the bottom and spread the filling on top. Place top cake on filling and press top cake down.

JUDY BARNES BAKER
APPETIZERS AND BEVERAGES

HERB ROASTED OLIVES

An Amuse Bouche is a flavorful, bite-sized appetizer that "entertains the mouth" as it awaits the main event. Toasting the olives makes them slightly chewy and concentrates the flavors in a way that is guaranteed to keep your bouche amused. Serve them solo with skewers for spearing or with my Parmesan Almond Chips, page 66.

1 cup pitted black olives (250 mL)
1 cup pitted Kalamata olives (250 mL)
1 cup green olives, stuffed with (250 mL)
  garlic, almonds, or pimento
8 to 10 whole garlic cloves, peeled
$^1/_4$ cup olive oil (60 mL)
1 tbsp Herbes de Provence, page 89 (15 mL)
1 tsp freshly-grated lemon zest (5 mL)
$^1/_4$ tsp freshly ground black pepper (1 mL)
Sprigs of fresh rosemary and/or thyme for garnish (optional)

Yield: 8 servings
1 serving
103 calories
0.5 g protein
10.5 g fat*
1.8 g net carbs

Preheat oven to 425°F (220°C).

Drain olives and place on small, rimmed baking sheet with garlic, olive oil, and Herbes de Provence, page 89. Toss together until well mixed. Bake 20 to 25 minutes or until olives are sizzling and garlic is starting to brown, stirring after first 10 minutes. Cool on pan until just warm. Transfer to a bowl, grate lemon zest and grind black pepper over olives and toss. Garnish with sprigs of herbs, if desired. Serve warm or at room temperature.

Helpful Hint: *Some of the fat included in the nutrition count stays in the pan.

~~Bits & Bites~~
I find it more economical to buy jarred olives at the big box stores like Costco. You can get a large jar for about the same price as a small one at the grocery store. I make this recipe often and they go quickly.

CHICKEN LIVER PATE

The secret ingredient that gives this silky pate *its savory depth of flavor is* anchovies. *Many people know them only as a strong, fishy-tasting pizza topping, but here in a supporting role, their sharp, salty taste is mellowed and subtle.* (*Recipe adapted from **Melissa Kronenthal, Beyond the Anchovy Aversion**, February 26, 2012,* The Seattle Times.)

1 lb chicken livers (0.45 kg)
$^1/_2$ cup butter, divided (125 mL)
$^1/_4$ cup minced shallot segments, (60 mL)
  about 3 medium, peeled and chopped
4 anchovy filets
$^1/_2$ cup dry sherry (125 mL)
$^1/_2$ tsp salt or to taste (2 mL)
$^1/_4$ tsp dried thyme (1 mL)
$^1/_8$ tsp ground allspice (0.5 mL)
$^1/_8$ tsp mace (optional) (0.5 mL)
Black pepper to taste
Sugar substitute equal to $^1/_4$ tsp sugar, optional (1 mL)
4 oz of cream cheese, softened (125 g)
1 or 2 fresh sage leaves for garnish (optional)

Yield: 16 servings
1 tbsp (15 mL) per serving
136 calories
13 g protein
12.5 g fat
1.7 g net carbs

Rinse livers and trim off any large pieces of fat, connective tissue, or dark spots. Drain and blot dry.

In heavy skillet, melt 1 tbsp (15 mL) butter over medium high heat. Add half the livers and sauté until browned but still pink in the center, about 2 minutes per side. Let cool slightly and transfer to a blender or processor. Wipe out skillet, add another tbsp (15 mL) butter to pan, and repeat with second batch of livers.

After livers are removed, wipe out skillet again and add 2 tbsp (30 mL) butter. Cook shallots until soft, about five minutes. Stir in anchovies and cook until they melt into a paste, about 2 minutes, then stir in sherry. Cook on medium high 5 or 6 minutes or until reduced to about 3 tbsp (45 mL) of liquid. Add shallot mixture to blender or processor. Add salt, thyme, allspice, mace if using, pepper, and sweetener, if using, and blend to a paste. Add cream cheese and 2 tbsp (30 mL) butter and blend until smooth. Taste and correct seasoning if needed. For an extra silky texture, press the mixture through a sieve.

Scrape pate into a 2-cup (500 mL) ceramic or glass container and smooth the surface. Refrigerate until firm, about four hours.

Melt remaining 2 tablespoons (30 mL) of butter over low heat. Place sage leaf, if using, on top of pate and pour butter over top. Tilt container so butter seals the entire surface. Chill until butter is firm and then cover with lid or plastic wrap.

Helpful Hints: Spread on toasted low-carb bread or crackers or use to fill celery sticks, cherry tomatoes, or tiny peppers.

Pate keeps refrigerated for about 2 weeks. After using some of the pate, melt additional butter and reseal exposed surface.

~~Bits & Bites~~

*Even Ancel Keys, the father of the **Lipid Hypothesis** (the theory that saturated fat causes heart disease), recognized the importance of including organ meats in the diet. His study of seven countries in the 1950s laid the foundation for the orthodoxy that continues today about the relationship between saturated fat and heart disease.*

*Keys and his wife, Margaret, invented the **Mediterranean Diet**, and although the modern perception is that it was an almost vegetarian regimen, an article in the 1961 issue of Time magazine that honored Keys as "Man of the Year," quoted him as saying that he and his wife ate steaks, chops, and roasts up to three times a week in addition to fish, chicken, Canadian bacon, and liver. He included liver because the Cretans, one of the two healthiest groups in his famous study were very fond of organ meats, like liver, spleen, and kidney. They also had the highest consumption of snails of anyone in the world.*

KALE CHIPS

Virtuous, crispy chips that taste fabulous! (I may try sneaking some of these into a movie!)

1¼ lbs black kale (0.57 kg)
¼ cup extra virgin olive oil (60 mL)
2 garlic cloves, peeled, and minced
Coarse salt and freshly ground black pepper
¼ cup finely grated Parmesan cheese (60 mL)
   OR to taste
Smoked finishing salt (optional)

Yield: 20 servings
1 serving
35 calories
0.9 g protein
3 g fat
0.9 g net carbs

Preheat oven to 350°F (180°C).

Fold kale leaves inward so center rib is on outside and use sharp knife to cut it off. Be sure to get all of rib as it is tough. Tear leaves into large pieces, rinse, and drain. Place in salad spinner and spin until completely dry. You will need to drain spinner and spin leaves more than once. Alternatively, place leaves in a large kitchen towel, roll up the towel and sling it around while holding the ends tightly.

Place olive oil in large bowl and mash garlic into oil. Add kale and toss until well coated on both sides. Spread kale out in one layer on two large baking sheets. Sprinkle with coarse salt and fresh pepper. Bake 6 to 8 minutes or until dry and crisp. Do not overcook or it will become bitter. Remove from oven and sprinkle with additional coarse salt or flavored finishing salt and grind more pepper over pan. Grate Parmesan over top and let cool. Store in airtight container.

Helpful Hints: For a final touch, I sprinkled my chips with mango-smoked sea salt that my daughter brought me from Hawaii. There are lots of specialty salts that you might try.

~~Bits & Bites~~
Black kale is also called lacinato or dinosaur kale. (Call them dinosaur chips if you want to lure the kids away from the Doritos!)

Dorot® makes frozen chopped basil, coriander, dill, parsley, and crushed garlic and ginger in trays of 20 cubes each. I especially like having the crushed garlic on hand. It thaws quickly and requires no peeling, measuring or chopping. There is a store locator on the website at www.mydorot.co.il.

PARMESAN ALMOND CHIPS

These remind me of Pringles®. Use them like chips with soup or burgers or like crackers with dips and spreads. They are perfect with the paté on page 63, or topped with a bit of caviar and crème frâiche as an hors d'oeuvre.

1 large egg white
1 cup almond flour, OR meal (250 mL)
3 tbsp finely grated Parmesan (45 mL)
  cheese
Sugar substitute equal to 2 tsp sugar (10 mL)
$^1/_8$ tsp freshly ground black pepper (0.5 mL)
$^1/_8$ tsp coarse salt, PLUS more (0.5 mL)
  for topping

> **Yield:** 48 chips
> 1 chip
> 16 calories
> 0.7 g protein
> 1.3 g fat
> *0.2 g net carbs*

Preheat oven to 325°F (160°C). Place a piece of parchment paper on large baking sheet. You will also need something for pressing the chips, like a flat meat pounder or a measuring cup with a flat bottom, and some plastic wrap.

Whisk egg white in a medium bowl until blended. Add almond flour, Parmesan, sugar substitute, pepper and salt and mix well. Form dough into 48 small balls, about $^1/_2$-inch (1.2 cm) in diameter. Place balls about 3 inches (7 cm) apart on parchment-lined pans. Cover with a sheet of plastic wrap and flatten balls into thin circles, roughly 2 inches (5 cm) across, with flat-bottomed glass or measuring cup. Make them as thin as possible without having them tear when plastic is removed.

Carefully remove plastic. Sprinkle chips with pepper and coarse salt and tap in place. Bake 10 to 12 minutes or until evenly golden brown and crisp. Repeat with remaining balls. Store in airtight container.

Helpful Hints: You will be tempted to eat these like potato chips. Make a few at a time and refrigerate the remaining dough to help with portion control or freeze some of the baked chips in serving-size containers to have on hand to accompany soup, chili, or salads.

~~Bits & Bites~~
The name, Parmegiano-Reggiano, can only be used for cheese imported from certain regions in Italy. It is made from raw milk from grass-fed cows and it is aged for 12 to 24 months. As it ages, the protein breaks down to produce crystals, giving it a characteristic crunchy texture. The longer it ages, the more grainy it becomes and the easier to digest.

STUFFED MUSHROOMS
No soggy mushrooms with this recipe!

12 medium-large brown or white mushrooms
$^1/_2$ tsp salt (2 mL)
6 oz (6 slices) bacon (180 g)
3 oz cream cheese, room temperature (90 g)
$^1/_4$ cup shredded Cheddar cheese (60 mL)
1 garlic clove, peeled and crushed
Additional salt, if desired
Pepper to taste
Chopped fresh chives and/or parsley for garnish (optional)

Yield: 12 servings
1 stuffed mushroom
104 calories
3.4 g protein
9.7 g fat
1.1 g net carbs

Lightly grease a shallow pan or baking sheet. Preheat oven to 425°F (220°C).

Rinse mushrooms and remove stems. Place, rounded side up, on lightly greased baking pan and sprinkle lightly with salt. Bake 10 minutes. Remove from oven and drain on paper towels. Blot with additional paper towels, pressing down into caps to soak up excess moisture. Lower oven temperature to 350°F (180°C).

Cook bacon until crisp and chop or crumble. Place cream cheese in medium bowl and work with spatula until creamy. Stir in bacon, Cheddar cheese, garlic, salt if using, and pepper. Fill mushroom caps with mixture and place on a shallow pan or baking sheet. Bake about 30 minutes. Let stand 5 minutes. Sprinkle with optional garnish and serve hot.

LIMEADE
Sweetened beverages are said to be the #1 source of calories in the diet of Americans. A 12-ounce serving of regular cola contains 10 teaspoons of sugar, usually high-fructose corn syrup. Why so much? Carbonated water tastes bitter and it takes a lot of sugar to counteract it. (Taste a flat Coke to see how sickeningly sweet it is.) Make your own drinks for your family using fresh ingredients and get the sugar and caffeine out.

1 cup water (250 mL)
1 lime or about 2 tbsp fresh (30 mL)
  lime juice
Sugar substitute equal to 2 tbsp sugar (30 mL)
Ice for serving
A sprig of mint OR a twist of lime, page 68
  (optional)

Yield: 1 serving
1 serving
6 calories
0 g protein
0 g fat
1.8 g net carbs

In container, mix together water, lime juice, and sweetener and serve over ice. Garnish with a sprig of mint or a twist of lime.

LIME RICKY

This old fashioned soda fountain drink is still the perfect summer cooler.

2 fresh limes, OR $^1/_4$ cup lime juice (60 mL)
Crushed or shaved ice
12 drops EZ-Sweetz®, OR
$^1/_4$ cup equivalent (60 mL)
Dash Angostura bitters
$^3/_4$ cup carbonated water (175 mL)
1 Lime Twist, below
1 cherry, with stem, for garnish (optional)

Yield: 1 serving
1 serving
7 calories
0 g protein
0 g fat
3.6 g net carbs

Lime Ricky: Roll limes on the counter or soak them in warm water for a few minutes to release more juice. Into a bowl, squeeze juice from limes. Fill a tall glass two-thirds full of crushed ice. Add lime juice, EZ-Sweetz®, OR equivalent and dash of bitters to the glass. Top with carbonated water. Stir and garnish with lime twist and fresh cherry, if using, and serve with a straw.

Lime Twist: Cut a $^1/_4$-inch (0.6 cm) slice from the center of a lime. Lay it flat and use a paring knife to cut around lime flesh and remove it, leaving a ring of rind with a small amount of white pith. Split one side of the ring and scrape away most of the pith with a spoon or paring knife. Roll up rind and rub colored side around the rim of the glass and then twist into a tight spiral and pull on ends to release the coil. Drop twist into drink or drape over side of glass.

~~Bits & Bites~~
A twist of lime is more than just a pretty garnish; it adds a burst of intensely-flavored citrus oil.

ROSE LASSI

A lassi is an Indian "milkshake" made with yogurt. Salty lassis, flavored with chili pepper and cumin, are popular in India, but most Westerners prefer the sweet ones like this fragrant version made with the distilled essence of rose petals and cardamom.

$^3/_4$ cup plain kefir, OR yogurt, (175 mL)
  whole milk if possible
2 tbsp heavy cream (30 mL)
$1^1/_2$ tsp rose water* (7 mL)
Sugar substitute equal to 3 tbsp (45 mL)
  sugar
$^1/_2$ tsp ground cardamom (2 mL)
5 standard ice cubes

Yield: 1 serving
1 serving
216 calories
6.6 g protein
17.1 g fat
3.8 g net carbs

In blender, put kefir, OR yogurt, cream, rose water, sugar substitute and cardamom and blend for about 30 seconds. Add ice cubes and blend for an additional 30 seconds or until frothy. (It will still have some chunks of ice.) Pour into tall glass and serve at once. Alternately, whisk ingredients together and pour over ice.

Helpful Hints: Nutrition data above excludes some of the sugar in the yogurt or kefir that has been eaten by the live cultures. About 4 grams per cup (250 mL) remains.

*Rose water can be found with the ethnic foods in some grocery stores or from Middle Eastern and Indian markets. It can be ordered online from Dyna's Market, where rose water is listed under the cooking aids: *http://www.daynasmarket.com/cooking_aids.html*

~~Bits & Bites~~
Kefir is liquid yogurt. Look for one made with whole milk that contains live cultures. Both yogurt and kefir are probiotics that provide "good" bacteria for the digestive tract and enhance the immune system by keeping the bad guys out. But while both yogurt and kefir contain friendly bacteria, kefir also contains beneficial yeast cultures. Kefir made from coconut milk is also available.

SALTY LASSI WITH MINT
A tangy, refreshing, and healthful probiotic drink.

$^3/_4$ cup plain kefir, OR yogurt with (175 mL)
  live cultures
2 tbsp heavy cream (30 mL)
6 fresh mint leaves, divided
$^1/_4$ tsp ground, toasted cumin (1 mL)
$^1/_4$ tsp coarse salt (1 mL)
4 to 5 standard ice cubes

Yield: 1 serving
1 serving
219 calories
6.8 g protein
17.1 g fat
4.1 g net carbs

In a blender, put kefir, OR yogurt, cream, and 4 of the mint leaves and blend for 30 seconds, or until mint is finely chopped. Add cumin, salt, and ice cubes and blend another 30 seconds until frothy. (It will still have some chunks of ice.) Pour into a tall glass. Lightly crush remaining mint leaves and place on top. Serve.

Helpful Hints: To toast cumin, heat and stir in a dry skillet over medium heat until fragrant, about 2 or 3 minutes.

Nutrition data excludes the sugar eaten by the live cultures in the kefir or yogurt.

~~Bits & Bites~~
Full-fat dairy products from pastured cows have several important health benefits. They contain the elusive vitamin K2, which along with the fat-soluble vitamins A and D, strengthens bones and reduces the risk of strokes and heart disease. They also contain CLA (conjugated linoleic acid), a powerful fatty acid believed to help with weight management and promote general health.

Fermented dairy products with live cultures must list the same number of carbohydrates as the milk that goes into them, but, according to Drs. Jack Goldberg and Karen O'Mara, authors of the Go-Diet, most of the sugar has been converted to lactic acid. That is why milk tastes sweet but buttermilk and yogurt taste sour. The amount of carbohydrate remaining after fermentation is about 4 grams per cup.*

*Jack Goldberg, Ph.D., and Karen O'Mara, D.O., GO-Diet: The Goldberg-O'Mara Diet Plan, the Key to Weight Loss & Healthy Eating, Go Corp, 1999.

SALADS AND SOUPS

ASPARAGUS RIBBONS WITH PARMESAN VINAIGRETTE

This salad is a revelation! Raw asparagus, shaved into beautiful green and white-striped strips, makes a delightful new salad green.

Salad:
12 large asparagus spears, about 1 lb (0.45 kg)
Parmesan Vinaigrette:
$^1/_4$ cup finely grated Parmesan cheese (60 mL)
$1^1/_2$ tbsp fresh lemon juice (22 mL)
Salt and freshly ground black pepper
$^1/_4$ cup extra virgin olive oil (60 mL)
Garnish:
$^1/_4$ cup toasted, sliced almonds (60 mL)

Yield: 4 servings
1 serving
193 calories
5 g protein
18.2 g fat
2.3 g net carbs

Salad: Snap off ends of asparagus stalks. They will naturally break at the point where they become tough.

Shave asparagus by working with one spear at a time. Hold down firmly, and starting at stem end, pull vegetable peeler down length of stalk, pressing down firmly and evenly to make long, thin shavings. Try to get some of tip on each strip, but if tips break off, just add them to salad. Transfer to a medium bowl.

Parmesan Vinaigrette: In small bowl, combine grated Parmesan, lemon juice, salt, and pepper. Slowly whisk in olive oil until thickened and well blended.

Drizzle vinaigrette over asparagus ribbons and toss gently to coat. Divide asparagus salad among chilled plates and scatter almonds over the top.

Helpful Hint: When shaving asparagus, it helps if you put the cutting board near the edge of the counter to make room for your knuckles.

~~Bits & Bites~~
"It ain't what we don't know that gives us trouble. It's what we know for sure that ain't so." - Variously attributed to Mark Twain, Josh Billings, and Artemus Ward.

CRANBERRY CHICKEN SALAD WITH CHAMPAGNE VINAIGRETTE

This crunchy, fruity salad is also perfect as a main dish for lunch or supper.

Cranberries:
1 oz freeze-dried cranberries, (30 g) (unsweetened)
$^1/_4$ cup water (60 mL)
Sugar substitute equal to 2 tbsp sugar, (30 mL) with bulk*

Salad:
2 cups cooked chicken, cubed (500 mL)
2 cups jicama, peeled and diced into $^1/_2$-inch (1.3 cm) cubes (500 mL)
2 cups celery, cut diagonally into $^1/_2$-inch (1.3 cm) slices (500 mL)
6 slices of bacon, cooked until crisp and chopped
4 or 5 green onions, white and light green parts only, chopped
$^1/_3$ cup sliced almonds, raw or toasted (75 mL)
Salt and fresh black pepper to taste
Champagne Vinaigrette, page 88

Yield: 6 servings
1 serving with vinaigrette
521 calories
18.7 g protein
45.8 g fat
5.1 g net carbs

Cranberries: In medium saucepan, combine cranberries with water and sweetener. Simmer until water is evaporated and berries are plump and sweet. Remove cranberries with slotted spoon and drain on paper towels.

Salad: In large bowl, add chicken, jicama, celery, bacon, onions, almonds, salt, pepper and cranberries. Toss to combine. Just before serving, add 1 cup (250 mL) of Champagne Vinaigrette, page 88, and toss again, or serve dressing with the salad.

Helpful Hints: *Sweeteners with bulk include Just Like Sugar®, LC-sweet®, Sweet Perfection®, Swerve®, and any of the stevia or sucralose blends with inulin or oligofructose. Granular Splenda® has been fluffed up with maltodextrin to give it volume, but it has almost no bulk.

~~Bits & Bites~~
Most "sugar-free" dried cranberries are sweetened with concentrated apple juice, not really an improvement over the sugar-sweetened ones. (Sugar is sugar whether it comes from a cane, a beet, an apple, or corn.) Freeze-dried, unsweetened cranberries are available from:
LC-Foods: www.holdthecarbs.com, Nuts.com: www.nuts.com, and Cherry Bay Orchards: www.cherrybayorchards.com.

LETTUCE WEDGE SALAD WITH BLUE CHEESE DRESSING

*Iceberg lettuce has been out of vogue in recent years, perhaps because it was so overused. I can't argue that it has much in the way of nutrients, and it is a bit bland compared to romaine or butterhead, but you can't do justice to this classic salad without the dense, crisp texture of iceberg lettuce. From **Nourished; A Cookbook for Health, Weight Loss, and Metabolic Balance.***

Blue Cheese Dressing:
$^1/_2$ cup real mayonnaise (125 mL)
$^1/_2$ cup plain Greek yogurt, OR (125 mL)
  sour cream
2 oz mild blue cheese, such as (60 g)
  Gorgonzola
1 tbsp lemon juice (15 mL)
Salt and fresh black pepper to taste

Salad:
16 slices bacon, about $^1/_2$ lb (250 g)
1 head iceberg lettuce, outer leaves removed
Coarse salt, to taste
Fresh black pepper, to taste
2 tbsp chopped, fresh chives, optional (30 mL)

> **Yield:** 8 servings
> 1 serving with dressing
> 186 calories
> 5.7 g protein
> 16.7 g fat
> *2.9 g net carbs*

Blue Cheese Dressing: In medium bowl, combine mayonnaise, yogurt, OR sour cream, blue cheese, and lemon juice, and whisk until just combined; small lumps of blue cheese should remain. Add salt and pepper to taste and chill. Dressing can be made ahead and refrigerated.

Salad: In skillet, cook bacon until crisp and drain. Rinse lettuce and blot dry. Cut head of lettuce vertically into 8 wedges. Remove core and place one lettuce wedge on each of 8 chilled salad plates. Top each with 3 tbsp (45 mL) of dressing and crumble 2 strips of bacon on top. Sprinkle with coarse salt and freshly ground black pepper. Garnish with chopped chives, if desired, and serve.

~~*Bits & Bites*~~
*"The public perception is that nitrite/nitrate are carcinogens but they are not....Many studies implicating nitrite and nitrate in cancer are based on very weak epidemiological data. If nitrites and nitrates were harmful to us, then we would not be advised to eat green leafy vegetables or swallow our own saliva, which is enriched in nitrate." - **Dr. Nathan Bryanm Ph.D., from the Institute of Molecular Medicine at the University of Texas in Houston.***

ROASTED RED PEPPER AND PRESERVED LEMON SALAD

I've updated this traditional salad from Morocco by using sweet, roasted red bell peppers instead of green peppers. Please do try this; it is sooo good!

3 Roasted Red Peppers, page 86
1 Preserved Lemon, page 91, pulp discarded,
  rind finely diced
2 garlic cloves, peeled and minced
3 tbsp chopped, fresh Italian parsley (45 mL)
1¹/₂ tbsp extra virgin olive oil (22 mL)
1 tbsp fresh lemon juice (15 mL)
Salt and freshly ground black pepper to taste

Yield: 4 servings
1 serving
87 calories
1.6 g protein
5.5 g fat
6.7 g net carbs

Roast peppers according to directions on page 86, using 3 rather than 2 peppers. Remove charred skin and dice. In medium bowl, combine peppers, Preserved Lemon rind, page 91, garlic, parsley, olive oil, lemon juice, salt and pepper. Toss to combine.

~~*Bits & Bites*~~
Several small salads (or mezze) are usually served together at the beginning of a Moroccan meal. Most often, they are made of cooked or roasted vegetables, like this one. This recipe will serve 2 or 3 as a solo starter salad or a side dish, 4 when used as one of several salads or as a relish or a condiment.

STRACCIATELLI SOUP WITH SPINACH

This healthful soup is the perfect way to use your own wonderful homemade chicken stock.

4 cups chicken stock (1 L)
4 large eggs
1 oz freshly-grated Parmesan cheese, (30 g)
  about $^1/_2$ cup (125 mL)
Pepper to taste
Ground nutmeg to taste
4 cups fresh baby spinach (1 L)
Salt if needed

Yield: 4 servings
1 serving
112 calories
11.2 g protein
62 g fat
0.9 g net carbs

In large saucepan, bring stock to a boil and then reduce heat to medium.

Break eggs into medium bowl and whisk until well blended. Whisk in cheese, pepper, and sprinkle of nutmeg.

Pour egg mixture in thin stream into simmering stock. Let cook for a few seconds and then whisk to break up strands of egg and whisk for about 2 minutes more. Add spinach and stir gently until spinach is wilted. Taste before adding salt, since stock and cheese may provide enough. Serve soup in heated bowls.

*~~**Bits & Bites**~~*
Stracciatelli means, "little rags," in Italian. It refers to the strands of egg in this Roman version of egg drop soup.

Most canned chicken broth or stock is mostly flavored water with MSG and sugar added to make it taste good. (Real stock will gel when it is cold.) Bouillon cubes are even worse; most of them list a small amount of chicken as one of the last ingredients, if at all. Make your own stock with chicken bones whenever possible. Add a little vinegar to the pot to draw the calcium out of the bones.

Dr. Ann Childers, also known as the NutriPsych, is a child and adult trained psychiatric physician. She helps her patients regain their physical and mental health through nutrition and sleep. She prescribes 2 cups (500 mL) of bone broth a day for her patients.

LANGOSTINO CREAM SOUP

Langostinos taste like tender, bite-sized lobsters. They are much less expensive and equally delicious. This recipe was adapted from **chef Jasper Mirabile Jr.'s Lobster Cappuccino.**

$^1/_2$ lb cooked langostino meat (250 g)
$^1/_3$ cup dry sherry (75 mL)
$^1/_4$ cup butter (60 mL)
$^1/_4$ onion, peeled and minced
2 cups organic, heavy cream (500 mL)
$^1/_2$ cup water or low-carb milk (125 mL)
$^1/_8$ tsp dried tarragon (0.5 mL)
Salt and pepper to taste
2 cups shredded Gruyere, Emmental, Fontina, OR Mozzarella cheese (500 mL)
$^1/_2$ cup organic, heavy cream, beaten to soft peaks (125 mL)
3 strips bacon, fried crisp, drained, and crumbled

> **Yield:** 4 servings
> 2 cups (500 mL) per serving
> 1,004 calories
> 33.3 g protein
> 95.1 g fat
> **5.8 g net carbs**

In small bowl, combine langostinos and sherry and set aside.

Melt butter in medium saucepan over low heat. Add onion and sauté until translucent. Gradually stir in cream and water. Season with tarragon, salt, and pepper and heat on low just until hot.

Stir in langostinos and sherry. Cover and heat gently over very low heat for 5 minutes. Add cheese of choice and stir until melted and well blended. Do not boil!

Ladle into heated soup bowls and top with whipped cream and bacon crumbles. Garnish with a sprig of fresh tarragon, if desired.

Helpful Hint: You can substitute cut-up lobster meat or shrimp in this recipe.

~~Bits & Bites~~

Langostino is Spanish for "little lobster." Several edible crustaceans that resemble small lobsters or large shrimp may be called langostinos, but in the US, it usually refers to the squat lobster.

It is especially important to buy organic dairy products. Most dairy cows are fed cottonseed to increase cream production. Cotton is not considered a food crop, so it can be treated with pesticides and chemicals that are not approved for use on plants used for food.

BREAKFASTS

CHEESE SOUFFLES

An easy and impressive dish that can be served for breakfast, as a main course for brunch or luncheon, as an appetizer, or the one I like best, as a delicious, low-carb side dish.

1 cup grated Gruyère cheese (250 mL)
$^1/_4$ cup Parmesan cheese (60 mL)
1 cup heavy cream (250 mL)
3 large eggs
$^1/_2$ tsp salt (2 mL)
$^1/_8$ tsp cayenne pepper (0.5 mL)

Yield: 4 servings
1 serving
363 calories
13.9 g protein
33.5 g fat
2.3 g net carbs

Preheat oven to 325°F (160°C). Butter 4, 1-cup (250 mL) capacity ramekins. Stir together Gruyère and Parmesan cheese and place one fourth of mixture in each buttered baking cup.

Heat cream until just warm. You should be able to comfortably touch the pan. If cream is too hot, it will cook the eggs. Whisk together cream, eggs, salt, and pepper until smooth. Pour custard mixture over cheese, filling cups almost to top. Put ramekins on baking sheet and place on middle rack in preheated oven. Bake 35 to 40 minutes or until puffed and brown. Check by looking through oven window; do not open oven door until custards are well risen. Place on a rack and let cool for about 5 minutes. Custards will sink a bit as they cool. Serve warm.

Helpful Hints: This recipe makes 2 servings as a main dish or 4 as a side.

~~Bits and Bites~~

The British Medical Journal reported that women who took calcium supplements had a higher risk of atherosclerosis, heart attack, and stroke than those who didn't. Vitamin K2, which is scarce in our modern food supply, is necessary to make sure calcium gets into the bones where it is needed rather than being deposited in soft tissues. Traditional societies obtained K2 from the meat, dairy products, and eggs of animals eating a natural diet of green plants.
*"When animals grazed on pasture, vitamin K2 was abundant in our food supply. The most common dietary staples, like butter, eggs, cheese, and meat, even when eaten in small quantities, easily met our needs. Now we consume large quantities of the mass-produced versions of these foods, but we are starving for the nutrients they no longer contain." – **Dr. Kate Rheaume-Bleue, Vitamin K2 and the Calcium Paradox, 2012.***

BACON LEEK SOUFFLE

I made only a few changes to the gorgeous soufflé pictured in the June/July 2011 issue of **Fine Cooking**. *The recipe says it makes 6 servings, but two of us ate half of it for supper with a green salad and finished off the rest for breakfast the next day. The recipe warned that it would deflate if not served at once, but mine was still firm and high after a night in the fridge and a few minutes in the microwave.*

5 slices bacon, thinly sliced crosswise
2 medium leeks, light green and white parts
  only, chopped
$1/2$ tsp dried thyme (2 mL)
$1/4$ tsp salt (1 mL)
$1/4$ tsp freshly ground black pepper (1 mL)
$1/2$ cup low-carb milk*, OR (125 mL)
  $1/4$ cup heavy cream and (60 mL)
  $1/4$ cup water (60 mL)
5 oz cream cheese, cut into cubes (150 g)
$1/2$ cup grated Parmesan cheese (125 mL)
5 large eggs, separated
1 large egg white

Yield: 6 servings
1 serving
329 calories
12.4 g protein
29.4 g fat
4.2 g net carbs

Preheat oven to 325°F (160°C). Grease 8-inch (20 cm) square baking pan.

In medium skillet, cook bacon crisp, about 8 minutes. Using slotted spoon, transfer bacon to a large bowl. Add leeks to skillet, reduce heat to medium low, cover, and cook, stirring occasionally, about 4 minutes or until softened. Place leeks in bowl with bacon and stir in thyme, salt, and pepper.

In skillet on medium low heat, gently warm milk or milk substitute. Stir in cream cheese and Parmesan and whisk until melted and smooth. Stir milk and cheese mixture into bowl with bacon and leeks. Let cool until just warm. Gently stir in egg yolks and set aside.

In medium bowl, beat 6 egg whites with electric mixer to medium-stiff peaks. With a large rubber spatula, carefully fold egg whites into leek and bacon mixture. Scrape mixture into greased pan and bake until puffed and brown on top, 22 to 24 minutes. Serve immediately.

Helpful Hints: Baking time may vary as oven temperatures tend to be somewhat different. If it is still soupy in the middle, put it back in the oven for another 5 minutes or so.

*You can use sugar-free coconut or almond milk, LC-Foods® or Hood's® low-carb milk, or "Milk" made using my recipe in my cookbook, *Nourished.*

MAIN COURSES AND SIDES

CHICKEN WITH PRESERVED LEMON AND ROSEMARY

Having Preserved Lemons, page 91, on hand lets you stir up this zesty chicken dish in a matter of minutes.

1$^1/_2$ lbs boneless, skinless chicken, (0.68 kg)
thighs or breasts cut across the grain into
$^1/_2$-inch strips (1.3 cm)
3 tbsp light olive oil, divided (45 mL)
2 tbsp finely chopped, fresh rosemary (30 mL)
leaves
$^1/_2$ tsp black pepper (2 mL)
1 Preserved Lemon, page 91, OR
purchased preserved lemon
2 leeks, white and light green parts, well rinsed and thinly sliced
2 garlic cloves, peeled and finely chopped
Sugar substitute equal to 1 tbsp sugar, optional (15 mL)
1 tbsp fresh lemon juice (15 mL)
Salt, if needed.

Yield: 4 servings
1 serving
309 calories
38.7 g protein
13.1 g fat
6.7 g net carbs

In large bowl, toss chicken with 1 tbsp (15 mL) of oil, the rosemary, and pepper.

Rinse preserved lemon well to remove salt and blot dry. Pull out and discard lemon flesh, leaving just the peel. Slice peel horizontally into $^1/_8$-inch (0.3 cm) slices.

Heat medium skillet over high heat. Add remaining 2 tbsp (30 mL) oil. When oil shimmers in pan, add lemon peel and stir-fry quickly until golden brown. Stir in leeks and reduce heat to medium high. Cook until leeks are soft, about 3 minutes. Stir in garlic and cook 1 minute more. Remove lemon peel, leek, and garlic mixture from the pan. Add chicken and sear, without moving, about 4 minutes. Stir leek mixture back into pan and continue to cook until chicken is done to taste, about 3 to 6 minutes more. Add sweetener, if using. Drizzle with lemon juice. Taste and add salt if needed (the preserved lemon may add enough salt).

~~Bits & Bites~~
Preserved lemons can be purchased in jars from Williams Sonoma or from Mediterranean and Middle Eastern markets. They can also be ordered online from Amazon.

CADDY GANTY

The wife of a fish packer who lived in Pelican Alaska is credited with creating this dish in the 1920s. Her name was Caddy Ganty. This version is based on one from the Gustavus Inn where we stopped over on our way to Glacier Bay, National Park a few years ago.

2 lbs fresh, skinless halibut fillets (0.9 kg)
  or other firm, white fish, at least 1-inch
  (2.5 cm) thick
1 tbsp coarse salt (15 mL)
1$^1/_2$ cups white wine (375 mL)
1 tbsp butter for the baking dish (15 mL)
2 cups sour cream, not low-fat (500 mL)
1 cup chopped green onion, green (250 mL)
  part only
1 cup mayonnaise (250 mL)
$^1/_4$ cup grated Parmesan cheese (60 mL)
1 tsp paprika (5 mL)

Yield: 4 servings
1 serving
878 calories
53 g protein
71.3 g fat
3.9 g net carbs

Preheat oven to 350°F (180°C).

Cut halibut fillets into 3 to 4-inch pieces (7.5 to 10 cm). Place cut up fish in high-rimmed baking dish, sprinkle with salt and add wine. Cover and place in refrigerator to marinate for 2 to 3 hours. Do not marinate longer, or wine will begin to break down the fish.

Butter shallow baking dish that is large enough to hold the fish in a single layer. Blot fish dry with paper towels and place in prepared baking dish.

In small bowl, combine the sour cream, chopped green onion, and mayonnaise. Spread the mixture evenly across top of fish, being careful to completely cover. Sprinkle with Parmesan and paprika.

Bake 25 to 30 minutes. Top should be lightly browned and bubbling and the fish should flake easily.

Helpful Hint: The nutrition count excludes 1.3 grams of carbohydrate per serving that have been eaten by the live cultures in the sour cream.

CRISP-BRAISED DUCK LEGS WITH VEGETABLES

A delicious, country-style, one-dish meal of crispy-skinned duck and meltingly tender vegetables.

1 large leek, white and light green parts only
4 whole duck legs (drumstick and thigh)
Salt and pepper to taste
1 lb rutabaga (3 or 4 small), peeled (0.45 kg)
  and cut into chunks
3 celery stalks, cut into $^1/_2$-inch (1.3 cm) slices
4 to 5 garlic cloves, peeled and lightly crushed
1 tsp dried thyme or several sprigs (5 mL)
  fresh thyme
2 cups chicken stock, preferably homemade, more as needed (500 mL)

> *Yield:* 4 servings
> 1 serving
> 154 calories
> 11.1 g protein
> 4.2 g fat
> *13.1 g net carbs*

Preheat oven to 400°F (200°C).

Split leek lengthwise and rinse well, checking between layers for dirt. Cut crosswise into $^1/_2$-inch (1.3 cm) wide slices.

Sprinkle duck legs with salt and pepper and place, skin-side down, in oven-proof skillet large enough to hold all ingredients. Place pan over medium heat and cook until skin is evenly browned. Turn duck legs over and sear for just a minute or two on cut side. Place on plate and set aside.

Remove all but 2 tbsp (30 mL) of fat from pan; reserve rest of fat for another purpose. Add leeks, rutabaga, celery, garlic and thyme to skillet and sprinkle with salt and pepper. Cook over medium high heat, stirring occasionally, until they begin to brown, 10 to 15 minutes. Return duck legs to pan skin-side up, and add stock until it comes about halfway up duck legs but does not cover them. Turn heat to high and bring to a boil. Remove pan from heat and transfer to preheated oven.

Cook 30 minutes, then lower heat to 350°F (180°C). Continue to cook, without turning, until duck is tender and liquid is reduced, at least another half hour. Duck is done when tip of a knife easily pierces meat and skin is very crisp. Duck can be held in warm oven for another hour, if necessary. Serve hot with vegetables and pan juices.

SLOPPY JOE STUFFED RED PEPPERS

*Trade those soggy buns for tender-crisp, baked red peppers. (Recipe adapted from **Linda Sue Genaw, www.genaw.com**.)*

1 lb ground beef, grass fed (0.45 kg)
  if possible
$^1/_4$ cup chopped onion (60 mL)
1 stalk celery, chopped
1 clove garlic, peeled and minced
$^1/_4$ cup dried tomatoes packed in (60 mL)
  garlic-flavored oil, snipped or diced
$^3/_4$ cup tomato sauce (175 mL)
$1^1/_2$ tsp white vinegar (7 mL)
$1^1/_2$ tsp Worcestershire sauce (7 mL)
Sugar substitute equal to 1 tsp sugar (5 mL)
$^1/_2$ tsp dry mustard (2 mL)
$^1/_2$ tsp salt (2 mL)
$^1/_8$ tsp black pepper (0.5 mL)
2 cups shredded Cheddar cheese, divided (500 mL)
3 red bell peppers, halved lengthwise and seeded

Yield: 6 servings
1 serving
335 calories
25.2 g protein
23 g fat
5 g net carbs

Preheat oven to 350°F (180°C). Grease a 9-inch (23 cm) baking pan or dish.

In large skillet, cook ground beef over medium heat until it starts to brown. Drain off extra fat and add onion, celery, and garlic (use an extra clove of garlic if dried tomatoes are not packed in garlic-flavored oil). Add dried tomatoes and some of the garlic-flavored oil. Stir in tomato sauce, white vinegar, Worcestershire sauce, sugar substitute, dry mustard, salt and pepper. Simmer 10 minutes. Stir half the cheese into hamburger mixture.

Place peppers in greased baking dish and fill with meat and cheese mixture. Top with remaining cheese. Bake 20 to 25 minutes until hot and bubbly and peppers are tender-crisp.

Helpful Hint: Use purchased dried tomatoes packed in garlic-flavored olive oil, OR increase garlic in recipe to 2 cloves and use plain dried tomatoes that have been covered with olive oil and heated until softened.

AVOCADO FRIES

"Crisp" is not a word that leaps to mind when you think of avocados. I had to try this to believe it. It works, it's easy, and they are delicious! (Recipe adapted from Chef Trey Foshee at George's in the Cove in La Jolla, California.)

1 large egg white
2 tbsp heavy cream (30 mL)
$^1/_8$ tsp hot sauce, optional (0.5 mL)
1 avocado, ripe but not mushy or bruised
Salt and freshly ground black pepper to taste
$^1/_2$-1 cup crushed pork rinds, (125 to 250 mL)
  more if needed
2 tbsp grated Parmesan cheese (30 mL)
Oil or fat for frying, as needed*

> **Yield:** 3 servings
> 1 serving
> 144 calories
> 6.2 g protein
> 12.8 g fat
> **0.8 g net carbs**

In small bowl, whisk egg white. Whisk in cream and hot sauce, if using. Reserve.

Cut avocado in half around seed. Carefully, smack the blade of a chef's knife into seed and twist out. Cut each half into two wedges and remove peel. Cut into $^1/_2$-inch wedges (1.3 cm) and sprinkle with salt and pepper.

Stir crushed pork rinds, Parmesan cheese, and more salt and pepper together in shallow dish. Dip avocado slices in egg white mixture, let excess drain away, and then dredge in pork rind mixture until completely coated. Place slices on wire rack to dry for 5 minutes.

Heat $1^1/_2$ inches (4 cm) of heat-stable oil in fryer or deep skillet to 375°F (190°C). Fry avocado slices for about 1 minute or until golden brown. Remove with slotted spoon or spider and drain on paper towels. Serve with lime wedges and ranch dressing or salsa.

Variation: You may use almond flour instead of pork rinds. The same size serving will have 223 calories, 20.6 g of fat, 6.9 g of protein, and **2.2 g net carbs** when made with almond flour.

Helpful Hints: One medium avocado makes 2 to 4 servings. Nutrition data is based on 3 servings per avocado. The fat content is estimated, as most of the fat will be left in the pan.

*Bacon fat makes wonderful avocado fries.

BAKED FENNEL IN CREAM

One of my favorite recipes from **Carb Wars** *is Braised Fennel. Here's an easy way to prepare fennel in the oven that is equally delicious.*

2 fennel bulbs, about $1^1/_2$ lbs total (680 g)
2 cups heavy cream (500 mL)
$1^1/_2$ cups finely grated Parmesan (375 mL)
  cheese, divided
Salt and freshly-ground black pepper, to taste
$^1/_4$ cup butter, cubed (60 mL)

Yield: 5 servings
1 serving
554 calories
14.2 g protein
53.1 g fat
5.8 g net carbs

Preheat oven to 425°F (220°C).

Remove stalks from fennel; reserve some of the feathery fronds for garnish, and discard the remainder. Cut the bulbs in half lengthwise, and then cut into $^1/_2$-inch (1.3 cm) wedges.

In large bowl, combine cream, 1 cup (250 mL) Parmesan, salt, and pepper. Add fennel slices and toss to coat. Transfer to a 3-quart (3 L) baking dish. Dot with butter and cover with lid or foil. Bake 1 hour. Uncover dish and sprinkle with remaining $^1/_2$ cup (125 mL) Parmesan cheese. Continue to bake until tender, about 30 minutes more. Finely chop some of reserved fronds and sprinkle over dish to garnish.

~~Bits & Bites~~

Fennel, a vegetable related to anise, becomes even sweeter when cooked. It can be used raw in salads or cooked with pot roast and in soups, but it is especially delicious when braised, sautéed, or fried.

There are two kinds of fennel: finocchio, or Florence fennel, has a bulbous base that is used as a vegetable. Fennel seeds that are used as a spice come from common fennel, which has no bulb. Fennel pollen, called "spice of the angels," is also used as a spice. The fern-like greens of either plant can be used as an herb.

"In Greek mythology, knowledge came to man from Olympus in the form of a fiery coal contained in a fennel stalk.... During the Italian Middle Ages agrarian cults of benandanti, or good witches, claimed that they fought nocturnal battles with evil witches, who were armed with stalks of sorghum, while benandanti were armed with bundles of fennel." -
from **Mediterranean Vegetables by Clifford Wright**

SAUTEED BLACK KALE WITH PARMESAN AND TOMATOES

Kale is at the top of the list of healthful vegetables. Don't assume you won't like it until you've tried this recipe.

$1^1/_2$ lbs black kale (0.68 kg)
2 tbsp bacon fat or light olive oil (30 mL)
Water, if needed
3 garlic cloves, peeled and sliced
4 tomatoes, seeded and diced
$^1/_2$ cup grated Parmesan cheese (60 mL)
Sugar substitute equal to $^1/_8$ tsp (0.5 mL) sugar
Salt and black pepper to taste

> *Yield:* 6 servings
> 1 serving
> 140 calories
> 7.2 g protein
> 7.7 g fat
> *10.6 g net carbs*

Wash kale, cut away heavy stems, and roughly chop. In large, heavy skillet over medium heat, heat bacon fat or oil. Add kale and increase heat to high. (You may need to cook it in batches.) Stir until kale starts to wilt, about 2 minutes, adding a little water if kale is very dry. Repeat with remaining batches, if divided. Add garlic and cook for 2 minutes more. Stir in tomatoes and cook for 1 minute. Stir in Parmesan, sweetener, salt, and pepper. Serve immediately.

~~Bits & Bites~~
Dark, blue-green kale, called black or lacinato kale, has deeply textured leaves that are sweeter and milder than regular kale. It may also be called dinosaur kale. See also my recipe for Kale Chips, page 65.

In Irish mythology, fairies were said to ride stalks of kale like horses during the new moon.

85

ROASTED RED PEPPERS

I use these in my Roasted Red Pepper and Preserved Lemon Salad, page 74, but they are also terrific on their own as a side or as part of an antipasto platter.

2 red bell peppers, 7 to 8 oz (220 to 250 g) each

Yield: 6 servings
$^1/_4$ cup (60 mL) per serving
16 calories
0.6 g protein
0.2 g fat
2.5 g net carbs

Cut $^1/_2$ inch (1.3 cm) off top of peppers. Cut around stem and pull it out. Cut $^1/_2$ inch (1.3 cm) off the bottom of peppers. Cut down through sides and open out into flat rectangles. Cut out seeds and membranes from all pieces. Flatten long side-wall pieces by breaking peppers where they naturally form segments, but leave skin intact.

Lay peppers, including top and bottom pieces, skin side up on broiler pan. Place under broiler, 2 to 3 inches (5 to 8 cm) from heat source. Broil 2 to 4 minutes, or until skin is blackened and blistered. Watch carefully and rotate pan for even heat, but do not turn the peppers over.

Put peppers in bowl and cover with plate or waxed paper. Leave to steam for 15 minutes to loosen skins. Peel off skins. Cut peppers into pieces and use in recipes or serve as appetizer or side.

Helpful Hint: You can also cook the peppers on a grill, in which case you would lay them skin side down.

*~~**Bits & Bites**~~*
"All I'm saying to obesity researchers is, pay attention to the hormonal and enzymatic regulation of the fat tissue. And if you do, you'll get a different answer for what causes obesity and what cures it." -
Gary Taubes, *author of* **Good Calories, Bad Calories** *and* **Why We Get Fat and What To Do About It.**

SAAG PANEER

Spinach with Paneer cheese is one of the most popular dishes in Indian cuisine.

1 10-oz package frozen spinach, OR (300 g)
2 cups cooked fresh spinach (500 mL)
1 medium red bell pepper, cored and seeded
2 tbsp light olive oil, OR coconut oil, (30 mL)
OR butter
2 leeks, white and light green part only, finely
chopped
1 to 4 seeded green chilies or to taste
(optional)
2 tbsp grated fresh ginger (30 mL)
1 tbsp minced garlic, about 3 cloves (15 mL)
1 tsp salt or to taste (5 mL)
$^1/_2$ tsp ground turmeric (2 mL)
$^1/_2$ cup water (125 mL)
8 oz Paneer cheese, cut into $^1/_2$-inch (1.3 cm) cubes (250 g)
$^1/_4$ cup heavy cream (60 mL)
$2^1/_2$ tsp Garam Masala, page 89 (12 mL)
1 to 2 tsp fresh lemon juice (5 to 10 mL)
Salt to taste

> *Yield:* 6 servings
> 1 serving
> 278 calories
> 13.3 g protein
> 21.2 g fat
> *7.8 g net carbs*

If using frozen spinach, thaw completely. Drain spinach and press out water. Place spinach in a food processor and blend to a smooth paste, scraping down sides of bowl frequently. Add red pepper to processor and blend until finely chopped but still visible. Set aside.

Heat oil in a large skillet. Add leeks to pan and fry over low heat for about 6 minutes or until softened. Add chilies, if using, ginger and garlic and cook and stir for another minute. Add salt and turmeric and cook for 30 seconds more. Stir in spinach and red pepper puree and water. Mixture should be loose, but not watery. Bring to a boil, reduce heat to low, and simmer for 3 minutes.

Add the Paneer cubes, cream, and Garam Masala, page 90 to pan. Stir and cook for a few minutes, or until spinach is creamy. Stir in lemon juice and salt. Transfer mixture to prewarmed dish and serve as a side dish or over cauli-rice as a main dish.

Helpful Hints: Paneer is an Indian cheese that can be found in many groceries or in Asian markets.

Garam masala is a spice mixture that can be bought ready-made in regular or ethnic stores. See my recipe for Garam Masala, page 90, to make your own.

MISCELLANEOUS

CHAMPAGNE VINAIGRETTE

An elegant dressing for any salad, but especially nice with my Cranberry Chicken Salad, page 72.

$1^1/_2$ cups extra virgin olive oil (375 mL)
$^1/_2$ cup champagne vinegar (125 mL)
1 shallot segment
1 garlic clove
1 tbsp prepared Dijon mustard (15 mL)
Sugar substitute equal to 2 tbsp sugar, (30 mL)
  OR more to taste
$^3/_4$ tsp salt (3 mL)
$^1/_2$ tsp freshly ground black pepper (2 mL)

Yield: 16 servings	
2 tbsp (30 mL) per serving	
183 calories	
0.1 g protein	
20.3 g fat	
0.4 g net carbs	

In a food processor, combine olive oil, vinegar, shallot, garlic, mustard, sugar substitute, salt, and pepper. Process until thickened and smooth.

Helpful Hints: Not all the dressing will be needed for my Cranberry Chicken Salad, 72. Use or refrigerate until needed and bring up to room temperature before using.

~~Bits & Bites~~

Olive oil has been a staple food in many cultures for thousands of years. It can be used with little processing, and in addition to its high oleic acid content (up to 75%), it also contains small amounts of both the essential fatty acids, omega-6 and omega-3. Expeller pressed, extra-virgin olive oil is an excellent choice for flavoring, for dipping, for low-temperature cooking, and for dressing salads, but it should not be used for high-heat cooking. Refined olive oil extra light can be heated to higher temperatures, but it will have lost some of its healthful compounds. Now for the bad news: the primary fatty acids in olive oil are the long-chain variety, which are more easily stored as body fat than medium- or short chain fatty acids, such as those found in butter and coconut oil.

"The deleterious effects of fat have been measured in the presence of high carbohydrate. A high-fat diet in the presence of high carbohydrate is different than a high-fat diet in the presence of low carbohydrate."
– Richard Feinman, Ph.D., Biochemistry, State University of New York, NY.

PROVENCAL HERBS

Herbs de Provence (Provencal herbs) is an aromatic seasoning blend made from the plants that thrive on the rocky, sun-drenched hillsides of Southern France. Make your own custom mix using some or all of the dried herbs listed below. Start with thyme, summer savory, rosemary, and either oregano or marjoram and choose which others to include.

1 tbsp dried thyme (15 mL)
1 tbsp dried chervil (15 mL)
1 tbsp dried rosemary (15 mL)
1 tbsp dried summer savory (15 mL)
1 tsp dried lavender (5 mL)
1 tsp dried tarragon (5 mL)
1 tsp dried marjoram (5 mL)
$^1/_2$ tsp dried oregano (2 mL)
$^1/_2$ tsp dried mint (2 mL)
$^1/_2$ tsp dried basil (2 mL)
$^1/_2$ tsp fennel seeds (2 mL)
$^1/_2$ tsp rubbed sage (2 mL)
$^1/_2$ tsp orange zest (2 mL)

Yield: 16 servings
1 tsp (5 mL) per serving
3 calories
0.1 g protein
0.1 g fat
0.3 g net carbs

Into a spice grinder or processor, place thyme, chervil, rosemary, summer savory, lavender, tarragon, marjoram, oregano, mint, basil, fennel seeds, sage and orange zest and blend until fine. Store in airtight container. To mix by hand, first chop or crush bay and rosemary leaves and fennel seeds.

Helpful Hints: Dried herbs and spices are much more economical from the bulk containers than from the small jars on the spice aisle, if you can find them that way. I recently looked at a little jar of dried chives that gave the per pound price on the shelf label. It cost over $600 per pound! At that rate, I have about a million dollars worth of chives growing in my flower bed!

~~Bits & Bites~~

If you have one of those cute little terra-cotta clay pots with a cork, keep some of your herbs on the countertop. If you have extra, it makes a great gift.

Frying, grilling, or cooking meat at high temperatures creates chemicals called heterocyclic amines. Herbs, such as rosemary, have been shown to reduce the formation of these toxins by up to 90%. A sprinkle of this mixture on your hamburgers or steaks before cooking may make them not only delicious, but more healthful as well.

GARAM MASALA
Use some or all of the spices on the list to make your own blend.

1, 2-inch piece of cinnamon stick (5 cm)
1 Turkish bay leaf
1 piece of star anise (1 whole star)
1 tbsp cardamom seeds (15 mL)
1 tsp black cumin (5 mL)
1 tsp whole cloves (5 mL)
1 tsp black peppercorns (5 mL)
1 tsp cumin seeds (5 mL)
$^1/_2$ tsp coriander seeds (2 mL)
$^1/_2$ tsp mace powder (2 mL)
$^1/_2$ tsp fennel seeds (2 mL)
$^1/_4$ tsp ground nutmeg (1 mL)
A few saffron threads

Yield: 12 servings
1 tsp (5 mL) per serving
5 calories
0.2 g protein
0.2 g fat
0.4 g net carbs

In dry skillet over low heat, toast cinnamon, Turkish bay leaf, star anise, cardamom seeds, cumin, cloves, peppercorns, cumin seeds, coriander seeds, mace powder, fennel seeds and ground nutmeg for about 2 minutes or until fragrant, shaking pan or stirring occasionally. Let cool and grind to powder in spice grinder or with mortar and pestle. Store in airtight container in a cool, dry place. Garam Masala will remain potent for several months.

Helpful Hints: When cooking with garam masala, add it to your dish toward the end of the cooking time.

ALMOND PIE CRUST
This tasty crust is excellent for any one-crust pie or tart.

$1^1/_4$ cups almond meal (300 mL)
2 tbsp butter, melted, PLUS more (30 mL)
   for buttering pan
Sugar substitute equal to 3 tbsp (45 mL)
   sugar

Yield: 8/10 servings
1 serving
129/103 calories
3.8/3 g protein
11.7/9.4 g fat
2/1.6 g net carbs

Preheat oven to 375°F (190°C). Butter bottom and sides of a 9-inch (23 cm) pie pan. In medium bowl, combine almond meal, melted butter, and sugar substitute. Mix well and press into bottom and up sides of pan. Bake 8 to 10 minutes or until lightly browned and fragrant. Remove from oven and let cool.

PRESERVED LEMONS

See my recipes for Chicken with Preserved Lemon and Rosemary, page 79, and Roasted Red Pepper and Preserved Lemon Salad, 74.

5 to 6 Meyer lemons
$^1/_2$ cup salt, PLUS (125 mL)
  2 tbsp for topping off (30 mL)
$1^1/_2$ - 2 cups fresh lemon juice (375 to 500 mL)

> *Yield:* 5 to 6 lemons
> 1 lemon, rind only
> 7 calories
> 0.2 g protein
> 0 g fat
> *0.8 g net carbs*

Wash and dry a one-quart (1 L) glass jar with a non-metallic lid. Wash lemons with soap, scrubbing to remove any wax and dirt. Rinse and blot dry.

Cut a thin slice from top of each lemon. This will remove stem button and allow lemons to sit flat. Place 1 lemon, cut-side down, on chopping board and cut lengthwise into quarters almost to base, but not all the way through, leaving lemon intact. Repeat with remaining lemons. Place lemons in single layer in large freezer bag and expel air. Seal and place in freezer overnight, then remove from freezer and transfer to fridge to thaw for 6 hours or overnight. This helps soften rind and speeds up the process of preservation.

In small bowl, place some salt. Set single lemon on salt and pour more salt over it, spreading open so lemon gets thoroughly coated inside and out. Repeat with remaining lemons. Push lemons tightly into jar and pour any salt left in bowl over them. Top off jar with extra 2 tbsp (30 mL) of salt.

Pour enough lemon juice over lemons to completely cover. Use glass or non-corrosive weight to keep lemons submerged if necessary. Seal jar, label and date. Store in cool place, away from direct sunlight, for 24 to 48 hours and then refrigerate for at least four weeks. Turn jar occasionally to keep salt distributed and add more lemon juice if needed to keep lemons covered. To use, remove lemon from brine and rinse under cold water. Pat dry. Pull out lemon flesh and discard. Slice peel into strips or use as directed in recipe.

Helpful Hints: I use a jar with a glass lid, a rubber gasket, and a wire bail and a thin glass paper weight that fits into the jar to keep the lemons submerged, which works well if you can find one. Once the lemons have settled in the jar, you might need to add more lemon juice to ensure the lemons remain covered; they will start to soften and might float up. As a result, they may not stay entirely covered with juice and may develop a harmless white mold. You may use regular lemons for this recipe, but you will need to scrape away the pith from the rind before using it in recipes.

SWEET ENDINGS

DEVONSHIRE CREAM WITH FRESH STRAWBERRIES

Provide a bowl of granular sugar substitute on the side for dipping. Just Like Sugar®, with its slight orange flavor, has a special affinity for fruit. LC Sweet Brown® is also nice. Devonshire cream makes a luscious topping for desserts or a dip for fresh berries.

Devonshire Cream:
8 oz cream cheese, softened to room (250 g)
temperature
$^1/_3$ cup real sour cream, (75 mL)
such as Daisy ® brand, OR Greek yogurt
Sugar substitute equal to 1 tbsp sugar (15 mL)
Serving Suggestion:
3 fresh strawberries, $^3/_4$ oz each (21 g each)
1 tbsp Devonshire Cream (15 mL)
Granular sugar substitute for dipping

Yield: 1 serving suggestion
3 strawberries, etc. per serv.
63 calories
1.1 g protein
4.7 g fat
3.6 g net carbs

Devonshire Cream: In medium bowl, beat the cream cheese with an electric mixer until fluffy. Fold in the sour cream and sweetener. Chill and serve with fresh berries or desserts.

Serving Suggestion: Dip the berries in the cream first and then in granular sweetener. (Use stemmed berries if you can get them.)

Helpful Hint: Recipe makes $1^1/_3$ cups (325 mL) of Devonshire Cream. (*0.6 g net carbs* per tablespoon (15 mL).

~~~Bits & Bites~~~
A study from Harvard School of Public Health of 18,555 young women concluded that the consumption of low-fat dairy products may increase the risk of infertility, while high-fat dairy products may decrease the risk. (A prospective study of dairy foods intake and anovulatory infertility, J.E. Chavarro et al, 2007.)

CHOCOLATE PEANUT BUTTER FUDGE

I love to eat this straight out of the freezer.

$^1/_2$ cup butter, OR part coconut oil (125 mL)
$^1/_2$ cup natural peanut butter, (125 mL)
  plain or chunky
2 oz cream cheese, (60 g)
  at room temperature
$^1/_2$ tsp sugar-free vanilla extract (2 mL)
Sugar substitute equal to 1 cup (250 mL)
  sugar (sucralose, OR stevia)
$^1/_3$ cup vanilla whey protein powder (75 mL)
$^1/_3$ cup cocoa powder (75 mL)
A few grains of salt
$^1/_4$ cup chopped walnuts, optional (60 mL)

> *Yield:* 20 servings
> 1 serving
> 107 calories
> 1.4 g protein
> 11.1 g fat
> *0.5 g net carbs*

Butter a 5 x 7-inch (13 x 18 cm) baking dish and line with parchment or wax paper, leaving an overhang on 2 sides to aid removal. Butter the paper also.

In medium saucepan or bowl, melt butter and peanut butter together on low heat or in microwave for 1 to 2 minutes. Mix together well.

In medium bowl, beat cream cheese to soften, and then beat into peanut butter mixture until blended and smooth. Add vanilla and sugar substitute.

In another bowl, whisk together whey protein powder, cocoa powder and salt until blended. Sift dry ingredients into wet ingredients and beat until smooth. Stir in nuts, if using.

Spread fudge in prepared pan and chill or freeze until set. Remove fudge from pan and cut into 20 squares. Store in refrigerator or freezer.

Helpful Hint: This confection may be eaten frozen.

CREAMY STRAWBERRY PIE
*This is an easy variation of my Lemon Icebox Pie from **Nourished.***

8 oz frozen strawberries (250 g)
2 tbsp lemon juice (30 mL)
16 oz whipped cream cheese (500 g)
8 oz plain, full fat, Greek yogurt (250 g)
 with live cultures
2 tsp sugar-free vanilla extract (10 mL)
Sugar substitute equal to 14 tbsp (210 mL)
 sugar, OR to taste (high intensity substitute)
$^1/_8$ tsp salt (0.5 mL)
10 oz fresh strawberries, hulled and sliced (300 g)
Almond Pie Crust, page 90, baked and cooled
Whipped cream and a strawberry to garnish, optional

Yield: 10 servings
1 serving
278 calories
6.2 g protein
25.3 g fat
6.7 g net carbs

In large saucepan over medium low heat, place frozen strawberries and cook, stirring frequently, until reduced to $^1/_2$ cup (125 mL) and as thick as jam, about 20 to 25 minutes. Whisk or stir with a fork to break up any large berry pieces. Stir in lemon juice and let cool.

In medium bowl, beat cream cheese and yogurt until smooth. Beat in vanilla, sweetener, and salt. Fold cooked berry puree and fresh berries into cream cheese and yogurt mixture. Spread evenly in baked pie shell and refrigerate until set, about 4 hours. (Filled pie can be refrigerated for 24 hours. Store filling and crust separately for longer storage.) Top with sugar-free whipped cream and garnish with a strawberry, if desired.

Helpful Hint: The nutrition count above excludes some of the sugar in the yogurt that has been eaten by the live cultures.

~~Bits & Bites~~
"Are wild strawberries really wild? Will they scratch an adult, will they snap at a child?... Or should we make a pet out of something less scary, like the Domestic Prune or the Imported Cherry, Anyhow, you've been warned and I will not be blamed if your Wild Strawberries cannot be tamed." –
Shel Silverstein, Where the Sidewalk Ends

SESAME SWEETS

Spiced, raw, nut and seed candy makes a yummy, guilt-free snack.

$^1/_2$ cup raw sesame seeds (125 mL)
$^2/_3$ cup raw sunflower seeds (150 mL)
$^1/_4$ cup xylitol *honey,* OR yacon syrup (60 mL)
Sugar substitute equal to 3 tbsp sugar (45 mL)
  (stevia, OR sucralose)
2 tbsp sesame paste (tahini), OR nut (30 mL)
  butter
1 tsp vanilla extract (5 mL)
$^3/_4$ tsp ground cardamom (3 mL)
$^1/_2$ tsp ground cinnamon (2 mL)
$^1/_2$ tsp grated fresh ginger, optional (2 mL)
$^1/_8$ tsp coarse salt (0.5 mL)
$^1/_4$ cup chopped walnuts (60 mL)
$^1/_2$ cup unsweetened, finely shredded, dried coconut for coating (125 mL)

Yield: 32 pieces
1 piece
50 calories
1.5 g protein
4.5 g fat
0.9 g net carbs

In blender, coffee grinder, or spice mill, coarsely grind sesame seeds and transfer to medium bowl. Grind sunflower seeds to a rough powder and add to bowl with sesame seeds. Add xylitol honey, OR yacon syrup, second sweetener, sesame paste or nut butter, vanilla, cardamom, cinnamon, fresh ginger, if using, and salt. Stir with wooden spoon to form stiff dough. Shape into 1-inch (2.5 cm) balls and roll in coconut to coat. Store, covered, in the refrigerator.

Helpful Hints: There are several brands of honey-flavored syrups made with xylitol or maltitol. (Both are sugar alcohols, but maltitol may cause more "digestive distress" than xylitol.) You can also buy honey flavoring and make your own syrup using a little xanthan gum, some water, and any of the sugar substitutes with bulk, such as Swerve®, LC-Sweet® or Just Like Sugar®.

Yacon is another option for a natural sweet syrup to use like honey. It is said to have the highest concentration of any food for fructooligosaccharide (FOS), a type of sugar that can't be absorbed by the body. FOS acts as a prebiotic fiber that feeds the friendly bacteria in the digestive tract. However, the nutrition data on most labels show yacon as being all sugar. That is almost certainly wrong, but I don't know how to get the true counts.

~~Bits & Bites~~

Both sesame and sunflower seeds are high in omega-6 oils. Most people who eat the standard American diet, heavy in grains and vegetable oils, get too much omega-6, and most of it is rancid or damaged. Omega-6 is one of the two essential fats, however, and fresh, raw seeds are a good source for low-carbers.

CHOCOLATE GLAZED PECANS

These are wonderful as a sweet treat or snack. Chopped, they make a crunchy topping for ice cream or desserts.

2 cups raw pecan halves (500 mL)
2 large egg whites
1 tsp sugar-free vanilla extract (5 mL)
Sugar substitute equal to $^1/_2$ cup (125 mL)
  sugar (high intensity substitute)
A few grains of salt
1 tbsp cocoa powder (15 mL)

Yield: 16 servings
$^1/_2$ oz (15 g) per serving
89 calories
1.6 g protein
8.9 g fat
0.6 g net carbs

Preheat oven to 300°F (150°C). Spread nuts in shallow pan and bake 5 minutes to crisp and dry. Let cool.

In medium bowl, whisk egg whites until foamy. Stir in vanilla, sweetener, and salt. Add nuts and toss until completely coated and sticky. Sift cocoa over nuts and toss again.

Spread nuts in single layer on cookie sheet and bake 12 minutes. Stir and break apart any nuts that stick together. Return to oven for 5 minutes more. Store in airtight container.

~~Bits & Bites~~

Natural saturated fats like butter and coconut oil have been demonized since Ancel Keys put forth his lipid hypothesis in the early 1950s. All his research has been debunked, but his theory lives on in the low-fat orthodoxy that survives to this day. Artificial fats, like shortening and margarine, and processed seed and grain oils (cottonseed, soy, and corn oil) are the real danger to health.

*A study from the World Health Organization called the **Multinational Monitoring of Trends in the determinants in Cardiovascular Disease** found that every single country in the top eight of saturated fat consumption had a lower rate of heart disease than every single country in the bottom eight of saturated fat consumption.*

JENNIFER ELOFF
APPETIZERS AND BEVERAGES

PEANUT BUTTER COOKIE DOUGH DIP

This very naughty, delightfully tasty cookie dough dip has many uses. Freshly made it makes a wonderful dip and refrigerated, it makes a wonderful spread for crackers. I can imagine this spread sandwiched between two plain cookies. It is also really wonderful spread in my crepes, page 111.

4 oz regular cream cheese, softened (125 g)
$^1/_2$ cup creamy peanut butter* (125 mL)
  (sugar-free)
$^1/_4$ cup butter, softened (60 mL)
Liquid sucralose to equal 1 cup (250 mL)
  SPLENDA® Granular
3 tbsp powdered erythritol (45 mL)
1 tsp molasses, optional (5 mL)
$^1/_2$ tsp vanilla extract (2 mL)
$^1/_2$ cup sugar-free chocolate chips (125 mL)

Yield: 26 servings
1 tbsp (15 mL) per serving
59.0 calories
1.5 g protein
5.5 g fat
0.9 g net carbs

In food processor, process cream cheese. Add peanut butter and butter; process. Add liquid sucralose, OR SPLENDA® Granular, erythritol, molasses, if using and vanilla extract; process until well combined. Stir in chocolate chips.

Serve with Cinnamon Cookie Crackers, page 98, *Low-Carbing Among Friends, Volume-2,* or Microwave Almond Crackers, page 139.

Helpful Hints: *If your peanut butter is quite a salty-tasting brand, then use unsalted butter or half unsalted and half salted butter. My hubby actually liked it a bit more on the salty side as he likes salty and sweet combinations.

~~Bits & Bites~~
Researchers in Denmark published a study (in 2000) which demonstrated that the in vitro hypoglycemic actions of stevioside and steviol are a result of their ability to stimulate insulin secretion via a direct action on beta cells. They concluded, "Results indicate that the compounds may have a potential role as anti-hyperglycemic agents in the treatment of type 2 diabetes mellitus." Folks with type 1 diabetes should typically not use stevia.

PECAN CHEESE RING

Pretty as a picture!

8 cups grated Cheddar cheese (2 L)
1 cup mayonnaise (250 mL)
1 tsp creamed horseradish (5 mL)
1 tsp prepared mustard (5 mL)
1 tsp cayenne pepper (5 mL)
1 cup chopped pecans (250 mL)
1 cup strawberry fruit spread, (250 mL)
  (optional)

Yield: 24 servings
1 serving
192.4 calories
10.3 g protein
16.4 g fat
1.2 g net carbs

In large bowl, combine Cheddar cheese, mayonnaise, horseradish, mustard and cayenne pepper. Stir well. Place 3-inch (7.6 cm) circumference ramekin in center of 9-inch (23 cm) springform pan. Sprinkle almost half the pecans in springform pan. Spread cheese mixture over top and smooth surface. Cover with plastic wrap.

Refrigerate until firm (about 2 hours). Remove ring. Place on pretty serving plate. Pat remaining pecans on top and around circumference of the cheese ring. Surround with Microwave Almond Crackers, page 139 and, if desired, spoon strawberry fruit spread in center.

SESAME HAM ROLL

Such an easy spread to whip up the night before a party.

8 oz regular cream cheese, (250 g)
  softened
1$^1/_2$ cups chopped, canned ham (375 mL)
2 tbsp finely chopped green onions (30 mL)
1 tsp Worcestershire sauce (5 mL)
1 tsp lemon juice (5 mL)
1 tsp dried parsley (5 mL)
3 tbsp toasted sesame seeds (45 mL)

Yield: 36 servings
1 serving
32.3 calories
1.6 g protein
2.7 g fat
0.6 g net carbs

In food processor, process cream cheese until smooth. Stir in ham, green onions, Worcestershire sauce, lemon juice and parsley. On oblong platter, form into log shape about 11 inches (28 cm) long and 2 inches (5 cm) wide. Sprinkle with sesame seeds. Refrigerate until firm. Slice and serve with Microwave Almond or Almond Sesame Crackers, page 139 or spread on cucumber slices or celery sticks.

EGGPLANT BRUSCHETTA

This is one of my favorite appetizers of all time. I love eggplant and especially Chinese eggplants which are a perfect size for appetizers and far less bitter than the larger variety of eggplants. There is no need to peel them.

7 tbsp olive oil (105 mL)
1 small onion, chopped
1 garlic clove, minced
14.5 oz can diced tomatoes (411 g)
$^1/_4$ cup water (60 mL)
Liquid sucralose to equal 2 tsp (10 mL)
 SPLENDA® Granular
$^1/_2$ tsp dried oregano (2 mL)
$^1/_2$ tsp dried basil (2 mL)
$^1/_2$ tsp salt (2 mL)
$^1/_2$ cup Gluten-Free Bake Mix 1, page 140, OR (125 mL)
 Gluten-Free Bake Mix 2, page 141
$^1/_3$ cup grated Parmesan cheese (75 mL)
$^1/_4$ tsp Italian seasoning (1 mL)
$^1/_4$ tsp salt (1 mL)
$^1/_8$ tsp black pepper (0.5 mL)
2 eggs
1 tbsp water (15 mL)
1 lb Chinese eggplant slices, about $^1/_4$-inch (0.6 cm) thick (0.45 kg)
1 cup grated Mozzarella cheese (250 mL)

Yield: 8 servings
1 serving
246.7 calories
8.5 g protein
20.4 g fat
8.0 g net carbs

In large skillet, in 1 tbsp (15 mL) olive oil, cook onion and garlic until translucent and tender. Stir in tomatoes, water, sucralose, OR SPLENDA® Granular, oregano, basil and salt. Simmer over low heat 10 minutes. On dinner plate, spread Gluten-Free Bake Mix 1, page 140, OR Gluten-Free Bake Mix 2, page 141, Parmesan cheese, Italian seasoning, salt and black pepper. In small bowl, beat eggs and water together with fork. Dip eggplant in egg wash and then lightly coat with Parmesan cheese mixture on both sides. In large, nonstick saucepan, in 1 tbsp (15 mL) hot oil, fry eggplant slices until golden brown on both sides. Repeat. Place a little tomato mixture along with some cheese on each eggplant round. They may be reheated if desired; however, they are tasty at room temperature as well.

Helpful Hints: If you think you will run out of "breading" then stir in some more Parmesan cheese and/or bake mix. You will need a good, nonstick saucepan that is still in good shape to use the amounts of oil indicated otherwise more oil will be required. You obviously don't need gelatin in Gluten-Free Bake Mix 2, page 141 for this recipe.

CINNAMON TEA
A tea popular in the Middle East.

3 cups water (750 mL)
1 large cinnamon stick
Zero-carb Sweetener, to taste

Yield: 2 servings
1 serving
0.0 calories
0.0 g protein
0.0 g fat
0.0 g net carbs

In medium saucepan, combine water and cinnamon stick. Bring to a full rolling boil and boil 5 minutes. Remove from heat. Serve immediately and leave cinnamon sticks in leftover tea, if desired.

Helpful Hint: I enjoy this tea with $1^1/_2$ tsp (7 mL) cream and zero carb sweetener, EZ-Sweetz®.

Fast Facts: A Pakistani study used people with diabetes as subjects. They consumed 1, 3 or 6 g cinnamon daily and had a significant drop in serum glucose, LDL (bad) cholesterol, triglycerides and total cholesterol, but no improvement in HDL (good) cholesterol. Scientists believe cinnamon has a component that may enable it to serve as an insulin substitute in Type 2 Diabetes.

STRAWBERRY LIMEADE
A refreshing summer drink!

2 cups frozen strawberries, (500 mL)
 (unsweetened)
$1^1/_2$ cups water (375 mL)
Liquid sucralose to equal $^2/_3$ cup (150 mL)
 SPLENDA® Granular
$^1/_3$ cup lime juice (75 mL)
1 cup carbonated spring water (250 mL)

Yield: 4 cups (1 L)
1 cup (250 mL) per serving
30.3 calories
0.4 g protein
0.1 g fat
6.5 g net carbs

In blender, combine strawberries, water, liquid sucralose, OR SPLENDA® Granular and lime juice. Blend. Carefully stir carbonated water into Strawberry Limeade. Pour slowly into container with tight-fitting lid.

SALADS AND SOUPS

COOL CUCUMBER SALAD
Cool, refreshing summertime salad; a classic from when I was a child.

1 cup grated English cucumber, OR (250 mL)
   finely diced
$^1/_2$ cup diced canned pineapple, (125 mL)
   optional (NOT fresh pineapple)*
1 tbsp grated onion (15 mL)
$^1/_3$ cup lemon juice (75 mL)
3 envelopes unflavored gelatin (45 mL)
1 cup boiling water (250 mL)
1 cup cold water (250 mL)
Liquid sucralose to equal $^1/_2$ cup SPLENDA® Granular (125 mL)
$^1/_3$ cup mayonnaise (75 mL)
1 tbsp vinegar (15 mL)
$^1/_8$ tsp salt (0.5 mL)
Green food coloring

> *Yield:* 6 servings
> with/without pineapple
> 113.5/107.0 calories
> 3.4/3.3 g protein
> 9.8/9.8 g fat
> *3.4/1.9 g net carbs*

Set aside the cucumber, pineapple, if using, and grated onion. In a large glass bowl, in lemon juice, soften gelatin. Add boiling water and stir until gelatin dissolves. Stir in cold water, liquid sucralose, OR SPLENDA® Granular, mayonnaise, vinegar, salt and green food coloring. Whisk the mixture really well until the mayonnaise dissolves. Pour into a jello mold. Chill the mixture about 30 minutes or more until thickened slightly. Fold cucumber, pineapple (if using) and onion into gelatin and chill at least 6 hours.

Helpful Hints: My food processor grater assembly made short work of grating the cucumber and onion.

To remove cucumber jello salad, fill up a basin with hot water and lower the jello mold into the water for 5 to 10 seconds. Place a pretty plate on top of the jello mold and invert. The salad should slide out easily.

*The bromelaine enzyme in fresh pineapple will prevent the gelatin from setting.

~~Bits & Bites~~
Scientific studies have proven that onions and garlic contain disulfides which play a role in decreasing blood sugar.

CHICKEN SALAD WITH AVOCADO DRESSING

Below is an alternate dressing that is also nice. Serve chicken salad in an avocado half, if desired. Add a few drops of hot sauce, if desired.

2 cups cubed, cooked chicken (500 mL)
$^1/_4$ cup cucumber, chopped (60 mL)
1 or 2 hard boiled eggs, chopped
1 Roma tomato (optional)
2 slices cooked, crisp bacon, crumbled
Avocado Dressing:
1 avocado, peeled and coarsely chopped
2 oz regular cream cheese (60 g)
$^1/_4$ cup sour cream 60 mL)
3 tbsp lemon juice (45 mL)
2 tbsp finely chopped onion (30 mL)
1 clove garlic, crushed
$^1/_2$ tsp salt (2 mL)
$^1/_8$ tsp black pepper (1 mL)

Yield: 4 servings
1 serving
273.5 calories
28.4 g protein
15.5 g fat
3.5 g net carbs

In medium bowl, combine chicken, cucumber, eggs, tomato and bacon. In blender, combine avocado, cream cheese, sour cream, lemon juice, onion, garlic, salt and black pepper. Blend. Pour dressing over salad and stir to combine. Serve in pretty wine glasses lined with lettuce leaves, if desired, as an hors d'oeuvre.

Variation: **Chicken Salad with Creamy Dressing:** In small bowl, combine $^1/_2$ cup (125 mL) sour cream, 2 tbsp (30 mL) Ranch dressing, 1 tbsp (15 mL) SPLENDA® Granular and $1^1/_2$ tsp (7 mL) prepared mustard. (*1.9 g net carbs*)

MARINATED CUCUMBER SALAD

Low-sodium pickles without sacrificing taste.

2 medium-sized field cucumbers
$^1/_2$ cup thinly sliced onion (125 mL)
1 cup water (250 mL)
1 cup white vinegar (250 mL)
Liquid sucralose to equal $^1/_2$ cup (125 mL)
 SPLENDA® Granular
$^1/_4$ tsp salt (1 mL)
$^1/_4$ tsp black pepper (1 mL)

Yield: 4 large servings
1 serving
30.5 calories
1.4 g protein
0.3 g fat
5.0 g net carbs

Peel and slice cucumbers thinly, but not quite as thinly as the onion. In medium bowl, combine water, vinegar, liquid sucralose, OR SPLENDA® Granular, salt and pepper. Stir in vegetables and leave to marinate at least 3 hours in the refrigerator. Drain vegetables and serve.

CONDENSED CREAM OF MUSHROOM SOUP

This is a handy soup for recipes instead of the commercial variety which is so high in sodium. Leave out the xanthan gum when using in place of commercial soups, as it could give an undesirable mouthfeel in some instances.

4 oz cream cheese (125 g)
$^1/_2$ cup heavy cream (125 mL)
2 tbsp water (30 mL)
1 tbsp olive oil (15 mL)
Liquid sucralose to equal 2 tsp (10 mL)
SPLENDA® Granular
1 tsp onion salt (5 mL)
1 tsp cornstarch, OR arrowroot powder (5 mL)
$^1/_4$ tsp xanthan gum (1 mL)
$^1/_8$ tsp salt (0.5 mL)
$^1/_8$ tsp white pepper (0.5 mL)
$^3/_4$ cup drained, canned mushrooms (175 mL)

> **Yield:** 2 servings
> $^3/_4$ cup concentrate per serv*
> 296.8 calories
> 3.5 g protein
> 25.5 g fat
> ***9.9 g net carbs***

In food processor or blender, process cream cheese, heavy cream, water, olive oil, liquid sucralose, OR SPLENDA® Granular, onion salt, cornstarch, OR arrowroot powder, xanthan gum, salt and white pepper until smooth. Add mushrooms and process, just until finely chopped.

To serve: In saucepan, add water cup-for-cup for condensed cream of mushroom soup. Heat until boiling. Serve. *The $^3/_4$ cup (175 mL) serving of soup is actually $1^1/_2$ cups (375 mL) when the equivalent amount of water is added.

~~Bits & Bites~~
Cinnamon has been shown to reduce lipids and have anti-inflammatory and platelet-adhesion properties. The results of a study demonstrated that the intake of small amounts of cinnamon per day (no more than six grams a day) reduced serum glucose, triglycerides, LDL cholesterol, and total cholesterol in people with type 2 diabetes. A study found that giving people with type 2 diabetes cinnamon extract significantly reduced their blood sugar levels. Remember if doing a low-carb diet for the first time to monitor blood sugar levels as you will almost certainly require less medication.

CONDENSED CREAM OF TOMATO SOUP

This is a handy soup for recipes instead of the commercial variety which is so high in sodium and usually contains MSG and other undesirable ingredients. The cream cheese is not apparent in the soup and the soup tastes remarkably similar to commercial varieties. The calories in this soup are not high either!

14.5 oz can diced tomatoes, (411 g)
Hunts®
8 oz regular cream cheese (250 g)
$^1/_4$ cup heavy cream (60 mL)
1 tsp salt (5 mL)
$^1/_4$ tsp hot sauce (1 mL)
$^1/_4$ tsp paprika (1 mL)
$^1/_4$ tsp black pepper (1 mL)

Yield: 3 cups (750 mL)
$^1/_2$ cup concentrate per serv.
173.0 calories
4.6 g protein
15.0 g fat
3.9 g net carbs

In blender, combine diced tomatoes, cream cheese, heavy cream, salt, hot sauce, paprika and black pepper. Blend until smooth.

To serve: Measure cup-for-cup with water and heat in the microwave oven until hot. Grind some black pepper over top and enjoy!

Helpful Hint: Use in recipes calling for condensed cream of tomato soup. There is usually 14 oz (414 mL) in a can of commercial condensed cream of tomato soup, so measure some out of this recipe accordingly.

~~Bits & Bites~~
Cinnamon has insulin-like activity and can actually enhance insulin sensitivity in the body. See my Cinnamon Tea, page 100.

Gelatin helps with skin tone, digestion, helps hair and fingernails to grow long and strong. Gelatin boosts muscle growth (contains an amino acid called lysine important for muscle growth)) and increases the metabolism, possibly because it contains an amino acid called arginine which is supposed to help the body's metabolism, so it could potentially help you to lose weight. These are some reasons to love the gelatin option in Splendid Gluten-Free Bake Mix, page 141.

FAUX POTATO AND ONION SOUP

This roasted cauliflower soup tastes so similar to potato soup; even the mouth feel is similar. It's great! I loved it. Try it and see if you agree.

1 medium head cauliflower, cut into chunks
1 large onion, cut into chunks
3 garlic cloves, peeled (4 if small)
$^1/_4$ cup olive oil (60 mL)
4 cups Chicken Stock, page 56 (1 L)
 Low-Carbing Among Friends, Volume-2, OR
 Traditional Chicken Bone Broth, page 252
1 tsp salt, OR to taste (5 mL)
1 cup coconut water, OR water (250 mL)
1 cup half and half, OR heavy cream if using water above (250 mL)
1 cup water (250 mL)
Black pepper, to taste

Yield: 6 servings
1 serving
221.6 calories
3.5 g protein
19.8 g fat
7.6 g net carbs

Preheat oven to 450°F (230°C). In medium bowl, toss cauliflower, onion and garlic with oil. Place on roasting pan and roast 30 minutes, or until turning golden. Turn veggies over after 15 minutes and continue roasting. In saucepan in Chicken Stock, page 56, *Low-Carbing Among Friends, Volume-2* combine cauliflower (reserve a few tiny florets for garnish), onion, garlic and salt and bring to a boil. Reduce heat and simmer until cauliflower is very tender. In blender, blend soup in batches. Hold the lid down and be careful as the liquid is very hot. Return to saucepan, and add 1 cup (250 mL) coconut water, OR water, half and half, OR heavy cream and remaining water and black pepper to taste. Heat soup over moderate heat just until heated through and serve.

Helpful Hints: Coconut water is the part of the canned coconut milk that is not creamy. The creamy part can have other uses.

If desired, add one capsule of glucomannan powder to one of the batches of soup being blended. Glucomannan powder helps with insulin sensitivity, but not everyone tolerates it well. After meal blood sugar levels are lower in people who take glucomannan with meals. It slows emptying of the stomach and, therefore, there is more gradual sugar absorption and lower blood sugar levels.

~~Bits & Bites~~
Avoid becoming famished during shopping trips and while traveling. Carry protein-rich snacks such as nuts, cheese or protein bars with you. If you shop on an empty tummy, chances are your grocery bill will be higher as your hunger will dictate what you buy!

FALL PUMPKIN SOUP

I can imagine enjoying this fabulous, low-calorie soup for lunch on Thanksgiving and having dinner later in the evening or the other way around – enjoying the soup in the evening in front of a roaring fire. And let's add some pretty, falling snow outside to complete the cozy scene inside the house!

2 tbsp unsalted butter (30 mL)
$^1/_2$ cup finely minced onion (125 mL)
2 tsp crushed garlic (10 mL)
1 tsp thyme, OR coriander (5 mL)
1 tsp molasses (5 mL)
$^1/_2$ tsp ground cumin (2 mL)
$^1/_4$ tsp nutmeg (1 mL)
$^1/_4$ tsp black pepper (1 mL)
4 cups Chicken Stock, 56 (1 L)
Low-Carbing Among Friends, Volume-2
15 oz can mashed pumpkin (425 g)
$^1/_4$ cup heavy cream (60 mL)
1 tsp salt, OR to taste (5 mL)
Black pepper, to taste
Garnish (optional):
Dollops of sour cream

Yield: 5 servings
1 serving
157.5.0 calories
6.3 g protein
10.2 g fat
9.4 g net carbs

In large skillet, melt butter over medium heat. Add onion and cook until soft and transparent. Add garlic and cook about a minute. Add thyme, OR coriander, molasses, cumin, nutmeg and black pepper. Stir well to combine.

Stir in Chicken Stock, page 56 *Low-Carbing Among Friends, Volume-2* and pumpkin and bring to a boil. Reduce heat and simmer 15 minutes. Stir in cream. Taste and add salt and pepper and heat gently over low heat (do not boil). Serve with a dollop of sour cream, if desired.

Helpful Hint: Stirring the sour cream into the hot soup will cool it down slightly and make it even thicker and richer-tasting.

Variation: Pumpkin Sausage Soup: Add warm, cooked slices of your favorite sausage.

~~Bits & Bites~~

Nothing says comfort quite like a steaming bowl of soup. Soup eaten before a meal is filling and helps one not to eat quite as much. Therefore, soup should have pride of place in our diet while trying to drop pounds.

BREAKFASTS

BLUEBERRY GRANOLA YOGURT PARFAIT

Here is a breakfast that is bound to make you feel special. It will give you enough energy for the morning and yet it will feel light.

$^1/_2$ cup plain yogurt (125 mL)
Liquid sucralose to equal 2 tbsp (30 mL)
 SPLENDA® Granular
$^1/_4$ cup Granola, page 108 (60 mL)
3 tbsp fresh, OR frozen blueberries (45 mL)

Yield: servings
1 serving
249.4 calories
9.7 g protein
18.1 g fat
6.1 g net carbs

In small bowl, combine yogurt and liquid sucralose, OR SPLENDA® Granular. In a pretty wine glass, layer yogurt, Granola, page 108 and fresh, OR frozen blueberries (slightly thawed and drained).

JUMBO RICOTTA PANCAKE

So quick and easy and absolutely delicious!

2 eggs
$^1/_4$ cup Ricotta cheese (60 mL)
Liquid sucralose to equal 1 tbsp (15 mL)
 SPLENDA® Granular
1 tsp vanilla extract (5 mL)

Yield: 1 serving
1 Jumbo Ricotta pancake
228.7 calories
19.2 g protein
13.1 g fat
5.5 g net carbs

In small bowl, beat eggs with fork. Whisk in ricotta cheese, liquid sucralose, OR SPLENDA® Granular and vanilla extract. Pour into 8-inch (20 cm) non-stick frying pan and as it begins to brown underneath, place lid over top. Cook until set on top, about 1 minute. Serve immediately with a dollop of Crème Fraiche, page 132, if desired.

Helpful Hint: If desired, replace sweetener with 1 tbsp (15 mL) Da Vinci® Sugar Free Vanilla Flavored syrup. (*4.5 g net carbs*)

Jennifer Eloff

CHUNKY, CRUNCHY, CHEWY GRANOLA OR GRANOLA BARS

I challenge you to find commercial granola or granola bars that are as tasty or healthy as these. Store in a cookie tin in the freezer. You don't need to make the Angel Coconut – just use regular, desiccated, unsweetened coconut.

1 cup finely chopped peanuts (250 mL)
1 cup finely chopped almonds (250 mL)
1 cup desiccated Angel Coconut*, (250 mL)
 OR plain desiccated, unsweetened coconut
$^1/_2$ cup chopped pecans (125 mL)
$^1/_2$ cup chopped cashews (125 mL)
$^1/_2$ cup Gluten-Free Bake Mix 1, (125 mL)
 page 140, OR Bake Mix 2, page 141
$^1/_3$ cup seedless raisins, OR Cranberry Raisins, page 128 (75 mL)
2 egg whites from 2 large eggs
Liquid sucralose to equal 1 cup (250)
 SPLENDA® Granular
$^1/_4$ cup butter, melted and cooled (60 mL)
$^1/_4$ cup powdered erythritol (60 mL)
1 tbsp sugar-free honey, OR (15 mL)
 natural honey (optional)
$^1/_2$ tsp salt, OR to taste (2 mL)
Angel Coconut:
$^1/_2$ cup unsweetened coconut (125 mL)
1$^1/_2$ tbsp boiling water (22 mL)
Liquid sucralose to equal 2 tbsp (30 mL)
 SPLENDA® Granular, OR to taste

Yield: 15 serv. or 25 bars
$^1/_3$ cup (75 mL)/1 bar
272.3/163.4 calories
7.5/4.5 g protein
23.6/14.1 g fat
6.8/4.1 g net carbs

Preheat oven to 300°F (150°C). Spray cookie sheet with nonstick cooking spray. Line cookie sheet with parchment paper and spray with nonstick cooking spray.

In large bowl, combine peanuts, almonds, Angel Coconut, OR plain coconut, pecans, cashews, Gluten-Free Bake Mix 1, page 140, OR Gluten-Free Bake Mix 2, page 141 and raisins, OR Cranberry Raisins, page 128. In small bowl, beat egg whites with a fork until frothy. Add liquid sucralose, OR SPLENDA® Granular, butter, erythritol, honey of choice, if using, and salt; combine well. Pour over granola and scrape all wet mixture out with spatula and then stir granola well to combine thoroughly. Place granola around the perimeter of the prepared cookie sheet, patting down firmly and leaving a big open rectangle in the center (to prevent soft spots) – see my blog, www.low-carb-news.blogspot.com for a photo. Bake 25 minutes, cover with parchment paper and bake 15 to 20 minutes more. Allow to cool completely before cutting into 25

108

granola bar shapes or breaking up into granola chunks. Place in cookie tin, seal and freeze. Eat them straight out of the freezer.

Angel Coconut: In small bowl, place coconut. In another small bowl, pour boiling water and stir in liquid sucralose, OR SPLENDA® Granular to taste. Pour over coconut and mix well. Cover bowl with plastic wrap and allow to sit for 15 minutes. This will turn dry, unsweetened coconut into the soft, sweet kind one buys in the grocery store. The Angel Coconut recipe is from **Barbara (Barbo) Goldstein.** This is a useful recipe for other purposes as well, but if you're going to keep the granola bars in the freezer for longer than a week, I'd use plain, unsweetened desiccated coconut to try and keep the crunchy texture – otherwise it changes to a chewier texture.

Helpful Hints: It is possible to change out the ingredients as you desire. You can add chopped apricots or sugar-free Cranberry Raisins, page 128 and use the nut combinations that you have on hand. I was able to source chopped peanuts and almonds at a kosher grocery store in the city, so that was a bonus.

FRENCH OMELET

A staple on the low-carb diet. Using cream instead of water makes for a very tasty omelet with enough fat to satiate the appetite for hours.

2 eggs
1 tbsp whipping cream (15 mL)
$^1/_8$ tsp salt (0.5 mL)
2 tsp butter (10 mL)

Yield: 1 omelet
1 serving without filling
234.2 calories
13.0 g protein
19.2 g fat
1.9 g net carbs

In small bowl, beat eggs, whipping cream and salt together with a fork or wire whisk. In medium skillet, melt butter and tilt pan to spread. Pour in egg mixture. Cook over medium heat. Fill slightly set omelet on one side with cheese and ham, bacon, tomato, green onions or whatever your heart desires. When omelet has almost set completely, fold one side over to cover filling and cook a few minutes more, until no runny egg remains.

PUFFY BAKED OMELET

A useful recipe to feed a crowd! This omelet served with spicy, chunky salsa has a distinct Mexican flavor. Spicy Salsa has been scientifically proven to raise the metabolism, as does drinking ice cold water!

12 eggs
$^2/_3$ cup sour cream (150 mL)
2 tbsp whipping cream (30 mL)
2 tbsp water (30 mL)
1 tsp salt (5 mL)
$^1/_4$ cup chopped green onions, OR (60 mL)
 canned jalapenos
1 cup Cheddar cheese (250 mL)
Salsa, optional

Yield: 8 to 12 servings
1 serving
213/142.2 calories
13.8/9.2 g protein
16.4/10.9 g fat
2.1/1.5 g net carbs

Preheat oven to 325°F (160°C). In blender, blend eggs, sour cream, whipping cream, water and salt. Liberally spray 9 x 13-inch (23 x 33 cm) glass baking dish with nonstick cooking spray. Pour omelet mixture into baking dish. Stir in green onions, OR jalapenos. Sprinkle Cheddar cheese overall. Bake 30 minutes, or until set. Serve with salsa, if desired.

BREAKFAST HASH

Delicious and different. Fried radishes lose that characteristic bite. A nice alternative to hash browns!

8 slices bacon, chopped
2 cups coarsely chopped red (500 mL)
 radishes, ends trimmed
$^1/_2$ cup chopped onion (125 mL)
$^1/_2$ tsp salt (2 mL)
$^1/_4$ tsp black pepper (1 mL)
$^1/_4$ tsp paprika (1 mL)
2 green onions, chopped

Yield: 4 servings
1 serving
104.5 calories
11.9 g protein
4.3 g fat
3.0 g net carbs

In skillet or wok, fry bacon until some of the fat releases. Add radishes and onion. Sprinkle with salt, pepper and paprika. Stir-fry about 7 to10 minutes, until radishes are tender. Add green onions during last 5 minutes of cooking.

Variation: **Deluxe Breakfast Hash:** Add 2 cups (500 mL) cubed, cooked ham or chicken.

CREPES WITH PEACH CUSTARD

Comfort Food for sure! The custard makes a nice pudding all by itself. I modified my crepe recipe from Low-Carbing Among Friends, Volume-1, and left out the whey protein powder, which depending on the whey protein that you use, could make the crepes a bit too thick.

Crepes:
1 cup Hood® Calorie Countdown (250 mL)
 milk, OR Carolyn's low-carb milk, page 278
6 large eggs
$^3/_4$ cup gluten-free oat flour (175 mL)
$^1/_4$ cup butter, melted (60 mL)
2 SPLENDA® packets
$^1/_4$ tsp xanthan gum (1 mL)
2 tbsp olive oil (30 mL)

Peach Custard:
2 cups half-and-half cream (500 mL)
Liquid sucralose to equal $^2/_3$ cup (150 mL)
 SPLENDA® Granular
6 egg yolks
1 tsp vanilla extract (5 mL)
$^1/_4$ tsp xanthan gum (1 mL)
12 oz canned peach halves in juice, drained and chopped (375 g)
$^1/_8$ tsp ground nutmeg, for garnish (0.5 mL)

Yield: 16 servings
1 serving
159.3 calories
5.5 g protein
12.1 g fat
6.4 g net carbs

Crepes: In food processor or blender, combine Hood® Calorie Countdown milk, OR Carolyn's low-carb milk, page 278, eggs, oat flour, butter, SPLENDA® and xanthan gum. Process well, stopping to scrape sides of food processor or blender a couple of times.

Into cereal bowl, pour olive oil. Using a pastry brush, brush a tiny amount of oil to cover a 6-inch (15 cm) nonstick pan. Pour 3 tbsp (45 mL) crepe batter in pan (tilt to cover) and cook over medium low heat until edges turn brown and bubbles form. Flip crepe and cook the other side briefly. Transfer to a dish with a lid to keep the crepes warm.

Peach Custard: In double boiler, combine half-and-half cream and liquid sucralose, OR SPLENDA® Granular. When scalding, pour into small bowl with 6 egg yolks; stir. Return to double boiler and stir constantly until custard begins to thicken (about 5 minutes). In food processor bowl, pour custard and add vanilla extract and xanthan gum; process until smooth and thickened. Stir in peaches. Place crepes (folded) in a single layer on an attractive, large platter. Pour custard with peaches over the top and down the center of the crepes. Sprinkle with nutmeg and serve.

111

MAIN COURSES AND SIDES

CHICKEN CREPE CASSEROLE
This is a very tasty casserole – comfort food for sure.

Double Crepe Recipe, page 111
{bigger crepes using scant $^1/_3$ cup (75 mL)}
Filling:
$2^1/_2$ cups cooked, diced chicken (625 mL)
$^2/_3$ cup Condensed Cream of (150 mL)
  Mushroom Soup, page 103
3 tbsp mayonnaise (45 mL)
2 tbsp grated onion, optional (30 mL)
2 tsp lemon juice (10 mL)
1 tsp curry powder (5 mL)
Salt and pepper, to taste
Topping:
$1^1/_2$ cups grated Cheddar cheese (375 mL)
3 tbsp heavy cream (45 mL)

Yield: 8 servings
1 serving
402.3 calories
24.7 g protein
30.1 g fat
6.8 g net carbs

Crepes: Prepare crepes on page 111. Into medium-sized, nonstick frying pan, pour a scant $^1/_3$-cupful (75 mL) of pancake batter. Cook until possible to flip easily. Cook other side very briefly. Repeat to make 10 crepes, each about 7 inches (18 cm) in diameter. You'll only need 8 crepes for this recipe.

Filling: In medium bowl, combine chicken, Condensed Cream of Mushroom Soup, page 103, mayonnaise, onion (if using), lemon juice and curry powder. Stir to combine well. Add salt and pepper to taste and mix in well.

Assembly: Divide filling into 8 even portions and place one portion down center of a crepe. Fold crepe over filling from either side and roll up. Place assembled crepes in shallow casserole dish.

Topping: Sprinkle crepes with Cheddar cheese and pour heavy cream over all. Bake in 350°F (180°C) oven 25 minutes with cover on. Remove cover and bake 5 minutes more, or until hot.

Helpful Hint: These days I make the crepes without the whey protein powder I used in my crepes in *Low-Carbing Among Friends, Volume-1.*

BRUSCHETTA CHICKEN

Here is an easy, tasty casserole dish of chicken breasts with all the familiar flavors of bruschetta.

2 eggs
2 tbsp water (30 mL)
$^1/_2$ cup Gluten-Free Bake Mix 1, (125 mL)
  page 140, OR Bake Mix 2, page 141
$^1/_3$ cup grated Parmesan cheese, (75 mL)
  (canned variety)
$^1/_2$ tsp Italian seasoning (2 mL)
$^1/_4$ tsp salt (1 mL)
$^1/_8$ tsp black pepper (0.5 mL)
6 chicken breasts
Black pepper, to taste
Bruschetta Topping:
2 large tomatoes, chopped
2 tbsp olive oil, divided (30 mL)
2 tsp crushed garlic (10 mL)
1 tsp basil (5 mL)
1 cup shredded Monterey Jack cheese (250 mL)

Yield: 6 servings
1 serving
295.5 calories
32.5 g protein
11.6 g fat
4.0 g net carbs

Preheat oven to 375°F (190°C). Spray 9 x 13-inch (23 x 33 cm) casserole dish with nonstick cooking spray. In medium bowl, combine eggs and water and beat with fork until frothy.

On dinner plate, combine Gluten-Free Bake Mix 1, page 140, OR Gluten-Free Bake Mix 2, page 141, Parmesan cheese, Italian seasoning, salt and black pepper and mix well. Push mixture to one side of the plate.

Rinse a chicken breast under running, cold water. Allow excess water to drip into sink and then coat the chicken breast with the egg wash. Place on dinner plate next to "flour" mixture and poke chicken breast with a fork in several places. Sprinkle with black pepper, to taste. Spoon "flour" mixture over chicken on both sides. Lay chicken breast in prepared casserole dish. Repeat with the remainder of the chicken breasts. Bake uncovered 25 minutes. Remove from oven. Place Bruschetta topping without cheese on chicken breasts. Drizzle with 1 tbsp (15 mL) olive oil. Bake lightly covered with foil 10 minutes. Remove; sprinkle Monterey Jack cheese over top of tomato topping. Place back in oven and bake uncovered a further 15 minutes, or until chicken is cooked and juices run clear. (You may need less time if the chicken breasts are not very thick.)

Bruschetta Topping: In medium bowl, combine tomatoes, 1 tbsp (15 mL) olive oil, crushed garlic and basil. Set aside. Drain in a colander just before using.

113

SEA BASS IN GARLIC BUTTER SAUCE

In the tropics, you would call this Corvina in garlic sauce. My husband is not a huge fish fan, but he is being converted with recipes like this one. Swai, similar to catfish, would work well in this recipe as well as Tilapia.

1 lb sea bass fillets (0.45 kg)
$^1/_4$ tsp paprika (1 mL)
$^1/_4$ tsp onion salt (1 mL)
$^1/_4$ tsp seasoning salt (1 mL)
$^1/_4$ tsp black pepper (1 mL)
1 tbsp olive oil (15 mL)
Lemon wedges

Garlic Butter Sauce:
$1^1/_2$ tbsp butter (22 mL)
1 tbsp olive oil (15 mL)
1 tsp dried parsley (5 mL)
1 tsp crushed garlic (5 mL)
$^1/_8$ tsp salt (0.5 mL)

Yield: 2 servings
1 serving
359.8 calories
42.1 g protein
20.0 g fat
0.7 g net carbs

Wash fish fillets under cold running water. Pat dry with paper towels. In small bowl, combine paprika, onion salt, seasoning salt and black pepper. Sprinkle seasoning on both sides of the fish.

Garlic Butter Sauce: In small saucepan, combine butter, olive oil, parsley, crushed garlic and salt. Heat until hot and sauce is bubbling.

In large frying pan, cook sea bass fillets about 5 minutes on the one side. Turn and coat with Garlic Butter Sauce and cook 4 to 5 minutes more, or until done. Serve immediately with lemon wedges.

~~Bits & Bites~~
When there is less sugar in the blood stream, less insulin (fat storing hormone) is secreted. Less insulin is produced on a low-carb diet and less insulin is produced during intermittent fasting as well. Scientists have discovered that when insulin levels drop, Hormone-Sensitive Lipase (HSL) rises in the body. This is literally a fat burning switch. Your body will burn fat when insulin levels are kept low.

BAKED CHICKEN WITH A DELICIOUS TOPPING

This chicken is so tasty and the best part? It could not be easier!

4 large boneless, skinless chicken breasts
$\frac{1}{2}$ cup mayonnaise (125 mL)
$\frac{1}{4}$ cup Parmesan cheese (60 mL)
$\frac{1}{4}$ cup ground almonds (60 mL)
4 tsp sesame seeds, (20 mL)
  toasted, if desired

Yield: 4 servings
1 serving
411.0 calories
31.9 g protein
29.9 g fat
1.4 g net carbs

Preheat oven to 425°F (220°C). Rinse chicken breasts under running, cold water and pat dry with paper towels.

In small bowl combine mayonnaise, Parmesan cheese and ground almonds. Place chicken breasts on greased cookie sheet. Spread mayonnaise mixture over top of chicken and sprinkle with sesame seeds.

Bake 20 to 30 minutes, or until cooked through (chicken meat must be white and not pink and the juices must run clear).

TANDOORI CHICKEN OR TURKEY

This mild, curried chicken you will often find in Indian restaurants.

8 chicken or turkey breasts without skin
2 cups sour cream (500 mL)
2 garlic cloves, crushed
1 tbsp medium curry powder (15 mL)

2 tsp ground ginger (10 mL)
$1\frac{1}{2}$ tsp ground cumin (7 mL)
$1\frac{1}{2}$ tsp ground coriander seed (7 mL)
1 tsp salt (5 mL)
$\frac{1}{2}$ tsp ground turmeric (2 mL)

Yield: 8 servings
1 serving
224.3 calories
32.2 g protein
8.6 g fat
3.1 g net carbs

With sharp knife, make shallow slits in top and underside of chicken. In medium bowl, combine sour cream, garlic, curry powder, ginger, cumin, coriander seed, salt and turmeric. Stir to combine well. In 9 x 13-inch (23 x 33 cm) glass baking dish, marinate chicken in curried mixture overnight. Wrap each chicken breast in foil. Bake in 350°F (180°C) oven 45 minutes, or until tender and no longer pink.

Remove chicken from foil; drain. Broil 6-inches (15 cm) from heat about 2 minutes (set timer to prevent burning) or until golden.

BAKED ALMOND PARMESAN SWAI FISH

This is so simple and yet incredibly tasty. Swai fish is very mild-tasting and is similar to catfish. It, therefore, needs good spices to make it flavorful. It is also quite inexpensive. Tilapia is another fish you could use here.

3 Swai fillets
5 tbsp olive oil, divided (75 mL)
Salt and black pepper, to taste
$^1/_3$ cup ground almonds (75 mL)
2 tbsp Parmesan cheese (30 mL)
$^1/_4$ tsp seasoning salt (1 mL)
$^1/_4$ tsp Italian herb seasoning (1 mL)
$^1/_8$ tsp black pepper (0.5 mL)
$1^1/_2$ tsp dried parsley (7 mL)
Seasoning salt, to taste
Small lemon wedges

Yield: 2 servings
1 serving
579.2 calories
53.7 g protein
39.5 g fat
1.6 g net carbs

Preheat oven to 350°F (180°C). Wash Swai fillets well under running cold water and pat dry with paper towels. Brush bottom of 9 x 13-inch (2 L) casserole dish with 1 tbsp (15 mL) olive oil. Brush both sides of fillets with 1 tbsp olive oil per fillet. Sprinkle both sides of fillets lightly with salt and pepper.

Place ground almonds, Parmesan cheese, seasoning salt, Italian herb seasoning and black pepper on a dinner plate. Mix well. Spoon Almond Parmesan mixture over fillets on both sides. Lay Swai fillets inside prepared casserole dish. Drizzle with last remaining 1 tbsp (15 mL) of olive oil. Bake uncovered 15 minutes. Sprinkle with half the parsley and gently flip fillets. Sprinkle top of fillets with seasoning salt and the remaining parsley. Bake another 5 to 7 minutes, or until fish is cooked in the middle.

Serving suggestion: Serve with lemon wedges, a nice salad and cauli-rice (mixed with cooked quinoa for those on maintenance-carbohydrate levels) or cauli-mash.

~~Bits & Bites~~
To enhance weight loss, eat a zero-carb breakfast or skip breakfast and eat a zero-carb lunch and a small supper with plenty of good carbs. The idea is to keep ketosis going for the night and a good part of the day.

CHICKEN STUFFED WITH BACON, ONIONS AND CHEDDAR AND COVERED IN GRAVY

This recipe may sound complicated from the title but it is actually so simple and quite quick to assemble.

2 tbsp olive oil (30 mL)
1 cup, thinly sliced onion (250 mL)
4 slices bacon
²/₃ cup shredded Cheddar cheese, (150 mL)
  OR Fontina cheese
3 lbs chicken breasts, four large (1.4 kg)
Seasoning salt, to taste
1 cup Chicken Stock, page 56
  Low-Carbing Among Friends, Volume-2
1 tbsp arrowroot starch, OR (15 mL)
  corn starch
¹/₃ cup white wine (75 mL)
¹/₂ tsp dried rosemary (2 mL)

Yield: 4 servings
1 serving
250.5 calories
33.7 g protein
7.9 g fat
5.5 g net carbs

In nonstick skillet, in olive oil over medium heat, cook onion (thinly sliced and chopped smaller) until golden brown. Set aside in small bowl to cool.

In same skillet, cook bacon over medium heat and set bacon aside to cool. Reserve bacon fat in skillet. Add Cheddar, OR Fontina cheese to cooled onions.

Slice chicken breasts horizontally along the long edge nearly to the opposite side. Open butterfly style and fill with about ¹/₄ cup (60 mL) of the onion cheese mixture per breast. Using one slice of bacon per breast, cut it up and add to the stuffing. Fold over to close.

Sprinkle top side of chicken breast lightly with your favorite seasoning salt. Place all 4 stuffed chicken breasts in skillet with bacon fat (add more olive oil if necessary) and cook over medium heat 5 minutes. Carefully turn them, sprinkle with seasoning salt and cook another 5 minutes on the other side.

Meanwhile in medium bowl, combine Chicken Stock, page 56, *Low-Carbing Among Friends, Volume-2* and arrowroot starch, OR corn starch. Use a wire whisk to combine well. Pour into another skillet and bring to a boil. Pour in white wine and add rosemary. Bring to a boil again. Pour over chicken breasts and cook another 4 or 5 minutes, covered, or until tender.

CHICKEN BACON RANCH WRAPS

Here is a tasty, simple-to-prepare wrap for lunch!

3$^1/_2$ cups diced chicken (875 mL)
1 cup shredded Monterey Jack, OR (250 mL)
  Mozzarella Cheese
8 slices cooked, chopped bacon
1 cup Ranch Dressing, page 129 (250 mL)
1 Roma tomato, chopped
$^1/_4$ cup chopped green onions, (60 mL)
  (optional)

Yield: 8 servings
1 serving
479.0 calories
24.5 g protein
38.1 g fat
7.6 g net carbs

2 tbsp chopped, canned jalapenos, OR to taste (30 mL)
Jiffy Flexible Microwave Tortillas, page 94, *Low-Carbing Among Friends, vol-2*
  (quadruple the recipe)
Mayonnaise
Light-tasting olive oil

In large bowl, combine chicken, Monterey Jack, OR Mozzarella Cheese, bacon, Ranch Dressing, page 129, Roma tomato, green onions (if using) and canned jalapenos.

Prepare Jiffy Flexible Microwave Tortillas, page 94, *Low-Carbing Among Friends, Volume-2*, OR Flexible Wraps, page 63 *Low-Carbing Among Friends, Volume-1*. Fill tortillas and use mayonnaise to seal edges closed. Fry in light-tasting olive oil on both sides in nonstick skillet.

Helpful Hint: Mayonnaise and olive oil are not included in the nutritional analysis as people will use as much or as little as they prefer.

~~Bits & Bites~~
Decreasing carbs results in lower insulin levels, which causes the body to burn stored fat for energy and ultimately helps one shed excess weight and reduce the risk factors for a number of health conditions.

CHICKEN IN HONEY ROASTED BARBECUE SAUCE

Bakes in the oven bathed in Lisa Marshall's Honey Roasted Barbecue Sauce, page 254, Low-Carbing Among Friends, Volume-1. Do not overcook chicken.

3 lbs chicken breasts (1.4 kg)
Salt and black pepper, to taste
Honey Roasted Barbecue Sauce:
$^1/_2$ cup light olive oil (125 mL)
$^1/_4$ cup sugar free honey substitute, (60 mL)
   OR sugar free maple pancake syrup
   (my tweak)
2 tbsp vinegar (30 mL)
1 tbsp Dijon mustard (15 mL)
1 tsp sugar free ketchup (5 mL)
1 packet sweetener
$^3/_4$ tsp liquid smoke (3 mL)
$^1/_4$ tsp paprika (1 mL)
$^1/_4$ tsp salt (1 mL)
$^1/_4$ tsp lemon juice (1 mL)
$^1/_8$ tsp pepper (0.5 mL)
$^1/_8$ tsp garlic powder (0.5 mL)
$^1/_8$ tsp onion powder (0.5 mL)
1 egg yolk, from a coddled egg (place in boiling water 50 sec.)
1 tsp water (5 mL)

Yield: 5 servings
1 serving
507.8 calories
63.6 g protein
26.2 g fat
1.1 g net carbs

Preheat oven to 400°F (200°C). Wash chicken breasts under running, cold water. Pat dry with paper towels. Sprinkle with salt and black pepper to taste on both sides. Place chicken breasts in 9 x 13-inch (23 x 33 cm) casserole dish. Pour "Honey" Roasted Barbecue Sauce over all. Bake 45 to 50 minutes or until meat thermometer registers 165°F (74°C) and juices run clear. Using a spoon, baste chicken with sauce drippings a couple of times during the baking period.

Honey Roasted Barbecue Sauce: In blender, combine olive oil, honey substitute, OR sugar free maple pancake syrup, vinegar, mustard, ketchup, sweetener, liquid smoke, paprika, salt, lemon juice, pepper, garlic powder, onion powder, egg yolk and water. Blend until smooth.

Helpful Hints: This recipe produces fabulous, moist chicken breasts with wonderful flavor. Lisa Marshall's sauce which mimics a special request item at Chick-Fil-A will also transcend ordinary, cut-up and warmed roast chicken from the grocery store into something special that you could even serve informal company with the right trimmings on the side. Pour the sauce over it. By the way, I simply blend the sauce in my blender, but Lisa cooks hers first.

Jennifer Eloff

SMOKEY MOUNTAIN MEATBALLS

These are terrific meatballs. If Worcestershire sauce is a source of migraines for you, then liquid smoke is a good alternative.

18 oz extra lean ground beef (510 g)
1 egg
3 oz onion, finely chopped (90 g)
1 tbsp gluten-free oat flour (15 mL)
1 tbsp low-carb ketchup (15 mL)
1 tbsp liquid smoke, OR (15 mL)
  Worcestershire sauce
1¹/₂ tsp white vinegar (7 mL)
1 clove garlic, crushed
³/₄ tsp salt (3 mL)
¹/₄ tsp white pepper (1 mL)
Chutney Sauce:
2 tbsp low-carb, sugar-free chutney* (30 mL)
1 tbsp liquid smoke, OR Worcestershire sauce (15 mL)
1 tbsp low-carb Ketchup (15 mL)
1 tbsp olive oil (15 mL)
1 tsp curry powder (5 mL)

Yield: 10 meatballs
1 meatball per serving
137.9 calories
10.5 g protein
9.5 g fat
1.6 g net carbs

In large bowl, combine ground beef with egg, onion, oat flour, ketchup, liquid smoke, OR Worcestershire sauce, white vinegar, garlic, salt and pepper. Form into 10 meatballs. Place in 2-quart (2 L) microwaveable baking dish. Pour sauce over meatballs. Microwave uncovered on high power 10 minutes (1 minute per meatball). Serve with extra sugar-free chutney, if desired – put a little on top of each meatball.

Chutney Sauce: In small bowl, whisk together low-carb chutney, liquid smoke, OR Worcestershire sauce, low-carb ketchup, olive oil and curry powder.

Helpful Hints: ***Sugar-Free Chutney:** You may use either a commercial product or a low-carb, sugar-free apricot or peach jam, stir in a little white vinegar and Worcestershire sauce to taste, and you have yourself a lovely, quick and easy low-carb, sugar-free chutney. It tastes really good too. Try it and see! If you like hot chutney, add some hot sauce to the chutney.

Double the recipe, if you like. You'll be glad you did!

120

SPICY SHRIMP

Spicy food speeds up the metabolism. Serve over Cauli-Fried Rice, if desired.

2 tbsp butter (30 mL)
1 cup fresh mushrooms, (250 mL)
  sliced
6 green onions, chopped
1 medium tomato, chopped
1 lb raw, medium-sized shrimp, (0.45 kg)
  shelled and deveined

Barbecue Sauce:
$^1/_2$ of $5^1/_2$ oz can tomato paste (78 g)
3 tbsp white vinegar (45 mL)
2 tbsp SPLENDA® Granular (30 mL)
1 tsp Hot Pepper sauce (5 mL)
$^1/_2$ tsp onion salt (2 mL)
$^1/_2$ tsp Worcestershire sauce (2 mL)
$^1/_4$ tsp liquid smoke (1 mL)
$^1/_8$ tsp garlic powder (0.5 mL)
$^1/_8$ tsp black pepper (0.5 mL)

Yield: 4 servings
1 serving
208.2 calories
24.8 g protein
8.1 g fat
7.7 g net carbs

In large skillet, in melted butter over medium heat, sauté mushrooms and green onions until softening. Add tomato and Barbecue Sauce; heat to boiling. Stir in shrimp. Stir frequently and simmer uncovered about 5 minutes, or until shrimp turns pink.

Barbecue Sauce: In small bowl, combine tomato paste, vinegar, SPLENDA® Granular, Hot Pepper sauce, onion salt, Worcestershire sauce, liquid smoke, garlic powder and black pepper.

Variations: Use a combination of shrimp and scallops. This recipe doubles easily for more servings. Great served in a two-egg omelet with Cheddar cheese.

Helpful Hint: If your tomato is very firm, add along with mushrooms and green onions.

~~Bits & Bites~~
Drinking the proper amounts of water can really help with weight loss during induction-style low-carbing. A ketogenic diet can dehydrate one fairly quickly, so drinking adequate amounts of water is imperative as is taking supplements to prevent an electrolyte imbalance.

MOLTEN CHEESE VEGGIE EGGPLANT BOATS

This is quicker than making Eggplant Parmigiana and almost as tasty! The presentation is fun and looks quite fancy.

3 Chinese eggplants
1 tbsp olive oil (15 mL)
1 small onion, chopped
1 tsp crushed garlic (5 mL)
14.5 oz can diced tomatoes (411 g)
$^1/_2$ tsp oregano (2 mL)
$^1/_2$ tsp basil (2 mL)
$^1/_2$ tsp salt (2 mL)
$^1/_2$ cup water (125 mL)
Liquid sucralose to equal 2 tsp SPLENDA® Granular (10 mL)
1 cup shredded Monterey Jack Cheese (250 mL)

Yield: 6 eggplant boats
1 boat (half eggplant)
110.3 calories
6.1 g protein
6.3 g fat
8.3 g net carbs

Preheat oven to 375°F (190°C). Wash eggplants, dry and cut them in half lengthwise. Cut out the pulp, leaving a skinny rim around the edges and on the bottom of the boat. Dice pulp.

In large saucepan, in olive oil, cook diced eggplant and onion a few minutes. Add crushed garlic; stir fry 1 minute. Add diced tomatoes, oregano, basil and salt. Allow to cook over medium low heat until moisture evaporates. Add water and liquid sucralose. Simmer until moisture evaporates.

Fill eggplant boats with veggie mixture and sprinkle with Monterey Jack cheese. Bake in oven 20 to 25 minutes, or until eggplant rims test soft to the tip of a paring knife and cheese is golden. If desired, sprinkle warm eggplant boats with more cheese.

~~Bits & Bites~~
Food intolerances can cause weight loss resistance, joint and body pain, and a whole host of issues, besides weight gain due to inflammation.

JUMBO EGGPLANT FRIES

These fries are so tasty! If you like eggplant then these fries are better than French Fries any day and so much better for you!

1 large Chinese eggplant
Breading:
$^1/_4$ cup Gluten-Free Bake Mix 1, (60 mL)
  page 140, OR Bake Mix 2, page 141
2 tbsp grated Parmesan cheese (30 mL)
$^1/_2$ tsp Italian seasoning (2 mL)
  (herb mixture)
$^1/_8$ tsp salt (0.5 mL)
$^1/_8$ tsp black pepper (0.5 mL)
Egg Wash:
2 eggs
1 tbsp water (15 mL)
$^1/_4$ cup olive oil (60 mL)

Yield: 2 to 4 servings
1 serving
408.6/204.3 calories
10.7/5.3 g protein
37.1/18.5 g fat
6.9/3.5 g net carbs

Wash eggplant. Slice in half horizontally and in half longitudinally again and again until you have nice jumbo-size fries and cut those fries in half to get the right length.

Breading: On dinner plate, combine Gluten-Free Bake Mix 1, page 140, OR Gluten-Free Bake Mix 2, page 141, Parmesan cheese, Italian seasoning, salt and black pepper.

Egg Wash: In small bowl, beat eggs and water with fork.

Dip eggplant fries in egg wash and then in "breading". Place in large nonstick skillet with 2 tbsp (30 mL) hot oil. Fry until brown on one side, turn over and fry on the other side until golden brown both sides and tender to the touch of a fork piercing them. Add a little extra oil if needed. Repeat with remaining oil and eggplant. Serve immediately or keep warm, uncovered, in a warm oven until serving time.

Helpful Hint: Use a good, nonstick skillet (i.e. relatively new) as it makes it easier to use much less oil when frying eggplant.

Jennifer Eloff

BUTTERNUT SQUASH CAKES

When I made these I was not prepared for just how tasty they would be. They are so substantial-tasting and carby-tasting that you will not miss potato or other starch on your dinner plate.

2 tbsp olive oil (30 mL)
1 cup chopped onion (250 mL)
2 tsp curry powder (10 mL)
1 tsp ground cumin (5 mL)
1 tsp salt (5 mL)
1 tsp black pepper (5 mL)
4 cups peeled, grated butternut squash,* (1 L)
  OR similar yellow squash
2 eggs, fork beaten
$^2/_3$ cup Gluten-Free Bake Mix 1, page 140, OR Bake Mix 2, page 141 (150 mL)
$^1/_4$ cup olive oil (60 mL)
Sour cream (optional)

> **Yield:** 10 squash cakes
> 1 squash cake
> 135.2 calories
> 2.4 g protein
> 11.2 g fat
> **6.2 g net carbs**

In nonstick frying pan, in olive oil and over medium heat, cook onion until soft and translucent. Stir in curry powder, ground cumin, salt and pepper.

To prepare butternut squash, see helpful hints. Place grated butternut squash in large bowl. Stir in cooked onion and spice mixture. Stir eggs in well. Stir in Gluten-Free-Bake Mix 1, page 140, OR Gluten-Free Bake Mix 2, page 141 until well combined. Form 10 patties or cakes.

In nonstick frying pan, in 2 tbsp (30 mL) olive oil over medium heat cook squash cakes until golden brown underneath, flip carefully using spatula and spoon or fork to stabilize. Firmly flatten squash cakes with back of spatula and continue to cook another 2 minutes or until golden brown on the other side. Serve immediately with sour cream, if desired.

Helpful Hints: *To peel the butternut squash, cut off the top and bottom ends, then halve lengthwise. Use a large spoon to scrape out the seeds and fibers. Place cut side down and cut off the outer skin with a sharp knife. One of the major hurdles to preparing winter squash, such as butternut, is cutting it in half. You can always use a heavy chef's knife or a cleaver and exert some pressure.

An easier method is probably to partially bake the whole squash until it is soft enough to yield more easily to a knife. Place the squash in a 350°F (180°C) oven for 15 minutes. Remove the squash, allow to cool and cut as directed and then grate it in a food processor using the grating assembly. I have not tried this method – just something I am certain will work. You want the squash to still be hard enough to shred easily. I use the grating assembly for my food processor.

124

CAULI-NUGGET CASSEROLE

This recipe is based on our friend, Margaret Wolf's hash brown potato casserole that she brought over for us to enjoy one Christmas day. It was a hit! The topping for the low-carb version of her dish is crunchy and very tasty indeed!

2.2 lb fresh cauliflower (1 kg)
Condensed Cream of Mushroom Soup,
  page 103
2 cups sour cream (500 mL)
1 cup grated Cheddar Cheese (250 mL)
$^1/_2$ cup chopped onion (125 mL)
2 tsp Mrs Dash® Seasoning (10 mL)
  Blend (Herb and Garlic)
$^3/_4$ tsp salt (3 mL)
$^1/_4$ tsp white pepper (1 mL)
2 tbsp butter, melted (30 mL)
Cheesy Almond Topping:
2 tsp butter (10 mL)
1 cup sliced almonds (250 mL)
$^1/_2$ cup grated Cheddar Cheese (125 mL)

Yield: 15 servings
1 serving
209.8 calories
7.2 g protein
17.2 g fat
6.0 g net carbs

Chop cauliflower florets really tiny – about the size of two hash browns – like little nuggets of cauliflower florets. Steam or boil cauliflower in water 20 to 30 minutes, or until just tender, but not mushy.

In large bowl, combine Condensed Cream of Mushroom Soup, page 103, sour cream, Cheddar cheese, onion, Mrs Dash® Seasoning Blend, salt and pepper. Stir in cooked cauliflower florets. Spread evenly in 9 x 13-inch (23 x 33 cm) glass baking dish. Sprinkle topping over top; distribute evenly. Drizzle with butter. Bake uncovered 40 minutes in 350°F (180°C) oven.

Cheesy Almond Topping: In skillet, melt butter and stir-fry almonds until turning brown. Remove from heat. Quickly stir in cheese.

Helpful Hints: If desired, just cover the casserole in plenty of cheese and skip the Cheesy Almond Topping to keeps things simple and quick. This casserole lasts a whole week in the refrigerator; however, it may also be frozen in an airtight container. It will not be quite as good as freshly made, but almost. This recipe may be halved and made in an 8-inch (20 cm) square glass dish.

EGGPLANT, TOMATO AND ONION SKILLET DISH

An easy veggie dish that takes minutes to prepare and then it simply cooks on the stove top while you prepare the rest of the meal.

1 cup diced onion (250 mL)
2 Chinese eggplants
Seasoning salt, to taste
Black pepper, to taste
14.5 oz canned, diced tomatoes (411 g)
1 cup water (250 mL)
2 tbsp grated Parmesan cheese (30 mL)

Yield: 6 servings
1 serving
45.9 calories
2.1 g protein
0.8 g fat
7.6 g net carbs

In large nonstick skillet, cook onion over medium heat until translucent. Peel Chinese eggplants and slice into $^1/_4$-inch (0.6 cm) thick rounds. In blender combine diced tomatoes and water; blend. Layer eggplant rounds over onion, sprinkle lightly with seasoning salt and black pepper and pour half tomato sauce over all; repeat. Cover with lid and simmer 10 minutes. Sprinkle with Parmesan cheese, place lid on skillet and continue cooking over low heat another 15 minutes, or until the eggplant is soft. If desired, sprinkle with a little more Parmesan cheese for garnish.

PARMESAN BROCCOLI

So simple, but to me this broccoli side dish looks fancy. Broccoli is high in vitamin A and vitamin K. For people needing to supplement with large doses of vitamin D, ample supply of vitamin K and A help keep our vitamin D metabolism in balance.

Yield: 4 to 6 servings
1 serving
91.8/61.2 calories
3.4/2.3 g protein
37.2/4.8 g fat
3.3/2.2 g net carbs

1 lb broccoli, chopped small (0.45 kg)
2 tbsp olive oil (30 mL)
$^1/_2$ tsp seasoning salt (2 mL)
$^1/_4$ tsp black pepper, OR to taste (1 mL)
$1^1/_2$ tbsp Parmesan cheese (22mL)

Bring a pot of water to a boil. Add broccoli and cook 2 minutes. Remove with a slotted spoon or pour over a colander placed over a larger bowl.

In large skillet, heat oil over medium high heat. Add broccoli and sprinkle with seasoning salt and black pepper. Stir fry 2 minutes or just until tender. Place broccoli in a serving dish, sprinkle with Parmesan cheese and serve.

MISCELLANEOUS

CREAMY ITALIAN DRESSING

For a non-creamy Italian Dressing, see Low-Carbing Among Friends, volume-1 page 36. It is so much fun to make one's own salad dressings.

$^1/_4$ cup olive oil (60 mL)
2 tbsp vinegar (30 mL)
2 tbsp mayonnaise (30 mL)
1 tbsp heavy cream (15 mL)
1 tbsp Parmesan cheese (15 mL)
$^1/_2$ tsp garlic powder (2 mL)
$^1/_2$ tsp onion powder (2 mL)
$^1/_2$ tsp salt (2 mL)
$^1/_2$ tsp black pepper (2 mL)
$^1/_8$ tsp Worcestershire sauce (0.5 mL)

Yield: 1 cup (250 mL)
1 tbsp (15 mL) per serving
74.7 calories
0.4 g protein
8.0 g fat
0.7 g net carbs

In blender, combine olive oil, vinegar, mayonnaise, heavy cream, Parmesan cheese, garlic powder, onion powder, salt, black pepper and Worcestershire sauce. Blend until smooth. Place in sealed container and refrigerate.

CRACKED PEPPER SALAD DRESSING

This salad dressing is so good and you won't believe it – it is almost like a mild-tasting Blue cheese dressing. I don't like Blue cheese dressing but I like this.

$^1/_2$ cup mayonnaise (125 mL)
$^1/_4$ cup heavy cream (60 mL)
1 tbsp lemon juice (15 mL)
1 tbsp Parmesan cheese (15 mL)
$1^1/_2$ tsp coarsely ground black pepper (7 mL)
$^1/_2$ tsp crushed garlic (2 mL)
$^1/_4$ tsp onion salt (1 mL)
1 tbsp finely chopped green onion (15 mL)

Yield: $^3/_4$ cup (175 mL)
1 tbsp (15 mL) per serving
85.9 calories
0.5 g protein
9.1 g fat
0.5 g net carbs

In medium bowl, combine mayonnaise, cream, lemon juice, Parmesan cheese, black pepper, crushed garlic and onion salt. Sprinkle with chopped green onion and perhaps grind a little more black pepper over the top.

Helpful Hint: Double the recipe, if desired.

CRANBERRY RAISINS

I am assuming that half the syrup is absorbed or clings to the cranberries for the nutritional analysis. Use in Chocolate Chip Cranberry Cookies, page 143.

12 oz package frozen cranberries, (340 g) unsweetened and slightly thawed
Syrup:
Liquid sucralose to equal $1^1/_2$ cups (375 mL) SPLENDA® Granular
1 cup water (250 mL)
$^1/_2$ cup powdered erythritol (125 mL)
1 tbsp butter (15 mL)
1 tbsp cornstarch (10 mL)
$^1/_8$ tsp salt (0.5 mL)
1 tsp vanilla extract (5 mL)

Yield: $1^3/_4$ cups (425 mL) 2 tbsp (30 mL) per serving 17.1 calories 0.1 g protein 0.5 g fat **2.3 g net carbs**

Using scissors cut cranberries in half; place in medium-size bowl.

Syrup: In small saucepan, stir together liquid sucralose, OR SPLENDA® Granular, water, erythritol, butter, cornstarch and salt. Bring to boil, stirring. Remove from heat. Stir in vanilla. Pour over cranberries. Cover and refrigerate for 48 hours. Drain lightly.

Line cookie sheet with parchment paper. Spread cranberries on parchment paper. Bake in 200°F (100°C) oven $4^1/_2$ hours, stirring after 2 hours and return to oven to complete the drying process. Turn off oven; leave cranberries uncovered in cool, dry place for 1 day or until preferred dryness. (Smaller berries will dry out first; they will be dehydrated and wrinkled, but still soft and pliable.) Store in small, covered plastic container or sealed plastic bag at room temperature for up to 2 weeks. Refrigerate or freeze no longer than 2 months.

Helpful Hint: A food dehydrator may be used instead of the oven. Convection ovens will make short work of dehydrating the cranberries – probably about half the time will be required.

~~Bits & Bites~~
My husband makes our yogurt every week and one of my favorite treats is making yogurt granola parfaits (see page 107) and adding a little of whatever fruit I happen to have in the house. Put it in a pretty wine glass to feel special. It makes a good, healthy breakfast or snack that is quite filling. These cranberries would be super in my Chunky, Crispy, Chewy Granola recipe, page 108.

MAYONNAISE

Commercial mayonnaise is often filled with sugar! This recipe is delicious and reminds me a bit of Miracle Whip® mayonnaise.

1 extra-large egg
  (organic, if possible)
2 tbsp white vinegar, OR (30 mL)
  lemon juice*
3 tbsp SPLENDA® Granular (45 mL)
1 tbsp water (15 mL)
2 tsp prepared mustard (10 mL)
$\frac{1}{2}$ tsp dry mustard powder (2 mL)
$\frac{1}{2}$ tsp salt (2 mL)
$\frac{1}{4}$ tsp white pepper (1 mL)
$\frac{1}{4}$ tsp xanthan gum, OR Thickening Agent, page 53, (1 mL)
  Low-Carbing Among Friends, Volume-1
1 cup light-tasting olive oil (250 mL)

Yield: $1\frac{1}{2}$ cups (375 mL)
1 tbsp (15 mL) per serving
84.3 calories
0.3 g protein
9.3 g fat
0.4 g net carbs

In blender, combine egg, vinegar, OR lemon juice, SPLENDA® Granular, water, mustard, dry mustard powder, salt and white pepper at low speed. Uncover blender or through hole in lid, add xanthan gum, OR Thickening Agent, page 53, *Low-Carbing Among Friends, Volume-1* and at low speed in slow, steady stream, add olive oil, until mayonnaise is thoroughly mixed and thickened.

Helpful Hints: Cider vinegar may be used instead of white vinegar, if desired. *If you suspect you have Candida, then using the lemon juice option would be a wise choice. For a bite to the mayonnaise add one more tablespoon (15 mL) vinegar or lemon juice.

RANCH DRESSING
An all-time favorite.

1 cup mayonnaise (250 mL)
$\frac{3}{4}$ cup buttermilk (175 mL)
$\frac{1}{2}$ cup sour cream (125 mL)
$\frac{1}{2}$ cup spreadable cream cheese (125 mL)
1 tbsp grated Parmesan cheese (15 mL)
2 tsp dried parsley (10 mL)
$\frac{1}{4}$ tsp garlic powder (1 mL)
$\frac{1}{4}$ tsp salt (1 mL)
$\frac{1}{4}$ tsp black pepper (1 mL)

Yield: $2\frac{3}{4}$ cups (675 mL)
1 tbsp (15 mL) per serving
49.8 calories
0.5 g protein
5.1 g fat
0.5 g net carbs

In blender, blend mayonnaise, buttermilk, sour cream, spreadable cream cheese, Parmesan cheese, parsley, garlic powder, salt and black pepper until smooth.

Jennifer Eloff

PEACH NECTARINE JAM

Imagine buttering my Cheddar Sandwich Bread, page 135, or Microwave Almond Crackers, page 139 and spreading one of these delightful jams on it.

4 cups chopped, ripe peaches (1 L)
2 cups chopped, ripe nectarines (500 mL)
3 tbsp lemon juice (45 mL)
3 cups SPLENDA® Granular* (750 mL)
  (not liquid sucralose – not sweet enough)
1 package Fruit Pectin for no-sugar** (49 g)
  jams
1 cup water (250 mL)
$^1/_2$ tsp butter (2 mL)

Yield: $5^1/_2$ cups (1.4 L)
1 tsp (5 mL) per serving
4.1 calories
0.0 g protein
0.0 g fat
0.9 g net carbs

In a 9 x 13-inch (23 x 33 cm) glass baking dish, cover six, 1-cup (250 mL) jars, lids and rings, long-handled spoon and tongs with boiling water to sterilize. In large pot, combine peaches, nectarines and lemon juice. Add SPLENDA® Granular and stir in well. Stir in pectin gradually. Stir in water. Cook over medium high heat and as fruit softens, mash with potato masher (fruit will mostly still be in tiny chunks). Bring to full rolling boil, stirring constantly. Add butter; boil 1 minute. Remove from heat. Skim off foam with long-handled spoon.

Carefully pick up jar with tongs and tip water out. Place jar on saucer and spoon hot jam to within $^1/_2$-inch (1.3 cm) of rim. Pick up lid with tongs; place on jar. Pick up ring with tongs and screw on jar tightly, using a clean dish towel. Allow to cool. Refrigerate sealed up to 1 year or freeze for much longer storage.

Variations: **Strawberry Jam:** Use 8 cups (2 L) frozen, unsweetened strawberries and 2 tbsp (30 mL) lemon juice. *(0.8 g net carbs)*

Strawberry Rhubarb Jam: Use 6 cups (1.5 L) frozen, unsweetened strawberries and 2 cups (500 mL) frozen unsweetened, chopped rhubarb, 1 cup (250 mL) water plus 3 tbsp (45 mL) extra water. Omit lemon juice. Chop rhubarb as it cooks and softens. *(0.7 g net carbs)*

Raspberry or Blueberry Jam: Use 8 cups (2 L) frozen, unsweetened raspberries or blueberries, in addition to, 1 tbsp (15 mL) lemon juice. (**Raspberry: 0.7 g net carbs**) (**Blueberry: 0.8 g net carbs**)

Helpful Hints: *If using a zero-carb sweetener, you will have to adjust the sweetness with another bulk sweetener. **If you're unable to find the particular pectin which is to be used with low-calorie sweeteners, then use light pectin and stir in 1 envelope (15 mL) gelatin softened in 2 tbsp (30 mL) water at the end of cooking. Opened jam should last about 1 month in the refrigerator.

CONDENSED MILK CHOCOLATE SAUCE

Decadent, rich and thick chocolate sauce as a topping for desserts.

$^{1}/_{2}$ cup whipping cream (125 mL)
Liquid sucralose to equal 1 cup (250 mL)
  SPLENDA® Granular
$^{1}/_{3}$ cup butter, melted (75 mL)
$^{1}/_{3}$ cup Da Vinci® Sugar Free (75 mL)
  French Vanilla, OR Vanilla Syrup
$^{1}/_{3}$ cup vanilla whey protein (75 mL)
$^{1}/_{3}$ cup skim milk powder, OR (75 mL)
  whole milk powder
$^{1}/_{8}$ tsp xanthan gum (0.5 mL)
1 oz unsweetened chocolate, melted (30 g)

> **Yield:** $1^{2}/_{3}$ cups (400 mL)
> 1 tbsp (15 mL) per serving
> 47.5 calories
> 1.4 g protein
> 4.5 g fat
> *0.8 g net carbs*

In blender, combine whipping cream, liquid sucralose, OR SPLENDA® Granular, butter, Da Vinci® Sugar Free French Vanilla, OR Vanilla Syrup, vanilla whey protein, skim, OR whole milk powder and xanthan gum. Blend until smooth. Add melted chocolate; blend. Serve immediately or refrigerate and use later.

Variations: **Condensed Milk Chocolate Frosting:** Use $^{1}/_{3}$ cup (75 mL) whipping cream and 2 tbsp (30 mL) Da Vinci® Sugar Free Vanilla Syrup.
Yield: 1 cup (250 mL). 12/16/36 servings:
92.6/69.5/30.9 calories, 2.9/2.2/1.0g pro, 8.6/6.4/2.9g fat, *1.7/1.3/0.6g net carbs*

Caramel Sauce/Frosting: Substitute Da Vinci® Sugar Free Caramel Syrup in main recipe and use cocoa butter instead of chocolate. Follow instructions for variation above for frosting as opposed to the sauce in the main recipe.

Any-Flavor Sauce or Frosting: Cocoa butter and Da Vinci® Sugar Free Syrup flavor of choice or chocolate and Da Vinci® Sugar Free Syrup flavor of choice.

Da Vinci® Alternative: Use water, appropriate flavored extract and 1 or 2 SPLENDA® packets.

Helpful Hints: This sauce is thick and becomes a little thicker upon chilling.

~~Bits & Bites~~
Anytime you make a treat and feel you cannot control your portions, quickly freeze the remainder and bring it out only when you feel your will power is stronger or you have others around to help you finish it.

SINGLE PIE CRUST

This is a lower-carb and more substantial crust that tastes great.

1¼ cups Gluten-free Bake Mix 1, (300 mL)
  page 140
3 oz cream cheese, softened (90 g)
2 tbsp powdered erythritol, optional (30 mL)
1 tbsp butter, softened (15 mL)
¼ tsp baking soda (1 mL)
⅛ tsp salt (0.5 mL)

Yield: 10 servings
1 serving
101.3 calories
3.1 g protein
8.3 g fat
3.2 g net carbs

In food processor or in bowl with electric mixer, process Gluten-Free Bake Mix 1, page 140, cream cheese, powdered erythritol (if using), butter, baking soda and salt until mixed. Form a ball with dough using your hands and cover with plastic wrap. Chill dough about 1 hour or freeze for quicker chilling.

Roll dough out (if crumbly, chill longer) between two sheets of parchment paper to fit shallow 9-inch (23 cm) glass pie dish. Remove top sheet of paper. Pick up sheet with dough and invert over pie dish. Remove paper. Use small rolling pin or small cylindrical object in pie dish, if necessary, to further roll dough. Patch dough where required. A straight edge up the sides is practical. Push down slightly from edge onto dough with thumbs and this will make a slightly thicker border for the crust. Bake in 350°F (180°C) oven 10 minutes.

CRÈME FRAICHE

Lovely sweetened whipped topping for serving with desserts or for garnishing desserts. It holds up better than plain whipped cream and tastes better. Add cocoa and you have a nice, creamy chocolate frosting!

1 cup whipping cream (250 mL)
Liquid sucralose to equal ½ cup (125 mL)
  SPLENDA® Granular
¼-½ tsp Thickening Agent, page, (1-2 mL)
  53, *Low-Carbing Among Friends, Volume-1*
⅔ cup regular sour cream, OR (150 mL)
  nonfat sour cream (to save calories)
½ tsp vanilla extract (2 mL)

Yield: 2⅛ cups (530 mL)
2 tbsp (30 mL) per serving
56.8 calories
0.6 g protein
5.8 g fat
0.9 g net carbs

In food processor, on low speed, process whipping cream with SPLENDA® Granular. While processing, sprinkle in Thickening Agent, LCAF's vol-1, page 53, OR xanthan gum through feed tube. Process until thick. Add sour cream and vanilla extract; process on medium high speed just until combined. It will keep at least one week or longer in the refrigerator.

BREADS, MUFFINS AND MORE

MINI BANANA LOAVES

Such cute loaves make a dainty, pretty display at the tea table, especially with the Cream Cheese Drizzle, which doesn't add much in the way of carbs.

3 eggs
1 cup mashed bananas (250 mL)
Liquid sucralose to equal 1 cup (250 mL)
 SPLENDA® Granular
$^1/_2$ cup light-tasting olive oil (125 mL)
$^1/_3$ cup buttermilk (75 mL)
$^1/_4$ cup granulated erythritol (60 mL)
$^1/_2$ tsp vanilla extract (2 mL)
2 cups Gluten-Free Bake Mix 1, page 140 (500 mL)
1 tsp baking soda (5 mL)
$^1/_2$ tsp salt (2 mL)
$^1/_4$ cup raisins, snipped in half, OR (60 mL)
 $^1/_2$ cup sugar-free chocolate chips (125 mL)
Cream Cheese Drizzle (optional):
2 oz cream cheese, softened (60 g)
2 tbsp powdered Steviva® Blend, OR erythritol, OR (30 mL)
 liquid sucralose, to taste
1 tbsp heavy cream (15 mL)

> ***Yield:*** 30 (10 x 3) slices
> 1 slice with raisins/choc.
> 85.2/94.0 calories
> 2.0/2.1 g protein
> 6.5/7.2 g fat
> ***4.4/3.6 g net carbs***

Preheat oven to 350°F (180°C).

Grease 3, $5^1/_4$ x $3^1/_4$ x $2^1/_4$-inch (13 x 8 x 6 cm) nonstick mini loaf pans. In food processor, process eggs. Add mashed bananas, liquid sucralose, OR SPLENDA® Granular, olive oil, buttermilk, granulated erythritol and vanilla extract; process.

In medium bowl, combine Gluten-Free Bake Mix 1, page 140, baking soda and salt. Add dry ingredients to wet ingredients and process about 1 minute, until thickened. Stir in raisins, OR chocolate chips.

Pour or scrape into prepared mini loaf pans. Bake 35 minutes, or until toothpick inserted in center comes out clean.

Cream Cheese Drizzle: In small bowl, combine softened cream cheese with powdered Steviva® Blend, erythritol, OR liquid sucralose, to taste, and heavy cream. Place in pastry bag with plain tip and pipe Cream Cheese Frosting over the mini banana loaves in a pretty, wavy pattern.

JIFFY CHEDDAR SANDWICH BREAD

This is very bread-like and is a variation on my Jiffy Sandwich Bread in Low-Carbing Among Friends, Volume-2. I made a sandwich with it and honestly it's very acceptable and quite tasty.

1 egg
1 tsp melted butter (5 mL)
1 tsp mayonnaise (5 mL)
1 tsp heavy cream, OR coconut milk (5 mL)
1 tsp water (5 mL)
$^1/_2$ tsp psyllium husk powder (2 mL)
3 tbsp Gluten-Free Bake Mix 1, (45 mL)
 page 140
$^1/_2$ tsp baking powder (2 mL)
$^1/_4$ cup shredded Cheddar cheese (60 mL)

Yield: 2 slices of bread
1 slice
170.1 calories
8.5 g protein
12.2 g fat
3.1 g net carbs

In small bowl, beat egg and butter with fork. Add mayonnaise, heavy cream, OR coconut milk and water and whisk into the egg with the fork until well combined. Add psyllium husks and whisk in well. Allow the psyllium husks to soak for 5 minutes (helps remove any grittiness that might be in the psyllium husks). Add Gluten-Free Bake Mix 1, page 140 and baking powder and combine well using the fork. Stir in shredded Cheddar cheese.

Using a rubber spatula to remove the batter completely, scrape it into a greased, square 4-inch (10 cm) glass dish. Spread batter evenly to all edges with the back of a spoon. Microwave on high power 1 minute. Invert onto a plate and microwave another 20 seconds. Allow to cool slightly and carefully with a large, serrated bread knife, slice horizontally into two slices. Allow to cool completely and dry out a bit on a wire rack.

Helpful Hints: My microwave oven is a Panasonic Inverter, 1200 watts. Your timing may differ quite substantially depending on the wattage of your microwave oven. When you touch the bread it should spring back and when you invert it and cook the last time, make sure there are no wet spots in the middle. If there are then stick it in the microwave oven in 10 second intervals until it is dry.

You will find the sweet spot for your microwave oven – just make a note next to the recipe for the next time. This bread toasts well.

The Cheddar cheese flavor is not particularly noticeable. I did try this bread with Monterey Jack cheese and I didn't like it as much.

CHEDDAR SANDWICH BREAD

This is my Jiffy Cheddar Sandwich bread made into a loaf.

8 eggs
2¹/₃ tbsp melted butter (35 mL)
{2 tbsp (30 mL) plus 1 tsp (5 mL)}
2¹/₃ tbsp mayonnaise* (35 mL)
2¹/₃ tbsp heavy cream, OR (35 mL)
coconut milk
2¹/₃ tbsp water (35 mL)
2 tsp psyllium husk powder (10 mL)
2 cups Gluten-Free Bake Mix 1, (500 mL)
page 140
2 tsp baking powder (10 mL)
2 cups shredded Cheddar cheese (500 mL)

Yield: 20 to 24 slices
1 slice
157.6/131.3 calories
7.3/6.1 g protein
12.7/10.6 g fat
2.8/2.3 g net carbs

Preheat oven to 350°C (180°F). In food processor or in bowl with mixer, process eggs and butter. Add mayonnaise, heavy cream, OR coconut milk, water and psyllium husk powder. Process on slow speed while preparing the rest of the recipe and continue processing 8 minutes. In medium bowl, combine Gluten-Free Bake Mix 1, page 140 and baking powder. Add to wet ingredients and process until thickened. Stir in Cheddar cheese.

Using a rubber spatula to remove the batter completely, scrape it into an 8 x 4-inch (20 x 10 cm) loaf pan lined with parchment paper. Spread batter evenly to all edges with the back of a spoon. If desired, put a little more batter on either end as this bread does dome slightly. Bake 50 minutes, or until knife inserted in center comes out clean. Cover with foil during last 10 minutes if necessary. Allow bread to cool 10 minutes in the pan. Remove to wire rack and carefully remove parchment paper. Slice when completely cool and allow the slices to air dry on a wire rack before refrigerating in a sealed container. Nuke a slice briefly and it is as if the bread was freshly baked again.

Helpful Hints: Some brands of psyllium husk powder have more grit than others and yet others can impart a slight purplish color. Allowing the psyllium husk powder to soften sufficiently in the wet ingredients helps remove grit. Apparently Jay Robb® makes great psyllium husks, which you can then grind into a powder in a coffee grinder or powerful blender. I used the NOW® brand which contains some grit. Allow the bread to cool completely before slicing. It is easier to slice uniform, thinner slices when the bread is cool. This bread does not need to be cut into thick slices. I much prefer thinner slices and, believe me; they are not too thin at all for this bread – just right! Great with butter and sugar-free preserves. See my Miscellaneous section for recipes. You can toast the slices.
*2¹/₃ tbsp (35 mL) is 2 tbsp (30 mL) and 1 tsp (5 mL).

JIFFY BANANA MUFFINS

Delicious muffins made in a jiffy. I love these muffins with the chocolate chips in them – especially the bottom part as many of the chips drop – pure fudgy, banana-and-chocolate-flavored heaven in a muffin.

5 tbsp Gluten-Free Bake Mix 1, (75 mL)
  page 140
2 tbsp erythritol (30 mL)
$^1/_2$ tsp baking powder (2 mL)
$^1/_8$ tsp salt (0.5 mL)
1 egg
2 tbsp mashed banana (30 mL)
1 tbsp heavy cream (15 mL)
Liquid sucralose to equal 2 tsp (10 mL)
  SPLENDA® Granular
1 tsp olive oil (5 mL)
$^1/_4$ tsp vanilla extract (1 mL)
1 to 2 tbsp sugar-free chocolate chips (15 to 30 mL)
  (optional - also sprinkle some chips on top of batter, if desired)

Yield: 2 muffins
1 muffin
154.0 calories
6.3 g protein
10.5 g fat
7.4 g net carbs

In small bowl, combine Gluten-Free Bake Mix 1, page 140, erythritol, baking powder and salt. In another small bowl, whisk egg with fork and whisk in banana, heavy cream, liquid sucralose, OR SPLENDA® Granular, olive oil and vanilla extract. Add to dry ingredients and whisk well with fork. Stir in chocolate chips, if using. Pour into two greased ramekins. Nuke approximately 1 minute and 10 seconds, or until top springs back when touched. Allow to cool almost completely for best taste experience.

Variation: **Jiffy Fudgy Pumpkin Muffins:** Use 3 tbsp (45 mL) canned pumpkin instead of banana, Liquid sucralose to equal 8 tsp (40 mL) SPLENDA® Granular, $^1/_2$ tsp (2 mL) cinnamon and $^1/_4$ tsp (1 mL) nutmeg. Nuke 1 minute 25 seconds or undercook slightly at 1 minute 15 seconds for a moist, fudgy muffin. *(6.2 g net carbs and with chocolate chips 6.7 g net carbs)*

Helpful Hints: My microwave oven is quite powerful - a Panasonic Inverter – 1200 Watts. Cooking times may vary quite a lot depending on your microwave oven. These muffins taste best if allowed to cool to room temperature. If you don't want the rest of the banana to spoil, slice the remainder of the banana and freeze it. One slice of banana = 1 gram of carbs. This recipe was only tested with the bake mix indicated.

COCONUT SCONE-LIKE MUFFINS

These will give you necessary fiber for the day at 7 grams of fiber per muffin. Most of my recipes have very little fiber – usually no more than 1 gram of fiber per serving and mostly a lot less. This muffin is high in fiber, so do be careful. Great with butter and sugar-free jam – see Peach Nectarine Jam, page 130.

6 eggs
$^1/_4$ cup butter, melted (60 mL)
$^1/_2$ cup coconut flour (125 mL)
$^1/_2$ cup ground almonds, OR (125 mL)
  almond flour
2 SPLENDA® packets
$^1/_2$ tsp baking soda (2 mL)
$^1/_4$ tsp xanthan gum (1 mL)
$^1/_4$ tsp salt (1 mL)
1 cup shredded Monterey Jack cheese (250 mL)

Yield: 6 to 9 muffins
1 muffin
304.1/202.7 calories
14.2/9.5 g protein
23.7/15.8 g fat
4.4/2.9 g net carbs

Preheat oven to 400°F (200°C). In food processor, process eggs and add butter; process. In medium bowl, combine coconut flour, ground almonds, OR almond flour, SPLENDA®, baking soda, xanthan gum and salt. Stir in Monterey Jack cheese. Stir in egg mixture and fill 6 large muffin cups or 9 regular-size muffin cups. Bake 15 to 20 minutes, or until knife inserted in center comes out clean.

~~Bits & Bites~~
Folks like body builders who make low-carbing a very high-protein diet can put themselves at risk for sudden death. According to Dr. Fuhrman, "It is well established in the medical literature that carbohydrate-restricted, high-protein diets can cause electrolyte deficiencies from enhanced urinary excretion, especially the loss of potassium that can lead to a cardiac arrhythmia and sudden cardiac death."

Do remember to eat lots of good carbs like vegetables and some fruits and plenty of good fats. This is exactly why the Meat Fast or Fat Fast taken to the extreme over a longer period of time can be very dangerous for those who would lose weight and water weight too quickly.

COCONUT PINEAPPLE MUFFINS

The pineapple makes these muffins! If you have the carb allowance, add a little more for sure, but dice it finely.

2¼ cups Gluten-Free Bake Mix 1, (560 mL)
  page 140
1½ tsp baking powder (7 mL)
½ tsp baking soda (2 mL)
½ tsp salt (2 mL)
2 eggs
Liquid sucralose to equal 1 cup (250 mL)
  SPLENDA® Granular
¼ cup granulated erythritol (60 mL)
1 tsp vanilla extract (5 mL)
14 fl oz-can coconut milk (414 mL)
⅔ cup finely desiccated, unsweetened coconut (150 mL)
⅔ cup finely diced pineapple, (150 mL)
  from canned pineapple in juice, drained

Yield: 12 muffins
1 muffin
215.3 calories
5.5 g protein
18.0 g fat
6.8 g net carbs

Preheat oven to 350°F (180°C). In large bowl, combine Gluten-Free Bake Mix 1, page 140, baking powder, baking soda and salt. In food processor, process eggs, liquid sucralose, OR SPLENDA® Granular, erythritol and vanilla extract. Add half coconut milk and half the dry ingredients; process briefly. Add remainder of coconut milk and dry ingredients and process until the batter thickens up. Stir in ½ cup (125 mL) coconut and all the diced pineapple.

Scoop batter into 12 greased muffin cups. Sprinkle batter with remaining coconut. Bake about 35 minutes. Keep an eye on them. After 25 minutes, test with a cake tester and cover lightly with foil during the last 5 to 10 minutes of baking.

Helpful Hints: The longer baking time is due to the high moisture content. No other fat is required thanks to the coconut milk. You can keep the remaining coconut aside and sprinkle on the baked muffins; looks pretty!

~~Bits & Bites~~
Huge changes occur in the body when switching to a ketogenic low-carb diet.
"The period of low-carb adaptation is that time between starting a low-carb diet and feeling great on a low-carb diet. It can take anywhere from just a day or so to two or three weeks. During this adaptation period people tend to fatigue easily, experience a slight lack of mental clarity and be tormented off and on by the unbidden lust for carbs that seems to rise up out of nowhere."-
Dr. Michael R. Eades, Protein Power.

MICROWAVE ALMOND CRACKERS

The sesame crackers are fairly bland as well, but more savory tasting than the almond crackers. Both are nice.

$1^{1}/_{4}$ cups ground almonds, OR (300 mL) almond flour
2 egg whites from large eggs
$^{1}/_{4}$ tsp salt (1 mL)

Yield: 56 crackers
1 cracker
12.8 calories
0.6 g protein
1.1 g fat
0.2 g net carbs

In medium bowl, place ground almonds, OR almond flour. In small bowl, whisk egg whites and salt with a fork. Add to ground almonds and stir to mix well. Turn out onto counter top onto a large piece of parchment paper. Flatten to a rough rectangular shape and cover with a similar-sized piece of parchment paper. Roll into an 11 x 12-inch (28 x 30 cm) rectangle. Place in microwave oven with parchment paper in place and nuke 2 minutes. Remove paper and cut into 56 crackers (8 x 7). Nuke another 3 to 4 minutes, or until hard, crunchy and slightly browned.

Variation: **Almond Sesame Crackers:** Use $1^{1}/_{8}$ cups (280 mL) ground almonds and $^{1}/_{4}$ cup (60 mL) toasted sesame seeds (toast in a dry nonstick skillet). Nuke 2 minutes, remove and cut into 56 cracker shapes and nuke another 5 minutes, or until crispy and browned. *(0.2 g net carbs)*

Helpful Hints: The crackers will crisp up slightly more as they cool. Store at room temperature in a cookie tin lined with parchment paper. Timing may vary depending on the wattage of your microwave oven. I have a Panasonic Inverter, 1200 watts microwave oven.

~~Bits & Bites~~
Make sure you consume enough fiber on your low-carb diet. Having sufficient fiber in the diet is associated with optimum health.

SPLENDID GLUTEN-FREE BAKE MIX 1

Almond flour versus almond meal produces slight differences. Since my husband is merely intolerant of gluten, we use oat flour by Arrowhead Mills®. * ¹/₄ Cup almond meal = 28 g. 1 cup Gluten-Free Bake Mix (almond meal) = 134 g.

1²/₃ cups almond flour, OR (400 mL; 182 g)
  (I use almond meal* – yield is greater with
  almond flour by up to ¹/₂ cup (125 mL) more,
  so then carbs would be **4.8 g** – bonus!)
³/₄ cup certified GF oat flour (175 ml; 100 g)
  (Bob's Red Mill®, *not* Legacy Valley®)
2 tbsp sifted coconut flour, (30 mL)
  (Bob's Red Mill®)
³/₄ tsp xanthan gum (3 mL)

> **Yield:** 2¹/₂ cups (625 mL)
> ¹/₄ cup (60 mL) per serving
> 125.7 calories
> 4.5 g protein
> 8.9 g fat
> **5.7 g net carbs**

In large bowl, combine almond flour, OR almond meal, oat flour (if you are intolerant to gluten-free oat flour then substitute another gluten-free flour like sorghum flour which others have had success with in the bake mix), coconut flour and xanthan gum. In container with airtight lid, place bake mix and shake the container well to combine. When measuring oat flour (not necessary with the other ingredients) into measuring cup, make sure to tap the cup on the counter top and fill to the top to get the correct yield for the bake mix. Keep bake mix at room temperature for up to one month or freeze for much longer storage.

Instructions for standard recipes: Add ¹/₄ cup (60 mL) additional bake mix when substituting for 1 cup (250 mL) or more than 1 cup (250 mL) flour and use 2 tbsp (30 mL) more if substituting for less than 1 cup (250 mL). Always begin by adding an extra egg in muffins, loaves, cakes and coffee cakes, except for cookies and except if bake mix required is less than or equal to 1 cup (250 mL). Withhold ¹/₄ cup (60 mL) of liquid/wet/fat ingredients; add in as needed (usually need it all). If batter after processing at least a minute is still too thick, add more of the liquid ingredients and if accidentally the batter ends up too sloppy, then add a little more bake mix. If all the liquid has been used and the batter is still too stiff, add another egg and another if necessary. Baking experience is helpful.

Helpful Hints: Great in muffins, loaves (with eggs!), cookies, squares or bars, coffee cakes, many cakes, pie crusts and a few other specialized applications, but will not be suitable for all applications, nor for most yeast applications. Xanthan gum has gluten-like properties, binding ingredients together to prevent crumbly outcomes. When substituting the Splendid Gluten-Free bake mix for some of my other bake mixes, 2 tbsp (30 mL) to ¹/₄ cup (60 mL) more bake mix may be required depending on if one is replacing less than 1 cup (250 mL) or 1 cup (250 mL) or more (last 2, latter amount). Follow the same rules above. It is convenient to double, triple or quadruple this bake mix.

SPLENDID GLUTEN-FREE BAKE MIX 2

For the older version of my bake mix using xanthan gum, see page 140. It was brought to my attention that many people do not tolerate xanthan gum well, or they balk at the price, or they just plain old don't trust it. Here is a very easy alternative. I need to test it more extensively in recipes, but for now here is what I have discovered and how you can use gelatin to help bind the wet ingredients and also the dry "flour" components of the bake mix to prevent crumbly outcomes, which is what the xanthan gum accomplished. If I only mention the former bake mix, it typically means the recipe has only been tested using it.

$1^2/_3$ cups almond flour, OR (400 mL; 182 g)
(I use almond meal* – yield is greater with
almond flour by up to $^1/_2$ cup (125 mL) more,
so then carbs would be *4.8 g* – bonus!)
$^3/_4$ cup certified GF oat flour, (175 ml; 100 g)
(Bob's Red Mill®, *not* Legacy Valley®)
2 tbsp coconut flour, (30 mL)
(Bob's Red Mill®)

Yield: $2^1/_2$ cups (625 mL)
$^1/_4$ cup (60 mL) per serving
125.0 calories
4.5 g protein
8.9 g fat
5.7 g net carbs

In large bowl, combine almond flour, OR almond meal, oat flour (if you are intolerant to certified gluten-free oat flour then substitute another gluten-free flour like sorghum flour which others have had success with in the bake mix), and coconut flour. In container with airtight lid, place bake mix and shake the container well to combine. When measuring oat flour (not necessary with the other ingredients) into measuring cup, make sure to tap the cup on the counter top and fill to the top to get the correct yield for the bake mix. Keep bake mix at room temperature for up to one month or freeze for much longer storage.

Instructions for substituting the bake mix in your own flour-containing recipes: Add $^1/_4$ cup (60 mL) additional bake mix when substituting for 1 cup (250 mL) or more than 1 cup (250 mL) flour in recipes and use 2 tbsp (30 mL) more if substituting for less than 1 cup (250 mL).

When using this bake mix in your regular flour-filled recipes keep the number of eggs the same and typically the liquid/fat/wet ingredients will remain the same, but if you want to be on the safe side, withhold $^1/_4$ cup (60 mL) of the liquid ingredients and add at the end. If the batter is too wet, add more bake mix 1 tbsp (15 mL) at a time, process and check the batter consistency. Very simple! If the batter is too thick and you've added all the liquid/fat/wet ingredients for the recipe, then add another egg and if it is still too thick, add some more liquid, 2 tablespoons (30 mL) at a time.

Adding Gelatin: You will need $1^1/_2$ tsp (7 mL) gelatin for every cup (250 mL) of Splendid Gluten-Free bake Mix 1*, page 140 or flour. Gelatin is added to wet

Jennifer Eloff

ingredients in food processor or mixer and mixed briefly. Let it sit and soften 10 minutes; process a few minutes. Add dry ingredients and process until well combined. Some math is needed to calculate the amount of gelatin needed. Hhere are some variations worked out for you. If **2$^1/_4$ cups** (560 mL) of bake mix is required, then you will require 1$^1/_2$ tsp (7 mL) gelatin x 2 (3 tsp (15 mL) **PLUS** 1$^1/_2$ ÷ 4 ($^3/_2$ x $^1/_4$ = $^3/_8$) = **3 tsp** (1 tbsp, 15 mL) gelatin **PLUS** $^3/_8$ **tsp** (1.5 mL).

For **1$^1/_2$ cups** (375 mL) bake mix, you would need **1$^1/_2$ tsp** (7 mL) gelatin **PLUS** you would need {1$^1/_2$ ÷ 2 = $^3/_4$ **tsp** (3 mL)}. **1$^3/_4$ cups** (425 mL) would require **1$^1/_2$ tsp** (7 mL) gelatin **PLUS** (remember $^1/_4$ cup (60 mL) requires $^3/_8$ tsp (1.5 mL) gelatin?), so $^3/_8$ x 3 = **1$^1/_8$ tsp** (5.5 mL) gelatin. **1$^1/_3$ cups** (325 mL) bake mix would need **1$^1/_2$ tsp** (7 mL) **PLUS** $^1/_2$ **tsp** (2 mL) (1$^1/_2$ ÷ 3 = $^1/_2$). With these few scenarios worked out for you, hopefully it should be easy to do the math for any other variations. *If this is bothersome to you, pretend 1 tsp (5 mL) per cup is required, do the math, and add $^1/_2$ tsp (2 mL) more; should still work favorably.*

Applications: Gelatin option works in muffins, cakes, loaves, bundt cakes, brownies and cupcakes, but not for cookies. The gluten-free bake mixes need eggs in almost all applications. *Sometimes I recommend both bake mixes in a recipe, but with regard to this bake mix option you will not always need gelatin; usually it is self-explanatory - for example, breading, cookies, crusts, etc.*

Cookies: For cookies simply leave out both the xanthan gum and gelatin option. Gelatin will make cookies too soft. Keep the number of eggs called for in the cookie recipe the same and follow the instructions for replacing flour with the bake mix. Cookies will be fragile straight out of the oven. Leave them to cool completely on the cookie sheet and using a thin metal spatula transfer cooled cookies to dinner plates and place in the freezer. Once frozen, place in a sealed container back in the freezer. If you're having trouble with a cookie recipe crumbling, add a tsp (5 mL) of honey or molasses to help bind the ingredients.

Helpful Hints: I buy the NOW® Brand gelatin in a 1 lb (0.45 kg) bag from Netrition.com. It is more economical. *When substituting the Splendid Gluten-Free bake mix 2 for some of my older bake mixes, then 2 tbsp (30 mL) to $^1/_4$ cup (60 mL) more bake mix will be required depending on if one is replacing less than 1 cup (250 mL) or 1 cup (250 mL) or more (last 2, latter amount). Follow same rules above. It is convenient to double, triple or quadruple this bake mix.

If you are using the gelatin application for my recipes that use the original Splendid Gluten-Free Bake Mix 1, page 140 with xanthan gum, don't change anything in the recipes other than withholding $^1/_4$ cup (60 mL) to $^1/_2$ cup (125 mL) of the wet ingredients and adding in as necessary. You will almost certainly need less of the wet ingredients. Xanthan gum requires more wet ingredients. *If you need to substitute Splendid Gluten-Free Bake Mix 1 for Splendid Gluten-Free Bake Mix 2 in recipes, you will need an extra egg, except for cookies.*

SWEET ENDINGS

CHOCOLATE CHIP CRANBERRY COOKIES

I love the cinnamon in this cookie. It is a substantial, crunchy cookie with a different flavor and the cranberries give it a distinctive, festive accent.

2 cups Gluten-Free Bake Mix 1,* (500 mL)
  page 140
1 tsp cinnamon (5 mL)
1 tsp baking soda (5 mL)
$^1/_4$ tsp baking powder (1 mL)
1 large egg
$1^1/_2$ sticks ($^3/_4$ cup) butter, softened (175 mL)
Liquid sucralose to equal 1 cup (250 mL)
  SPLENDA® Granular
$^1/_4$ cup granulated erythritol (60 mL)
1 tsp vanilla extract (5 mL)
$1^1/_2$ cups sugar-free chocolate chips (375 mL)
$^1/_2$ cup dried, sugar-free cranberries, OR raisins (use half the amount) (125 mL)

> **Yield:** 28 cookies
> 1 cookie
> 124.9 calories
> 1.9 g protein
> 9.9 g fat
> **2.3 g net carbs**

Preheat oven to 375°F (190°C). In medium bowl, combine Gluten-Free Bake Mix 1, page 140, cinnamon, baking soda and baking powder. Stir to mix well.

In food processor with metal blade, process egg. Add butter, sucralose, OR SPLENDA® Granular, erythritol and vanilla extract; process.

Add dry ingredients to wet ingredients and process about 1 minute. Stir in chocolate chips and sugar-free cranberries, OR raisins. Using heaping tablespoonfuls, place dough on greased cookie sheet. Flatten dough with back of spoon. Bake 10 to 12 minutes or until turning brown. Allow to cool 5 minutes. Transfer to freezer or refrigerator.

Helpful Hints: *If you cannot tolerate xanthan gum – leave it out and read the instructions for cookies under Gluten-Free Bake Mix 2, page 141. If desired increase the dried, sugar-free cranberries to 1 cup (250 mL) and reduce the chocolate chips accordingly for a chewier cookie.

~~Bits & Bites~~
Heavy consumption of green vegetables leads to fewer food cravings.

CHEWY HOLIDAY BARS

These tasty, chewy squares are very satisfying. If you like, you could also add a couple of tablespoons of snipped raisins or dried apricots.

Crust:
1 cup Gluten-Free Bake Mix 1, (250 mL)
  page 140, OR Bake Mix 2, page 141
$^1/_2$ cup ground almonds (125 mL)
7 tbsp butter, melted (105 mL)
Topping:
8 oz regular cream cheese (250 g)
$^1/_4$ cup sour cream (60 mL)
Liquid sucralose to equal $^1/_2$ cup SPLENDA® Granular (125 mL)
1 egg
$^1/_4$ tsp vanilla extract (1 mL)
$^3/_4$ cup unsweetened shredded coconut (175 mL)
$^1/_4$ cup SPLENDA® Granular (60 mL)
6 oz sugar-free chocolate chips (180 g)
$^1/_2$ cup chopped walnuts (125 mL)

Yield: 36 servings
1 serving
111.5 calories
2.4 g protein
9.8 g fat
1.7 g net carbs

Crust: In medium bowl, combine Gluten-Free Bake Mix 1, page 140, OR Gluten-Free Bake Mix 2, page 141, ground almonds and melted butter. Press onto bottom of 13 x 9-inch (23 x 33 cm) baking dish. Bake at 350°F (180°C) 10 minutes.

Topping: In food processor, process cream cheese and sour cream until smooth. Add liquid sucralose, OR SPLENDA® Granular, egg and vanilla extract; process until smooth. Spread evenly over crust. In small bowl, combine coconut and SPLENDA® Granular. Stir in chocolate chips and walnuts. Sprinkle cream cheese layer with the mixture of sweetened coconut, chocolate chips and walnuts. Press into cream cheese layer slightly. Bake 17 minutes at 350°F (180°C). Refrigerate when cool.

~~Bits & Bites~~
A number of recent, good scientific studies have shown that a low-carb, high-fat diet makes it easier to lose weight and control blood sugar. This is not news to most of us who have been low-carbing for a number of years, but it is good to hear that scientists are finding out the truth about low-carbing and that hopefully sooner rather than later the medical profession will embrace it as a treatment protocol for many people with carbohydrate intolerance issues.

JIFFY CHOCOLATE CHIP COOKIES

Sometimes you only want one or two chocolate chip cookies and not the temptation of a whole batch of cookies! These simple cookies fit the bill. Choose tasty chocolate chips for an extra-special treat!

1 egg yolk
1 tbsp butter, melted
Liquid sucralose to equal 2 tbsp (30 mL)
 SPLENDA® Granular
$^1/_4$ tsp vanilla extract (1 mL)
$^1/_4$ cup Gluten-Free Bake Mix 1, (60 mL)
page 140, OR Bake Mix 2, page 141*
$^1/_4$ tsp baking powder (1 mL)
$^1/_8$ tsp salt (0.5 mL)
2 tbsp sugar-free chocolate chips (30 mL)

> **Yield:** 2 cookies
> 1 cookie
> 193.5 calories
> 4.1 g protein
> 15.4 g fat
> *3.7 g net carbs*

In small bowl, combine egg yolk, butter, liquid sucralose, OR SPLENDA® Granular and vanilla extract. In another small bowl, combine Gluten-Free Bake Mix1, page 140, OR Gluten-Free Bake Mix 2, page 141, baking powder and salt. Stir dry ingredients into egg yolk mixture until well combined. Stir in chocolate chips. Form 2 equal-sized dough balls.

Spray 2 small ramekins with nonstick cooking spray. Press a dough ball evenly in bottom of each ramekin. Microwave 45 seconds for a crunchy, slightly browned cookie. Enjoy!

Helpful Hints: My microwave oven is 1200 Watts. Your timing may vary depending on the wattage of your microwave oven. Do not use Truvia® or Steviva Blend® in these cookies – they will burn too easily.

If your chocolate chips have been kept in the freezer or refrigerator, briefly nuke them before stirring them into the cookie dough for best results.

Freeze one of the cookies and see if you prefer them after they have been frozen – most of my low-carb cookies have a great texture straight out of the freezer.

*You don't need xanthan gum in the bake mix for this recipe for those of you sensitive to xanthan gum. Don't use gelatin either.

JIFFY CREAMY CHEESECAKES

This has got to be the easiest cheesecake to make, the quickest and, believe it or not, one of the yummiest cheesecakes from a creamy, delicate point of view. The most difficult part will be waiting for the cheesecake to chill.

4 oz regular cream cheese, softened (125 g)	**Yield:** 2 huge servings
1 cup sour cream (250 mL)	1 serving
$^1/_4$ cup egg whites (60 mL)	384.3 calories
$^1/_4$ cup powdered erythritol (60 mL)	12.3 g protein
Liquid sucralose to equal 2 tbsp (30 mL)	33.9 g fat
SPLENDA® Granular	***7.5 g net carbs***

1 tsp lemon juice (5 mL)
$^1/_2$ tsp vanilla extract (2 mL)
$^1/_4$ tsp xanthan gum (1 mL)
2 tsp sugar-free jam of choice (divided), optional (10 mL)
Crumb Topping (optional):
2 tbsp ground almonds, OR Gluten-Free Bake Mix 1, page 140, OR (30 mL)
  Gluten-Free Bake Mix 2 page 141
1 SPLENDA® packet
1 tsp butter, melted (5 mL)

In blender or food processor, process *softened* cream cheese, sour cream, egg whites, powdered erythritol, liquid sucralose, OR SPLENDA® Granular, lemon juice, vanilla extract and xanthan gum until smooth.

Pour evenly into 2 small ramekins and drop blobs of jam on the surfaces, if using. Swirl in (not stir in) with a knife. Microwave individually on high (can try medium power, but will need longer to cook) 33 seconds in a 1200 watt microwave oven. (You want to stop the cooking before the cheesecake surface "breaks." The surface must look smooth after cooking.) If the wattage is half that amount, you may need to microwave the cheesecake a lot longer. Look through the microwave door and just as the cheesecake starts to rise, stop the cooking. Chill in the freezer about one hour to speed the chilling process. If you forget your cheesecakes in the freezer and they accidentally freeze solid, do not worry, place in the refrigerator until softer.

Crumb Topping (optional): In small bowl, combine ground almonds, OR Gluten-Free Bake Mix 1, page 140, OR Gluten-Free Bake Mix 2, page 141, SPLENDA® and melted butter. Sprinkle chilled cheesecakes with crumb topping

Helpful Hints: Overcooked cheesecake will still be good but the texture is different. It may take one or two tries to get the timing right, but once you do, this will be your go-to recipe for cheesecake in a jiffy! The cheesecake servings are huge. You can swirl in melted chocolate chips instead of jam.

JIFFY CHOCOLATE PEANUT BUTTER LAVA CAKE

Serve with Ice Cream Custard (one of the most popular recipes on my blog), page 75, Low-Carbing Among Friends, Volume-1 and Strawberry Sauce, page 26 of volume 1, if desired. Obviously those additions need to be made ahead of time. My son, Jonathan, loved this recipe. I served it with the ice cream and strawberry sauce.

2 eggs
3 tbsp smooth peanut butter, (45 mL)
  (sugar-free)
Liquid sucralose to equal ¼ cup (60 mL)
  SPLENDA® Granular, OR to taste
2 tbsp granulated erythritol (30 mL)
2 tbsp heavy cream (30 mL)
1 tbsp water (15 mL)
1 tsp vanilla extract (5 mL)
¼ cup Hershey's® cocoa (60 mL)
¾ tsp baking powder (3 mL)

> *Yield:* 2 to 3 servings
> 1 serving
> 285.8/191.2 calories
> 13.8/9.2 g protein
> 22.3/14.9 g fat
> *6.4/4.3 g net carbs*

In food processor, process eggs. Add peanut butter, liquid sucralose, OR SPLENDA® Granular, erythritol, heavy cream, water and vanilla extract; process. Add cocoa and baking powder and process again. In medium, microwaveable bowl, pour batter (which will be quite thin) and microwave 1 minute. Serve immediately with suggestions below the title of the recipe or on its own with a tablespoon or two (15 to 30 mL) of heavy cream.

Helpful Hints: My microwave oven is 1200 Watts. You may need to cook yours a little less or a little longer depending on the wattage of your microwave oven. This cake becomes more brownie-like if you eat it later. It's very good.

~~Bits & Bites~~
People with diabetes who take insulin will need to monitor their blood sugar closely when they begin a low-carb diet. They will not need as much and can easily become hypoglycemic by overmedicating. Do check with your doctor when you begin your low-carb diet and have him help monitor the situation.

Jennifer Eloff

PUMPKIN PECAN CHEESE PIE
Thanksgiving would not be Thanksgiving for some folks without Pumpkin Pie.

Pecan Crust:
$^1/_2$ cup ground pecans (125 mL)
2 tbsp SPLENDA® Granular (25 mL)
2 tbsp vanilla whey protein powder (30 mL)
2 tbsp butter, melted (25 mL)
1 egg yolk*

Cream Cheese Layer:
8 oz light cream cheese, softened (250 g)
Liquid sucralose to equal $^1/_3$ cup SPLENDA® Granular (75 mL)
$^1/_4$ cup powdered erythritol (60 mL)
1 egg
1 tsp vanilla extract (5 mL)

Pumpkin Layer:
1 cup canned pumpkin (250 mL)
2 eggs
Liquid sucralose to equal $^3/_4$ cup SPLENDA® Granular (175 mL)
2 tbsp powdered erythitol (30 mL)
1 tsp cinnamon (5 mL)
$^1/_2$ tsp ginger (2 mL)
$^1/_4$ tsp nutmeg, optional (1 mL)
$^1/_2$ cup half-and-half cream (125 mL)
$^1/_2$ cup heavy cream (125 mL)

Yield: 10 servings
1 serving
228.9 calories
6.6 g protein
20.5 g fat
4.7 g net carbs

Pecan Crust: In medium bowl, combine pecans, SPLENDA® Granular and vanilla whey protein powder. Stir in butter and egg yolk. Spread in deep 9-inch (23 cm) pie plate. Cover with plastic wrap and press crust out evenly; remove plastic wrap. Bake in 350°F (180°C) oven 10 minutes.

Cream Cheese Layer: In food processor with sharp blade, blender or in bowl with electric mixer, process cream cheese, liquid sucralose, OR SPLENDA® Granular, erythritol, egg and vanilla extract until smooth. Pour over crust evenly.

Pumpkin Layer: In medium bowl, combine pumpkin, eggs, liquid sucralose, OR SPLENDA® Granular, erythritol, cinnamon, ginger and nutmeg. Beat well with wire whisk. Whisk in half-and-half cream and heavy cream. Pour over cream cheese layer. Bake in 350°F (180°C) oven 40 minutes or until cake tester inserted in center comes out clean. Garnish with whipped cream and additional pecan halves, if desired.

Helpful Hints: For a more substantial crust, double crust *(5.7 g net carbs)*.
*You can skip the egg yolk and simply add enough melted butter to moisten.

PEANUT BUTTER FUDGE

Very rich, fudgy confection for Christmas or anytime. I used Peter Pan® peanut butter (sweetened with sucralose).

$^1/_2$ cup SPLENDA® Granular (125 mL)
$^1/_2$ cup cup peanut butter (125 mL)
$^1/_3$ cup granulated erythritol (75 mL)
$^1/_4$ cup whole, OR skim milk powder (60 mL)
3 tbsp heavy cream, OR evap. milk (45 mL)
2 tbsp unsalted butter (30 mL)
1 tbsp water (15 mL)
$^1/_4$ cup vanilla whey protein (60 mL)

Yield: 25 small, thick pieces
1 serving
54.6 calories
2.1 g protein
4.4 g fat
1.8 g net carbs

In medium, nonstick saucepan, stir together SPLENDA® Granular, peanut butter, erythritol, whole milk powder, OR skim milk powder, heavy cream, OR evaporated milk, butter and water. Keep stirring until the butter has melted, then stir less than a minute longer, or until the peanut butter smells a little toasty, and the fudge pulls away slightly from the sides, when stirring with a long-handled wooden or plastic mixing spoon.

In food processor with sharp blade, process fudge with vanilla whey protein until smooth. Quickly transfer to a small, square container (I used a 5-inch (12.7 cm) square plastic container) as the fudge begins to harden almost immediately. Place in the freezer until set and then transfer to the refrigerator. Keep refrigerated.

~~Bits & Bites~~
Cutting out sugar and starch may be a better way to lower mildly elevated blood pressure than by using medication. In fact, cutting out gluten for folks who have gluten intolerance will naturally lower blood pressure. This is what happened to my husband. He retains a lot of water when he eats anything with gluten and that places pressure on the vascular system, raising blood pressure.

FRUIT COCKTAIL CHEESECAKE
A fruity, pretty cheesecake, popular with friends and family.

Coconut Almond Crust:
$^2/_3$ cup ground almonds (150 mL)
$^1/_3$ cup SPLENDA® Granular (75 mL)
$^1/_4$ cup desiccated coconut,* (60 mL)
  (unsweetened)
3 tbsp vanilla whey protein powder (45 mL)
3 tbsp butter, melted (45 mL)
1 egg yolk

Yield: 12 servings
1 serving
252.4 calories
7.5 g protein
21.9 g fat
6.2 g net carbs

Filling:
16 oz regular cream cheese, softened (500 g)
1 cup sour cream (250 mL)
Liquid sucralose to equal 1 cup SPLENDA® Granular (250 mL)
1 tsp vanilla extract (5 mL)
2 tbsp water (30 mL)
1 envelope unflavored gelatin (15 mL)
$1^1/_4$ cups canned fruit cocktail in unsweetened juice (300 mL)

Coconut Almond Crust: In medium bowl, combine ground almonds, SPLENDA® Granular, coconut and whey protein powder. Stir in butter and egg yolk. Press into 9-inch (23 cm) glass pie dish and also up sides about $^1/_2$ inch (1.3 cm). Bake in 350°F (180°C) oven 10 minutes.

Filling: In food processor with sharp blade, blender or in bowl with electric mixer, process cream cheese until smooth. Add sour cream, liquid sucralose, OR SPLENDA® Granular and vanilla extract; process. In small saucepan, combine water and gelatin. Dissolve gelatin over medium heat. Add to cheesecake mixture; process briefly. Make sure there is no more than $^1/_2$ cup (125 mL) liquid with the canned fruit. Stir fruit into cheesecake mixture. Pour over prepared crust. If desired, garnish top with a few more pieces of fruit, pressing fruit into cheesecake slightly. Chill until set.

Helpful Hints: *If desired, skip the coconut in the crust and just use ground almonds or almond flour.

~~*Bits and Bites*~~
Cheesecakes are a near-perfect dessert for low-carbers. You can easily adapt your favorite recipes. Replace the graham cracker crust with a nut crust and replace the sugar with your sweetener of choice in the filling and make sure to use full-fat dairy as we are not afraid of fat on a low-carb diet.

VANILLA CUPCAKES

These buttery cupcakes do not have a very fluffy texture; however the texture is fine and a bit denser than a regular cupcake. These are best served at room temperature. They will become quite firm in the refrigerator, so take them out about 2 hours before serving for the best texture or serve them freshly baked, cooled to room temperature and frosted decoratively.

$1^3/_4$ cups Gluten-Free Bake Mix 2, (425 mL)
  page 141 (use almond flour)
2 tsp baking powder (10 mL)
$^1/_2$ cup regular butter, softened (125 mL)
$^1/_2$ cup sour cream (125 mL)
Liquid sucralose to equal $^3/_4$ cup (175 mL)
  SPLENDA® Granular
$^1/_4$ cup powdered erythritol (60 mL)
2 eggs
2 large egg yolks
$2^1/_2$ tsp PLUS $^1/_8$ tsp unflavored gelatin (12.5 mL)
2 tsp vanilla extract (10 mL)
Almond Butter Cream Cheese Frosting:
Peanut Butter Cookie Dough Dip, page 97
  (Use almond butter, only 1 tbsp (15 mL) butter and omit chocolate chips)

> ***Yield:*** 12 cupcakes
> 1 cupcake
> 240.4 calories
> 12.1 g protein
> 15.1 g fat
> ***4.9 g net carbs***

Preheat oven to 350°F (180°C). In medium bowl, combine Gluten-Free Bake Mix 2, page 141 and baking powder.

In food processor, or in bowl with mixer, process butter, sour cream, liquid sucralose, OR SPLENDA® Granular, powdered erythritol, eggs, egg yolks, gelatin and vanilla extract a few minutes. Allow to sit 10 minutes to soften the gelatin. Process again for a few minutes. Add the dry ingredients and process until well combined.

Fill 12, foil-lined muffin cups about $^3/_4$ full. Bake 20 minutes, or until cake tester comes out clean. Cool and frost decoratively using a pastry bag and tip.

Helpful Hints: You can use Condensed Milk Chocolate Frosting, page 131 instead, if desired, or my Betty Crocker-like Frosting, which you will find on my blog, www.low-carb-news.blogspot.com. I experimented using the Gluten-Free Bake Mix 2, page 141 with the gelatin option. Using the calculations on page 142, I worked out the amount of gelatin I would need for this recipe. It is quite possible that in the future I will suggest using less gelatin to make the math calculations much easier, but I need to do more experimenting to verify if that will work satisfactorily. The bake mix option 2 was a last minute insertion in the book. Gelatin is very healthy and a good alternative to xanthan gum.

CHOCOLATE ECSTASY CHEESECAKE

Tunnels of gooey chocolate sauce built into a velvety-smooth cheesecake makes for a very sensual experience. Jeanne Lobsinger, who was like a mother to me described it as such and hence the name was given to this cheesecake!

Graham Cracker-like Crust:
²/₃ cup Gluten-Free Bake Mix 1, (150 mL)
  page 140, OR Bake Mix 2, page 141
²/₃ cup ground almonds (150 mL)
2 SPLENDA® packets
¹/₃ cup butter, melted (75 mL)
Filling:
16 oz regular cream cheese, (500 g)
  softened
Liquid sucralose to equal 1 cup SPLENDA® Granular (250 mL)
1 cup whipping cream (250 mL)
¹/₄ cup water (60 mL)
1¹/₂ envelopes unflavored gelatin (22 mL)
Condensed Milk Chocolate Sauce, *page 131*

Yield: 16 servings
1 serving
348.9 calories
7.7 g protein
34.1 g fat
4.2 g net carbs

Graham Cracker-like Crust: In medium bowl, combine Gluten-Free Bake Mix 1, page 140, OR Gluten-Free Bake Mix 2, page 141, ground almonds, SPLENDA® and butter. Press into 9-inch (23 cm) springform pan. Bake in 350°F (180°C) oven 10 minutes, or until turning brown.

Filling: In food processor with S-blade, blender or in bowl with electric mixer, process cream cheese and liquid sucralose, OR SPLENDA® Granular until smooth. Add whipping cream gradually while processing. In cereal bowl, combine water and gelatin. Microwave 45 seconds. Add gelatin mixture to cream cheese mixture along with ²/₃ cup (150 mL) Condensed Milk Chocolate Sauce, page 131; process.

Pour over prepared crust. Pour remaining sauce over cheesecake in 5 blobs, placed randomly. Use flat, dinner knife to gently swirl between the blobs. Chill.

Condensed Milk Chocolate Sauce: Prepare as directed on page 131.

Variations: **Frozen Chocolate Ecstasy Cheesecake:** Freeze cheesecake and let thaw at room temperature at least 20 minutes, or until easy to slice, before serving.

Caramel Ecstasy Cheesecake: Use 1¹/₂ tsp (7 mL) vanilla extract in filling and Caramel Sauce, page 131. **(4.0 g net carbs)**

CHERRY CHEESE PIE

This fabulous pie is perhaps something one might find in a German or Austrian bakery. Use fresh cherries, pitted, and cut in half during cherry season.

Single Pie Crust, page 132
unbaked
Filling:
1 cup fresh cherries, pitted, OR (250 mL)
canned sweet cherries*
1¹/₂ cups cottage cheese (375 mL)
5 oz regular cream cheese (150 g)

Yield: 10 servings
1 serving
229.8 calories
10.0 g protein
17.9 g fat
6.7 g net carbs

Liquid sucralose to equal ²/₃ cup SPLENDA® Granular (150 mL)
2 tbsp powdered erythritol (30 mL)
1 tbsp certified gluten-free oat flour (15 mL)
1 egg
Topping:
1 cup Crème Fraiche, page 132 (250 mL)

Single Pie Crust: Prepare the Single Pie crust as directed on page 132 in 9-inch (23 cm) glass pie dish. Do not bake. Spread pitted, coarsely chopped cherries over piecrust.

Filling: In food processor with sharp blade, blender or in bowl with electric mixer, process cottage cheese until smooth. Add cream cheese, liquid sucralose, OR SPLENDA® Granular, erythritol and oat flour; process. Add egg; process just until smooth. Pour over cherries.

Bake in 350°F (180°C) oven 25 minutes, or until pie is set. Chill. Garnish chilled pie with Crème Fraiche, page 132. Sprinkle with a little grated unsweetened chocolate or garnish with chocolate curls and a few fresh cherries, if desired.

Helpful Hints: *Canned sweet cherries can come in a light sugar solution. Drain syrup off. Place cherries in colander and rinse well under running water. Toss cherries with a little granular sweetener after rinsing, if desired.

~~Bits & Bites~~
If you feel that you cheated on your diet, don't use it as an excuse to go off your diet for the rest of the day, or worse yet, for weeks. That is self-sabotage.

PEANUT BUTTER CUPS

There is a taste explosion when one bites into one of these substantial treats!
They look really attractive too.

1.5 oz cocoa butter* (45 g)	*Yield:* 10 servings
1 oz unsweetened chocolate (30 g)	1 serving
$^1/_4$ cup peanut butter, softened (60 mL)	139.8 calories
$^1/_4$ cup butter, melted (60 mL)	2.2 g protein
10 SPLENDA® packets	13.7 g fat
2 tbsp whole, OR skim milk (30 mL)	*3.0 g net carbs*
powder	
1 tbsp whipping cream (15 ml)	

In medium microwaveable bowl, microwave cocoa butter and chocolate on high power 2 minutes. Stir cocoa butter until it melts. If necessary, nuke in microwave oven 30 to 60 seconds more, however be careful of overheating chocolate, or it could seize and taste really bitter as a result. Heat in smaller second increments. In another cereal bowl, soften peanut butter 30 seconds on high power in microwave oven. Stir peanut butter, butter, SPLENDA®, whole, OR skim milk powder and whipping cream into chocolate mixture. Pour into small milk jug.

Carefully pour and half fill 10, medium paper baking cups (double up for extra strength) placed on two dinner plates or a cookie sheet. Keep them in the freezer. Remove paper to serve.

Variation: **Almond Butter Cups:** Use almond butter instead of peanut butter. (*3.1 g net carbs*).

Helpful Hints: I used finely ground whole milk powder. Carnation® skim milk powder will be fine, but really coarse skim milk powder may have to be blended finely first in a blender for best results. *Purchase cocoa butter at Netrition.com or check your local health food store. A double boiler may be used to melt cocoa butter and chocolate, which will ensure chocolate does not easily seize.

~~*Bits & Bites*~~
*Yogurt is very beneficial for weight loss. 1 cup (250 mL) has only 4 g carbs, since the live bacteria have changed the lactose into lactic acid, and this is not taken into account in the nutritional analysis. The Authors of the **Go Diet, Jack Goldberg and Karen O'Mara,** made me aware of this fact, when they brought to light definitive laboratory research.*

DECADENT COCOA BROWNIES

These brownies are so decadent-tasting – very close to the real thing!

4 eggs
$^3/_4$ cup melted butter (175 mL)
Liquid sucralose to equal 1 cup (250 mL)
 SPLENDA® Granular
$^1/_2$ cup granulated erythritol (125 mL)
$1^1/_2$ tsp vanilla extract (7 mL)
1 cup Gluten-Free Bake Mix 1, (250 mL)
 page 140
$^1/_2$ cup cocoa (125 mL)
$^1/_2$ tsp baking powder (2 mL)
$^1/_4$ tsp salt (1 mL)
Condensed Milk Chocolate Frosting, page 131

Yield: 25 servings
1 serving
113.5 calories
2.6 g protein
10.5 g fat
2.2 g net carbs

In food processor, process eggs. Add butter, liquid sucralose, OR SPLENDA® Granular, erythritol and vanilla extract; process.

In medium bowl, combine Gluten-Free Bake Mix 1, page 140, cocoa, baking powder and salt. Add to egg mixture; process. Spread in greased 8-inch (20 cm) square baking pan. Bake at 350°F (180°C) for 25 to 30 minutes, or until a cake tester comes out clean. Cool, frost and refrigerate.

~~Bits & Bites~~
A chocolate brownie is a flat, baked square or bar first developed in America at the end of the 19th century and then became very popular in the 20th century in both the U.S. and Canada.

A brownie can be either fudgy or cakey, depending on its density and it may include nuts, frosting, chocolate chips or other ingredients. A variation of a brownie with no chocolate in it is called a blondie.

HAZELNUT CHOCOLATE BUNDT CAKE

Bundt cakes usually look so impressive and are perfect for special company.

$2^1/_2$ oz sugar-free chocolate chips, (45 g)
$^1/_3$ cup butter (75 mL)
6 extra-large eggs, separated
$^1/_4$ tsp lemon juice (1 mL)
Liquid sucralose to equal $^3/_4$ cup (175 mL)
  SPLENDA® Granular
$^1/_3$ cup powdered erythritol (75 mL)
$1^2/_3$ cups ground hazelnuts (400 mL)
1 cup Crème Fraiche, page 132 (250 mL)
Few raspberries for garnish, (optional)
Chocolate Drizzle:
$^1/_4$ cup sugar free chocolate chips, (60 mL)
1 tbsp unsalted butter (15 mL)
1 tbsp whipping cream (15 mL)

Yield: 16 servings
1 serving
207.2 calories
4.6 g protein
18.3 g fat
2.0 g net carbs

Spray 10-inch (25 cm) bundt pan with nonstick cooking spray and line with wax paper or parchment paper (leaving edges high). Spray liberally with nonstick cooking spray. Set aside.

In double boiler, melt chocolate and butter. In food processor, process egg whites and lemon juice until stiff. In small bowl, whisk egg yolks and liquid sucralose, OR SPLENDA® Granular and erythritol together until smooth. Whisk in chocolate mixture.

Fold ground hazelnuts and chocolate mixture into beaten egg whites. Pour batter into prepared pan. Bake in 350°F (180°C) oven 30 to 40 minutes, or until cake tester comes out clean. Lift cake out of bundt pan by holding onto the wax or parchment paper and place cake on wire rack. Carefully remove wax paper.

Chocolate Drizzle: In double boiler, melt chocolate chips and butter. Stir in whipping cream.

Spread cooled cake with Crème Fraiche, page 132, add a few fresh raspberries, if desired and drizzle with chocolate.

Variation: **Almond Chocolate Bundt Cake:** Use ground almonds instead of ground hazelnuts.

.

RHUBARB CHIFFON PIE

Excellent, pretty in pink, and slightly tart! My son, Jonathan, loved this pie.

Single Pie Crust, page 132
Filling:
2$^1/_2$ cups chopped rhubarb (625 mL)
$^1/_2$ cup water (125 mL)
$^1/_4$ cup DaVinci® Sugar-Free Syrup, (60 mL)
  strawberry, OR raspberry
$^2/_3$ cup SPLENDA® Granular (150 mL)
$^1/_3$ cup powdered erythritol (75 mL)
1 envelope unflavored gelatin, (15 mL)
  PLUS 1$^1/_2$ tsp (7 mL)
2 tbsp water (30 mL)
1 cup whipping cream (250 mL)

Yield: 10 servings
1 serving
189.9 calories
4.8 g protein
16.0 g fat
6.9 g net carbs

Sinble Pie Crust: Prepare pie crust, page 132 and bake in 350°F (180°C) oven 10 to 12 minutes.

Filling: In medium saucepan, combine rhubarb, $^1/_2$ cup (125 mL) water, DaVinci® Sugar-Free Syrup, SPLENDA® Granular and erythritol. Bring to boil, reduce heat slightly and cook until rhubarb is soft. In small bowl, soften the gelatin in 2 tbsp (30 mL) water. Stir into hot rhubarb sauce until dissolved. Remove from heat. Pour into medium bowl and chill until syrupy. Meanwhile whip cream until stiff. Fold into cooled rhubarb. Pour into prepared pie crust. Chill. Serve with Crème Fraiche, page 132, if desired.

Helpful Hints: Instead of DaVinci® Sugar-Free Syrup, you could add water, Kool-Aid® unsweetened flavoring and extra sweetener to taste.

~~Bits & Bites~~
It's a good idea to get into the habit of reading nutrition labels on products.
You'd be amazed how often you would put the product back on the shelf!

PEANUT BUTTER BANANA OAT COOKIES

I get a crate of bananas every week to feed the birds and critters that visit our home here in the tropical jungle/rain forest. Sometimes the temptation to use them in baking becomes overwhelming. These are a maintenance-style cookie and a good cookie for children.

1³/₄ cups Gluten-Free Bake Mix 1, (425 mL) page 140
2 tbsp gluten-free instant rolled oats (30 mL)
³/₄ tsp baking soda (3 mL)
1 egg
Liquid sucralose to equal 1 cup (250 mL) SPLENDA® Granular
¹/₂ cup mashed banana (125 mL)
¹/₄ cup granulated erythritol (60 mL)
¹/₄ cup butter, softened (60 mL)
¹/₄ cup peanut butter (60 mL)
1 tsp vanilla extract (5 mL)
³/₄ cup sugar-free chocolate chips (175 mL)

> **Yield:** 25 cookies
> 1 cookie
> 98.6 calories
> 2.4 g protein
> 7.1 g fat
> *3.5 g net carbs*

Preheat oven to 375°F (190°C). In medium bowl, combine Gluten-Free Bake Mix 1, page 140, oats and baking soda.

In food processor, process egg. Add liquid sucralose, OR SPLENDA® Granular, mashed banana, erythritol, butter, peanut butter and vanilla extract; process well. Add dry ingredients and process 1 minute. Stir in chocolate chips.

When the oven is hot, place cookie sheet in oven 10 minutes. Allow dough to rest while cookie sheet is warming up in the oven. Allowing the dough to rest also makes for bigger cookies.

Place slightly rounded tablespoonfuls on greased (spray with nonstick cooking spray) hot cookie sheet. Flatten dough with back of spoon. Bake about 10 minutes, or until brown underneath.

Helpful Hints: If you skip warming the cookie sheet, the cookies will simply be less spread out and chunkier and will rise more. Those were good as well – it just depends on how you like your cookies to appear – wider or smaller and chunkier.

~~Bits & Bites~~
It is now generally accepted that non-contaminated, gluten-free oats are safe for a celiac disease diet, with the exception of a small minority of people with celiac disease who have an additional intolerance to Avenin.

FUDGEY PRUNE CHIP SPICE BARS

Dark and mysterious-looking, these bars are so very delicious, gooey and fudge-like. They have got to be one of my favorites! Just be careful not to eat too much on account of the prunes, to avoid a sore tummy! Prunes are fantastic for one's skin, especially as one gets older.

2 eggs
Liquid sucralose to equal $^{1}/_{2}$ cup (125 mL)
  SPLENDA® Granular
$^{1}/_{2}$ cup water (125 mL)
6 tbsp butter, melted (90 mL)
$^{1}/_{4}$ cup granulated erythritol (60 mL)
2 tsp lemon juice (10 mL)
$1^{1}/_{4}$ cups Gluten-Free Bake Mix 1, (300 mL)
  page 140, PLUS 2 tbsp (30 mL)
$^{1}/_{2}$ tsp baking soda (2 mL)
$^{1}/_{2}$ tsp nutmeg (2 mL)
$^{1}/_{2}$ tsp cinnamon (2 mL)
$^{1}/_{4}$ tsp ground cloves (1 mL)
$^{1}/_{4}$ tsp salt (1 mL)
$^{2}/_{3}$ cup dried, pitted prunes, (150 mL)
  cut up quite finely
$^{1}/_{2}$ cup sugar-free chocolate chips (125 mL)

Yield: 25 bars
1 bar
131.9 calories
2.6 g protein
9.8 g fat
2.5 g net carbs

Preheat oven to 350°F (180°C). In food processor, process eggs, liquid sucralose, OR SPLENDA® Granular, water, butter, erythritol and lemon juice.

In medium bowl, combine Gluten-Free Bake Mix 1, page 140 {plus the extra 2 tbsp (30 mL)}, baking soda, nutmeg, cinnamon, cloves and salt. Add to food processor and process 1 minute. Stir in prune chips and chocolate chips. Scoop into greased 8-inch (20 cm) square glass baking dish.

Bake approximately 35 minutes or until brown on top and knife comes out clean.

~~*Bits & Bites*~~

Prunes help keep skin elastic, thereby preventing wrinkles, and the high boron content helps to keep bones strong, which is especially beneficial during menopause. Prunes are low on the Glycemic Index, have good fiber and besides boron contain potassium, magnesium, iron and vitamin E. Due to their high magnesium content, they have a similar relaxing effect to eating chocolate. The Greek Hippocrates (460-377 BC) mentions prunes in the preparation of medicine for the sick.

CREAMY WHITE FREEZER FUDGE

This creamy, chewy fudge with a subtle peanut butter and honey flavor is very sweet and thus rather addictive for those with a sweet tooth. Ian and I had a friendly race to the freezer for the last few blocks, which we then shared.

3 tbsp melted butter (45 mL)
Liquid sucralose to equal $^1/_2$ cup (125 mL)
  SPLENDA® Granular
3 tbsp water (45 mL)
2 tbsp creamy peanut butter (30 mL)
  (sugar-free)
1 tbsp honey, OR sugar-free honey (15 mL)
$^1/_4$ cup whole milk powder (60 mL)
$^1/_4$ cup powdered erythritol, OR (60 mL)
  Steviva Blend®
3 tbsp vanilla whey protein powder (45 mL)
$^1/_2$ tsp cornstarch (2 mL)
4 oz cocoa butter, melted (120 g)

Yield: 36 servings
1 serving
49.7 calories
0.8 g protein
4.8 g fat
1.1 g net carbs

Line an 8 x 4 x 3-inch (1.5 L) loaf pan with parchment paper (spray pan with nonstick cooking spray first). In blender, combine melted butter, Liquid sucralose, OR SPLENDA® Granular, water, peanut butter, honey, OR sugar-free honey, whole milk powder, powdered erythritol, OR Steviva Blend®, vanilla whey protein and cornstarch. Blend until smooth. In deep microwave-safe bowl, place cocoa butter. Microwave 4 to 5 minutes, or until melted.

Use oven mitts to retrieve bowl from microwave oven after a couple of minutes to allow it to cool a bit and be extremely careful. Add contents of blender to cocoa butter and using a whisk, whisk it all in until creamy, smooth and thick. Pour into prepared loaf pan and freeze for 1 hour. Remove and score into 36 small squares. Freeze again.

Helpful Hint: Instead of honey, you can use sugar-free maple pancake syrup.

~~Bits & Bites~~
Fudge is thought to be an American invention but before 1886, the origin and history of fudge is unclear. Most believe the first batch was as a result of an accidental, "fudged" batch of caramels, hence the name, "fudge." Whey protein powder is very useful in making low-carb, fudge-like confections.

KYNDRA HOLLEY
APPETIZERS

HOT SHRIMP AND ARTICHOKE DIP

This dish is a great make-ahead. Take this to the next gathering you attend and it is sure to be the first empty dish.

6 oz cooked shrimp, chopped (180 g)
2 tbsp butter (30 mL)
1 tsp crushed red pepper flakes (5 mL)
14 oz can artichoke hearts, drained (397 g)
  and chopped
1^1/$_4$ cups Parmesan cheese, (300 mL)
  shredded
1 cup sharp Cheddar cheese, (250 mL)
  shredded
^{1}/$_2$ cup mayonnaise (125 mL)
^{1}/$_2$ cup sour cream (125 mL)
6 green onions, chopped
1 tbsp fresh garlic, minced (15 mL)
1 tsp garlic powder (5 mL)
1 tsp onion powder (5 mL)

Yield: 10 servings
1 serving
207 calories
11.2 g protein
15.7 g fat
2.6 g net carbs

Preheat oven to 350°F (180°C).

If shrimp have tails, remove before chopping. In medium sauté pan, sauté 5 to 10 minutes over medium heat with butter and red pepper flakes.

In large mixing bowl, combine shrimp, artichoke hearts, Parmesan cheese, Cheddar cheese, mayonnaise, sour cream, green onions, fresh garlic, garlic powder, and onion powder.

Bake in an 8-inch (20 cm) square glass baking dish 30 minutes or until the top is bubbling and golden brown. For extra crispiness, finish by broiling for 2 to 3 minutes.

~~Peace, Love and Low-Carb Quick Tips~~
Even though the shrimp are precooked, sautéing them with the butter and red pepper flakes will lend extra flavor to the dish.

CHORIZO QUESO DIP
This dip is also great to eat on taco salads.

1 lb Mexican pork chorizo (0.45 kg)
1 shallot, finely chopped
8 oz cream cheese, softened (250 g)
$^1/_2$ cup Pepper Jack cheese, (125 mL)
  shredded
$^1/_2$ cup extra sharp white Cheddar, (125 mL)
  shredded
$^1/_2$ cup salsa (125 mL)

Yield: 12 servings
1 serving
225 calories
10 g protein
18 g fat
2 g net carbs

Heat large skillet over medium high heat. Remove chorizo from casings and crumble into skillet. Add chopped shallot to the pan. Cook until chorizo is fully cooked. Drain excess grease.

In large mixing bowl, combine chorizo and shallots, cream cheese, Pepper Jack cheese, white Cheddar cheese and salsa. Mix until all ingredients are well combined

Transfer mixture to 8-inch (20 cm) square glass baking dish and bake at 350°F (180°C) for 20 minutes.

~~Peace, Love and Low-Carb Quick Tips~~
Chorizo comes in many variations, short, long, hard, soft etc. The leaner versions are meant to be eaten at room temperature and would make a great appetizer served with cheese. The fattier versions are typically used for cooking. Although not always the case, a good rule of thumb is that long, thin chorizos are typically sweet, whereas the shorter chorizo is typically spicy.

ROASTED RED PEPPER, SPINACH, AND ARTICHOKE DIP

This warm, deliciously rich dip is very easy to prepare. It is wonderful served alongside mixed, fresh vegetables.

14 oz can of artichokes (397 g)
3$^1/_2$ oz roasted red peppers (105 g)
10 oz package frozen spinach, thawed (300 g) and drained
8 oz package cream cheese, softened (250 g)
1 cup Parmesan cheese, divided (250 mL)
$^1/_3$ cup mayonnaise (75 mL)
$^1/_4$ cup minced garlic (60 mL)
Salt and pepper, to taste

> *Yield:* 6 servings
> 1 serving
> 286 calories
> 9.5 g protein
> 24 g fat
> *5.0 g net carbs*

Preheat oven to 350°F (180°C).

Chop artichokes and roasted red peppers.

In large mixing bowl, combine artichokes, roasted red peppers, spinach, cream cheese, $^3/_4$ cup (175 mL) Parmesan cheese, mayonnaise, garlic, salt and pepper. Mix until all ingredients are well incorporated.

Place mixture in an 8-inch (20 cm) glass baking dish and bake 20 minutes. Remove from oven and sprinkle remaining Parmesan cheese on top. Bake an additional 10 to 15 minutes or until Parmesan on top is a nice golden brown.

~~Peace, Love and Low-Carb Quick Tips~~
Spinach is very low in calories, fat, and carbs. 2 cups (500 mL) of fresh spinach leaves contain only 20 calories, 0 grams of fat, and 2 net grams of carbs. It also contains a good amount of dietary fiber.

BUFFALO BLUE CHICKEN MEATBALLS

These meatballs are a great party appetizer. They can be made ahead of time and then heated and tossed in the sauce just before serving. They are also delicious served on top of Caesar salad.

2 large ribs celery, divided
1 lb ground chicken (0.45 kg)
$^1/_2$ cup Franks® RedHot® Buffalo (125 mL)
  sauce, divided
$^1/_4$ cup Blue cheese crumbles (60 mL)
2 tbsp garlic, minced (30 mL)
1 tsp onion powder (5 mL)
Salt and pepper to taste
2 tbsp butter (30 mL)
Garnish (optional):
2 large green onions, chopped

Yield: 4 servings
4 meatballs per serving
163 calories
29 g protein
3 g fat
2.5 g net carbs

Preheat oven to 400°F (200°C).

Dice up one rib of celery for meatball mixture. Cut other rib into dipping stick-sized pieces.

In large mixing bowl, combine ground chicken, diced celery, 2 tbsp (30 mL) Franks®, Blue cheese crumbles, garlic, onion powder, salt and pepper.

Form mixture in 16 meatballs and bake in a lightly greased, glass baking dish 15 minutes.

In saucepan, while meatballs are baking, heat remainder of hot sauce and butter over low heat, until the butter is completely melted and is well combined.

When meatballs have finished cooking, gently toss them in sauce until they are generously coated. Serve and Enjoy!

Garnish: Sprinkle chopped green onions over meatballs before serving.

~~Peace, Love and Low-Carb Quick Tips~~
This recipe would be equally as delicious with ground turkey. Ground turkey is slightly firmer and easier to form into meatballs.

CAJUN TRINITY CRAB CAKES

My husband and I love New Orleans. In Nola the Cajun trinity of onions, bell pepper, and celery is present in so many of the classic dishes.

1 large rib celery, chopped
1 mini yellow bell pepper, chopped
1 mini red bell pepper, chopped
1 mini orange bell pepper, chopped
1 shallot, chopped
2 tbsp butter (30 mL)
1 tsp garlic salt (5 mL)
1 large egg
2 tbsp mayonnaise (30 mL)
1 tbsp Worcestershire sauce (15 mL)
1 tsp sweet hot mustard (5 mL)
1 tsp hot sauce (5 mL)
$^1/_2$ cup Parmesan cheese, grated (125 mL)
$^1/_2$ cup pork rinds, crushed (125 mL)
16 oz lump crab meat (500 g)
3 tbsp olive oil (45 mL)

Yield: 4 servings
2 cakes per serving
252 calories
14 g protein
10.4 g fat
4 g net carbs

Sauté celery, yellow, red and orange peppers and shallot in butter and garlic salt until soft.

In large mixing bowl, combine egg, mayonnaise, Worcestershire sauce, mustard, and hot sauce. Mix in Parmesan cheese and crushed pork rinds. Fold crab into mixture.

Line large plate or cookie sheet with waxed paper and spray with cooking spray. Form mixture into 8 equal patties. Refrigerate one hour.

Panfry in olive oil over medium high heat. Be careful not to flip them too often or they will fall apart. Fry until they are golden brown and crispy on both sides, approximately 5 minutes each side.

~~Peace, Love and Low-Carb Quick Tips
This recipe works best with the refrigerated crab meat found in the deli section of your local grocer. It is not packed in liquid and tastes very fresh. You can use lump crab meat or even claw meat.

CARAMELIZED ONION BACON DIP

This dip is great served hot or cold. It is easy to prepare and perfect for summer barbecues.

2 tbsp butter (30 mL)
2 tbsp olive oil (30 mL)
2 tbsp cooking sherry (30 mL)
2 tbsp minced garlic (30 mL)
2 large onions, thinly sliced
10 slices thickly cut bacon
8 oz cream cheese, softened (250 g)
$^3/_4$ cup sour cream (175 mL)
$^1/_4$ cup Parmesan cheese, shredded (60 mL)
A few sprigs of Italian flat-leaf parsley, chopped

Yield: 10 servings
1 serving
151 calories
4.6 g protein
12.2 g fat
3.3 g net carbs

In large sauté pan over low medium heat, add butter, olive oil, sherry, and garlic. Add onions and cook until nice and caramelized; about 30 to 40 minutes.

While onions are caramelizing, in large skillet, fry bacon over medium high heat until crispy; 5 to 8 minutes Let cool on paper towel to remove excess grease. Crumble bacon and set aside.

In large mixing bowl, combine softened cream cheese, sour cream, Parmesan cheese, and chopped parsley.

Add in bacon and onions. Mix until all ingredients are well incorporated.

~~Peace, Love and Low-Carb Quick Tips~~
This dip is also great served hot. Simply follow the directions above and then bake the mixture for 20 minutes at 350°F (180°C).

ALMOND PARMESAN CRUSTED ZUCCHINI CRISPS

This recipe makes for a great appetizer, side dish or snack. With only a few ingredients, it is very easy to prepare. These are great served with ranch dressing or cucumber sauce.

2 medium zucchini
$^1/_2$ cup almonds (125 mL)
$^1/_2$ cup grated Parmesan cheese (125 mL)
1 large egg
$^1/_2$ tsp garlic powder (2 mL)
$^1/_2$ tsp onion powder (2 mL)
3 tbsp butter (45 mL)

| *Yield:* 4 servings |
| 1 serving |
| 190 calories |
| 11 g protein |
| 14 g fat |
| *4.3 g net carbs* |

Slice zucchini into $^1/_4$- to $^1/_2$-inch (0.6 cm to 1.3 cm) slices. Slice on a slight bias.

Grind almonds in food processor until they are a fine powder. In small bowl, combine ground almonds and Parmesan cheese.

On large plate, spread almond mixture into thin layer.

In medium bowl, whisk the egg, garlic powder and onion powder with a fork.

In large nonstick pan, heat butter over medium high heat, until melted and bubbling. Press zucchini slices into the almond/parmesan mixture, coating both sides. Next, dredge each slice in the egg wash. Coat with almond Parmesan mixture a second time. Panfry until breading is golden brown on both sides, about 2 to 3 minutes on each side.

~~Peace, Love and Low-Carb Quick Tips~~
When frying something with almond flour breading, take care not to flip it too much. Because almond flour lacks gluten, the crust is more fragile and you will lose quite a bit if you flip too often.

SALADS AND SOUPS

CHICKEN CLUB SALAD

This chicken salad is great on top of lettuce or inside a low-carb wrap.

1 lb chicken, cooked and cubed (0.45 kg)
6 strips bacon, cooked and crumbled
1 avocado, peeled, pitted and cubed
8 grape tomatoes, halved
$^1/_4$ cup red onion, diced (60 mL)
$^1/_4$ cup mayonnaise (60 mL)
Salt and pepper to taste

Yield: 4 servings
1 serving
352 calories
27 g protein
26 g fat
4 g net carbs

In large bowl, combine chicken, bacon, avocado, tomatoes, red onion, mayonnaise, salt and pepper. Mix until all ingredients are well incorporated. Eat as is, or serve on top of lettuce or in a low-carb, gluten-free wrap.

SPICY AVOCADO TUNA SALAD

This tuna salad is great served over a bed of greens or sliced tomatoes

1 large avocado, peeled, pitted, and mashed
3 tbsp creamy horseradish (45 mL)
2, 5-oz cans of tuna, drained (300 g)
$^1/_4$ cup shallot, finely chopped (60 mL)
1 tbsp garlic, minced (15 mL)
1 rib celery, finely chopped
Salt and pepper, to taste

Yield: 4 servings
1 serving
154 calories
18 g protein
8 g fat
4 g net carbs

In large bowl, combine mashed avocado and creamy horseradish. Add tuna, shallot, minced garlic and celery. Mix until all ingredients are well incorporated.

Serve on top of mixed greens, sliced tomatoes or even use a gluten-free tortilla to make this into a delicious tuna quesadilla.

GREEK SALAD

This is not your average Greek salad.

12 slices peppered salami
1 large head romaine lettuce, shredded
$^2/_3$ cup grape tomatoes (150 mL)
$^1/_2$ large cucumber, sliced
1 avocado, peeled, pitted and cubed
$^1/_2$ cup Feta cheese (125 mL)
$^1/_2$ cup lightly salted cashews (125 mL)
$^1/_3$ cup thinly sliced red onion (75 mL)
$^1/_3$ cup Kalamata olives (75 mL)

Yield: 4 servings
1 serving
328 calories
16 g protein
25 g fat
8 g net carbs

Slice salami into thin strips. In skillet, fry until crispy. Place fried salami strips on a paper towel to soak up excess grease.

In large mixing bowl, combine romaine lettuce, salami, tomatoes, cucumber, avocado, Feta, cashews, red onion and Kalamata olives. Toss together until all ingredients are well combined. Mix in low-carb dressing of choice, and serve.

ITALIAN CHOPPED SALAD

This salad tastes great topped with balsamic vinaigrette.

1 large head romaine lettuce, shredded
8 oz chicken, cooked and chopped (250 g)
4 oz salami, thinly sliced strips (125 g)
4 oz smoked Mozzarella cheese, (125 g)
 shredded
$^1/_3$ cup Kalamata olives (75 mL)
$^1/_3$ cup sun-dried tomatoes (75 mL)
$^1/_3$ cup garbanzo beans (75 mL)
$^1/_4$ cup pepperoncini, sliced (60 mL)

Yield: 4 servings
1 serving
360 calories
41 g protein
15 g fat
8 g net carbs

In large mixing bowl, combine romaine lettuce, chicken, salami, smoked Mozzarella cheese, Kalamata olives, sun-dried tomatoes, garbanzo beans, and pepperoncini. Top with low-carb vinaigrette before serving.

CHICKEN CAESAR LETTUCE WRAPS WITH GARLIC PARMESAN CROUTONS

Now you won't have to miss croutons any longer.

1 cup Parmesan cheese, shredded (250 mL)
1 tbsp garlic powder (15 mL)
1 tbsp Italian seasoning (15 mL)
1 lb chicken breasts, boneless and (0.45 kg)
 skinless
Salt and pepper, to taste
3 tbsp olive oil (45 mL)
1 head romaine lettuce
4 strips bacon, cooked and crumbled
$^1/_4$ cup Caesar dressing (60 mL)

Yield: 4 servings
1 serving
294 calories
31 g protein
15.5 g fat
2.5 g net carbs

Preheat oven to 350°F (180°C).

Line a baking sheet with parchment paper that has been lightly oiled on both sides. Spread Parmesan cheese in thin layer on parchment paper. Sprinkle garlic powder and Italian seasoning evenly over Parmesan.

Bake cheese on middle rack until golden brown and crispy, 15 to 20 minutes. Let cool and break into pieces. Set aside.

Sprinkle chicken breasts with salt and pepper on each side. Heat grill pan with olive oil over medium high heat. Grill chicken until cooked all the way through; approximately 15 to 20 minutes, depending on thickness. Let cool and cut into cubes.

Pull 6 large leaves off head of romaine. Chop remaining lettuce.

In large mixing bowl, combine chopped romaine, crumbled bacon, chicken, and Caesar dressing. Divide evenly among 6 romaine leaves and top with Parmesan croutons.

~~Peace, Lov, and Low-Carb Quick Tips~~
Cooking cheese in this manner is known as "Frico". Frico is an Italian term for cheese crisp.

SLOW COOKER BEEF STEW

This stew is rich and hearty and completely worth the wait.

4 mini bell peppers, 2 red, 2 orange
6 oz cremini mushrooms (180 g)
2 ribs celery
1 leek, washed and sliced
2 Roma tomatoes
3 small carrots
$^1/_2$ large onion
4 cloves garlic, minced
2 cups beef broth, divided (500 mL)
2 lbs stewing beef (0.9 kg)
Sprinkle of salt and pepper
3 tbsp olive oil (45 mL)
8 oz beef bacon, cooked and crumbled (250 g)
1 tbsp Worcestershire sauce
1 tbsp kosher salt (15 mL)
1 tsp black pepper (5 mL)
1 tsp garlic powder (5 mL)
1 tsp oregano (5 mL)
1 bay leaf

Yield: 10 servings
1 serving
225 calories
28.3 g protein
8.4 g fat
5.9 g net carbs

Heat slow cooker on low setting.

Chop mini bell peppers, cremini mushrooms, celery, leek, tomatoes, carrots, onion, and minced garlic and add to slow cooker with 1 cup (250 mL) beef broth. Cover and let the veggies sweat for one hour.

Sprinkle salt and pepper over stewing beef. In large skillet, over medium high heat, sear stewing beef in olive oil and brown on both sides.

To slow cooker add stewing beef, bacon, remaining 1 cup (250 mL) beef broth, Worcestershire sauce, kosher salt, pepper, garlic powder, oregano and bay leaf. Mix all ingredients together. Cover and cook on low for 8 hours.

Remove bay leaf before serving.

~~Peace, Love and Low-Carb Quick Tips~~
For an even heartier stew, peel and chop one large rutabaga and add to slow cooker when adding the other vegetables. This will increase the carb count but will simulate potatoes nicely.

BREAKFASTS

SPICY BREAKFAST SAUSAGE

It is so easy to make your own breakfast sausage and then you know exactly what is going into it.

1 lb ground pork (0.45 kg)
3 cloves garlic, minced
1 tsp dried thyme (5 mL)
1 tsp ground sage (5 mL)
1 tsp salt (5 mL)
$^1/_2$ tsp cayenne pepper (2 mL)
$^1/_2$ tsp onion powder (2 mL)
$^1/_2$ tsp crushed red pepper flakes (2 mL)

Yield: 4 servings
1 serving
 253 calories
22 g protein
16.25 g fat
2 g net carbs

In medium bowl, combine ground pork, minced garlic, dried thyme, ground sage, salt, cayenne pepper, onion powder, and red pepper flakes. By hand, mix until all ingredients are well incorporated.

Form mixture into 8 equal patties. Heat large skillet over medium high heat and drizzle pan with a little olive oil. Once oil is hot, place sausage patties in the pan and cook until brown on both sides and cooked all the way through.

~~Peace, Love and Low-Carb Quick Tips~~
If you do not eat pork, you can easily substitute ground chicken or ground turkey in this recipe. Also, you can easily adjust the level of spiciness by simply adding or subtracting the amount of cayenne and crushed red pepper flakes in this breakfast sausage recipe.

PEPPER JACK DENVER EGG MUFFINS

Egg muffins are great for doing food prep for the week. Pop them in the fridge or even the freezer and just heat and eat!

9 large eggs
6 oz Canadian bacon, diced (180 g)
$^1/_2$ cup Pepper Jack cheese, (125 mL) shredded
5 baby bella mushrooms, finely chopped
$^1/_3$ cup green bell peppers, diced (75 mL)
$^1/_3$ cup sweet onion, diced (75 mL)
$^1/_2$ tsp salt (5 mL)
$^1/_2$ tsp black pepper (5 mL)
$^1/_2$ cup salsa (125 mL)

Yield: 6 servings
2 muffins per serving
188 calories
16 g protein
11 g fat
3.5 g net carbs

Preheat oven to 350°F (180°C). Spray a 12-muffin nonstick tin with cooking spray.

In large bowl, crack eggs and whisk with fork. Add Canadian bacon, Pepper Jack cheese, mushrooms, bell peppers, onions, salt and pepper. Mix until all ingredients are well combined.

Ladle the egg mixture into the muffin cups, filling each one $^3/_4$ of the way full.

Bake 25 minutes. Allow to cool and remove egg muffins from muffin tin. Top each egg muffin with salsa before serving.

~~Peace, Love and Low-Carb Quick Tips~~
These muffins are a great make ahead for breakfasts throughout the week. Make a batch on the weekend, portion and freeze. Then, simply reheat and eat.

MAIN COURSES AND SIDES

CHICKEN DIJON WITH MUSHROOMS AND ARTICHOKES

This dish would be great served atop zucchini noodles or cauliflower rice.

$1^1/_2$ lbs chicken breast, cut into (0.68 kg) tenders
Salt and pepper, to taste
3 tbsp butter (45 mL)
$^1/_2$ cup chicken stock (125 mL)
1 tbsp chicken bouillon granules (15 mL)
$^1/_8$ tsp dried tarragon (0.5 mL)
1 cup heavy cream (250 mL)
8 oz artichoke hearts, quartered (250 g)
4 oz sliced baby Portobello mushrooms (125 g)
2 tbsp Dijon mustard (30 mL)
Salt and pepper, to taste

Yield: 4 servings
1 serving
469 calories
35 g protein
32 g fat
5 g net carbs

Liberally sprinkle both sides of chicken breasts with salt and pepper.

In large sauté pan over medium high heat, melt butter. When butter is hot, sauté chicken tenders until golden brown on both sides, about 3 minutes each side. Remove chicken from the pan and set aside. Chicken will not be fully cooked at this stage.

Deglaze pan with chicken stock. Use rubber spatula to scrape off and mix in all bits of chicken and butter.

To chicken stock, mix in chicken bouillon granules and tarragon. Reduce heat to low and let simmer 5 minutes.

Add heavy cream, artichoke hearts, mushrooms and Dijon mustard and let simmer 10 to 15 minutes.

Add the chicken back to the pan and let simmer until the chicken is cooked all the way through, 5 to 8 minutes. Season with salt and pepper.

CHILI LIME RUBBED CHICKEN WITH AVOCADO FETA SALSA

This dish tastes best prepared over the flames of an outdoor grill.

Avocado Feta Salsa, page 186
1$^1/_2$ lbs bonelss, skinless chicken (0.68 kg)
  breasts, about 4 breasts total
2 tbsp fresh lime juice (30 mL)
2 tbsp olive oil (30 mL)
3 cloves garlic, minced
1 tsp fresh cilantro, chopped (5 mL)
1 tbsp cumin (15 mL)
1 tbsp chili powder (15 mL)
$^1/_2$ tsp garlic powder (2 mL)
$^1/_2$ tsp onion powder (2 mL)
$^1/_2$ tsp sea salt (2 mL)
$^1/_8$ tsp black pepper (0.5 mL)

> **Yield:** 4 servings
> 1 serving
> 287 calories
> 41 g protein
> 6 g fat
> *4 g net carbs*

Prepare Avocado Feta Salsa, page 186 and refrigerate while you prepare the chicken.

Preheat barbecue or on the stove top, heat grill pan over medium high heat.

In small bowl, combine lime juice, olive oil, garlic, and cilantro. In another small bowl, stir together cumin, chili powder, garlic powder, onion powder, sea salt and black pepper.

Baste one side of each chicken breast with lime mixture, and then sprinkle seasoning mixture on each basted breast. Place basted, seasoned side down on grill. Baste and season the other side of each breast. Flip as needed to prevent burning.

Grill until chicken is cooked all the way through; about 10 minutes each side. Top with Avocado-Feta Salsa, and enjoy!

~~Peace, Love and Low-Carb Quick Tips~~
Cumin seeds are known for their distinctive flavor and aroma. It is globally popular and is an essential flavoring in many cuisines, such as South Asian, Northern African and Latin American cuisines.

.

175

TURKEY TACO BURGERS

This recipe puts a fun new twist on "Taco Tuesdays".

1 lb lean ground turkey (0.45 kg)
$^1/_2$ cup salsa (125 mL)
4 oz sharp white Cheddar cheese, (125 g)
  shredded, divided
3 mini bell peppers, diced
2 tbsp chili powder (25 mL)
1 tbsp cumin (15 mL)
1 tbsp onion powder (15 mL)
1 tbsp garlic powder (15 mL)
1 tsp kosher salt (5 mL)
1 tsp crushed red pepper flakes (5mL)
$^1/_2$ tsp cayenne pepper (2 mL)
$^1/_2$ small onion
1 medium, ripe avocado, peeled and pitted
1 Roma tomato, chopped
$^1/_2$ cup sour cream (125 mL)
8 large black olives, sliced

Yield: 4 servings
1 serving
423 calories
30 g protein
25.5 g fat
7.5 g net carbs

In a large bowl, combine ground turkey, salsa, 2 oz (60 g) cheese, diced peppers, chili powder, cumin, onion powder, garlic powder, kosher salt, crushed red pepper flakes and cayenne pepper. Use a microplane grater to grate the onion into mixture. Mix until all ingredients are well combined. Score the mixture into 4 even portions and form into 4 patties.

Spray a grill pan with cooking spray and cook patties over medium high heat until they are cooked through.

Top each patty with cheese, avocado, tomato, sour cream and olives.

Serve and Enjoy!

~~Peace, Love and Low-Carb Quick Tips~~
For years I bought prepackaged taco seasoning and thought nothing of it. Making your own taco seasoning is simple, not to mention healthier and can be done with spices you probably already have on hand. Simply mix the spices in the proportions listed in the ingredients and use that to prepare all of your favorite taco recipes.

ITALIAN MEATBALLS

These meatballs are moist and flavorful. They make a great dish all on their own topped with a low-carb marinara sauce.

1 lb ground beef (0.45 kg)
1 lb ground pork (0.45 kg)
$^1/_2$ cup crushed pork rinds (125 mL)
$^1/_2$ cup Parmesan cheese, grated (125 mL)
$^1/_4$ cup tomato paste (60 mL)
1 large egg
2 cloves garlic, minced
2 tsp dried oregano (10 mL)
2 tsp dried basil (10 mL)
2 tsp dried parsley (10 mL)
$^1/_2$ small onion
1 tsp kosher salt (5 mL)
$^1/_2$ tsp black pepper (2 mL)

Yield: 10 servings 2 meatballs 202 calories 42 g protein 10 g fat *1.5 g net carbs*

Preheat oven to 350°F (180°C).

In large bowl, combine ground beef, ground pork, pork rinds, Parmesan cheese, tomato paste, egg, garlic, oregano, basil, and parsley. Using a microplane grater, grate onion into mixture. Mix until all ingredients are well incorporated.

Heat a large nonstick skillet over medium high heat.

Form mixture into 20 evenly-sized meatballs. Sprinkle each meatball with a little kosher salt and black pepper.

Once skillet is hot, place meatballs in pan. Quickly brown meatballs on all sides, 2 to 3 minutes. Remove from pan and set aside.

Once all meatballs are browned, place them on a greased baking sheet. Bake for 20 minutes.

~~Peace, Love and Low-Carb Quick Tips~~
The term "meatball" is rather vague. But there is something about meatballs that make them universally loved. In Afghanistan a meatball is called kebab, in Germany, a konigsberger klopse, In Italy a meatball is known as a polpette, in Greece they are keftedes and in Mexico they are albondigas. Whatever you call them, they are delicious in their many variations.

BEEF STROGANOFF PATTIES

This stroganoff is delicious served over mashed or riced cauliflower.

1¹/₂ lbs ground beef (0.68 kg)
3 tbsp Italian flat-leaf parsley, (45 mL) chopped
2 tbsp Worcestershire sauce (30 mL)
2 tbsp garlic, minced divided (30 mL)
1 tsp onion powder (5 mL)
1 tsp garlic powder (5 mL)
¹/₂ tsp kosher salt (2 mL)
¹/₂ tsp black pepper (2 mL)
2 tbsp butter (30 mL)
2 tbsp cooking sherry (30 mL)
1 small white onion, chopped
1 cup beef broth (250 mL)
2 tbsp beef bouillon granules (30 mL)
6 oz cremini mushrooms, sliced (180 g)
¹/₄ cup heavy cream (60 mL)
³/₄ cup sour cream (175 mL)

Yield: 4 servings
1 serving
670 calories
49 g protein
25.5 g fat
6.3 g net carbs

In large bowl, combine ground beef, chopped parsley, Worcestershire sauce, 1 tbsp (15 mL) garlic, onion powder, garlic powder, kosher salt, and pepper. Form into 4 even patties.

In a large sauté pan over medium low heat, add butter, cooking sherry, remaining 1 tbsp (15 mL) garlic, and chopped onions. Sauté onions until they are a nice caramel color, about 20 minutes.

While onions are sautéing, start cooking beef patties over medium high heat, flipping as necessary. After 10 minutes, remove from heat and set aside. They will finish cooking in the sauce.

When the onions are nice and caramelized, deglaze pan with beef broth. Use a rubber spatula to scrape all the bits of onion and garlic from the pan and mix into the broth. Add beef bouillon granules and stir until dissolved.

To sauce, add sliced mushrooms and let simmer over medium low heat for 5 to 8 minutes.

Stir heavy cream and sour cream into sauce. Add burger patties to the sauce and let the whole dish simmer, uncovered on low for 10 minutes

LEMON SHERRY CHICKEN

This dish is so quick and easy to prepare. There is a good chance that you may already have all of the ingredients on hand. You can throw in your favorite low-carb vegetables and turn this dish into a one-pot wonder.

$^1/_4$ cup cooking sherry (60 mL)
$1^1/_2$ lbs chicken breasts, boneless, (0.68 kg)
  skinless, cut into tenders
$^2/_3$ cup heavy cream (150 mL)
$2^1/_2$ tbsp lemon juice (37 mL)
1 tbsp lemon pepper seasoning (15 mL)
1 cup Mozzarella cheese, shredded (250 mL)
A few sprigs of Italian flat-leaf parsley,
  chopped and divided

Yield: 4 servings
1 serving
497 calories
61 g protein
26 g fat
2.5 g net carbs

In large sauté pan over medium heat, heat cooking sherry. Add chicken and sauté until nearly cooked through; about 10 to 15 minutes.

Add heavy cream, lemon juice and lemon pepper seasoning and stir in. Reduce heat to low and let simmer until chicken is cooked through; about 5 to 10 minutes more.

Add Mozzarella cheese and half the chopped parsley to sauce. Stir occasionally and allow sauce to thicken.

Garnish with remaining parsley.

~~Peace, Love and Low-Carb Quick Tips~~
Sherry is a type of fortified wine, which means that a stronger liquor such as brandy is added to the wine. The primary advantage of cooking sherry is that it can be stored in the cupboard for quite some time after opening it. Since few recipes call for an entire bottle of sherry, it is nice to be able to open a bottle, use a small amount, and replace the bottle in the cupboard until it is needed again.

HALIBUT SUPREME

This recipe produces an incredibly moist halibut with a rich, creamy sauce.

2 lbs fresh halibut (0.9 kg)
Salt and pepper, to taste
1 cup sharp Cheddar cheese, (250 mL)
 shredded
$^1/_2$ cup mayonnaise (125 mL)
$^1/_2$ cup sour cream (125 mL)
2 cloves garlic, minced
1 tsp lemon pepper seasoning (5 mL)
1 tsp onion powder (5 mL)
1 cup bay shrimp, pre-cooked (250 mL)
Salt and pepper, to taste
Garnish (optional):
6 green onions, sliced

> *Yield:* 6 servings
> 1 serving
> 459 calories
> 49 g protein
> 27 g fat
> *2 g net carbs*

Preheat oven to 400°F (200°C).

Lightly grease a 9 x 13-inch (2 L) glass baking dish and arrange halibut in a single layer. Sprinkle salt and pepper over halibut.

In large mixing bowl, combine sharp Cheddar cheese, mayonnaise, sour cream, minced garlic, lemon pepper seasoning, and onion powder.

Pour mixture over top of halibut, covering evenly. Bake 20 minutes.

Remove from oven and spread bay shrimp evenly across the top of entire dish. Bake 10 additional minutes or until halibut can be easily flaked with a fork. Season with salt and pepper.

Garnish (optional): Sprinkle sliced green onion over the top, after plating.

~~Peace, Love and Low-Carb Quick Tips~~
Halibut is prized for its sweet, delicate flavor, snow-white color and firm, flaky meat. It is also an excellent source of protein and minerals, low in sodium, fat and calories and contains a minimum of bones making it easy to clean and prepare the fish.

SOUR CREAM SMOTHERED CHICKEN

I am always trying to think of new ways to dress up chicken. What better way to dress it up than by smothering it with all of my favorite things?

1 medium sweet onion, thinly sliced
8 oz mushrooms, sliced (250 g)
4 tbsp butter, divided (60 mL)
4 tbsp olive oil, divided (60 mL)
Garlic salt, to taste
Pepper, to taste
1¹/₂ lbs boneless, skinless chicken (0.68 kg)
  breasts
1 cup chicken stock (250 mL)
1 cup sour cream (250 mL)
¹/₃ cup shredded Mozzarella cheese (75 mL)
6 slices bacon, cooked and crumbled
6 green onions, chopped

Yield: 4 servings
1 serving
459 calories
16 g protein
32 g fat
7.3 g net carbs

In large sauté pan, combine onions, mushrooms, 2 tbsp (30 mL) butter, 2 tbsp (30 mL) olive oil, garlic salt and pepper. Sauté over medium heat until mushrooms and onions are nice and caramelized, about 30 minutes.

In large skillet, heat remaining 2 tbsp (30 mL) butter, and 2 tbsp (30 mL) olive oil over medium high heat. Pan sear chicken breasts until cooked through and golden brown on both sides, about 10 minutes each side.

While chicken is searing, add chicken stock and sour cream to onion and mushrooms. Allow to come to a boil over medium high heat. Reduce heat to low and allow sauce to simmer and thicken, about 15 to 20 minutes.

Once chicken is cooked through, plate it, top with sauce, Mozzarella cheese, bacon, and green onions.

~~Peace, Love and Low-Carb Quick Tips~~
This dish can easily be made in a slow cooker on those busy days where you don't have much time to spend in the kitchen. Simply precook the bacon and caramelized onions per the directions, add all ingredients to slow cooker and cook on low 6 to 8 hours.

PARMESAN DIJON CRUSTED PORK CHOPS

These pork chops are great served with a cauliflower mash.

4 pork loin chops, boneless
$1/4$ tsp kosher salt (1 mL)
$1/4$ tsp black pepper (1 mL)
$1/4$ cup Dijon Mustard (60 mL)
2 tbsp spicy brown mustard (30 mL)
2 tbsp olive oil (30 mL)
$1/2$ tsp garlic powder (2 mL)
$1/2$ tsp thyme (2 mL)
$1/4$ tsp onion powder (1 mL)
$1/4$ tsp dried oregano (1 mL)
$1/4$ tsp dried basil (1 mL)
$1/4$ tsp Italian seasoning (1 mL)
1 cup Parmesan cheese, grated (250 mL)

Yield: 4 servings
1 serving
336 calories
44 g protein
14 g fat
1.5 g net carbs

Preheat oven to 400°F (200°C).

Season chops on both sides with kosher salt and pepper.

In shallow mixing bowl, combine Dijon mustard, spicy brown mustard, olive oil, garlic powder, thyme, onion powder, dried oregano, dried basil, and Italian seasoning. Dredge each chop in the mustard mixture, liberally coating both sides.

On large plate, spread Parmesan cheese into thin layer. Coat mustard covered chops liberally with Parmesan cheese on both sides.

Place a cooling rack on top of a cookie sheet and place chops on cooling rack. This will allow them to get crisp on both sides.

Bake 20 minutes. Then broil on high, on the top oven rack for 3 to 4 minutes or until chops are nice and crisp and golden brown.

~~Peace, Love and Low-Carb Quick Tips~~
If you are not a fan of pork, you can substitute chicken in this recipe and the end result will be equally as delicious.

ASIAN LETTUCE WRAPS

The lettuce wraps are fresh and light and make for a great lunch, dinner, or midday snack.

2 tbsp olive oil (30 mL)
1, 8-oz can water chestnuts (250 g)
4 oz baby Portobello mushrooms (125 g)
1 large rib celery, chopped
$^{1}/_{2}$ medium sweet onion, diced
1 clove garlic, minced
1 lb lean ground turkey (0.45 kg
2 tbsp soy sauce (30 mL)
2 tbsp hoisin sauce (30 mL)
1 tsp Chinese five spice (5 mL)
6 large iceberg lettuce leaves

Yield: 6 servings
1 serving
148 calories
15 g protein
6 g fat
6 g net carbs

In large nonstick pan over medium high heat in olive oil, sauté water chestnuts, Portobello mushrooms, chopped celery, diced onion and minced garlic, in olive oil until vegetables are tender.

Add ground turkey to pan and cook until turkey is browned and cooked all the way through; about 10 minutes. Mix in soy sauce, hoisin sauce, and Chinese five spice. Reduce heat to low and cook for an additional 10 minutes.

Divide mixture evenly among the lettuce leaves and pile mixture into the center of the leaves.

~~Peace, Love and Low-Carb Quick Tips~~
In the past, hoisin sauce could only be found in specialty markets or in Chinese markets. However with the expansion of international cuisines, hoisin sauce is now readily available in most major grocery stores. Look for it in the international/ethnic foods section of your local grocer.

TUNA GREEN BEAN CASSEROLE

I love tuna casserole and I love green bean casserole. I thought it would be a fun experiment to combine the two into one casserole. The results were surprisingly delicious.

1 medium head cauliflower
$^1/_2$ cup cream of mushroom soup (125 mL)
$^1/_2$ cup cream of chicken soup (125 mL)
1 tbsp garlic, minced (15 mL)
Salt and pepper, to taste
2 ribs celery, chopped
2, 5 oz cans of tuna (300 g)
3.5 oz canned green beans (105 g)
1 cup sharp Cheddar cheese, (250 mL)
  shredded
$^1/_4$ cup crushed pork rinds (60 mL)

Yield: 6 servings
1 serving
175 calories
14 g protein
11 g fat
6.0 g net carbs

In large, covered saucepan, steam whole head of cauliflower in 1 inch (2.5 cm) of water, until fork tender, about 15 minutes.

Preheat oven to 400°F (200°C).

When cauliflower is tender, drain water from pan and leave the cauliflower in the hot pan.

In large bowl, combine cream of mushroom soup, cream of chicken soup, garlic, salt and pepper. Fold in celery, tuna, and green beans.

Fork mash cauliflower and layer in 8-inch (20 cm) square glass baking dish. Layer soup mixture on top of cauliflower. Using a fork, poke through mixture in several spots to allow some of soup mixture to blend in with cauliflower.

Bake 20 minutes. Layer Cheddar cheese on top and bake 10 additional minutes. Layer pork rinds on top of the cheese and bake for 10 additional minutes.

Helpful Hint: Leaving the cauliflower in the hot pan helps draw out some of the excess water from the cauliflower.

LOADED GARLIC BAKED FAUXTATO

This is a great substitution for those loaded baked potatoes we all miss so much.

1 medium head of cauliflower, whole
1 cup chicken broth (250 mL)
2 tbsp garlic, minced (30 mL)
4 oz cream cheese (125 g)
$^1/_2$ cup sour cream (125 mL)
$1^1/_4$ cups sharp Cheddar cheese, (300 mL)
  shredded
7 green onions, chopped
7 strips of bacon, cooked crisp and crumbled
$^1/_8$ tsp garlic pepper seasoning (0.5 mL)

> *Yield:* 6 servings
> 1 serving
> 281 calories
> 14 g protein
> 23 g fat
> *3 g net carbs*

Preheat oven to 350°F (180°C).

In a large covered pot over high heat, steam cauliflower in chicken broth and minced garlic until fork tender, about 15 minutes.

Drain broth and garlic while leaving cauliflower in the hot pot. This will help pull some of the excess moisture from cauliflower.

Mash cauliflower with the cream cheese and sour cream. Once well mashed, mix in Cheddar cheese, green onions, crumbled bacon, and garlic pepper seasoning.

Bake in an 8-inch (20 cm) casserole dish, uncovered 15 to 20 minutes.

ROASTED RANCH "POTATOES"

Once I realized what a great substitution rutabaga is for potato, my mind began swimming in all the delicious possibilities.

$1^1/_2$ lbs rutabaga (0.68 kg)
$1^1/_2$ oz package dry Ranch dressing mix (45 g)
  (gluten-free)
$^1/_4$ cup olive oil (60 mL)

> *Yield:* 6 servings
> 1 serving
> 125 calories
> 0 g protein
> 10 g fat
> *9 g net carbs*

Preheat oven to 400°F (200°C).

Wash rutabaga and cut ends off. Slice into wedges. Toss with ranch dressing mix and olive oil. Bake on an ungreased baking sheet for 40 minutes.

MISCELLANEOUS

AVOCADO FETA SALSA

This is a light, fresh take on a traditional salsa. It is wonderful as a dip or even as a topping for chicken.

1 ripe avocado, peeled, pitted, and cubed
1 Roma tomato, diced
$^1/_4$ cup red onion, finely chopped (60 mL)
$^1/_4$ cup artichoke hearts, chopped (60 mL)
$^1/_4$ cup capers (60 mL)
1 tbsp chopped cilantro (15 mL)
3 cloves of garlic, minced
$^1/_4$ cup Feta cheese (60 mL)
3 tbsp olive oil (45 mL)
Juice of $^1/_2$ a lime
Sea salt and pepper, to taste

Yield: 6 servings
1 serving
77 calories
0.5 g protein
4 g fat
3.2 g net carbs

In medium bowl, combine avocado, tomato, red onion, artichoke hearts, capers chopped cilantro, and garlic.

Add Feta, olive oil, lime juice and salt and pepper. Lightly toss until all ingredients are well incorporated. Allow salsa to refrigerate at least one hour before serving. Doing so will allow the vibrant flavors in this salsa to come together.

~~Peace, Love and Low-Carb Quick Tips~~
Did you know that Cilantro is also referred to as Coriander and Chinese Parsley? No matter what you call it, it is a very strong-flavored herb. Many people are not fond of cilantro. If you are one of those people, simply substitute the cilantro with some Italian flat-leaf parsley. It is a much milder herb, belonging to the same family.

ROASTED RED PEPPER AIOLI

This sauce is unbelievably easy to prepare and can accompany so many different foods.

6 slices of marinated, roasted red peppers
$^3/_4$ cup mayonnaise (175 mL)
3 tbsp minced garlic (45 mL)
2 tbsp lemon juice (30 mL)
A few sprigs of Italian flat-leaf parsley
Salt and pepper to taste

Yield: 1 cup (250 mL)
2 tbsp (30 mL) per serving
140 calories
0 g protein
15 g fat
1.8 g net carbs

In food processor, combine roasted red peppers, mayonnaise, minced garlic, lemon juice, parsley, salt and pepper. Pulse until well blended and creamy. Alternatively, this may be done in a blender.

Refrigerate at least 30 minutes before serving.

CAPER AND ARTICHOKE TARTAR SAUCE

This is a delicious spin on your traditional tartar sauce.

1 cup mayonnaise (250 mL)
$^1/_2$ small dill pickle, chopped
A few sprigs of Italian flat-leaf parsley
2 tbsp capers (30 mL)
1 tbsp lemon juice (15 mL)
1 tbsp Dijon mustard (15 mL)
1 tsp dried minced onion flakes (5 mL)
$^1/_2$ tsp garlic salt (2 mL)
$^1/_8$ tsp black pepper (0.5 mL)
$^1/_4$ cup artichoke hearts, quartered (60 mL)

Yield: 10 servings
1 serving
150 calories
1.0 g protein
16.0 g fat
0.5 g net carbs

In a food processor, combine mayonnaise, pickle, parsley, capers, lemon juice, Dijon mustard, onion flakes, garlic salt, and pepper. Pulse until well blended and creamy. Add in artichokes and give a few quick pulses. Alternatively, this can be done in a blender.

Refrigerate at least 30 minutes before serving.

ASIAN MARINADE

This marinade is great on pork but would also be amazing on chicken, beef, and seafood as well.

$^1/_4$ cup soy sauce (60 mL)
2 tbsp rice vinegar (30 mL)
Juice of one small key lime
1 tbsp minced garlic (15 mL)
1 tbsp chopped shallot (15 mL)
1 tsp crushed red pepper flakes (5 mL)
1 tsp grated ginger (5 mL)
1 tsp sesame oil (5 mL)
1 tsp toasted sesame seeds (5 mL)
$^1/_2$ packet SPLENDA®

Yield: 4 servings
1 serving
38 calories
2 g protein
1 g fat
2 g net carbs

In small bowl, mix soy sauce, rice vinegar, lime juice, minced garlic, chopped shallot, crushed red pepper flakes, grated ginger, sesame oil, toasted sesame seeds, and SPLENDA® together. Pour over meat and allow at least 3 hours to marinate.

TERIYAKI SAUCE

This recipe makes for a great glaze or a marinade.

$^1/_2$ cup water, divided (125 mL)
$^1/_4$ cup soy sauce (60 mL)
1 tbsp rice wine vinegar (15 mL)
2 SPLENDA® packets
1 tbsp SPLENDA® Brown Sugar (15 mL)
  Blend
1 tbsp garlic, minced (15 mL)
1 tsp fresh ginger, peeled and grated (5 mL)
1 tsp xanthan gum (5 mL)

Yield: 4 servings
1 serving
32 calories
2 g protein
0 g fat
4.5 g net carbs

In a saucepan, mix together $^1/_4$ cup (60 mL) water, soy sauce, rice wine vinegar, SPLENDA® packets, brown sugar SPLENDA®, garlic and ginger. Stir and heat over medium high heat.

In glass, mix remaining $^1/_4$ cup (60 mL) water and xanthan gum. It will not dissolve and will be clumpy.

Pour xanthan gum slurry into sauce. Whisk constantly until xanthan gum is no longer visible and sauce has begun to thicken. Reduce heat to low and allow sauce to thicken to the consistency of syrup, about 5 minutes.

PEPPER JACK CREAM SAUCE

This sauce is wonderful over chicken or on any type of faux pasta dish.

$^1/_4$ cup butter, salted (60 mL)
1 tbsp garlic, minced (15 mL)
1 cup heavy cream (250 mL)
4 oz Pepper Jack cheese, shredded (125 g)
4 oz Parmesan cheese, grated (125 g)
Few sprigs of Italian, flat-leaf parsley,
  chopped
Salt and pepper, to taste

Yield: 8 servings
1 serving
266 calories
9.5 g protein
25 g fat
2 g net carbs

In large sauté pan, brown butter and garlic over medium heat. Add heavy cream, reduce heat to low and let simmer 5 minutes.

Add Pepper Jack cheese, Parmesan cheese and chopped parsley. Stirring often, continue simmering on low until sauce has thickened. Season with salt and pepper to taste.

SUN-DRIED TOMATO PESTO CREAM SAUCE

This sauce is delightful over chicken or halibut.

$^1/_4$ cup butter, salted (60 mL)
2 tbsp garlic, minced (30 mL)
1 cup heavy cream (250 mL)
4 oz Parmesan cheese, grated (125 g)
$^1/_2$ cup sun-dried tomatoes, chopped (125 mL)
$^1/_4$ cup pesto (60 mL)
Salt and pepper to taste

Yield: 8 servings
1 serving
225 calories
8 g protein
17 g fat
2.5 g net carbs

In large sauté pan, brown butter and garlic over medium heat. Add heavy cream, reduce heat to low and let simmer 5 minutes.

Add Parmesan cheese, sun-dried tomatoes and pesto. Stirring often, continue simmering on low until sauce has thickened. Add salt and pepper as needed.

CAROLYN KETCHUM
APPETIZERS AND BEVERAGES

SRIRACHA HOT WINGS

Sriracha is fast becoming one of the most popular condiments in North America and it adds a wonderful heat to any dish without the added sugars in ketchup.

$^1/_4$ cup Sriracha (60 mL)
2 tbsp olive oil (30 mL)
2 cloves garlic, minced
1 tsp ground cumin (5 mL)
$^1/_2$ tsp salt (2 mL)
$^1/_4$ tsp pepper (1 mL)
$2^1/_2$ lbs chicken wings (1.1 kg)

Yield: 4 servings
1 serving
419 calories
28 g protein
31 g fat
4 g net carbs

In large bowl, whisk together Sriracha, olive oil, minced garlic, ground cumin, salt and pepper to combine. Add chicken wings and toss thoroughly to coat. Let marinate in refrigerator at least one hour and up to 24 hours.

Spread chicken wings in single layer, skin side down, on broiling pan. Bake in 425°F (220°C) oven 25 minutes, flipping wings halfway through. Remove from oven and let stand 5 to 10 minutes before serving.

Helpful Hint: For really crispy wings, turn off the oven and let the wings sit inside for up to 20 minutes. This helps crisp up the skin without drying out the chicken.

~~Bits & Bites~~
Never underestimate the power of exercise in improving your mood and boosting your immune system.

CHIPOTLE LIME COCKTAIL NUTS

The tang of the lime offsets the wonderful heat of the chipotle and chili powder in this delicious snack.

2 small limes
$1^1/_4$ cups raw almonds (300 mL)
$1^1/_4$ cups raw pecans (300 mL)
$^1/_2$ cup raw cashews (125 mL)
1 tbsp chili powder (15 mL)
1 tbsp chipotle powder (1 mL)
2 tsp kosher salt (10 mL)
$^1/_2$ tsp cayenne (2 mL)

Yield: 12 servings
$^1/_4$ cup (60 mL) per serving
201 calories
5 g protein
18 g fat
6 g net carbs

Wash limes carefully and grate zest from them. Set zest aside. Squeeze lime juice into medium bowl and add almonds, pecans and cashews. Toss to coat, and then drain in colander or sieve.

Sprinkle nuts with chili powder, chipotle powder, kosher salt and cayenne. Toss to coat evenly. Add grated lime zest and toss again. Spread nuts in single layer on parchment-lined baking sheet. Bake in 350°F (180°C) oven until browned and fragrant, 12 to 15 minutes, stirring occasionally. Remove from oven and let cool 10 minutes before serving.

SMOKED SALMON AND WASABI BITES

These easy-to-make appetizers take all the best flavors of sushi without the carb-filled rice.

$^1/_3$ cup mayonnaise (75 mL)
1 tbsp wasabi paste (15 mL)
1 medium cucumber
8 oz smoked salmon, thinly sliced (250 g)
2 tbsp toasted sesame seeds (30 mL)

Yield: 8 servings
1 serving
117 calories
6 g protein
10 g fat
1 g net carbs

In small bowl, whisk together mayonnaise and wasabi paste. Set aside. Cut cucumber into $^1/_4$-inch (0.6 cm) slices. Cut smoked salmon into 1-inch (2.5 cm) pieces. Spread each cucumber slice with about $^1/_2$ tsp (2 mL) of mayonnaise-wasabi mixture. Top each with a piece of smoked salmon, and then lightly sprinkle with sesame seeds. Serve immediately.

GARLIC AND HERB NUT THINS

*The basic recipe for these comes from **Birgit Kerr** of **Birgit's Daily Bytes** (http://birgitkerr.blogspot.com/). They are incredibly easy to make and a great replacement for chips and crackers.*

$^2/_3$ cup almonds (150 mL)
$^1/_3$ cup sunflower seeds (75 mL)
$^1/_3$ cup whole flax seeds (75 mL)
1 tsp salt (5 mL)
$^1/_2$ tsp garlic powder (2 mL)
$^1/_2$ tsp dried rosemary, OR basil (2 mL)
1 large egg white

> *Yield:* 8 servings
> 1 serving
> 138 calories
> 5 g protein
> 11 g fat
> *2 g net carbs*

In food processor fitted with metal S-blade, combine almonds, sunflower seeds and flax seeds. Process until finely ground, 1 to 2 minutes. Transfer to medium bowl and add salt, garlic powder and rosemary, OR basil. Stir well. Stir in egg white until dough comes together.

Roll out dough as thin as possible between two large pieces of parchment paper. Score into desired size of cracker and bake in 325°F (160°C) oven until edge pieces are beginning to brown, about 10 minutes. Remove from oven and remove outer, browned pieces, and then return to the oven. Repeat when more crackers are lightly browned, until all crackers are done.

MATCHA GREEN TEA SMOOTHIE

Matcha powder is the form of green tea used in Japanese tea ceremonies. The powder is expensive but a little goes a long way and makes for a healthy, refreshing smoothie.

2 tbsp boiling water (30 mL)
2 tsp matcha powder (10 mL)
1 cup Greek yogurt (250 mL)
1 cup unsweetened almond milk (250 mL)
$^1/_2$ cup crushed ice (125 mL)
3 tbsp granulated erythritol (45 mL)
2 tbsp vanilla whey protein powder (30 mL)

> *Yield:* 2 servings
> 1 serving
> 112 calories
> 17 g protein
> 2 g fat
> *6 g net carbs*

In small bowl, whisk together boiling water and matcha powder until mixture is smooth. Set aside.

In blender, combine Greek yogurt, almond milk, crushed ice, erythritol and vanilla whey protein powder. Add matcha mixture and blend until smooth.

192

SALADS AND SOUPS

FENNEL WALNUT CHICKEN SALAD

Fresh fennel bulbs and lightly toasted walnuts add a lovely crunch.

3 boneless, skinless chicken breasts, cooked
1$\frac{1}{2}$ cups fresh fennel bulbs, (375 mL)
  coarsely chopped
$\frac{1}{4}$ cup toasted walnuts, chopped (60 mL)
$\frac{1}{4}$ cup mayonnaise (60 mL)
2 tbsp walnut oil (30 mL)
2 tbsp freshly-squeezed lemon juice (30 mL)
2 tbsp chopped fennel fronds (30 mL)
2 cloves garlic, minced
$\frac{1}{8}$ tsp cayenne (0.5 mL)
$\frac{1}{2}$ tsp salt (2 mL)
$\frac{1}{4}$ tsp pepper (1 mL)

Yield: 6 servings
1 serving
287 calories
28 g protein
18 g fat
2 g net carbs

Cube chicken breasts into $\frac{1}{2}$-inch (1.3 cm) cubes. In large bowl, toss together chicken, chopped fennel and chopped walnuts to combine. In medium bowl, whisk together mayonnaise, walnut oil, lemon juice, chopped fennel fronds, garlic and cayenne until smooth. Pour dressing over chicken mixture and toss to coat thoroughly. Season with salt and pepper.

VICHYSSOISE

Let's face it; this is really just cold potato and leek soup. Without the potatoes!

1 tbsp butter (15 mL)
3 cups diced daikon radish (750 mL)
1 leek, washed, trimmed and thinly sliced
$\frac{3}{4}$ tsp salt (3 mL)
$\frac{1}{2}$ tsp freshly ground pepper (2 mL)
4 cups chicken, OR vegetable stock (1 L)
$\frac{3}{4}$ cup heavy cream (175 mL)

Yield: 6 servings
1 serving
151 calories
2 g protein
13 g fat
4 g net carbs

In large stock or soup pot, melt butter over medium heat. When hot, add daikon radish and leek and season with salt and pepper. Cook 2 to 3 minutes. Add stock, cover and bring to a simmer. Cook until vegetables are soft, about 20 minutes.

Working in two batches, transfer to blender or food processor and puree until smooth. Stir in cream. Let chill in refrigerator until cold, about 2 hours.

193

LOADED "BAKED POTATO" SOUP

This soup is truly amazing – thick, rich and filling, you wouldn't have any idea that there are no potatoes in it at all.

$^1/_2$ lb bacon, cut into small pieces (250 g)
Soup:
$^1/_2$ cup onion, minced (125 ml)
1 medium head cauliflower, cut
   into 2-inch (5 cm) florets
2 cloves garlic, minced
$^1/_2$ tsp salt (2 mL)
$^1/_4$ tsp pepper (1 mL)
4 cups chicken, OR vegetable stock (1 L)
1 bay leaf
$^1/_2$ cup whipping cream (125 mL)
1 egg yolk, lightly beaten
$^1/_2$ cup grated Cheddar cheese (125 mL)
Garnish:
Cooked Bacon pieces
$^1/_2$ cup grated Cheddar cheese (125 mL)
$^1/_4$ cup chopped chives (60 mL)

Yield: 6 servings
1 serving
398 calories
18 g protein
33 g fat
3 g net carbs

In large stock pot over medium heat, cook bacon pieces until very crisp, about 10 minutes. Remove bacon pieces with slotted spoon and let drain on paper towel-lined plate.

Soup: Drain all but 2 tbsp (30 mL) bacon grease from pot. Add onion and cook until translucent, about 5 minutes. Add cauliflower, garlic, salt and pepper and cook until garlic is fragrant, about 1 minute. Add chicken or vegetable stock and bring to a boil over medium high heat. Add bay leaf. Cover and reduce heat to medium low, and continue to cook 30 minutes. Remove from heat and remove bay leaf. Puree until smooth using an immersion blender or by transferring soup in two batches to blender or food processor.

In medium bowl, whisk together cream and egg yolk until smooth. Slowly whisk in 1 cup (250 mL) of pureed soup until well combined. Slowly whisk cream mixture back into soup. Return to medium heat, stirring continuously. Stir in grated Cheddar in two batches, and continue stirring until thoroughly melted.

Garnish: Ladle hot soup into 6 bowls and garnish each with bacon pieces, grated Cheddar cheese and chopped chives.

THAI COCONUT PUMPKIN SOUP

This rich, creamy soup derives its heat from Thai red curry paste.

1 tbsp vegetable oil (15 mL)
2 tbsp grated ginger (30 mL)
2 tbsp Thai red curry paste (30 mL)
3 cups chicken broth (750 mL)
1, 15-oz can pumpkin puree (425 g)
$\frac{1}{4}$ tsp salt (1 mL)
$\frac{1}{8}$ tsp cayenne pepper (0.5 mL)
1, 15-oz can coconut milk (444 mL)
3 tbsp fresh lime juice (45 mL)
$\frac{1}{4}$ cup fresh cilantro, chopped, for garnish (60 mL)

Yield: 6 servings
1 serving
242 calories
3 g protein
22 g fat
8 g net carbs

In large saucepan over medium heat, heat oil until shimmering but not smoking. Stir in ginger and red curry paste until fragrant, about 1 minute.

Add $\frac{1}{2}$ cup (125 mL) of the chicken broth and stir to dissolve curry paste. Stir in remaining broth, then pumpkin puree, salt and cayenne pepper, and bring to a simmer. Simmer gently, uncovered, for 10 minutes.

Add coconut milk and stir to combine. Continue to cook until heated through, about 5 minutes. Remove from heat and stir in lime juice. Sprinkle each bowl with chopped cilantro before serving.

~~Bits & Bites~~
Breast cancer gets a great deal of recognition as a serious disease, and well it should. But diabetes is the underlying cause of almost twice as many deaths in the United States each year (71,000). And diabetes is a contributing factor in four times as many deaths than breast cancer. But diabetes awareness is far more limited, and many people don't realize just how deadly a disease it is.

BREAKFASTS

BACON, GRUYERE AND MUSHROOM BREAKFAST QUICHES

I love eggs for breakfast, but making an omelet every morning is time-consuming. Having these ready to go makes things a lot simpler.

12 slices bacon
8 oz mushrooms (250 g)
2 cloves garlic, minced
6 oz Gruyere cheese (180 g)
12 large eggs
$1^1/_2$ cups whipping cream (375 mL)
$^1/_2$ tsp salt (2 mL)
$^1/_4$ tsp pepper (1 mL)

Yield: 8 servings
1 serving
357 calories
16 g protein
31 g fat
3 g net carbs

In large skillet over medium heat, cook bacon until very crisp. Remove and drain on paper towel-lined plate. Pour off all but 2 tbsp (30 mL) bacon fat from skillet and return skillet to heat. Add mushrooms and sauté 5 to 8 minutes, until tender and browned. Add minced garlic and cook until fragrant, about 30 seconds. Remove from heat. Crumble bacon into small pieces and divide among 8 well-greased, $^3/_4$-cup (175 mL) ramekins. Divide mushrooms among ramekins and sprinkle each with shredded Gruyere cheese.

In large bowl, whisk together eggs, whipping cream, salt and pepper until well combined. Divide mixture evenly among prepared ramekins. Place ramekins on baking sheet and bake in 325°F (160°C) oven 25 to 30 minutes, or until tops are puffed and center is set. Remove and let cool 10 minutes. Run sharp knife around inside of each ramekin to loosen, and then carefully flip out onto serving plate.

~Bits & Bites~
The American Diabetes Association estimates that 7 million people are suffering from undiagnosed diabetes, and another 79 million people have pre-diabetes. Diabetes is on the rise in Western society and our carb, sugar and gluten-filled diet is largely to blame.

PEANUT BUTTER PROTEIN PANCAKES

I have a slight obsession with all things peanut butter, and these pancakes really hit the spot. Try them with a little sugar-free maple or caramel syrup.

1 cup peanut flour, (250 mL)
(partially defatted)
$^1/_3$ cup vanilla whey protein powder (75 mL)
$^1/_4$ cup flax seed meal (60 mL)
2 tbsp granulated erythritol (30 mL)
$^1/_2$ tsp baking powder (2 mL)
$^1/_4$ tsp salt (1 mL)
$^1/_4$ cup creamy peanut butter (60 mL)
$^1/_4$ cup butter (60 mL)
4 large eggs, lightly beaten
$^1/_2$ cup unsweetened almond milk (125 mL)
1 tbsp butter, OR coconut oil for pan (15 mL)

Yield: 6 servings
2 pancakes per serving
237 calories
16 g protein
17 g fat
4 g net carbs

In large bowl, whisk together peanut flour, whey protein powder, flax seed meal, granulated erythritol, baking powder and salt. In small, microwave-safe bowl, melt peanut butter and butter together, stirring until smooth. Add peanut butter mixture and eggs to peanut flour mixture and stir vigorously to combine. Stir in almond milk until well combined. Let batter rest and thicken, 3 to 5 minutes.

In large skillet, heat 1 tsp (5 mL) butter, OR coconut oil over medium heat until butter is melted and froth begins to subside. Using 3 to 4 tbsp (45 to 60 mL) of batter per pancake, spoon into hot pan. Cook until bottom of each pancake is golden brown, about 3 minutes, then carefully flip and cook until second side is golden brown, 2 to 3 minutes more. Repeat with remaining butter, OR coconut oil and remaining batter.

Helpful Hints: Like traditional wheat-based pancakes, these will bubble slightly on the top as the first side cooks. Flip the pancake when you see bubbles appear around the edges, but do not wait until bubbles appear in the center or the first side will be overcooked.

Peanut flour comes in several varieties, both defatted and non-defatted, as well as in different roasts. Each variety behaves a little differently and you may need to adjust your liquid content if your batter is overly thick. If it is too thin and your pancakes flatten out too much, add just a little more peanut flour and/or flax seed meal to your batter.

BLUEBERRY RICOTTA BREAKFAST PUDDING

I call this pudding for lack of a better term. It really has the consistency of cooked oatmeal and makes a hearty, satisfying breakfast.

$^1/_4$ cup whole milk ricotta cheese (60 mL)
2 tbsp flax seed meal (30 mL)
1 large egg
2 tsp granulated erythritol (10 mL)
$^1/_8$ tsp vanilla extract (0.5 mL)
2 tbsp frozen blueberries (30 mL)

Yield: 1 serving
1 serving
252 calories
16 g protein
18 g fat
4 g net carbs

In small microwave-safe bowl, stir together ricotta, flax seed meal, egg, erythritol and vanilla extract until well-combined. Stir in blueberries. Cook on high in microwave for 2 to 4 minutes, until pudding is mostly set, but center is still slightly soft. Let cool 5 minutes.

~~Bits & Bites~~

The word "Ricotta" translates as "recooked" in Italian. Traditional ricotta is made from the leftover whey when making firmer cheeses like Mozzarella and Provolone. The whey is allowed to ferment and become more acidic, or acids are added in, and then the whey is reheated until tiny curds form.

ALMOND FLOUR FRENCH TOAST

French toast is one of my all-time favorite breakfast foods. I had to find a way to make a decent, low-carb version, so I could still enjoy it. I developed my Basic Almond Flour Bread recipe specifically with this French toast in mind, but it's good on its own too.

8 slices Almond Flour Bread, page 216,
 $^1/_2$ inch (1.3 cm) thick each
2 large eggs
1 tbsp heavy cream (15 mL)
 $^1/_2$ tsp ground cinnamon (2 mL)
 $^1/_8$ tsp ground nutmeg (0.5 mL)
2 tsp butter, OR coconut oil for pan (10 mL)

Yield: 4 servings
2 slices per serving
432 calories
11 g protein
21 g fat
7 g net carbs

Arrange slices of bread on wire rack set over baking sheet and place in 200°F (100°C) oven. Let dry out for at least one hour and up to 3 hours.

In medium bowl, whisk together eggs, cream, ground cinnamon and ground nutmeg until well combined. Pour batter into large, shallow dish. Place two slices of bread into batter and let sit 30 seconds to 1 minute to soak. Flip over and let sit another 30 seconds to one minute.

Meanwhile, heat large, nonstick skillet over medium heat. Add butter and cook until butter just begins to brown, swirling to coat bottom of pan. Remove bread from batter and shake lightly to remove excess. Place in skillet and cook until golden brown on both sides, 2 to 3 minutes per side. Transfer to wire rack and keep warm in 200°F (100°C) oven. Repeat with remaining batter and remaining bread.

~~Bits & Bites~~
French toast is typically made with stale, dry bread because it soaks up the egg mixture better. Because almond flour is moister than wheat bread, you need to dry it out a lot first. Make sure the bread is dry to the touch before dredging it in the eggs.

MAIN COURSES AND SIDES

LEMON GINGER CHICKEN THIGHS

Marinating the chicken thighs in lemon juice makes them incredibly tangy and delicious.

Chicken:
6 chicken thighs, bone-in, skin on
$1/4$ cup fresh lemon juice (60 mL)
$1/2$ tsp salt (2 mL)
$1/4$ tsp pepper (1 mL)
Lemon Honey Glaze:
$1/4$ cup fresh lemon juice (60 mL)
1 tbsp honey (15 mL)
2 cloves garlic
2 tsp freshly grated ginger (10 mL)

Yield: 6 servings
1 serving
216 calories
16 g protein
14 g fat
5 g net carbs

Chicken: In large gallon (4 L) freezer bag, combine chicken thighs and freshly-squeezed lemon juice. Place bag in large bowl and refrigerate for at least one hour, turning bag once or twice to coat chicken well. Remove chicken from bag, pat dry with paper towels, and sprinkle with salt and pepper.

Place chicken thighs, skin-side up, in 9 x 13-inch (23 x 33 cm) glass or ceramic baking dish.

Lemon Honey Glaze: In small bowl, whisk together freshly-squeezed lemon juice, honey, garlic and ginger. Using pastry brush, brush half of glaze onto chicken thighs. Bake in 350°F (180°C) oven 35 minutes, brushing with remaining glaze halfway through. Heat broiler on high and broil 4 to 5 minutes or until skin is golden brown and crisp.

~~Bits & Bites~~
Dark poultry meat, like the meat found in chicken thighs, is often eschewed because it's higher in fat and calories than white meat. Dark meat is rich in myoglobin, an iron-packed compound, whereas white meat has none. Dark meat also has higher amounts of zinc and B vitamins.

200

NEW MEXICAN-STYLE SMOTHERED PORK CHOPS

New Mexico is famous for its green chili hamburgers, so I decided to recreate the flavors with tender pork chops.

Green Chili Sauce:
1 tbsp olive oil (15 mL)
$^1/_4$ cup onion, chopped (60 mL)
1 jalapeno, minced
1 clove garlic, minced
$^1/_2$ tsp ground cumin (2 mL)
3, 4-oz cans mild green diced chilies (375 g)
$^1/_4$ cup water (60 mL)
$^1/_4$ tsp salt (1 mL)
$^1/_2$ tsp dried oregano (2 mL)
Pork Chops:
1 tbsp olive oil (15 mL)
6 bone-in pork chops, 1 inch (2.5 cm) thick
Salt and pepper to taste
$1^1/_2$ cups shredded Cheddar, Monterey Jack, OR a combination (375 mL)

Yield: 6 servings	
1 serving	
409 calories	
30 g protein	
29 g fat	
5 g net carbs	

Green Chili Sauce: In medium saucepan, heat olive oil over medium heat until shimmering but not smoking. Add onion and cook until soft, stirring frequently, about 4 minutes. Add jalapeno, garlic and ground cumin and cook until fragrant, about 30 seconds. Stir in green chilies, water and salt and bring to a simmer. Simmer gently for 5 minutes. Remove from heat and stir in oregano. Let cool 5 minutes. Transfer sauce to a blender and blend until smooth. Set aside.

Pork Chops: In large skillet, heat olive oil over medium high heat until shimmering. Pat pork chops with paper towel and sprinkle with salt and pepper on both sides. Brown chops on both sides, about 3 minutes per side. Continue to cook until center registers 140°F (60°C) on an instant read thermometer, about 7 minutes.

Lay pork chops in large, glass baking dish and divide sauce evenly over each. Sprinkle chops with shredded cheese. Broil on high, 3 to 4 inches from heat source, until cheese is melted and bubbly, 3 to 4 minutes.

Helpful Hints: For really tender, juicy pork chops, brine them in a large bowl containing 2 tbsp (30 mL) kosher salt and enough water to cover the chops. Let them sit for 1 hour before patting dry with paper towels.

CHILI RUBBED STEAKS WITH CILANTRO BUTTER

This is so simple, I almost hesitate to call it a recipe! Boneless or semi-boneless rib eye steaks are perfect for this recipe. Grilled or broiled, they will turn out juicy and flavorful.

Cilantro Butter:
2 tbsp butter, softened (60 mL)
2 tbsp fresh cilantro leaves, chopped (60 mL)
$^1/_4$ tsp salt (1 mL)
Steaks:
2 tbsp chili powder (30 mL)
1 tsp kosher salt (5 mL)
$^1/_2$ tsp freshly ground pepper (2 mL)
4 small boneless rib eye steaks, about 8 oz each (250 g each)
4 wedges of lime

Yield: 4 servings
1 serving
630 calories
37 g protein
51 g fat
2 g net carbs

Cilantro Butter: In small bowl, whisk softened butter with chopped cilantro and salt. Refrigerate until firm.

Steaks: In another small bowl, whisk together chili powder, kosher salt and pepper. Rub well into both sides of steaks. Place on pre-heated grill and cook 7 minutes on the first side, then flip and cook another 4 to 5 minutes. Steaks should register about 135°F (57°C) on an instant read thermometer for medium rare. Transfer to a platter and dollop each steak with 1 tbsp (15 mL) cilantro butter. Let sit 5 minutes.

Serve with wedge of lime for squeezing over steak.

~~Bits & Bites~~
Continual exposure to high blood glucose levels can cause damage to both blood vessels and nerve fibers, leading to peripheral neuropathy. Pain, numbness or tingling and burning sensations in the feet are often the first symptoms of diabetic neuropathy.

CHICKEN PICCATA

Chicken cutlets breaded with almond flour and served with a lemony, buttery caper sauce.

1 large egg
1 cup almond flour (250 mL)
$^1/_2$ tsp salt (2 mL)
$^1/_4$ tsp pepper (1 mL)
8, 4-oz boneless chicken cutlets (125 g each)
$^1/_4$ cup vegetable oil (60 mL)
2 cloves garlic, minced
1 cup chicken broth (250 mL)
Half a lemon, sliced $^1/_4$ inch thick (0.6 cm)
  and cut crosswise
$^1/_4$ cup freshly squeezed lemon juice (60 mL)
2 tbsp capers (30 mL)
$^1/_4$ cup butter, cut into 4 chunks (60 mL)
$^1/_2$ tsp salt (2 mL)
$^1/_4$ tsp pepper (1 mL)

Yield: 8 servings
1 serving
309 calories
26 g protein
21 g fat
3 g net carbs

In shallow dish, beat egg with fork until slightly frothy. In another shallow dish, whisk together almond flour, salt and pepper. Dip cutlets in beaten egg and shake off excess. Then dip cutlets into almond flour on both sides and shake off excess.

In large 12-inch (30 cm) skillet, heat 2 tbsp (30 mL) oil over medium high heat until shimmering. Add half the cutlets and cook until golden brown, about 4 minutes per side. Transfer to wire rack set above cookie sheet and keep warm in 200°F (100°C) oven. Repeat with remaining cutlets.

Add minced garlic to skillet and cook until fragrant, about 1 minute. Stir in broth and lemon slices and bring to a simmer. Cook until sauce is thickened and reduced by about half.

Stir in lemon juice and capers until combined. Reduce heat to low and whisk in butter, one piece at a time. Season with salt and pepper. Spoon sauce over chicken before serving.

SHEPHERD'S PIE

Leave out the flour in the filling and top it with mashed cauliflower and this classic dish becomes a delicious low-carb, gluten-free dinner.

Filling:
1 tbsp olive oil (15 mL)
2 medium carrots, peeled and sliced
1 medium onion, chopped
1$^1/_2$ lbs ground beef (0.68 kg)
1 lb ground lamb (0.45 kg)
1 tsp salt (5 mL)
$^1/_2$ tsp pepper (2 mL)
$^1/_4$ cup chicken or beef broth (60 mL)
$^1/_4$ cup dry red wine (60 mL)
1 tbsp Worcestershire sauce (15 mL)
1 tbsp chopped fresh rosemary, OR thyme (15 mL)

Topping:
2 medium heads cauliflower, cut into 1$^1/_2$-inch (4 cm) florets
2 cups water (500 mL)
2 garlic cloves
3 tbsp butter, melted (45 mL)
1 large egg, lightly beaten
$^1/_2$ tsp salt (2 mL)
$^1/_4$ tsp pepper (1 mL)

Yield: 12 servings
1 serving
318 calories
17 g protein
26 g fat
2 g net carbs

Filling: Heat oil in large skillet over medium high heat until shimmering. Add carrots and onion and cook until just softened, about 3 minutes. Add beef and lamb and cook until browned and cooked through, 7 to 10 minutes. Spoon off as much liquid from pan as possible and season with salt and pepper. Stir in broth, red wine, Worcestershire sauce and rosemary, OR thyme. Bring to a simmer, stirring to coat, and then remove from heat. Spread filling evenly in 9 x 13 inch (23 x 33 cm) glass or ceramic baking dish.

Topping: In large stockpot, combine cauliflower, water and garlic cloves over high heat. Bring to a boil, and then reduce heat to low and simmer until cauliflower is soft, 6 to 8 minutes. Drain in colander and transfer half of cauliflower to a food processor. Process until smooth and transfer to a large bowl. Repeat with remaining cauliflower. Stir in melted butter, egg, salt and pepper until well combined. Spread cauliflower mixture over filling, pressing to edges to create a seal. Bake in 400°F (200°C) oven 20 to 25 minutes, or until topping is lightly browned and pie is warmed through.

BRIE AND GREEN APPLE STUFFED CHICKEN BREASTS

This dish is actually modeled after one of my all-time favorite flavors of Panini, and it crossed over to stuffed chicken very well!

4 chicken breasts
2 tbsp kosher salt (30 mL)
$^1/_2$ small Granny Smith apple, thinly sliced
4 oz Brie cheese, thinly sliced (125 g)
$^1/_3$ cup mayonnaise (75 mL)
2 tbsp Dijon mustard (30 mL)
$^1/_4$ cup almond flour (60 mL)
$^1/_2$ tsp salt (2 mL)
$^1/_4$ tsp pepper (1 mL)

Yield: 4 servings
1 serving
533 calories
62 g protein
30 g fat
3 g net carbs

Fill large bowl halfway with water and add kosher salt. Stir until most of the salt has dissolved. Add chicken breasts and refrigerate one hour. Don't let chicken sit much longer, as it will get very salty. Remove breasts from brine and pat dry with paper towels. Lay chicken flat on cutting board and cut deep, horizontal pocket into thickest part of breast. Lay slices of green apple in single layer in each pocket, then brie in single layer. Seal edge of each breast with two toothpicks.

In small bowl, whisk together mayonnaise and Dijon mustard. Lay chicken in well-greased 9 x 13-inch (23 x 33 cm) glass or ceramic baking dish and spread mayonnaise mixture over top of each breast. Sprinkle breasts with almond flour, then salt and pepper. Bake in 425°F (220°C) oven 30 to 35 minutes, or until chicken registers 165°F (75°C) in thickest part of breast with an instant read thermometer. Remove and let cool 5 minutes before serving.

Variation: **Brie, Ham and Green Apple Stuffed Chicken Breasts:** Add two slices of thin-sliced Black Forest ham into pocket of each chicken breast before sealing and cooking. *(3 g net carbs)*

~~Bits & Bites~~
The moldy rind on Brie cheese forms after the cheese has been sprayed with Penicillin candidum, a healthy mold. The bacteria then penetrate the cheese, turning it into the smooth, semi-soft texture people love.

COFFEE-SPICED PORK TENDERLOIN

Ground coffee adds a depth of flavor to a spicy rub for pork. This recipe isn't overly spicy, and the pork is wonderfully moist and tender.

1 tsp finely ground coffee (5 mL)	**Yield:** 4 servings
¹/₂ tsp chili powder (2 mL)	1 serving
¹/₂ tsp salt (2 mL)	197 calories
¹/₄ tsp ground cumin (1 mL)	24 g protein
¹/₄ tsp garlic powder (1 mL)	11 g fat
¹/₈ tsp cayenne (0.5 mL)	**0 g net carbs**
1 lb pork tenderloin (0.45 kg)	
2 tbsp olive oil (30 mL)	

In small bowl, whisk together ground coffee, chili powder, salt, cumin, garlic powder and cayenne. Pat pork tenderloin dry with paper towels and place on broiling pan. Rub tenderloin all over with spice mixture, and then drizzle with olive oil.

Bake in 425°F (220°C) oven 20 to 22 minutes, or until thickest part of tenderloin reads 140°F (60°C) on an instant read thermometer. Remove from oven, tent with foil and let meat rest for 5 to 10 minutes. Slice into ¹/₂-inch (1.3 cm) slices and serve.

*~~**Bits & Bites**~~*
The health news about coffee seems to be ever-changing. Is it good for us or not? Like almost anything, coffee has its health benefits along with a few health risks. The Mayo Clinic points out that on the whole, the benefits outweigh the risks for most people. It can help protect against Parkinson's, type 2 Diabetes and certain cancers. But high consumption (2 or more cups per day) is also associated with an increase in heart disease in people who have a certain genetic mutation that slows the breakdown of caffeine in the body.

JALAPENO AND CHEDDAR STUFFED HAMBURGERS

Chopped, fresh jalapeno and sharp Cheddar right inside the burgers means you don't need any sugary ketchup or other condiments.

1 lb ground beef (0.45 kg)
1 lb ground pork (0.45 kg)
$^3/_4$ tsp salt (3 mL)
$^1/_2$ tsp freshly ground pepper (2 mL)
4 oz sharp Cheddar, (125 g)
  cubed into $^1/_4$-inch (0.6 cm) pieces
2 medium jalapeno peppers, finely chopped

Yield: 6 servings
1 serving
476 calories
31 g protein
38 g fat
1 g net carbs

In large bowl, mix together ground beef, ground pork, salt and pepper. Use hands to work together so ground meat holds together well. Divide into 6 even portions.

Using hands shape about two-thirds of each portion into flat patties with slight wells in center. Divide Cheddar cubes and chopped jalapenos evenly into wells. Top each well with remaining meat and shape into flat patty, making sure to have no cheese or jalapeno exposed.

Cook burgers on pre-heated grill about 5 to 6 minutes per side for medium. Cook slightly less for medium-rare and slightly more for medium-well. Meat should register at least 125°F (50°C) to 130°F (55°C) on an instant-read thermometer. Remove from grill and let sit 5 minutes

~~Bits & Bites~~
It's not always easy to get your hands on grass-fed beef, but the benefits can be well worth the effort and the price tag. Grass-fed animals have a higher concentration of Omega-3 fatty acids, they are free from antibiotics and many other toxins, and they are easier on our fragile environment. And many people claim it tastes better too!

GREEK SHRIMP WITH FETA AND CAULI-RICE

This is my low-carb version of a beloved family favorite that was originally made with orzo.

Cauliflower Rice:
1 head cauliflower
1 tbsp olive oil (15 mL)
$^1/_2$ cup crumbled Feta cheese (125 mL)
$^1/_4$ cup grated Parmesan cheese (60 mL)
2 tbsp fresh basil, chopped (30 mL)

Greek Shrimp:
2 tbsp olive oil (30 mL)
2 cloves garlic, minced
1 lb shrimp, peeled and deveined (0.45 kg)
$^1/_2$ cup dry white wine (125 mL)
14 oz can diced tomatoes, drained (411 g)
$^1/_2$ tsp red pepper flakes (2 mL)
$^1/_2$ tsp salt (2 mL)
$^1/_4$ tsp pepper (1 mL)
$^1/_2$ cup crumbled Feta cheese (125 mL)

Yield: 6 servings
1 serving
254 calories
21 g protein
15 g fat
5 g net carbs

Cauliflower Rice: Cut cauliflower into 1-inch (2.5 cm) florets. Place half in food processor and pulse until it resembles rice grains. Transfer to large microwave-safe bowl and repeat with remaining cauliflower. Cover bowl with tight-fitting lid or plastic wrap and microwave on high 5 minutes. Let sit 5 to 10 minutes, covered, to steam. Drain cauliflower in sieve to remove excess liquid, then return to bowl and toss with olive oil, Feta, grated Parmesan cheese and basil. Spread mixture evenly in greased 11 x 17-inch (28 x 43 cm) inch glass or ceramic baking dish.

Greek Shrimp: Heat oil in large skillet over medium high heat until shimmering but not smoking. Add garlic and sauté until fragrant, about 30 seconds. Add shrimp and sauté until just barely pink, about 1 minute. Arrange shrimp in single layer over cauliflower rice.

Add white wine to skillet and cook until reduced to a few tablespoons, 4 to 5 minutes. Add drained tomatoes, red pepper flakes, salt and pepper and cook until sauce thickens, about 2 minutes more. Pour sauce over shrimp and bake in 350°F (180°C) oven 10 minutes. Remove from oven and sprinkle with remaining crumbled Feta.

MUSHROOM SPINACH TORTA

This high-sided egg torta makes a wonderful entrée or brunch item. It is just as good cold as it is served warm.

2 tbsp olive oil (30 mL)
1, 10-oz package frozen spinach, (300 g)
  thawed and well drained*
8 oz mushrooms, sliced (250 g)
$^1/_4$ tsp hot pepper flakes (1 mL)
$^1/_4$ tsp salt (1 mL)
8 oz cream cheese, softened (250 g)
6 large eggs
$^1/_4$ cup whipping cream (60 mL)
2 cloves garlic, minced
$^1/_4$ tsp salt (1 mL)
$^1/_4$ tsp pepper (1 mL)
1 cup Parmesan cheese, grated (250 mL)

Yield: 8 servings
1 serving
271 calories
13 g protein
23 g fat
3 g net carbs

In large skillet over medium heat, heat oil until hot but not smoking. Add spinach, mushrooms, hot pepper flakes and salt and sauté 5 minutes. Set aside.

In large bowl, beat cream cheese until smooth. Beat in eggs until combined (batter may be a little lumpy). Beat in whipping cream. Stir in garlic, salt and pepper. Add sautéed vegetables to egg mixture and stir until well combined, then stir in Parmesan cheese.

Spread mixture in well-greased 9-inch (23 cm) springform pan lined with greased parchment paper. Wrap outside of pan in aluminum foil.

Bake in 325°F (160°C) oven 60 to 65 minutes or until top is puffy and golden brown and center no longer jiggles when pan is shaken. Remove from oven and let cool in pan 10 minutes, and then run a sharp knife around edges of torta to loosen. Gently remove pan sides.

Helpful hint: *The spinach should be very well drained and pressed to remove as much moisture as possible otherwise the torta may become soggy and take much longer to cook.

CAULIFLOWER AU GRATIN

It took a lot of trial and error to get a thick, cheesy sauce without using any flour.
But it was worth all the effort!

1 medium head cauliflower
2 tbsp butter (30 mL)
2 cloves garlic, minced
$^1/_2$ cup half and half (125 mL)
$^1/_2$ cup whipping cream (125 mL)
1 tbsp arrowroot starch (15 mL)
$1^1/_4$ cups grated Cheddar cheese, (300 mL)
  divided
$^1/_2$ tsp salt (2 mL)
$^1/_4$ tsp pepper (1 mL)

Yield: 6 servings
1 serving
253 calories
9 g protein
23 g fat
3 g net carbs

Cut cauliflower into even, 1-inch (2.5 cm) florets. Place florets in steam basket in large saucepan and steam lightly until tender but still firm, about 5 minutes. Drain and set aside.

In medium saucepan over medium high heat, cook butter until melted and golden brown, 1 to 2 minutes. Stir in minced garlic and sauté until fragrant, 30 seconds. Reduce heat to medium. In glass measuring cup, whisk together arrowroot starch, half and half and whipping cream. Add mixture to browned butter and cook until thickened considerably, about 4 minutes. Stir in 1 cup (250 mL) grated Cheddar cheese until melted. Season with salt and pepper.

Spread cauliflower florets in well-greased baking dish and pour cheese sauce evenly over top. Sprinkle with remaining grated Cheddar cheese. Bake in 350°F (180°C) oven for 20 to 25 minutes. Serve hot.

~~Bits & Bites~~
Like all cruciferous vegetables, cauliflower can get somewhat bitter and lose nutrients when overcooked. The trick is to steam it lightly until it can be pierced with a fork but doesn't crumble or become mushy. Light cooking makes it more easily digestible as well.

JICAMA FRIES WITH JERK MAYONNAISE

Jicama makes for great fries and Jamaican jerk seasoning really spices up the mayonnaise for a flavorful snack.

Fries:
1 large jicama
3 to 4 cups vegetable oil (750 mL to 1 L)
2 tsp salt (10 mL)
Jerk Mayonnaise:
$^1/_4$ cup mayonnaise (60 mL)
2 tsp jerk seasoning (10 mL)
   (Walkerswood® recommended)

Yield: 8 servings
1 serving
201 calories
1 g protein
20 g fat
3 g net carbs

Fries: Peel jicama and slice into $^1/_4$-inch (0.6 cm) slices. Cut slices into $^1/_4$-inch (0.6 cm) strips. Heat vegetable oil in large, heavy saucepan over medium high heat and bring temperature to 350°F (180°C). Use candy or instant read thermometer to measure temperature.

When oil is hot, carefully add half of the jicama strips and fry until crispy, about 7 to 9 minutes. Using a slotted spoon, remove jicama from oil and drain on paper towel-lined plate. Sprinkle with half of the salt. Repeat with remaining jicama, bringing oil back up to 350°F (180°C) before frying.

Jerk Mayonnaise: In small bowl, whisk together mayonnaise and jerk seasoning until well combined. Serve with jicama fries.

SESAME ROASTED BROCCOLI

Roasting is a great way to cook broccoli without making it mushy, and toasted sesame oil adds a wonderful nuttiness.

1 lb broccoli, stems discarded (0.45 kg)
2 tbsp toasted sesame oil (30 mL)
2 cloves garlic, minced
$^1/_2$ tsp salt (2 mL)
$^1/_4$ tsp pepper (1 mL)
2 tbsp toasted sesame seeds (30 mL)

Yield: 4 servings
1 serving
121 calories
4 g protein
9 g fat
3 g net carbs

Cut broccoli into 1-inch (2.5 cm) florets and place in medium bowl. Toss with sesame oil, minced garlic, salt and pepper. Place in even layer in glass or ceramic baking dish and sprinkle with toasted sesame seeds. Roast in 425°F (220°C) oven 8 to 10 minutes, or until just tender.

SPICY THAI PEANUT NOODLES

These spicy noodles make a great side dish alongside any chicken or beef.

Peanut Sauce:
$^1/_3$ cup smooth peanut butter (75 mL)
3 tbsp hot water (45 mL)
2 tbsp apple cider vinegar (30 mL)
1 tbsp soy sauce (15 mL)
1 clove garlic, minced
1 tsp ground ginger (5 mL)
$^1/_2$ tsp red pepper flakes (2 mL)

Yield: 4 servings
1 serving
192 calories
9 g protein
15 g fat
6 g net carbs

4 cups water (1 L)
2, 8-oz packages shiratake noodles (500 g each)
3 tbsp salted peanuts, chopped (45 mL)

Peanut Sauce: In medium bowl, whisk together peanut butter, water, cider vinegar, soy sauce, garlic, ginger and pepper flakes until well combined and smooth. Set aside.

In medium saucepan, bring 4 cups (1 L) water to a boil. Add shirataki noodles and cook 3 to 4 minutes. Drain well. Toss with peanut sauce and garnish with chopped peanuts.

~~Bits & Bites~~
Peanuts are a surprisingly good source of resveratrol, a polyphenol antioxidant that is also found in red wine. Resveratrol is associated with reduced risk of heart disease, Alzheimer's and stroke.

MISCELLANEOUS

SUGAR-FREE CANDIED GINGER

Candied ginger is so wonderful in baked goods that I had to find a way to make it without sugar.

$^1/_2$ cup water (125 mL)
$^3/_4$ cup granulated erythritol, (175 mL) divided
$^1/_2$ cup peeled fresh ginger, (125 mL) sliced into $^1/_8$-inch slices (0.3 cm)

Yield: 8 servings
1 tbsp (15 mL) per serving
4 calories
0.0 g protein
0.0 g fat
1 g net carbs

In small saucepan over medium high heat, bring water and $^1/_2$ cup (125 mL) granulated erythritol to a boil, stirring until erythritol dissolves. Add sliced ginger and lower heat to medium. Simmer, stirring frequently, until much of the liquid has evaporated, about 20 to 30 minutes.

Using slotted spoon, transfer ginger to wire rack set over cookie sheet. Let cool 5 minutes.

Place remaining $^1/_4$ cup (60 mL) erythritol in small bowl. Dip each piece of ginger in erythritol, covering completely. Shake off excess erythritol and return to rack to dry, about 3 hours. Store in airtight container in refrigerator.

~~Bits & Bites~~
Fresh ginger root can be stored for up to a month in the refrigerator. When purchased, it should be firm and free of mold. Mature ginger root, which is most commonly available, has a tough skin that requires peeling before it can be used. I find that a sharp knife works best.

HOMEMADE CHOCOLATE HAZELNUT SPREAD

I adore all things chocolate and hazelnut, and this spread is great used in other recipes as well.

$^1/_2$ cup hazelnuts (125 mL)
2 tbsp hazelnut, OR other nut oil (30 mL)
2 tbsp cocoa powder (30 mL)
1 tbsp powdered erythritol (15 mL)
$^1/_2$ tsp vanilla extract (2 mL)
$^1/_8$ tsp stevia extract, OR (0.5 mL)
 2 tbsp equivalent (30 mL)

Yield: 8 servings
1 tbsp (15 mL) per serving
89 calories
1 g protein
9 g fat
1 g net carbs

Spread hazelnuts in single layer on large, rimmed baking sheet. Bake in 350°F (180°C) oven 8 to 10 minutes, or until nuts are browned and fragrant. Remove and let cool 10 minutes. Roll hazelnuts between fingers until husks fall away. Some husks will remain.

Grind hazelnuts in food processor fitted with metal S-blade until finely ground and just beginning to clump together. Add oil, cocoa powder, powdered erythritol, vanilla extract and stevia extract, OR equivalent and continue to process until creamy and smooth, scraping down sides of processor with rubber spatula as needed. If mixture continues to clump together, add another 1 to 2 tsp (5 to 10 mL) of oil until a spreadable consistency is achieved.

STRAWBERRY RHUBARB SAUCE

This sweet, tangy sauce is delicious over ice cream or the Earl Grey Panna Cotta on page 242. It also makes a great alternative to pancake syrup.

$1^1/_2$ cups sliced rhubarb (375 mL)
1 cup strawberries, chopped (250 mL)
3 tbsp granulated erythritol (45 mL)
2 tbsp plus 2 tsp water, divided (40 mL)
1 tsp arrowroot starch (5 mL)

Yield: 8 servings
$^1/_4$ cup (60 mL) per serving
11 calories
0 g protein
0 g fat
1 g net carbs

In large saucepan over medium heat, bring rhubarb, strawberries, erythritol and 2 tbsp (30 mL) water to a boil. Reduce heat to low and simmer until fruit is tender, 5 to 10 minutes. Mash large chunks of fruit with the back of a wooden spoon for a chunky sauce. Alternatively, use an immersion blender to puree until smooth.

In small bowl, whisk together arrowroot starch and remaining 2 tsp (10 mL) water. Add to sauce and return to a boil. Cook until thickened, about 2 minutes. Let cool to room temperature.

BREADS, MUFFINS AND MORE

CHEDDAR BEER BREAD

This bread has quickly become a family favorite and a staple in our house. My kids love it and we even use it for toast and sandwiches. It's actually wonderful spread with peanut butter.

2 cups almond flour (500 mL)
$^1/_3$ cup coconut flour (75 mL)
$^1/_4$ cup whey protein powder (60 mL)
  (unflavored)
1 tbsp granulated erythritol (15 mL)
2 tsp baking powder (10 mL)
$^1/_2$ tsp baking soda (2 mL)
$^1/_2$ tsp salt (2 mL)
$1^1/_2$ cups finely grated Cheddar cheese, divided (375 mL)
3 large eggs, lightly beaten
$^1/_4$ cup butter, melted (60 mL)
1 cup gluten-free beer (250 mL)

Yield: 15 servings
1 serving
186 calories
9 g protein
15 g fat
2 g net carbs

In a large bowl, whisk together almond flour, coconut flour, whey protein powder, granulated erythritol, baking powder, baking soda and salt. Stir in $1^1/_4$ cups (300 mL) of the Cheddar cheese. Add eggs and butter and mix until well combined. Add beer and stir vigorously until batter is smooth.

Spread batter in well-greased 9 x 5 x 3-inch (2 L) loaf pan and sprinkle top with remaining $^1/_4$ cup (60 mL) Cheddar cheese. Bake in 325°F (160°C) oven 45 minutes, or until tester inserted in center comes out clean. Let cool in pan 10 minutes, and then flip out onto a wire rack to cool completely.

~~Bits & Bites~~
Most varieties of beer are not gluten-free, as the hops and grains used in making them can be cross-contaminated with wheat. But many brewers are starting to put out good gluten-free beer, so there is hope!

BASIC ALMOND FLOUR BREAD

This is a basic almond flour bread recipe that is great plain, with a little bit of butter, or in other recipes such as French toast or stuffing.

$2^1/_2$ cups almond flour (625 mL)
$^1/_4$ cup coconut flour (60 mL)
$^1/_4$ cup whey protein powder (60 mL)
   (unflavored)
1 tbsp granulated erythritol (15 mL)
2 tsp baking powder (10 mL)
1 tsp xanthan gum (5 mL)
$^1/_2$ tsp baking soda (2 mL)
$^1/_2$ tsp salt (2 mL)
6 oz Greek yogurt (180 g)
6 tbsp butter, softened (90 mL)
4 large eggs
6 tbsp almond milk (90 mL)

Yield: 15 servings
1 serving
182 calories
8 g protein
15 g fat
3 g net carbs

In medium bowl, whisk together almond flour, coconut flour, whey protein powder, granulated erythritol, baking powder, xanthan gum, baking soda and salt. In large bowl, beat together yogurt and butter until smooth. Beat in eggs, one at a time, scraping down sides of bowl and beaters as needed. Add almond flour mixture and beat until well combined. Beat in almond milk until thoroughly combined.

Spread batter in well-greased 9 x 5 x 3-inch (2 L) loaf pan and bake in 325°F (160°C) oven 45 to 50 minutes, or until top is golden brown and tester inserted in center comes out clean. Let cool in pan 15 minutes and then flip out onto wire rack to cool completely.

~~Bits & Bites~~
Type 1 diabetes and Celiac disease are both auto-immune disorders. Celiac disease occurs with much greater frequency in people with Type 1 diabetes than in the general population.

PUMPKIN CARDAMOM BREAD

Pumpkin bread is one of my favorite baked goods, and ground cardamom gives it a slightly exotic flair.

$2^1/_4$ cups almond flour (560 mL)
$^1/_2$ cup granulated erythritol (125 mL)
6 tbsp whey protein powder (90 mL)
  (unflavored)
2 tsp baking powder (10 mL)
$1^1/_2$ tsp ground cardamom (7 mL)
1 tsp xanthan gum (5 mL)
$^3/_4$ tsp baking soda (3 mL)
$^1/_2$ tsp salt (2 mL)
1 cup pumpkin puree (250 mL)
6 tbsp coconut oil, melted (90 mL)
3 large eggs
$^1/_3$ cup almond milk (75 mL)
$^1/_8$ tsp stevia extract, OR (0.5 mL)
  2 tbsp equivalent (30 mL)

Yield: 12 servings
1 serving
218 calories
9 g protein
19 g fat
4 g net carbs

In medium bowl, whisk together almond flour, granulated erythritol, whey protein powder, baking powder, cardamom, xanthan gum, baking soda and salt. In large bowl, beat pumpkin and coconut oil until smooth. Beat in eggs, almond milk and stevia extract, OR equivalent until combined. Add almond flour mixture to pumpkin mixture and stir until batter is just combined.

Spread batter in well-greased 9 x 5 x 3-inch (2 L) loaf pan, smoothing the top. Bake in 325°F (160°C) oven 34 to 40 minutes, or until top is set and tester inserted in the center comes out clean. Let cool in pan for 20 minutes, and then transfer to a wire rack to cool completely.

Variation: **Pumpkin Spice Bread:** Substitute 2 tsp (10 mL) pumpkin pie spice for the cardamom. *(4 g net carbs)*

~~Bits & Bites~~
Like other bright orange vegetables, pumpkin is loaded with beta-carotenes. An anti-oxidant, beta-carotene is associated with a reduced risk of heart disease and certain cancers, and may also protect against other degenerative diseases.

SESAME HAMBURGER BUNS

What's a burger without a bun? I wanted a flavorful bun that would stand up to a juicy burger and not fall to pieces. These did the trick!

2 cups almond flour (500 mL)
$^1/_4$ cup coconut flour (60 mL)
$^1/_4$ cup whey protein powder, (60 mL)
  (unflavored)
2 tsp baking powder (10 mL)
1 tsp baking soda (5 mL)
1 tsp garlic powder (5 mL)
$^1/_2$ tsp salt (2 mL)
3 large eggs, lightly beaten
6 tbsp butter, melted (90 mL)
$^1/_4$ cup almond milk (60 mL)
$^1/_4$ cup toasted sesame seeds (60 mL)

Yield: 8 servings
1 serving
300 calories
11 g protein
27 g fat
4 g net carbs

In large bowl, whisk together almond flour, coconut flour, whey protein powder, baking powder, baking soda, garlic powder and salt. Stir in beaten eggs, melted butter and almond milk until dough comes together. Dough will be very sticky and thick.

Using wet hands to keep dough from sticking, shape into 8 equal balls and lay on parchment-lined baking sheet. Press dough down with palm of hand to about $^3/_4$ inch (2 cm) thick. Sprinkle tops with sesame seeds and press lightly to adhere. Bake in 325°F (160°C) oven 15 to 20 minutes, or until buns are firm to the touch and lightly browned. Remove and let cool.

~~Bits & Bites~~
Sesame seeds are high in healthy fatty acids, but because of this, they can go rancid when stored improperly. Store in air-tight containers in dark, cool places or in the freezer to help them last longer.

GOLDEN FLAX WALNUT MUFFINS

*This recipe comes from reader, **Ellen Grasso**. We tried them out and the whole family loved them! And since flax seed is almost all fiber, these muffins have virtually no carbs but are incredibly filling. A wonderful breakfast or snack with a slathering of organic butter.*

1 1/4 cups golden flax seed meal (300 mL)
1/4 cup granulated erythritol (60 mL)
1 tbsp baking powder (15 mL)
1 tsp ground cinnamon (5 mL)
1/2 tsp ground nutmeg (2 mL)
1/4 tsp salt (1 mL)
1/4 tsp sucralose powder, OR (1 mL)
  1/8 tsp stevia extract, OR (0.5 mL)
  2 tbsp equivalent (30 mL)
3 large eggs, lightly beaten
1/3 cup coconut oil (75 mL)
2 1/2 tbsp water (37 mL)
2 1/2 tbsp heavy cream (37 mL)
1/4 cup chopped walnuts (60 mL)

Yield: 10 servings	
1 serving	
179 calories	
6 g protein	
16 g fat	
1 g net carbs	

In large bowl, whisk together golden flax seed meal, granulated erythritol, baking powder, cinnamon, nutmeg, salt and sucralose powder, if using. Stir in stevia extract, if using, OR equivalent, eggs, coconut oil, water and cream. Mix well until fully combined.

Divide batter among 10 paper-lined muffin cups. Sprinkle with chopped walnuts. Bake in 350°F (180°C) oven 16 to 18 minutes or until set and a tester inserted in the center comes out clean. Let cool in pan.

Helpful Hints: Ellen suggests buying flax meal from a vendor who keeps it refrigerated because it tastes bitter if it has been on the shelf for any period of time. At home, I store it in the freezer.

~~Bits & Bites~~
There is little nutritional difference between golden flax seed and brown flax seed, so they can really be used interchangeably. Because of its lighter color, golden flax seed meal can blend in with other ingredients a little better.

Carolyn Ketchum

CRANBERRY CINNAMON CRUMB MUFFINS

Cranberry and cinnamon are wonderful together and the streusel crumb topping makes these muffins a great treat.

Muffins:
2 cups almond flour (500 mL)
$^1/_4$ cup granulated erythritol (60 mL)
$^1/_4$ cup whey protein powder (60 mL)
 (unflavored)
2 tsp baking powder (10 mL)
1 tsp ground cinnamon (5 mL)
$^1/_2$ tsp baking soda (2 mL)
$^1/_2$ tsp salt (2 mL)
$^1/_2$ tsp xanthan gum (2 mL)
6 oz Greek yogurt (180 g)
2 large eggs
$^1/_4$ cup butter, melted (60 mL)
$^1/_2$ tsp vanilla extract (2 mL)
$^1/_4$ tsp stevia extract, OR (1 mL)
 $^1/_4$ cup equivalent (60 mL)
$^1/_4$ cup unsweetened almond milk (60 mL)
1 cup cranberries (250 mL)

Crumb Topping:
$^1/_4$ cup almond flour (60 mL)
3 tbsp granulated erythritol (45 mL)
1 tsp cinnamon (5 mL)
$1^1/_2$ tbsp butter, chilled and cut into small pieces (22 mL)

Yield: 12 servings
1 serving
202 calories
9 g protein
17 g fat
4 g net carbs

Muffins: In medium bowl, whisk together almond flour, granulated erythritol, whey protein powder, baking powder, cinnamon, baking soda, salt and xanthan gum. In large bowl, beat yogurt and eggs together until smooth. Stir in melted butter, vanilla and stevia extract, OR equivalent. Add almond flour mixture in two batches, alternating with almond milk, until batter is well combined. Stir in cranberries. Divide batter among 12 muffin tins lined with paper liners.

Crumb Topping: In small bowl, whisk together almond flour, granulated erythritol and cinnamon. Cut in butter until mixture resembles fine crumbs. Sprinkle muffins with topping.

Bake in 325°F (160°C) oven 25 to 30 minutes, or until muffins are set and crumb topping is lightly browned. Remove from oven and let cool in pan.

GINGER WALNUT PEAR MUFFINS

These muffins were inspired by the big, beautiful pears that were picked fresh from a friend's tree.

2 cups almond flour (500 mL)
$^1/_4$ cup flax seed meal (60 mL)
$^1/_4$ cup granulated erythritol (60 mL)
$^1/_4$ cup whey protein powder (60 mL)
  (unflavored)
1 tbsp ground ginger (15 mL)
2 tsp baking powder (10 mL)
$^1/_2$ tsp baking soda (2 mL)
$^1/_2$ tsp ground cinnamon (2 mL)
$^1/_2$ tsp salt (2 mL)
3 oz cream cheese, softened (90 g)
$^1/_4$ cup butter, softened (60 mL)
3 large eggs
$^1/_4$ tsp stevia extract, (1 mL)
  OR $^1/_4$ cup equivalent (60 mL)
$^1/_4$ cup unsweetened almond milk (60 mL)
1 cup diced pear (250 mL)
$^1/_2$ cup walnuts, chopped (125 mL)

Yield: 12 servings	
1 serving	
243 calories	
9 g protein	
21 g fat	
5 g net carbs	

In medium bowl, whisk together almond flour, flax seed meal, granulated erythritol, unflavored whey protein, ground ginger, baking powder, baking soda, ground cinnamon and salt.

In large bowl, beat cream cheese and butter together until smooth. Beat in eggs and stevia extract, OR equivalent until combined. Beat in almond flour mixture in two additions, alternating with almond milk and scraping down beaters and sides of bowl as needed. Stir in diced pears and chopped walnuts.

Divide batter between 12 muffin cups lined with paper liners. Bake in 325°F (160°C) oven 18 to 22 minutes, or until tops are set and tester inserted in center comes out clean. Let cool in pan 5 minutes, then transfer to wire rack to cool completely.

~~Bits & Bites~~

Having some low-carb baked goods on the go helps curb those cravings in times of temptation. Consider making double batches of muffins and keeping them in the freezer. 45 Seconds in the microwave and they taste freshly baked.

CHOCOLATE GINGER SCONES

I love the combination of chocolate and ginger, and these scones make a delicious breakfast treat.

Scones:
1³/₄ cups almond flour (425 mL)
¹/₃ cup cocoa powder (75 mL)
3 tbsp granulated erythritol (45 mL)
2 tsp baking powder (10 mL)
¹/₂ tsp baking soda (2 mL)
¹/₂ tsp salt (2 mL)
¹/₃ cup Candied Ginger, page 213, chopped fine (75 mL)
¹/₃ cup coconut oil, melted (75 mL)
1 large egg, lightly beaten
2 tbsp heavy cream (30 mL)
¹/₂ tsp vanilla extract (2 mL)
¹/₈ tsp stevia extract, OR (0.5 mL)
  2 tbsp equivalent (30 mL)

Chocolate Glaze:
¹/₄ cup powdered erythritol (60 mL)
1 tbsp cocoa powder (15 mL)
1¹/₂ tbsp almond milk (22 mL)
¹/₄ tsp vanilla extract (1 mL)

Yield: 8 servings
1 serving
252 calories
7 g protein
24 g fat
4 g net carbs

Scones: In large bowl, whisk together almond flour, cocoa powder, granulated erythritol, baking powder, baking soda and salt in large bowl. Add chopped, Candied Ginger, page 213 making sure to break up any pieces that clump together to get even distribution. Add coconut oil, egg, heavy cream, vanilla extract and stevia extract, OR equivalent and stir vigorously until dough comes together.

Turn dough out onto parchment-lined baking sheet and shape by hand into rough circle, 7 or 8 inches (18 to 20 cm) in diameter. Slice into 8 even wedges and separate carefully, then space evenly around baking sheet. Bake in 325°F (160°C) oven 20 to 25 minutes, or until scones are firm and lightly browned, keeping an eye on bottoms to make sure they don't burn. Transfer to wire rack to cool.

Chocolate Glaze: In small bowl, whisk together powdered erythritol and cocoa powder until combined, breaking up any clumps with the back of a fork. Whisk in milk and vanilla extract until mixture is smooth. Drizzle or spread over cooled scones.

ROSEMARY LEMON SCONES

Rosemary is such a surprising, fresh flavor in a sweet baked good. I was going to put a glaze on these but they were so good just plain.

2^1/$_4$ cups almond flour (560 mL)
^{1}/$_4$ cup granulated erythritol (60 mL)
2 tsp baking powder (10 mL)
^{1}/$_2$ tsp baking soda (2 mL)
^{1}/$_4$ tsp salt (1 mL)
1 tbsp fresh rosemary, chopped (15 mL)
1 tbsp freshly grated lemon zest (15 mL)
1 large egg, lightly beaten
^{1}/$_4$ cup butter, melted (60 mL)
2 tbsp heavy cream (30 mL)

Yield: 8 servings
1 serving
255 calories
8 g protein
24 g fat
3 g net carbs

In large bowl, whisk together almond flour, granulated erythritol, baking powder, baking soda and salt. Stir in fresh rosemary and lemon zest to distribute evenly. Add egg, butter and cream and stir until dough comes together.

Turn out dough onto baking sheet lined with parchment paper or silicone mat. Shape into a rough circle, 7 or 8 inches (18 or 20 cm) in diameter. Slice into 8 even wedges and separate carefully, then space evenly around prepared baking sheet. Bake in 325°F (160°C) oven 18 to 22 minutes, or until scones are firm and lightly browned. Keep an eye on bottoms to make sure they don't burn. Remove from oven, transfer to a wire rack and let cool.

~~Bits & Bites~~
Insulin resistance is the condition whereby the body's cells no longer uptake insulin properly. As both fat and muscle cells require insulin to absorb glucose, insulin resistance results in elevated blood glucose levels. If you are overweight, losing 5% to 10% of your body weight can decrease insulin resistance dramatically.

SOUR CREAM, CHEDDAR AND BASIL DROP BISCUITS

Cheddar and basil make these sour cream-based biscuits a flavorful addition to any soup or stew.

1 cup almond flour (250 mL)
$^1/_3$ cup gluten-free oat fiber (75 mL)
2 tbsp fresh basil, chopped fine (30 mL)
2 tsp baking powder (10 mL)
$^1/_2$ tsp salt (2 mL)
1 cup shredded Cheddar cheese (250 mL)
2 large eggs, room temperature
$^1/_3$ cup sour cream, room temperature (75 mL)
$^1/_4$ cup butter, melted (60 mL)

Yield: 8 servings
1 serving
230 calories
9 g protein
21 g fat
2 g net carbs

In large bowl, whisk together almond flour, oat fiber, basil, baking powder and salt. Stir in shredded Cheddar cheese. In small bowl, whisk together eggs, sour cream and melted butter until well combined. Add egg mixture to almond flour mixture and stir until dough comes together.

Drop large spoonfuls of dough, about $^1/_4$ cup (60 mL) each, onto baking sheet lined with parchment paper or a silicone liner. Bake in 400°F (200°C) oven 12 to 15 minutes, or until tops are golden brown and spring back to the touch. Cool on pan for 10 minutes.

Variations: **Sour Cream, Cheddar and Dill Drop Biscuits:** Substitute 2 tbsp (30 mL) fresh, chopped dill for the basil. *(2 g net carbs)*

Sour Cream, Cheddar and Chive Drop Biscuits: Substitute 2 tbsp (30 mL) chopped chives for the basil. *(2 g net carbs)*

~~Bits & Bites~~
You will often hear diabetics refer to their A1C numbers. A1C measures the percentage of hemoglobin that is glycated, or covered in sugar. It represents a patient's overall blood glucose control for the past 2 to 3 months. The lower the A1C, the better the blood glucose control.

MAPLE GLAZED DONUTS

My favorite donut flavor, rendered low-carb and gluten-free.

Donuts:
1$\frac{1}{2}$ cups almond flour (375 mL)
$\frac{1}{4}$ cup granulated erythritol (60 mL)
$\frac{1}{2}$ tsp baking powder (2 mL)
$\frac{1}{2}$ tsp baking soda (2 mL)
$\frac{1}{2}$ tsp xanthan gum (2 mL)
$\frac{1}{4}$ tsp salt (1 mL)
2 large eggs, room temperature
2 tbsp butter, melted (30 mL)
$\frac{1}{2}$ tsp vanilla extract (2 mL)
$\frac{1}{4}$ tsp stevia extract (1 mL) OR $\frac{1}{4}$ cup equivalent (60 mL)
6 tbsp almond milk (90 mL)
Maple Glaze:
6 tbsp powdered erythritol (90 mL)
1 tsp maple extract (5 mL)
2 tbsp heavy cream (30 mL)

Yield: 8 servings
1 serving
179 calories
6 g protein
16 g fat
3 g net carbs

Donuts: In large bowl, whisk together almond flour, granulated erythritol, baking powder, baking soda, xanthan gum and salt. In another small bowl, whisk together eggs, melted butter, vanilla extract and stevia extract, OR equivalent. Add egg mixture to almond flour mixture and stir until thoroughly combined. Add almond milk and stir until smooth.

Fill holes of well-greased donut tin $\frac{2}{3}$ full. Bake in 325°F (160°C) oven 18 to 20 minutes, or until set and donuts spring back when touched. Let cool in pan 5 minutes and then flip out onto a wire rack to cool completely. Repeat with remaining batter.

Maple Glaze: In small bowl, whisk together powdered erythritol, maple extract and heavy cream until smooth. Spread over cooled donuts and let set, about 20 minutes.

Helpful Hint: The size of your donut pan may vary slightly and will determine how many you get from this recipe and how long you have to bake the donuts.

BLUEBERRY CREAM CHEESE COFFEE CAKE

I had a craving for a dense, rich coffee cake and this fit the bill perfectly!

Blueberry Filling:
1 cup frozen blueberries (250 mL)
2 tsp water (10 mL)
1 tsp arrowroot starch (5 mL)
Cream Cheese Filling:
8 oz cream cheese (250 g)
1 large egg
2 tbsp granulated erythritol (30 mL)
$^1/_4$ tsp stevia extract (1 mL), OR $^1/_4$ cup equivalent (60 mL)
Cake:
2 cups almond flour (500 mL)
$^1/_4$ cup granulated erythritol (60 mL)
$^1/_4$ cup vanilla whey protein powder (60 mL)
2 tsp baking powder (10 mL)
1 tsp xanthan gum (5 mL)
$^1/_2$ tsp baking soda (2 mL)
$^1/_2$ tsp salt (2 mL)
6 oz greek yogurt (180 g)
$^1/_4$ cup butter, softened (60 mL)
3 large eggs
$^1/_8$ tsp stevia extract (0.5 mL), OR 2 tbsp equivalent (30 mL)
$^1/_4$ cup unsweetened almond milk (60 mL)

Yield: servings
1 serving
307 calories
13 g protein
26 g fat
6 g net carbs

Blueberry Filling: In small saucepan over medium heat, bring blueberries to a simmer and cook until they release their juices, about 3 minutes. In small cup, mix together water and arrowroot starch until well combined. Add starch mixture to blueberries and cook until thickened, about 1 minute. Set aside.

Cream Cheese Filling: In medium bowl, beat cream cheese until smooth. Beat in egg until well combined, and then beat in erythritol and stevia extract, OR equivalent. Set aside.

Cake: In medium bowl, whisk together almond flour, granulated erythritol, vanilla whey protein powder, baking powder, xanthan gum, baking soda and salt. In large bowl, beat yogurt and butter together until smooth. Add eggs one at a time, beating lightly after each addition, then beat in stevia extract, OR equivalent. Beat in almond flour mixture in two additions, alternating with almond milk and scraping down beaters and sides of bowl as needed

Spread batter in well-greased, 9-inch (23 cm) springform pan with removable bottom, pushing batter up sides of pan to create center well for filling. Sides should be about 1 inch (2.5 cm) wide. Spread cream cheese mixture evenly into center well, and then spread blueberry mixture over top of cream cheese. Bake in 350°F (180°C) oven 30 to 35 minutes, or until sides are set. Center will still jiggle somewhat. Let cool in pan. Run a sharp knife around cake in pan to loosen, and remove sides. Cover tightly with plastic wrap and refrigerate for at least one hour.

Helpful Hints: Because the filling is made with cream cheese, keep this cake refrigerated. It also takes on a lovely, dense quality when it has been in the fridge for a while.

~~*Bits & Bites*~~

Gluten is a protein, and in its absence, it is necessary to replace the protein to help give the baked good some structure. I like to use whey protein powder, but you can use hemp, soy or flax protein powder instead.

Gluten is often found in unexpected foods such as soy sauce, ketchup, ice cream and beer. Gluten is not always listed on a product label, so if you do react to a product, it might be a good idea to search for a product that specifically says gluten-free on the label. A phone call to the manufacturer of a product might confirm your suspicions of gluten in a product. With enough calls from concerned people, that manufacturer might remove gluten from their product.

SWEET ENDINGS

CHOCOLATE PEPPERMINT CUPS

These chocolate cups are filled with a delicious peppermint buttercream and make a festive addition to any dessert table.

Chocolate Coating:
$^1/_4$ cup butter (60 mL)
3 oz unsweetened chocolate (90 g)
2 tbsp powdered erythritol (30 mL)
2 tbsp cocoa powder (30 mL)
$^1/_4$ tsp vanilla extract (1 mL)
$^1/_8$ tsp stevia extract, OR (0.5 mL)
  2 tbsp equivalent (30 mL)

Peppermint Filling:
6 tbsp butter, softened (90 mL)
1 cup powdered erythritol (250 mL)
$^1/_4$ tsp peppermint extract (1 mL)
$^1/_4$ cup heavy cream (60 mL)

Garnish:
4 sugar-free peppermint candies, crushed (optional)

Yield: 18 servings
2 pieces per serving
94 calories
1 g protein
10 g fat
1 g net carbs

Chocolate Coating: In small saucepan over low heat, melt butter, unsweetened chocolate and powdered erythritol together, stirring until smooth. Stir in cocoa powder, vanilla and stevia extract, OR equivalent. Let cool 5 to 10 minutes, until thickened. Use back of small spoon to spread chocolate mixture on bottom and up sides of foil-lined petit fours cups. Place cups on baking sheet or platter and freeze until firm, about 20 minutes.

Peppermint Filling: In medium bowl, beat butter until smooth. Beat in powdered erythritol, peppermint extract and cream until smooth. Fill chilled chocolate cups with peppermint filling almost to top, and smooth the top.

Rewarm chocolate coating over low heat until melted. Use spoon to pour chocolate over peppermint filling to cover. If desired, place small piece of crushed peppermint candy on top to garnish. Refrigerate until set, about half an hour.

~~Bits & Bites~~

Peppermint extract typically comes in 2 kinds; the extract made with alcohol, or peppermint oil. I like the peppermint oil for most recipes, but be warned that it's not useful for meringues. The oil makes the whipped egg whites deflate.

ALMOND JOY TART

A buttery, shortbread crust topped with coconut buttercream and rich chocolate ganache.

Almond Crust:
1$^1/_2$ cups almond flour (375 mL)
$^1/_4$ cup granulated erythritol (60 mL)
1 tsp xanthan gum (5 mL)
5 tbsp butter, chilled (75 mL)
$^1/_8$ tsp stevia extract, OR (0.5 mL)
   2 tbsp equivalent (30 mL)
1 tsp almond extract (5 mL)

Yield: 12 servings	
1 serving	
375 calories	
5 g protein	
38 g fat	
4 g net carbs	

Filling:
$^1/_2$ cup butter, softened (125 mL)
2 cups powdered erythritol (500 mL)
2 tbsp heavy whipping cream (30 mL)
1 tbsp dark rum (15 mL)
2 cups unsweetened, shredded coconut (500 mL)

Chocolate Ganache:
6 tbsp butter (90 mL)
2$^1/_2$ oz unsweetened chocolate (75 g)
2 tbsp powdered erythritol (30 mL)
2 tbsp cocoa powder (30 mL)
$^1/_2$ tsp vanilla extract (2 mL)
$^1/_4$ tsp stevia extract (1 mL), OR $^1/_4$ cup equivalent (60 mL)

Crust: In food processor fitted with metal S-blade, combine almond flour, granulated erythritol, and xanthan gum. Pulse 4 or 5 times to combine. Cut chilled butter into small $^1/_2$-inch (1.3 cm) pieces and sprinkle over almond flour mixture. Sprinkle with stevia and almond extracts. Process until mixture resembles fine crumbs. Press evenly into bottom and sides of very well-greased tart pan. Bake in 350°F (180°C) oven 12 to 15 minutes or until crust is golden brown. Remove and let cool.

Filling: In medium bowl, cream butter until fluffy. Add powdered erythritol, 1 cup (250 mL) at a time, until well combined. Mixture will be dry. Add cream and rum and beat until smooth. Stir in shredded coconut. Spread filling evenly in cooled tart shell.

Chocolate Ganache: In small saucepan, melt butter, chocolate, eythritol and cocoa powder together over low heat, stirring until smooth. Remove from heat and stir in vanilla extract and stevia extract, OR equivalent. Pour over coconut buttercream, spreading to edges of tart using a knife or offset spatula. Let cool and set, about 30 minutes.

TRULY FUDGY BROWNIES

It took me a long time to figure out how to get truly fudgy, low-carb brownies.
As it turns out, the trick is not to use any sort of flour at all and make them with
almond butter.

1 oz unsweetened chocolate, chopped (30 g)
$1^1/_2$ cups almond butter (375 mL)
6 tbsp granulated erythritol (90 mL)
$^1/_3$ cup cocoa powder (75 mL)
3 large eggs
3 tbsp almond milk (45 mL)
$^1/_2$ tsp vanilla extract (2 mL)
$^1/_4$ tsp salt (1 mL)
$^1/_4$ tsp stevia extract, OR (1 mL)
  $^1/_4$ cup equivalent (60 mL)
$^1/_3$ cup walnuts, chopped (75 mL)

Yield: 16 servings
1 serving
192 calories
6 g protein
18 g fat
5 g net carbs

In small, microwave-safe bowl, melt chocolate in microwave by heating on high for 30 second intervals. Stir between each interval until smooth.

In large bowl, stir together almond butter, melted chocolate, erythritol and cocoa powder until combined. Mixture will be very thick. Stir in eggs, almond milk, vanilla extract, salt and stevia, OR equivalent until batter is well combined. Stir in chopped walnuts.

Spread batter in 8-inch (20 cm) square pan and smooth the top with a knife or offset spatula. Bake in 325°F (160°C) oven 18 to 20 minutes or until just barely set in center. Do not overbake. Remove from oven and let cool in pan.

~~Bits & Bites~~
The American Diabetes Association estimated that in 2007, the total cost of diabetes on the healthcare system in the US was $174 billion dollars. And that number only includes diagnosed cases. The total amount including undiagnosed diabetes, prediabetes and gestational diabetes comes in at $218 billion.

GRASSHOPPER BARS

A brownie base topped with mint buttercream and rich chocolate ganache.

Base:
1 cup almond flour (250 mL)
1 tsp baking soda (5 mL)
$^1/_2$ tsp baking powder (2 mL)
$^1/_2$ tsp salt (2 mL)
$^1/_2$ tsp xanthan gum (2 mL)
$^1/_2$ cup butter, melted (125 mL)
$^1/_4$ cup cocoa powder (60 mL)
4 oz cream cheese, softened (125 g)
2 large eggs
$^1/_4$ cup granulated erythritol (60 mL)
$^1/_8$ tsp stevia extract (0.5 mL), OR 2 tbsp equivalent (30 mL)
$^1/_3$ cup almond milk (75 mL)

Filling:
$^1/_2$ cup butter, softened (125 mL)
$1^1/_2$ cups powdered erythritol (375 mL)
1 tsp peppermint extract (5 mL)
1 to 2 drops green food coloring gel
$^1/_3$ cup heavy cream (75 mL)

Ganache:
5 tbsp butter (75 mL)
$^1/_4$ cup powdered erythritol (60 mL)
2 oz unsweetened chocolate, finely chopped (60 g)
$^1/_4$ cup cocoa powder (60 mL)

Yield: 16 servings
1 serving
200 calories
4 g protein
20 g fat
3 g net carbs

Base: In medium bowl, stir together almond flour, baking soda, baking powder, salt and xanthan gum. In small bowl, stir together melted butter and cocoa powder. In large bowl, beat cream cheese until smooth. Beat in eggs until well combined. Add cocoa mixture and beat until smooth. Add erythritol, stevia extract, OR equivalent and almond milk. Beat in almond flour in two batches until thoroughly combined. Spread batter in well-greased, 8-inch (20 cm) square pan and bake in 350°F (180°C) oven 18 to 22 minutes or until top is just set. Cool in pan.

Filling: To food processor, add butter, powdered erythritol, peppermint extract and food coloring. Process until combined. Add cream a little bit at a time until spreadable consistency is achieved. Spread over cooled base.

Ganache: Melt butter, powdered erythritol, unsweetened chocolate and cocoa together in small saucepan over low heat, stirring until smooth. Spread over filling and let set, at least one hour.

PEANUT BUTTER AND CHOCOLATE COOKIE CUPS

Peanut butter cookie dough baked in mini-muffin tins and filled with rich chocolate ganache. A perfect, bite-sized treat.

Cookie Cups:
1 cup non-defatted peanut flour (250 mL)
$^1/_2$ cup almond flour (125 mL)
$^1/_3$ cup granulated erythritol (75 mL)
1 tsp baking soda (5 mL)
$^1/_2$ tsp salt (2 mL)
$^1/_2$ cup butter (125 mL)
$^1/_2$ cup peanut butter (125 mL)
1 large egg
$^1/_2$ tsp vanilla extract (2 mL)
$^1/_8$ tsp stevia extract (0.5 mL), OR 2 tbsp equivalent (30 mL)

Chocolate Ganache:
5 tbsp butter (75 mL)
2 oz unsweetened chocolate, chopped (60 g)
2 tbsp powdered erythritol, OR xylitol (30 mL)
$^1/_4$ cup cocoa powder (60 mL)
$^1/_4$ tsp vanilla extract (1 mL)
$^1/_8$ tsp stevia extract (0.5 mL), OR 2 tbsp equivalent (30 mL)

Yield: 12 servings	
2 cookies per serving	
257 calories	
7 g protein	
25 g fat	
4 g net carbs	

Cookies: In medium bowl, whisk together peanut flour, almond flour, granulated erythritol, baking soda and salt. In large bowl, beat butter and peanut butter together until smooth. Beat in egg, vanilla extract and stevia extract, OR equivalent until just incorporated. Add half of peanut flour mixture and beat until just incorporated, and then repeat with remaining peanut flour mixture.

Divide dough between 24 paper-lined mini muffin tins. Using fingers, press dough to bottom and up sides of paper liners. Bake in 350°F (180°C) oven 12 minutes, or until cookie cups are puffed and golden brown. Remove from oven and use handle of wooden spoon to create a well in center of each. Let cool in pan.

Chocolate Ganache: In small saucepan over low heat, melt butter, chocolate and powdered erythritol, OR xylitol together. Stir in cocoa powder, vanilla and stevia extract, OR equivalent until smooth. Remove from heat and let sit 5 to 10 minutes, until thickened but still pourable. Spoon chocolate ganache into well of each cookie cup and let set, about 2 hours.

STRAWBERRY SHORTCAKE

Soft, sweet biscuits served with sweetened whipped cream and fresh strawberries.

Shortcakes:
2 cups almond flour (500 mL)
$^1/_4$ cup granulated erythritol (60 mL)
3 tbsp whey protein powder, (45 mL)
  (unflavored)
2 tsp baking powder (10 mL)
1 tsp baking soda (5 mL)
$^1/_2$ tsp salt (2 mL)
1 tbsp freshly grated lemon zest (15 mL)
2 large eggs, lightly beaten
$^1/_4$ cup butter, melted (60 mL)

Whipped Cream Topping:
$^3/_4$ cup whipping cream (175 mL)
2 tbsp powdered erythritol (30 mL)
$^1/_2$ tsp vanilla extract (2 mL)
$^1/_8$ tsp stevia extract (0.5 mL) OR 2 tbsp equivalent (30 mL)
2 cups fresh strawberries, hulled and chopped (500 mL)

Yield: 8 servings
1 serving
328 calories
10 g protein
30 g fat
6 g net carbs

Shortcakes: In large bowl, whisk together almond flour, granulated erythritol, whey protein powder, baking powder, baking soda and salt. Add lemon zest and stir well to evenly distribute. Add in eggs and butter and stir until dough comes together. Dough will be quite sticky.

Drop by large spoonfuls onto baking sheet lined with parchment paper to make 8 mounds, at least 2 inches apart. Bake in 325°F (160°C) oven 16 to 18 minutes, or until biscuits are firm and just beginning to brown. Let cool on pan 5 minutes, then transfer to wire rack to cool completely.

Whipped Cream Topping: In large bowl, beat cream, powdered erythritol, vanilla extract and stevia extract, OR equivalent until stiff peaks form. Do not overbeat.

Cut each biscuit horizontally in half. Top with large spoonful of whipped cream and some berries. Lay second half of biscuit over, top with small spoonful of whipped cream and a few more berries. Serve immediately.

CHOCOLATE WALNUT CARAMEL BARS

Walnuts are some of my favorite nuts and I am always dreaming up new ways to use them.

Chocolate Crust:
1 cup almond flour (250 mL)
$^1/_3$ cup cocoa powder (75 mL)
$^1/_4$ cup granulated erythritol (60 mL)
$^1/_2$ tsp xanthan gum (2 mL)
$^1/_2$ tsp salt (2 mL)
$^1/_8$ tsp stevia extract, OR (0.5 mL)
  2 tbsp equivalent (30 mL)
5 tbsp butter, chilled and cut into small pieces (75 mL)

Walnut Caramel Filling:
2 cups walnuts, lightly toasted (250 mL)
$^1/_2$ cup granulated erythritol (125 mL)
1 tbsp agave nectar, OR honey (15 mL)
$^1/_2$ cup whipping cream (125 mL)
1 tbsp butter (15 mL)
$^1/_2$ tsp vanilla extract (2 mL)

Yield: 16 servings
1 serving
215 calories
6 g protein
20 g fat
6 g net carbs

Chocolate Crust: In food processor fitted with metal S-blade, add almond flour, cocoa powder, granulated erythritol, xanthan gum, salt and stevia extract, OR equivalent. Pulse quickly to combine. Sprinkle pieces of butter over other crust ingredients and pulse until mixture just begins to clump together. Transfer to 8-inch (20 cm) square pan. Use flat-bottomed glass or measuring cup to press evenly into bottom of pan. Bake in 350°F (180°C) oven for 15 minutes, or until crust is slightly puffed and browned. Remove from oven and let cool.

Walnut Caramel Filling: Sprinkle cooled crust with toasted walnuts. In small saucepan over medium heat, combine granulated erythritol and agave nectar, OR honey. Cook, stirring frequently, until erythritol has dissolved and mixture bubbles, about 5 to 7 minutes. Remove from heat and stir in whipping cream, butter and vanilla extract. Mixture will boil vigorously. Return to heat, bring to a boil and stir until smooth, about 2 minutes. Pour mixture over walnuts and crust and let cool completely, about 1 hour.

Helpful Hint: The caramel mixture will smoke, but you must make sure it actually bubbles before proceeding or it won't set properly

NUTELLA SWIRL CHEESECAKE ICE CREAM

Ice cream made with cream cheese is rich and delicious, especially with a ribbon of homemade Nutella running through it.

8 oz cream cheese, softened (250 g)
6 oz Greek yogurt (180 g)
$^1/_2$ cup whipping cream (125 mL)
$^1/_4$ cup powdered erythritol (60 mL)
$^1/_2$ tsp vanilla extract (2 mL)
$^1/_8$ tsp stevia extract, OR (0.5 mL)
 2 tbsp equivalent (30 mL)
$^1/_8$ tsp salt (0.5 mL)
$^1/_2$ cup Homemade Chocolate Hazelnut Spread, page 214 (125 mL)

Yield: 6 servings
1 serving
307 calories
7 g protein
30 g fat
4 g net carbs

In food processor fitted with metal S-blade, combine cream cheese, Greek yogurt, whipping cream and powdered erythritol and process until smooth. Add vanilla extract, stevia extract, OR equivalent and salt and continue to process until fully combined.

Refrigerate mixture until well chilled, about 2 hours. Transfer to canister of an ice cream maker and churn according to manufacturer's directions. Once churned, transfer to an air-tight container. Swirl Homemade Chocolate Hazelnut Spread, page 214 into mixture. Place plastic wrap flush to the surface of ice cream, close container and freeze until firm but not rock hard, about 1 hour.

~~Bits & Bites~~
I recently discovered that making your own cream cheese is incredibly simple, and the taste far surpasses store-bought. It's simply a matter of bringing some cream and milk to a boil, then simmering with the addition of something acidic like vinegar. When the mixture curdles, you simply scoop out the curds and let them drain in cheesecloth. 4 hours later, you have creamy, rich, sweet cheese.

CHOCOLATE HAZELNUT BISCOTTI
Crisp biscotti always make the perfect treat for dipping in hot coffee or tea.

1³/₄ cups hazelnut flour (425 mL)
¹/₄ cup cocoa powder (60 mL)
¹/₄ cup granulated erythritol (60 mL)
¹/₂ tsp baking powder (2 mL)
¹/₂ tsp xanthan gum (2 mL)
¹/₄ tsp salt (1 mL)
¹/₄ cup butter, melted (60 mL)
1 large egg, lightly beaten
1 tsp hazelnut extract (5 mL)
¹/₈ tsp stevia extract (0.5 mL), OR 2 tbsp equivalent (30 mL)
¹/₃ cup toasted hazelnuts, finely chopped (75 mL)

Yield: 15 servings
1 serving
137 calories
3 g protein
13 g fat
2 g net carbs

In large bowl, whisk together hazelnut flour, cocoa powder, granulated erythritol, baking powder, xanthan gum, and salt. Stir in melted butter, beaten egg, hazelnut extract and stevia extract, OR equivalent and stir vigorously until dough comes together. Stir in chopped hazelnuts.

Turn out dough onto baking sheet lined with a silicone mat or parchment paper, and shape into low, flat log, 10 x 4 inches (25 x 10 cm). Bake in 325°F (160°C) oven 20 to 25 minutes or until lightly browned and firm to the touch. Remove from oven and let cool 30 minutes. Reduce oven temperature to 250°F (120°C).

With sharp knife, gently cut into 15 even slices. Place slices, cut-side down, back onto baking sheet and bake 15 minutes, then flip each slice over and bake for another 15 minutes. Turn off oven and let biscotti sit inside until cool.

Helpful Hints: Using commercially ground hazelnut flour will make your biscotti much finer and easier to cut. Also cut with a straight, up-and-down motion, and do not saw back and forth or your biscotti might crumble.

~~Bits & Bites~~
Many recipes call for skinned hazelnuts, and it's really easy to do when they are freshly toasted. Simply let the hazelnuts cool to the point where they can be touched, about 10 minutes. Then simply roll them between your fingers until the dark skins fall off. A few are stubborn and the skin won't come off, but it doesn't make much difference to the taste or texture of most recipes.

CAPPUCCINO CUPCAKES

These coffee-flavored cupcakes topped with cinnamon whipped cream are like the coffeehouse drink in solid form!

Cupcakes:
$^1/_2$ cup almond milk (125 mL)
2 tbsp instant coffee (30 mL)
2 cups almond flour (500 mL)
6 tbsp whey protein powder (90 mL)
  (unflavored)
$^1/_4$ cup granulated erythritol (60 mL)
2 tsp baking powder (10 mL)
1 tsp xanthan gum (5 mL)
$^1/_2$ tsp baking soda (2 mL)
$^1/_2$ tsp salt (2 mL)
6 oz Greek yogurt (180 g)
$^1/_4$ cup butter, softened (60 mL)
2 large eggs
$^1/_2$ tsp vanilla extract (2 mL)
$^1/_4$ tsp stevia extract (1 mL), OR $^1/_4$ cup equivalent (60 mL)

Cinnamon Cream Frosting:
1 cup whipping cream, chilled (250 mL)
6 tbsp powdered erythritol (90 mL)
1 tsp ground cinnamon (5 mL)
$^1/_2$ tsp vanilla extract (2 mL)

Yield: 12 servings
1 serving
246 calories
9 g protein
22 fat
4 g net carbs

Cupcakes: In small bowl, combine almond milk and instant coffee and stir until coffee is dissolved. Set aside.

In medium bowl, whisk together almond flour, whey protein powder, erythritol, baking powder, xanthan gum, baking soda and salt. In large bowl, beat yogurt and butter together until smooth. Beat in eggs, vanilla extract and stevia extract, OR equivalent until well mixed. Beat in almond flour mixture in two additions, alternating with almond milk/coffee mixture. Scrape down beaters and sides of bowl as necessary. Divide batter among 12 paper-lined muffin cups and bake in 325°F (160°C) oven 23 to 25 minutes, or until tops are puffed and set, and tester inserted in the center comes out clean. Let cool completely in pan.

Cinnamon Cream Frosting: Beat whipping cream, powdered erythritol, cinnamon and vanilla extract until stiff peaks form. Pipe or spread onto cooled cupcakes. Garnish with a sprinkle of cinnamon or cocoa powder.

CLASSIC CHOCOLATE BIRTHDAY CAKE WITH CHOCOLATE SOUR CREAM FROSTING

A classic layer cake, perfect for birthdays and other special occasions.

Cake:
$2^1/_4$ cups almond flour (560 mL)
$^3/_4$ cup cocoa powder (175 mL)
$^1/_2$ cup granulated erythritol (125 mL)
$^1/_2$ cup vanilla whey protein powder (125 mL)
1 tbsp instant coffee (15 mL)
2 tsp baking powder (10 mL)
1 tsp baking soda (5 mL)
1 tsp xanthan gum (5 mL)
$^1/_2$ tsp salt (2 mL)
6 oz Greek yogurt, room temperature (180 g)
$^1/_2$ cup butter, softened (125 mL)
5 large eggs, room temperature
$^1/_4$ tsp stevia extract (1 mL), OR $^1/_4$ cup equivalent (60 mL)
$^2/_3$ cup almond milk (150 mL)

Chocolate Sour Cream Frosting:
4 oz unsweetened chocolate, chopped (125 g)
$1^1/_2$ cups sour cream, room temperature (375 mL)
3 cups powdered erythritol (750 mL)
$^1/_4$ cup cocoa powder (60 mL)
1 tsp vanilla extract (5 mL)
$^1/_8$ tsp stevia extract (0.5 mL), OR 2 tbsp equivalent (30 mL)
$1^1/_2$ tsp xanthan gum (7 mL)

Yield: 16 servings
1 serving
279 calories
11 g protein
25 g fat
5 g net carbs

Cake: In large bowl, whisk together almond flour, cocoa powder, granulated erythritol, vanilla whey protein powder, instant coffee, baking powder, baking soda, xanthan gum and salt. In another large bowl, beat Greek yogurt and butter together until combined. Beat in eggs and stevia extract, OR equivalent. Beat in almond flour mixture in two additions, alternating with almond milk, and scraping down beaters and sides of bowl as needed.

Divide batter between two well-greased, 8-inch (20 cm) diameter, round cake pans lined with parchment and bake in 325°F (160°C) oven 30 to 35 minutes, or until cakes are set and a tester inserted in center comes out clean. Let cool in pans 10 minutes, and then flip out onto wire racks to cool completely. Once cool, use a large, serrated knife to cut each layer in half horizontally.

Chocolate Sour Cream Frosting: In small saucepan over low heat, melt chocolate and stir until smooth. Set aside. In large bowl, beat sour cream and powdered erythritol until smooth. Beat in cocoa powder, then vanilla extract and stevia extract, OR equivalent. Sprinkle xanthan gum over mixture and beat in until frosting thickens slightly. Stir in melted chocolate, scraping down sides of bowl, until well combined.

Place one layer of cake on a serving platter and top the cake with $^1/_2$ to $^3/_4$ cup (125 to 175 mL) frosting, using knife or offset spatula to spread evenly. Repeat with remaining layers and frosting. For final layer, top with any remaining frosting and spread down and over sides of cake, smoothing with knife or offset spatula. If desired, use back of small spoon to create swirled effect on top of cake.

Chill cake in refrigerator for at least one hour. Any leftover cake should be wrapped in plastic and kept in the refrigerator.

Helpful Hints: You can skip cutting the layers in half and just do two layers of cake, but you will want to make less frosting. If you find your icing too gummy after adding the xanthan gum, add some liquid like whole milk, 1 tbsp (15 mL) at a time until it thins out.

*~~ **Bits and Bites**~~*
Xanthan gum is incredibly useful in gluten-free baking, as it helps bind the baked good together in the absence of gluten. It's also useful as an alternative to cornstarch and other higher carb thickeners in puddings, salad dressings, gravies, and even ice cream.

FROZEN CAPPUCCINO MOUSSE

This dessert is light in texture but tastes rich and decadent. Fitting the ramekins with paper collars allows it to rise elegantly above the top of the dish.

$^1/_2$ cup hot water (125 mL)
1 tbsp instant coffee (15 mL)
4 large eggs, separated
$^1/_8$ tsp salt (0.5 mL)
$^1/_8$ tsp stevia extract , OR (0.5 mL)
  2 tbsp equivalent (30 mL)
$^1/_4$ tsp xanthan gum (1 mL)
$^3/_4$ cup whipping cream (175 mL)
1 tsp ground cinnamon (5 mL)
$^1/_2$ tsp vanilla extract (2 mL)
$^1/_8$ tsp cream of tartar (0.5 mL)
$^1/_4$ cup granulated erythritol (60 mL)

Yield: 4 servings
1 serving
232 calories
7 g protein
21 g fat
2 g net carbs

In small bowl, combine hot water and instant coffee and stir until coffee dissolves. Let cool to room temperature.

In medium glass or ceramic bowl, whisk together egg yolks, coffee mixture, salt and stevia extract, OR equivalent. Set over saucepan of barely simmering water, but do not allow bottom of bowl to touch water. Whisk constantly until mixture just begins to thicken, 8 to 12 minutes. Remove bowl from heat and sprinkle with xanthan gum, whisking vigorously to combine. Press plastic wrap flush to surface of mixture and refrigerate until completely chilled, at least 2 hours.

Prepare four 1-cup (250 mL) capacity ramekins by fitting with paper collars. Cut strips of parchment 1 inch (2.5 cm) longer than diameter of ramekin and 1 inch (2.5 cm) higher than height of ramekin. Wrap paper strip around top of ramekin and secure with tape.

When coffee mixture is chilled, whip cream, cinnamon and vanilla extract in large bowl until stiff peaks form when beaters are lifted. In another large bowl, combine egg whites and cream of tartar. With clean beaters, beat whites until foamy. Gradually add erythritol and continue to beat until stiff peaks form.

Whisk the coffee mixture until smooth and add to whipped cream, folding in gently until just combined. Add egg whites and fold in until combined. Divide mixture among prepared ramekins. Freeze mousse 2 hours, until firm but not rock hard. Remove collars and serve.

Helpful Hint: If you will be freezing them longer than 2 hours, remove from freezer 15 minutes before serving to allow them to soften.

PEANUT BUTTER CARAMEL SHORTBREAD BARS

When I made these, my husband said they tasted exactly like Tagalongs, the Girl Scout Cookies made with peanut butter and chocolate.

Almond Crust:
1¼ cups almond flour (300 mL)
¼ cup butter, chilled (60 mL)
¼ cup granulated erythritol (60 mL)
½ tsp xanthan gum (2 mL)
⅛ tsp stevia extract, OR (0.5 mL)
  2 tbsp equivalent (30 mL)

Peanut Butter Caramel Filling:
½ cup granulated erythritol (125 mL)
1 tsp agave nectar (5 mL)
½ cup whipping cream (125 mL)
½ cup smooth peanut butter (125 mL)
½ tsp vanilla extract (2 mL)

Chocolate Topping:
6 tbsp butter (90 mL)
2½ oz unsweetened chocolate (75 g)
2 tbsp powdered erythritol (30 mL)
2 tbsp cocoa powder (30 mL)
½ tsp vanilla extract (2 mL)
⅛ tsp stevia extract (0.5 mL), OR 2 tbsp equivalent (30 mL)

Yield: 16 servings
1 serving
215 calories
5 g protein
21 g fat
4 g net carbs

Crust: In food processor fitted with metal blade, combine almond flour, butter, erythritol, xanthan gum and stevia extract, OR equivalent. Pulse until mixture resembles fine crumbs. Press mixture evenly into the bottom of 8-inch (20 cm) square pan and bake in 350°F (180°C) oven 15 minutes or until light golden brown. Set aside and let cool.

Peanut Butter Caramel Filling: In small saucepan over medium heat, combine erythritol and agave nectar. Cook, stirring frequently, until erythritol has dissolved and mixture bubbles, about 5 to 7 minutes. Remove from heat and stir in cream. Mixture will bubble vigorously. Return to heat and boil one minute. Stir in peanut butter and vanilla extract until smooth. Pour over cooled crust and spread evenly with offset spatula.

Chocolate Topping: In small saucepan over low heat, melt butter together with chopped chocolate and powdered erythritol, stirring continuously until smooth. Add cocoa powder and stir until smooth. Stir in vanilla and stevia extract, OR equivalent. Pour chocolate over cooled peanut butter filling and spread evenly with an offset spatula. Let set at room temperature for about 1 hour.

EARL GREY PANNA COTTA

Lightly infused with Earl Grey tea, this creamy dessert makes an elegant finish to any meal.

1¹/₂ cups heavy cream (375 mL)	***Yield:*** 6 servings
2 tbsp Earl Grey loose tea leaves (30 mL)	1 serving
¹/₄ cup granulated erythritol (60 mL)	223 calories
1¹/₂ cups unsweetened almond milk, (375 mL) divided	3 g protein
	23 g fat
2 envelopes unflavored gelatin (15 g)	***2 g net carbs***
¹/₈ tsp stevia extract, OR (0.5 mL) 2 tbsp equivalent (30 mL)	

In medium saucepan over medium heat, combine cream, tea leaves and granulated erythritol. Bring to a boil, stirring frequently, then remove from heat and let steep 30 minutes. Pour through a fine-mesh sieve into bowl to remove solids, pressing on solids to push as much liquid through as possible.

Pour ¹/₂ cup (125 mL) of the almond milk into another medium saucepan. Sprinkle with gelatin and let sit 3 minutes. Add remaining almond milk and heat on medium, stirring constantly. Cook until gelatin dissolves and steam begins to rise from the milk, but do not let it come to a boil.

Remove from heat and gently stir in cream mixture and stevia extract, OR equivalent. Divide among 6 lightly-greased, ³/₄-cup (175 mL) ramekins or custard cups. Refrigerate until set, about 4 hours.

To unmold, sit bottom of each ramekin in hot water for 30 seconds. Run sharp knife around inside of ramekin to loosen, and flip out onto plate. Serve with fresh berries or Strawberry Rhubarb Sauce, page 214.

Helpful Hints: You can use bagged tea, if necessary. Simply cut open the bags and proceed as directed. It is finer than loose leaf tea, so you may find a little more of the actual tea leaves come through into your panna cotta.

SNICKERDOODLE BLONDIES

One of my favorite readers, **Guiliana of Cooking By Correspondence**
*(http://cookingbycorrespondence.blogspot.com) took my recipe and improved on
it. She says they get even better after two to three days in the fridge.*

Blondies:
1$\frac{1}{2}$ cups almond flour (375 mL)
$\frac{1}{2}$ cup granulated erythritol (125 mL)
$\frac{1}{4}$ cup coconut flour (60 mL)
2 tsp ground cinnamon (10 mL)
1 tsp baking powder (5 mL)
$\frac{1}{2}$ tsp salt (2 mL)
$\frac{1}{4}$ tsp ground nutmeg (1 mL)
1 large egg
$\frac{1}{2}$ cup butter, melted and cooled (125 mL)
$\frac{1}{4}$ cup water (60 mL)
$\frac{1}{2}$ tsp vanilla extract (2 mL)
$\frac{1}{8}$ tsp stevia extract (0.5 mL), OR 2 tbsp equivalent (30 mL)

Topping:
1 tbsp granulated erythritol (15 mL)
1 tsp cinnamon (5 mL)

Yield: 16 servings
1 serving
131 calories
3 g protein
12 g fat
2 g net carbs

Blondies: In large bowl, whisk together almond flour, erythritol, coconut flour,
cinnamon, baking powder, salt and nutmeg. In medium bowl, whisk egg until
frothy, and then whisk in melted butter, water, vanilla extract and stevia extract,
OR equivalent.

Make well in center of almond flour mixture and slowly pour egg and butter
mixture into well. Stir gently until all ingredients are just combined. Batter will
be quite thick. Press batter into greased 8-inch (20 cm) square pan.

Bake in 325°F (160°C) oven 25 to 30 minutes, watching to make sure edges
don't brown too quickly.

Topping: In small bowl, whisk together granulated erythritol and cinnamon.
Sprinkle over bars while still hot from oven. Let bars cool completely before
cutting into squares.

CHOCOLATE COCONUT MILK PUDDING

This pudding is rich and creamy, with a slight hint of sweet coconut. Garnish
with toasted coconut and a macadamia nut for a tropical treat.

Pudding:
1, 14-oz can coconut milk, (414 mL)
 (NOT light)
$^1/_4$ cup granulated erythritol (60 mL)
3 large egg yolks
$^1/_2$ tsp xanthan gum (2 mL)
$^1/_4$ cup cocoa powder (60 mL)
1 oz unsweetened chocolate, chopped (30 g)
3 tbsp butter, in 3 pieces (45 mL)
$^1/_2$ tsp vanilla extract (2 mL)
$^1/_8$ tsp stevia extract (0.5 mL), OR 2 tbsp equivalent (30 mL)
Garnish:
$^1/_4$ cup whipping cream (60 mL)
1 tbsp powdered erythritol (15 mL)
2 tbsp flaked, unsweetened coconut, lightly toasted (30 mL)
4 macadamia nuts

Yield: 4 servings
1 serving
295 calories
6 g protein
29 g fat
5 g net carbs

Pudding: In medium saucepan over medium heat, combine coconut milk and granulated erythritol. Bring to a simmer, stirring occasionally.

In medium bowl, whisk egg yolks until smooth. Slowly add $^1/_2$ cup (125 mL) of hot coconut milk mixture into egg yolks, whisking continuously. Slowly whisk tempered egg yolks back into saucepan of hot coconut milk. Reduce heat to medium low and sprinkle with xanthan gum, whisking continuously. Stir in cocoa powder and cook until mixture thickens, about 3 to 4 minutes.

Remove from heat and stir in chopped chocolate and butter until smooth. Stir in vanilla extract and stevia extract, OR equivalent. Divide between 4 custard cups or ramekins and chill in refrigerator until set, 2 to 3 hours.

Garnish: In medium bowl, beat whipping cream and powdered erythritol until soft peaks form. Divide among prepared puddings and sprinkle with toasted coconut. Top each with one macadamia nut.

CRANBERRY UPSIDE DOWN CAKE

This cake was inspired by a recipe from Martha Stewart.

Topping:
1 tbsp butter, room temperature (15 mL)
2 tbsp granulated erythritol (30 mL)
$\frac{1}{2}$ tsp ground cinnamon (2 mL)
$\frac{1}{4}$ tsp allspice (1 mL)
1 cup fresh cranberries (250 mL)
$\frac{1}{3}$ cup chopped pecans (75 mL)

Cake:
2 cups almond flour (500 mL)
$\frac{1}{4}$ cup unflavored whey protein powder (60 mL)
1 tsp baking powder (5 mL)
$\frac{1}{2}$ tsp baking soda (2 mL)
$\frac{1}{4}$ tsp salt (1 mL)
$\frac{1}{3}$ cup butter, room temperature (75 mL)
$\frac{1}{3}$ cup granulated erythritol (75 mL)
2 large eggs, room temperature
$\frac{1}{2}$ tsp vanilla extract (2 mL)
$\frac{1}{4}$ tsp stevia extract (1 mL), OR $\frac{1}{4}$ cup equivalent (60 mL)
$\frac{1}{3}$ cup almond milk (75 mL)

Yield: 10 servings
1 serving
250 calories
8 g protein
22 g fat
4 g net carbs

Topping: Rub butter on bottom and sides of 8-inch (20 cm) round cake pan to coat thickly. In small bowl, mix granulated erythritol, cinnamon and allspice together and sprinkle over bottom of pan. Arrange cranberries and pecans in even layer on bottom of pan.

Cake: In medium bowl, whisk together almond flour, whey protein powder, baking powder, baking soda and salt. Set aside.

In large bowl, beat butter and granulated erythritol together until light and fluffy. Beat in eggs one at a time, scraping down beaters and sides of bowl as needed. Beat in vanilla extract and stevia extract, OR equivalent. Beat in half of almond flour mixture, then almond milk, and then remaining almond flour mixture until thoroughly combined. Spread batter carefully over topping in pan. Bake in 325°F (160°C) oven 45 to 50 minutes, or until cake is golden brown and a tester inserted in the center comes out clean.

Let cool in pan 10 minutes, and then run sharp knife around edges to loosen. Flip out onto serving plate.

VANESSA ROMERO
APPETIZERS AND BEVERAGES

HAZELNUT BRUSCHETTA WITH TOMATO, BASIL AND BLACK OLIVE SALSA

Traditional bruschetta is toasted French bread with garlic and olive oil. We can forgo the gluten and carbs by making our own tasty Bruschetta with a hazelnut twist. If hazelnut isn't your thing, use blanched almond flour.

Salsa:
3 plum tomatoes, chopped and seeded
$^1/_4$ cup chopped black olives (60 mL)
8 basil leaves, chopped
1 tbsp extra virgin olive oil (15 mL)
1 tsp balsamic vinegar (5 mL)
$^1/_4$ tsp salt (1 mL)
$^1/_4$ tsp black pepper (1 mL)

Hazelnut Bruschetta:
2 large eggs
$^1/_2$ cup hazelnut flour (125 mL)
$^1/_4$ cup golden flaxseed meal (60 mL)
1 tsp aluminum-free baking powder (5 mL)
$^1/_8$ tsp Celtic® sea salt (0.5 mL)
1 clove garlic
Extra virgin olive oil

Yield: 6 servings
2 bruschetta with salsa
114 calories
4.6 g protein
9.2 g fat
2.2 g fiber
1.8 g net carbs

Salsa: Mix together tomatoes, black olives, basil leaves, olive oil, vinegar, salt and pepper and refrigerate until ready for serving.

Bruschetta: In small bowl, whisk eggs together. In medium bowl, sift together hazelnut flour, flaxseed meal, baking powder and salt. Add eggs to dry ingredients and mix. Pour into a mini loaf pan sprayed with nonstick spray. Bake at 350°F (180°C) for 22 minutes.

Remove from oven and cool on wire rack. Slice bread into 12 slices and return to oven for 15 minutes or until dry and crisp, turning once.

Cut garlic in half and rub each piece of bruschetta, then brush with olive oil. Place bread on platter and salsa on the side for serving on top.

COCKTAIL FRANKS WITH CRANBERRY CHILI SAUCE

Classic holiday appetizer made healthy. Instead of buying high-fructose corn syrup-laden cranberries and chili sauce, make your own. It's easy and the guests at your party will never know the difference.

Cranberry Sauce:
12 oz fresh cranberries (375 g)
1 cup water (250 mL)
$^3/_4$ cup granulated erythritol, (175 mL)
$^1/_2$ tsp stevia extract powder, OR (2 mL)
  $^2/_3$ cup equivalent (150 mL)
Chili Sauce:
2 cups tomato sauce (500 mL)
$^1/_2$ cup vinegar (125 mL)
6 tbsp granulated erythritol (90 mL)
$1^1/_2$ tsp molasses (7 mL)
$^1/_2$ tsp cinnamon (2 mL)
$^1/_4$ tsp stevia extract powder, OR (1 mL)
  $^1/_3$ cup equivalent (75 mL)
$^1/_8$ tsp ground cloves (0.5 mL)
$^1/_8$ tsp allspice (0.5 mL)
$^1/_8$ tsp cayenne pepper (0.5 mL)
Franks
24 oz uncured beef cocktail franks (680 g)

Yield: 12 servings
4 cocktail franks with sauce
177.5 calories
7.9 g protein
12.0 g fat
1.4 g fiber
6.2 g net carbs

Cranberry Sauce: In medium saucepan on medium high heat, combine cranberries, water, erythritol and stevia, OR equivalent and cranberries. Cook cranberries until they all pop. Mash popped cranberries with a slotted spoon.

Chili Sauce: To cooked cranberries, whisk in tomato sauce, vinegar, erythritol, molasses, cinnamon, stevia, OR equivalent, cloves, allspice and cayenne pepper. Bring to a boil and then reduce temperature and simmer 30 minutes.

Franks: In slow cooker, combine cocktail franks and sauce. Cover and turn to low for one hour or until franks are hot.

Helpful Hint: This is a fantastic cranberry sauce that can also be used as an accompaniment for turkey or pork.

DAIRY-FREE MOCHA COFFEE COOLER

Add a scoop of your favorite protein powder to this coffee cooler and you have the perfect low-carb breakfast-on-the-go. Or turn it into an afternoon treat with a dollop of Dairy-Free Whipped Cream, page 263.

$^1/_2$ cup raw almonds (125 mL)
2 cups filtered water (500 mL)
4 cups cold strong brewed coffee (1 L)
$^1/_4$ cup dark cocoa powder (60 mL)
1 tsp vanilla extract (5 mL)
$^1/_8$ tsp Celtic® sea salt (0.5 mL)
$^1/_8$ tsp liquid vanilla stevia, OR (0.5 mL)
  2 tbsp equivalent (30 mL)

Yield: 4 servings
1 cup (250 mL) per serving
99.5 calories
3 g protein
7.5 g fat
4 g fiber
3 g net carbs

Place raw almonds in jar with lid. Fill jar with filtered water and cover. Soak almonds 8 hours or overnight. Drain and rinse and then place in high-powered blender. Add coffee to blender and blend on high for 3 minutes.

Line a fine mesh sieve with a clean, old t-shirt or kitchen towel and strain. Squeeze to remove all of the liquid and then discard pulp. Pour coffee cooler in quart (1 L) jar, add cocoa powder, vanilla, salt and stevia, OR equivalent, cover, and shake well. Chill until ready for use.

~~Bits & Bites~~
Recent research is showing trans fats and the inflammation it promotes in our bodies is what is most threatening to our overall health and well-being. Trans fats, commonly found in heavily processed foods, lower HDL and raise LDL levels. When reading labels, look for the word "hydrogenation" as this indicates trans fats are in the product.

SPARKLING CRANBERRY JUICE

Among the fruits richest in health-promoting antioxidants, cranberries rank right up there at the top. According to Rui Hai Liu, M.D., Ph.D., a leader in the area of cranberry research, "Cranberry extracts have been shown to exhibit potent antioxidant activity, inhibit LDL oxidation and have anti-bacterial and anti-cancer activities. The phytochemicals present in cranberries, especially phenolics and flavonoids, appear responsible for these health benefits."

Cranberry Syrup:
4 cups water (1 L)
12 oz fresh or frozen cranberries (375 g)
Sparkling Cranberry Juice:
8 to 10 fl. oz club soda (250 to 300 mL)
2 fl. oz Cranberry Syrup (60 mL)
$^1/_8$ tsp liquid stevia, OR (0.5 mL)
  2 tbsp equivalent (30 mL)

> *Yield:* 20 servings
> 2 fl. oz syrup per serving
> 8 calories
> 0 g protein
> 0 g fat
> *2 g net carbs*

Cranberry Syrup: In medium saucepan on medium high, combine water and cranberries. Cook cranberries until they all pop. Mash popped cranberries with a slotted spoon and remove from heat. Let stand for 5 minutes. Pour cranberries into high-powered blender and blend on high 1 minute. Strain syrup through a fine mesh sieve, cool on counter in glass jar. Cover and refrigerate.

Sparkling Cranberry Juice: Fill a pint glass with ice and combine club soda, Cranberry Syrup and stevia, OR equivalent, stir and enjoy.

CRANBERRY MARGARITA

You can really impress your friends with a complete low-carb fiesta. Serve up Carnitas, page 260, Mexican Cauli-Rice, page 261, a side of Refried Beans with Bacon, page 261, and top it off with this tasty Cranberry Margarita.

2 fl. oz Cranberry Syrup, page 249 (60 mL)
$1^1/_2$ fl. oz tequila (45 mL)
1 fl. oz fresh lime juice (30 mL)
$^1/_4$ tsp pure orange extract (1 mL)
$^1/_8$ tsp liquid stevia, OR (0.5 mL)
  2 tbsp equivalent (30 mL)
Club soda

> *Yield:* 1 margarita
> 1 serving
> 113 calories
> 0 g protein
> 0 g fat
> *4.6 g net carbs*

In cocktail shaker, stir together Cranberry Syrup, in recipe above, tequila, lime juice, orange extract and stevia, OR equivalent. Pour in club soda and gently stir. Fill Margarita glass with ice and pour mixture over top.

SALADS AND SOUPS

BROCCOLI AND BACON SALAD

This is a very pretty holiday salad with the green broccoli and red cranberries. It's a family classic I made low-carb by using sugar-free cranberries instead of raisins and alternative sweetener.

Mayonnaise Dressing:
1 cup mayonnaise, page 264 (250 mL)
2 tbsp white vinegar (30 mL)
3 tbsp granulated erythritol, (45 mL)
 powdered
$^1/_8$ tsp stevia extract powder (0.5 mL)
 OR $2^1/_2$ tbsp equivalent (37 mL)
Salad:
1 lb bacon (0.45 kg)
2 large heads of broccoli
$^1/_4$ cup purple onion, diced (60 mL)
$^1/_2$ cup hulled and salted sunflower seeds (125 mL)
$^1/_2$ cup sugar-free dried cranberries (125 mL)

Yield: 8 servings
$^1/_2$ cup (125 mL) per serving
156.8 calories
7.3 g protein
10.8 g fat
3.6 g fiber
5.8 g net carbs

Mayonnaise Dressing: In small mixing bowl, whisk together mayonnaise and vinegar. In a coffee grinder, add erythritol granules and stevia, OR equivalent and pulse until powdered. Mix sweeteners with mayonnaise and vinegar and set aside.

Salad: In cast iron skillet over medium heat, fry bacon. Once cool cut into bits. While bacon is frying, chop broccoli and onion. In serving bowl, combine broccoli, onion and dressing and refrigerate for one hour. Mix in bacon, sunflower seeds and cranberries before serving.

Helpful Hints: Sugar-free, dried cranberries are hard to find. You can source them on the internet or make your own. You can find a pictorial for making sugar-free, dried cranberries on my blog, www.healthylivinghowto.com.

Editor's note: Also find, Cranberry Raisins on page 128.

SLOW COOKER BEEF STEW

Great for the cold days of fall and winter! This is marvelous over top of a heaping pile of Garlic Mashed Fauxtatoes, page 262 and topped with a dollop of Dairy-Free Sour Cream, page 266.

4 lbs beef chuck roast, cubed (1.8 kg)
4 large carrots, sliced
4 large celery stalks, sliced
1 medium onion, chopped
8 oz tomato sauce (250 g)
4 cups water (1 L)
2 tbsp tapioca starch (30 mL)
2 tsp Celtic® sea salt (10 mL)
1 tsp black pepper (5 mL)

Yield: 8 servings
1 cup (250 mL) per serving
340 calories
46 g protein
11 g fat
1.8 g fiber
8.4 g net carbs

To slow cooker, add cubed roast, carrots, celery and onion. In medium bowl, whisk together tomato sauce, water, tapioca, salt and pepper and pour over roast and vegetables. Cover and cook on high 5 hours.

SLOW COOKER CHICKEN TACO SOUP

Top this Taco Soup with a Mexican flair with avocado slices, Dairy-Free Sour Cream, page 266 and an oven-toasted Tortilla, page 268 on the side.

4 cups Chicken Bone Broth, page 252 (1 L)
1 cup salsa (250 mL)
8 oz tomato paste (250 g)
$^1/_2$ cup onions, diced (125 mL)
1 clove garlic, crushed
1 tbsp chili powder (15 mL)
$1^1/_2$ tsp ground cumin (7 mL)
1 tsp Celtic® sea salt (5 mL)
1 tsp black pepper (5 mL)
$^1/_2$ tsp paprika (2 mL)
$^1/_4$ tsp garlic powder (1 mL)
$^1/_4$ tsp onion powder (1 mL)
$^1/_4$ tsp crushed red pepper flakes (1 mL)
$^1/_4$ tsp dried oregano (1 mL)
2 lbs boneless skinless chicken thighs (0.9 kg)

Yield: 6 servings
1 cup (250 mL) per serving
268.6 calories
30 g protein
11.3 g fat
3 g fiber
8.5 g net carbs

In large bowl whisk together Chicken Bone Broth, page 252, salsa, tomato paste, onions, garlic, chili powder, cumin, salt, black pepper, paprika, garlic powder, onion powder, red pepper flakes and oregano. Place chicken thighs in bottom of slow cooker and top with liquid. Cover and cook on low 8 hours. Remove chicken thighs, shred and return to slow cooker.

TRADITIONAL CHICKEN BONE BROTH

Research supports what grandmothers everywhere have known for ages, chicken soup is rich in medicinal properties. It promotes healing, supports digestion, contains highly absorbable minerals (calcium, magnesium, potassium), bolsters bone and joint healing, aids in detoxification and supports the immune system. This liquid gold is truly medicine and the best part is you can't overdose on it and it carries no ill side effects!

3 to 5 lb whole chicken carcass (1.4 to 2.3 kg) (including skin, meat remnants and cooking juices)
2 stalks celery
2 whole carrots, roughly chopped
$^1/_2$ medium yellow onion, sliced
1 garlic clove
1 tbsp Celtic® sea salt (15 mL)
8 to 12 cups cold water (2 to 3 L)
1 tbsp apple cider vinegar (15 mL)

Yield: varies
8 fl. oz (250 mL) per serving
26.0 calories
1.0 g protein
2.0 g fat
0.0 g fiber
1.0 g net carbs

Into a stock pot, slow cooker or pressure cooker place whole chicken carcass, celery, carrots, onion, garlic and sea salt. Add enough cold water until chicken carcass is fully submerged. Add apple cider vinegar.

Stock Pot Method: Bring to boil, turn to low, cover and simmer for 12 hours.

Slow Cooker Method: Cover, cook on high for 2 hours, turn to low and simmer for a total of 12 hours.

Pressure Cooker Method: Bring to high pressure, turn to low and set timer for 1 hour.

Strain broth into glass jars, let come to room temperature, cover and then refrigerate overnight. Skim hardened fat off top.

~~Bits and Bites~~
Fat is a precursor to many essential hormones in the body and a component of all cell membranes. Our body needs fat to be healthy.

BREAKFASTS

SCOTCH EGGS

These are a fun breakfast to make on the weekends. Spicy sausage and hard-boiled egg combined into one, with a light breading on the outside. On the side have a palate-cleansing bowl of fresh berries with a splash of coconut milk.

Sausage:
1 lb ground pork (0.45 kg)
1 tsp Celtic® sea salt (5 mL)
1 tsp sage (5 mL)
1 tsp thyme (5 mL)
1 tsp paprika (5 mL)
1 tsp black pepper (5 mL)
$^1/_2$ tsp cayenne pepper (2 mL)
$^1/_2$ tsp nutmeg (2 mL)
4 hard-boiled eggs, peeled

Breading:
$^1/_2$ cup coarse ground almond meal (125 mL)
2 tbsp coconut flour (30 mL)
2 large eggs

> **Yield:** 4 servings
> 1 Scotch egg
> 346.5 calories
> 28 g protein
> 24.6 g fat
> 2.1 g fiber
> *1.8 g net carbs*

Sausage: In medium mixing bowl, using your hand, mix together pork, salt, sage, thyme, paprika, black pepper, cayenne pepper and nutmeg. Divide sausage into 4 equal portions.

Make a patty with sausage and then place hard-boiled egg in center and wrap sausage evenly around egg.

Breading: In pie plate, mix together almond meal and coconut flour. In separate small bowl, whisk together eggs. Roll Scotch egg in whisked egg and then roll in almond-coconut mixture.

Place on parchment-lined baking sheet. Repeat until all 4 Scotch eggs are coated with breading. Bake at 375°F (190°C) 25 minutes and then increase oven temperature to 400°F (200°C) and continue baking until coating is lightly browned.

SUPERFOOD GRANOLA

Looking for a low-carb breakfast alternative to eggs and bacon, then give this superfood granola a try. High in fiber and loaded with nutrients, this will keep you going well past lunchtime.

$^1/_2$ oz raw cacao nibs (15 g)
$^1/_2$ oz unsweetened coconut flakes (15 g)
$^1/_2$ oz chia seeds (15 g)
$^1/_2$ oz sunflower seeds, hulled (15 g)
$^1/_2$ oz hemp seeds (15 g)
$^1/_2$ cup unsweetened almond milk (125 mL)
5 drops liquid stevia, OR
  1 tsp equivalent (5 mL)
1 oz wild blueberries (30 g)

Yield: 1 serving
1 serving
447 calories
15.3 g protein
35.4 g fat
15.2 g fiber
7.3 g net carbs

Place a cereal-sized bowl on kitchen scale and measure out cacao nibs, coconut flakes, chia seeds, sunflower seeds and hemp seeds individually. Add unsweetened almond milk and stevia, OR equivalent. Finally top with blueberries and enjoy.

ZUCCHINI HASH ROUNDS

Zucchini is a delicious and versatile low-carb vegetable. Ditch the starchy potatoes at breakfast and instead make zucchini hash rounds. For a double dose of zucchini make a batch of Double Dark Chocolate Muffins, page 267 to go along with your eggs and hash rounds.

1 large egg
$^1/_4$ tsp garlic powder (1 mL)
$^1/_4$ tsp onion powder (1 mL)
$^1/_8$ tsp Celtic® sea salt (0.5 mL)
$^1/_8$ tsp black pepper (0.5 mL)
1 cup zucchini rounds (250 mL)
2 tbsp bacon grease (30 mL)

Yield: 4 servings
1 hash round
81.7 calories
2 g protein
7.7 g fat
0.3 g fiber
1 g net carbs

In small bowl, whisk together egg, garlic powder, onion powder, salt and pepper. Add zucchini and mix well. In medium skillet over medium high heat, melt bacon grease. Spoon four equal-sized zucchini rounds into skillet and cook, turning once brown. Sprinkle with a little additional salt and serve.

BREAKFAST SAUSAGE

Who needs the convenience of prepackaged breakfast sausage full of unhealthy ingredients, when making your own is not only easy but also healthier? These sausage patties are just the perfect size to be tucked inside an easy breakfast biscuit (recipe above).

1 lb ground pork (0.45 kg)
1 tsp Celtic® sea salt (5 mL)
1 tsp sage (5 mL)
1 tsp thyme (5 mL)
1 tsp paprika (5 mL)
1 tsp black pepper (5 mL)
$^1/_2$ tsp cayenne pepper (2 mL)
$^1/_2$ tsp nutmeg (2 mL)

Yield: 12 patties
1 sausage
77.5 calories
6.7 g protein
5.5 g fat
0.2 g fiber
0.4 g net carbs

In large bowl, add ground pork. In small bowl, measure and mix together salt, sage, thyme, paprika, black pepper, cayenne pepper and nutmeg and then add to ground pork. With hands, mix spices and pork together. Form into 12 equal-size patties. In cast iron skillet, over medium high heat, pan fry 3 to 4 minutes per side or until no longer pink in the center.

~~Bits & Bites~~
Ample protein and fat in one's diet leads to increased satiety and therefore, encourages decreased cravings for excessive carbohydrate consumption.

MAIN COURSES AND SIDES

SKILLET LAMB AND CABBAGE WITH SUN-DRIED TOMATOES

This Greek-inspired dish is reminiscent of a Gyro and its fragrant spices. It's not necessary to dirty the dishes to make this meal as it all goes in one skillet. A dollop of Dairy-Free Sour cream, page 266 is the perfect topping.

1 lb ground lamb (0.45 kg)
2 tsp Celtic® sea salt (10 mL)
$1^1/_2$ tsp parsley (7 mL)
$1^1/_2$ tsp dill (7 mL)
$1^1/_2$ tsp oregano (7 mL)
1 tsp black pepper (5 mL)
$^3/_4$ tsp coriander (3 mL)
$^3/_4$ tsp cumin (3 mL)
4 cups cabbage, chopped (1 L)
$^1/_4$ cup yellow onion, chopped (60 mL)
1 tbsp Dijon mustard (15 mL)
2 cloves garlic, crushed
$1^1/_2$ oz sun dried tomatoes, chopped (45 g)
$^1/_4$ cup sliced black olives (60 mL)

Yield: 4 servings
1 serving
277.7 calories
21.3 g protein
17.1 g fat
3.7 g fiber
6.8 g net carbs

To large skillet, add ground lamb and cut up into chunks. Top lamb with salt, parsley, dill, oregano, black pepper, coriander and cumin and then top with cabbage and onion. Cover skillet and cook over medium high heat for 5 minutes until it begins to steam and the steam starts to soften the cabbage.

Remove cover and mix cabbage and lamb, cooking until cabbage is soft, about another 5 minutes. Once cooking is complete, mix in mustard and crushed garlic and top with sun dried tomatoes and black olives.

~~Bits & Bites~~
Spices and herbs often have more antioxidants than fruits and vegetables. Eating food rich in antioxidants is an important part of being healthy. In fact, Dr. Bharat B. Aggarwal, Professor of Cancer Research at the University of Texas, says, "Countless studies have linked culinary spices to the prevention and treatment of more than 150 health problems."

CRUNCHY TURKEY MEATBALLS WITH ASIAN DIPPING SAUCE

The sauce for these meatballs is so amazing; you will want to make it again and again. Try it over Oven-Baked Chicken Thighs, page 259. This dish is excellent alongside a pan of cauliflower fried rice, using toasted sesame oil to fry it in, add a little crushed garlic, soy sauce and some green onions.

Turkey Meatballs:
1$^1/_2$ lbs ground turkey, dark meat (680 g)
1 large egg
8 oz canned water chestnuts, drained (250 g)
  and chopped
1 tsp Celtic® sea salt (5 mL)
1 tsp sage (5 mL)
1 tsp thyme (5 mL)
1 tsp paprika (5 mL)
1 tsp black pepper (5 mL)
$^1/_2$ tsp cayenne pepper (2 mL)
$^1/_2$ tsp nutmeg (2 mL)
Asian Dipping Sauce:
3 tbsp almond butter (45 mL)
1 tbsp white vinegar (15 mL)
1 tbsp gluten-free soy sauce (15 mL)
1 tbsp water (15 mL)
1 tbsp toasted sesame oil (15 mL)
1 tbsp sriracha sauce (15 mL)
$^1/_4$ tsp ground ginger (1 mL)
5 drops liquid stevia, OR 1 tsp equivalent* (5 mL)

Yield: 4 servings
3 meatballs with sauce
387.2 calories
23.3 g protein
27.6 g fat
4.1 g fiber
6.3 g net carbs

Meatballs: In large mixing bowl, with your hands, combine turkey, egg, water chestnuts, salt, sage, thyme, paprika, black pepper, cayenne pepper and nutmeg. Roll into 12 equal-size balls. Place each ball in a regular-size muffin tin and bake at 375°F (190°C) 20 to 22 minutes.

Asian Dipping Sauce: While meatballs are baking, whisk together almond butter, vinegar, soy sauce, water, sesame oil, sriracha sauce, ginger and stevia, OR equivalent. Serve alongside meatballs.

Helpful Hints: If sauce is too thick, thin out with a little extra water. Thickness is going to depend on brand of almond butter. *Add stevia, OR equivalent to taste to the Asian Dipping Sauce.

OVEN-BAKED SALMON WITH RAINBOW SALSA

Food not only nourishes our body, it can be a work of art. Bell peppers come in all colors and when made into a simple salsa, it livens up just about any dish. Try this salsa with your morning eggs or with Oven-Baked Chicken Thighs, page 259. It is delicious.

Oven-Baked Salmon:
1$^1/_2$ lbs wild salmon filets (680 g)
Celtic® sea salt, to taste
Black pepper, to taste
Rainbow Salsa:
$^1/_2$ cup red bell pepper, diced (125 mL)
$^1/_2$ cup yellow bell pepper, diced (125 mL)
$^1/_2$ cup orange bell pepper, diced (125 mL)
$^1/_2$ cup purple bell pepper, diced (125 mL)
$^1/_2$ cup cilantro, chopped (125 mL)
$^1/_4$ cup yellow onion, minced (60 mL)
1 medium California avocado, diced
1 clove garlic, crushed
1 tsp Celtic® sea salt (5 mL)
Half a lime, juiced

Yield: 6 servings
1 serving
218.2 calories
25.5g protein
7.3 g fat
2.5 g fiber
2.8 g net carbs

Salmon: Place salmon, skin side down, on a baking sheet lined with parchment paper. If desired, season with a little salt and pepper to taste. Bake at 400°F (200°C) 12 to15 minutes, depending on thickness of salmon filets.

Rainbow Salsa: In medium bowl, combine red, yellow, orange and purple bell peppers, cilantro, onion and avocado. Mix garlic, salt and lime juice with veggies and chill. Top each salmon filet with salsa and serve.

~~Bits & Bites~~
Research available today on low-carb living clearly shows a benefit for health, weight management and even certain types of performance enhancement. However, it only works when it's followed on a daily basis. To be effective, low-carbing needs to be a lifestyle, not a diet.

OVEN-BAKED CHICKEN THIGHS WITH BUTTERY BUFFALO SAUCE

Did you know celery is an excellent source of Vitamin K, a fat-soluble vitamin that allows your blood to clot, protects bones from fracture, prevents bone loss and calcification of the arteries? Quick and delicious describes this meal and an easy way to eat more celery. If you want to really indulge, make a side of Dairy-Free Ranch Dressing, page 266 and double dip.

Oven Baked Chicken Thighs:
Celtic® sea salt,
Black pepper
$1^1/_2$ lbs boneless skinless chicken (680 g) thighs
Buttery Buffalo Sauce:
$^1/_3$ cup red hot sauce (75 mL)
$^1/_3$ cup Ghee, page 265 (75 mL)
2 tbsp xylitol honey (30 mL)
1 tbsp Worcestershire sauce (15 mL)
Garnish
4 celery stalks

Yield: 4 servings
1 serving
410.5 calories
32.4 g protein
30.5 g fat
0 g fiber
0 g net carbs

Oven Baked Chicken Thighs: Salt and pepper chicken thighs, to taste. In a large ovenproof baking dish, bake chicken thighs at 375°F (190°C) 40 minutes.

Buttery Buffalo Sauce: In small saucepan over medium heat, whisk together red hot sauce, Ghee, page 265, honey and Worcestershire until melted and well combined. Turn to low and keep warm, whisking periodically. Before serving, brush baked thighs with sauce and serve remaining sauce on the side for dipping.

Garnish with celery sticks.

~~Bits & Bites~~
The real goal is to change how you view food. If you look at something and say, "That's going to make me feel good. I want that," your brain's going to get activated. If you look at it and say, "Ugh, that's disgusting. I'd rather have something else," your brain's not going to be activated. You have to take the power out of the food by changing how you view the stimulus. ~ David A. Kessler, MD, Former Commissioner of the FDA and author of the book, The End of Overeating.

259

PULLED PORK CARNITAS

For a complete Mexican meal, pair these pulled pork carnitas with Mexican Cauli-Rice, page 261, a dollop or two of Dairy-Free Sour Cream, page 266 and some Refried Beans With Bacon, page 261. If you are feeling really indulgent have a Cranberry Margarita, page 249 to wash it down.

Pork Roast:
2 cups water (500 mL)
1 tsp hickory liquid smoke (5 mL)
1 bay leaf
3 lbs boneless pork shoulder roast (1.4 kg)
Seasonings:
1 tbsp chili powder (15 mL)
1 tsp Celtic® sea salt (5 mL)
1 tsp garlic powder (5 mL)
1 tsp onion powder (5 mL)
$^1/_2$ tsp dried oregano (2 mL)
$^1/_4$ tsp cinnamon (1 mL)

Yield: 6 servings
4 oz (125 g) per serving
139.8 calories
28.9 g protein
15.5 g fat
0.6 g fiber
0.9 g net carbs

There are three different methods to cook the pork roast.

Pressure Cooker: In pressure cooker, place water, liquid smoke and bay leaf. Add trivet to bottom of pressure cooker and then the steamer basket. Cut roast into large chunks. Set meat in steamer basket, cover cooker, bring to high pressure then reduce temperature and cook for 55 minutes.

Slow Cooker: In slow cooker, reduce water to 1 cup (250 mL), and add liquid smoke, bay leaf and pork roast. Cover and cook on low 8 hours.

Oven Method: In roasting pan, reduce water to 1 cup (250 mL), and add liquid smoke, bay leaf and pork roast. Cover with foil and bake at 275°F (135°C) 8 hours.

Seasonings: While pork is cooking, in small bowl, measure and mix chili powder, Celtic® sea salt, garlic powder, onion powder, oregano and cinnamon. Once pork is cooked, place in serving dish and shred with fork. Add about $^1/_4$ cup (60 mL) of reserved liquid and spices and mix well.

REFRIED BEANS WITH BACON

Low-carb doesn't necessarily mean no-carb. Sometimes we don't have to give up our starchy favorites if we pay attention to serving size. While a $^1/_4$ cup (60 mL) of beans doesn't sound like much, these are so flavorful that a small amount will do. Try some refried beans inside a Mexican-style omelet topped with salsa and Dairy-Free Sour Cream, page 266.

2 medium strips bacon
15 oz can pinto beans (425 g)
1 clove garlic, crushed
1 tbsp bacon grease (15 mL)
$^1/_2$ tsp Celtic® sea salt (2 mL)

> **Yield:** 5 servings
> $^1/_4$ cup (60 mL) per serving
> 105 calories
> 5.3 g protein
> 4.6 g fat
> 4.2 g fiber
> **8.4 g net carbs**

In cast iron skillet over medium heat, cook bacon until crisp, reserving bacon grease. Chop bacon into bits and set aside. Add pinto beans, crushed garlic and salt to bacon grease and heat on medium high. As beans heat up, with a potato masher, smash beans until desired consistency. Stir in bacon bits and serve.

MEXICAN CAULI-RICE

My Mexican grandmother spoke very little English, could not read or write, but boy could she cook. Mexican rice was a staple in all of her dishes. I watched my grandmother make rice many times; she'd throw white rice in a pan with lard and brown it, then add water, onions, garlic and tomatoes. Never used a measuring cup or spoon, just her hands, and every batch was as good as the next. This rice is the perfect accompaniment to Carnitas, page 260.

1 large head cauliflower
1 tbsp non-hydrogenated lard (15 mL)
1 medium tomato, chopped
$^1/_4$ cup yellow onion, chopped (60 mL)
3 to 4 tbsp chili powder (45 to 60 mL)
1 tsp Celtic® sea salt (5 mL)
1 clove garlic, crushed

> **Yield:** 6 servings
> $^1/_2$ cup (125 mL) per serving
> 63.4 calories
> 2.6 g protein
> 2.9 g fat
> 4 g fiber
> **4.6 g net carbs**

Remove core from cauliflower and with a box grater, grate flowerettes down to the stem. In cast iron skillet over high heat, melt lard and add cauliflower. Fry cauliflower rice, stirring frequently, until it is starting to lightly brown, and then turn heat to medium high. Add chopped tomato, onion, chili powder, salt and garlic. Cook until cauliflower rice is soft.

GARLIC MASHED FAUXTATOES

I had the opportunity to go on the 2012 Low-Carb Cruise
www.lowcarbcruiseinfo.com. At our pre-sail dinner we had the most amazing
low-carb fauxtatoes made with cauliflower and celeriac root. There is just
something about adding the celeriac root that lends not only a starchier
consistency but a more potato-like mouth feel. Give these a go with a dollop of
Dairy-Free Sour Cream, page 266.

1 large head cauliflower
2 cups celeriac root, peeled (500 mL)
  and chopped
$^1/_4$ to $^1/_2$ cup Chicken Bone (60 to 125 mL)
  Broth, page 252
2 tbsp Ghee, page 265 (30 mL)
1 tsp Celtic® sea salt (5 mL)
1 clove garlic, crushed

Yield: 6 servings
$^1/_2$ cup (125 mL) per serving
63.4 calories
2.6 g protein
2.9 g fat
4 g fiber
4.6 g net carbs

Remove core from cauliflower, cut into flowerettes and in pressure cooker or vegetable steamer, steam until tender. With a vegetable peeler, peel celeriac root and chop into 1-inch (2.5 cm) chunks. In pressure cooker or vegetable steamer, steam celeriac until tender. This takes longer than the cauliflower, so do them separately. In high-powdered blender or food processor, add steamed vegetables, $^1/_4$ cup (60 mL) hot Chicken Bone Broth, page 252, Ghee, page 265, salt and garlic and process on high until creamy. You can add an additional $^1/_4$ cup (60 mL) of broth, if necessary.

Helpful Hint: I use a pressure cooker to steam my vegetables, but a vegetable steamer works just fine.

~~Bits & Bites~~
A diet full of natural foods with little to no adulteration lays the foundation for optimal health and well-being.

MISCELLAENOUS

DAIRY-FREE WHIPPED CREAM

*This recipe was originally created by **Patty** at www.followingmynose.com as a dairy-free alternative to coffee creamer. After making it several times, I got the idea to get out my iSi® Cream Whipper and see if I could make whipped cream. Amazingly, it worked. The only change I made to the original recipe was adding some stevia to sweeten it up.*

13.5 oz can coconut milk (400 mL)
2 tbsp extra virgin coconut oil (30 mL)
1 large egg
1 tsp vanilla extract (5 mL)
$^1/_8$ tsp liquid stevia, (0.5 mL)
   OR 2 tbsp equivalent (30 mL)

Yield: 32 servings
2 tbsp (30 mL) per serving
32.4 calories
0.2 g protein
3.2 g fat
0 g fiber
0.7 g net carbs

To a high-powered blender, add coconut milk, coconut oil, egg, vanilla extract and liquid stevia, OR equivalent. Blend on highest speed for 30 seconds, no more, no less. Pour cream into iSi® Cream Whipper and charge. Before dispensing, refrigerate for 8 hours or until well chilled.

Helpful Hint: If you don't have a cream whipper, you can still make this recipe. After blending, pour into pint jar, cover and place in refrigerator to thicken.

~~Bits and Bites~~
Leptin is a hormone that signals us that we're full. Studies show leptin is elevated in many overweight individuals, which means they may become leptin resistant the way they become resistant to insulin. The body keeps secreting the hormone to say, "hey, you don't need to eat anymore." Yet, the brain doesn't get the signal. There are many theories around this phenomenon, including the idea that processed foods may block leptin signaling.

DAIRY-FREE ALMOND CREAM CHEESE

Dairy-free cream cheese alternative that is great smeared on Double Chocolate Zucchini muffins, page 267 or sweetened up and used as a frosting for Gingerbread Men Cookies, page 271.

1 cup raw almonds (250 mL)
$^1/_3$ cup water, PLUS more for (75 mL)
  soaking and blanching
2 tbsp extra-virgin coconut oil (30 mL)
1 tsp apple cider vinegar (5 mL)
1 tsp lemon juice (5 mL)
$^1/_2$ tsp Celtic® sea salt (2 mL)

> *Yield:* $1^1/_2$ cups (375 mL)
> 2 tbsp (30 mL) per serving
> 88.1 calories
> 2.5 g protein
> 8.3 g fat
> 1.4 g fiber
> *1.0 g net carbs*

Place almonds in glass jar with lid, fill with water, cover and let soak for 8 hours. Rinse and drain. Blanch soaked almonds by pouring near-boiling water on them and letting sit for 10 minutes. Remove skins by pinching almonds between your fingers. To high-powered blender or food processor, add blanched almonds, $^1/_3$ cup (75 mL) water, coconut oil, apple cider vinegar, lemon juice and salt and process until smooth.

MAYONNAISE

If you want a healthy dressing or mayonnaise that tastes better than store bought with soybean oil, then you are going to have to make it yourself. Don't despair; it is really quite simple to do. Your efforts will be rewarded with great health, less inflammation and a yummy salad dressing.

1 cup extra light olive oil, divided (250 mL)
1 large egg
2 tbsp white vinegar (30 mL)
$^1/_2$ tsp dry mustard (2 mL)
$^1/_4$ tsp Celtic® sea salt (1 mL)
$^1/_8$ tsp cayenne pepper (0.5 mL)
5 drops liquid stevia, OR
  1 tsp equivalent (5 mL)

> *Yield:* 20 servings
> 1 tbsp (15 mL) per serving
> 99 calories
> 0 g protein
> 11 g fat
> 0 g fiber
> *0 g net carbs*

In a high-powered blender, add $^1/_4$ cup (60 mL) olive oil, egg, vinegar, mustard, salt and cayenne pepper. Cover and remove center cap from blender. Turn on high and as slowly as possible, pour in remaining oil in a thin and steady stream until emulsion forms and mayonnaise is complete. Transfer mayonnaise to a glass jar with lid and stir in stevia to taste.

Helpful Hint: The key to making mayonnaise is to make sure all ingredients are at room temperature.

GHEE

For those of us allergic or sensitive to bovine dairy, ghee is the alternative to butter. Ghee is simply butter with the allergenic proteins, casein and whey, removed. What's left behind is the butter fat, rich in butyric acid, which is amazing for calming inflammation in the gut.

1 lb unsalted organic grass fed butter (0.45 kg)

Yield: 75 servings
1 tsp (5 mL) per serving
45.0 calories
0.0 g protein
5.0 g fat
0.0 g fiber
0.0 g net carbs

In stainless steel pot, place butter and over medium heat, slowly melt the butter.

Once all the butter is melted, there will be three layers forming; a foamy layer on top, a butterfat layer in the middle and solids that start to fall to the bottom.

The butter will then start to erupt like little volcanoes. Turn heat down to medium low.

When butter is done erupting, it should be at a low boil. Foam will temporarily dissipate; however, more is going to appear on the top of the surface. Swirl butter around and take note of milk solids that have settled to bottom of pan.

With a spoon, remove the foam. Check bottom of the pan; the milk solids should be brown.

When most of the foam has been removed and no more is forming, remove the butter from the heat.

Place a small mesh sieve over a heat-proof container. Line the sieve with a kitchen "flour" towel, then pour the ghee, slowly, into the sieve.

Transfer ghee to glass container with a lid. Cover once it has come to room temperature and solidified. Ghee will last 6 months or longer and does not require refrigeration.

Helpful Hint: Not as a hard and fast rule, but to give you a general idea of when your ghee should be done, set your kitchen timer for 30 minutes.

DAIRY-FREE SOUR CREAM

Since finding out I am sensitive to bovine-derived dairy, I've been longing for sour cream. Would you believe me if I told you, you can easily make your own healthy dairy-free sour cream with just two ingredients? Piled atop a bowl of Mexican Cauli-Rice Rice page 261, Carnitas, page 260 and diced avocados, it is simply too amazing for words.

13.5 oz. can coconut milk (400mL)
2 tbsp white vinegar (30 mL)

Yield: 8 servings
1 tbsp (15 mL) per serving
22.5 calories
0 g protein
2.5 g fat
0 g fiber
0 g net carbs

Refrigerate full can of coconut milk for an hour or two (be careful not to shake). Open can and scoop out the hardened coconut cream on the top, about a $^1/_2$ cup (125 mL). With a spoon, mix well, coconut cream and vinegar. Return to refrigerator for an hour. Stir before serving.

DAIRY-FREE RANCH DRESSING

Did you know there really was a "Hidden Valley Ranch"? It was a resort in California, owned by Steve and Gayle Henson, the place where ranch dressing was invented. Steve Henson's simple mixture of mayonnaise, buttermilk and herbs has become our favorite way to liven up lettuce.

1 tbsp white vinegar (15 mL)
1 cup canned coconut milk (250 mL)
$^1/_2$ cup Mayonnaise, page 264 (125 mL)
$^1/_2$ tsp dried chives (2 mL)
$^1/_2$ tsp dried parsley (2 mL)
$^1/_2$ tsp dried dill weed (2 mL)
$^1/_4$ tsp onion powder (1 mL)
$^1/_4$ tsp garlic powder (1 mL)
$^1/_8$ tsp Celtic® sea salt (0.5 mL)
$^1/_8$ tsp black pepper (0.5 mL)

Yield: 12 servings
2 tbsp (30 mL) per serving
100.1 calories
0.1 g protein
10.5 g fat
0 g fiber
1.3 g net carbs

In a 1-cup (250 mL) measuring cup, add 1 tbsp (15 mL) vinegar and then fill to the top with coconut milk. Let stand for 5 minutes. In medium bowl, whisk together coconut milk, Mayonnaise, page 264, chives, parsley, dill weed, onion powder, garlic powder, salt and pepper. Pour into a pint jar with a lid. Refrigerate for at least an hour before serving.

BREADS, MUFFINS AND MORE

DOUBLE CHOCOLATE ZUCCHINI MUFFINS

Split these muffins in half and slather with Ghee, page 265 for a wonderful breakfast treat.

$^1/_2$ cup golden flaxseed meal (125 mL)
$^1/_4$ cup coconut flour (60 mL)
$^1/_4$ cup granulated erythritol (60 mL)
2 tbsp dark cocoa powder (30 mL)
1 tsp aluminum-free baking powder (5 mL)
$^1/_4$ tsp Celtic® sea salt (1 mL)
$^1/_8$ tsp cinnamon (0.5 mL)
$^1/_8$ tsp nutmeg (0.5 mL)
$^1/_8$ tsp ground cloves (0.5 mL)
$^1/_8$ tsp stevia extract powder (0.5 mL), OR $2^1/_2$ tbsp equivalent (37 mL)
$^1/_2$ cup zucchini, grated and packed (125 mL)
2 large eggs, room temperature
$^1/_4$ cup warm water (60 mL)
2 tbsp extra-virgin coconut oil, melted (30 mL)
$^1/_2$ tsp vanilla extract (2 mL)
1 oz 65% dark chocolate chips, (30 g)
(optional)

> **Yield:** 6 muffins
> 1 muffin per serving
> 122 calories
> 5.8 g protein
> 8.8 g fat
> 6.2 g fiber
> **3.3 g net carbs**

In medium mixing bowl, sift together flaxseed meal, coconut flour, erythritol, cocoa powder, baking powder, salt cinnamon, nutmeg, cloves, and stevia, OR equivalent and set aside. In small bowl, whisk together zucchini, eggs, water, coconut oil and vanilla extract.

Mix wet ingredients into dry ingredients, eliminating all clumps and stir in chocolate chips. Divide batter evenly between six muffin tins, lined and sprayed with nonstick spray. Bake at 350°F (180°C) 25 minutes. Cool, serve and enjoy.

~~Bits & Bites~~
Zucchini is the best known of the summer squashes. It resembles the cucumber in size and shape with a thin green or yellow skin. Summer squash provides a fair amount of potassium, carotene, and vitamin C.

267

EASY BREAKFAST BISCUIT

The closest I've ever gotten to making biscuits were the unhealthy refrigerator kind that you peeled the label off until the can popped open. So whether or not my healthy biscuits actually taste like their unhealthy high-carb relative, I'll leave that up to you to decide. However, truth be told, these easy breakfast biscuits are amazing with egg and Breakfast Sausage, page 255, tucked inside.

1 large egg
2 tbsp golden flaxseed meal (30 mL)
1 tbsp coconut flour (15 mL)
$^1/_2$ tsp aluminum-free baking powder (2 mL)
$^1/_8$ tsp Celtic® sea salt (0.5 mL)
1 tsp ghee, page 265 (5 mL)

Yield: 1 biscuit
1 serving
164 calories
9.6 g protein
12.2 g fat
5.1 g fiber
3 g net carbs

In small bowl, whisk egg and set aside. In a separate, small bowl, sift together flaxseed meal, coconut flour, baking powder and sea salt. To the dry ingredients, add Ghee, page 265 and with a fork, mash together until small crumbles form. Add egg and mix together. Spoon into greased $4^1/_2$-inch (11.4 cm) ramekin. Microwave for 1 minute or bake at 350°F (180°C) 15 minutes.

TORTILLAS

Try stuffing one of these with scrambled eggs and a smear of Refried Beans With Bacon, page 261, a little Dairy-Free Sour Cream, page 266 and dip in salsa.

$^1/_2$ cup coconut flour (125 mL)
1 tbsp psyllium seed husk powder (15 mL)
$^1/_2$ tsp aluminum-free baking powder (2 mL)
$^1/_4$ tsp Celtic® sea salt (1 mL)
2 tbsp lard, non-hydrogenated (30 mL)
1 cup warm water (250 mL)

Yield: 6 tortillas
1 serving
72 calories
2.3 g protein
5.2 g fat
5.1 g fiber
2.5 g net carbs

In medium bowl, sift together coconut flour, psyllium, baking powder, and sea salt. With a pastry cutter, cut in lard until small crumbles form. Add warm water and mix until a dough ball forms. Cover bowl with kitchen towel and let sit for 30 minutes.

Divide dough into six equal balls and roll out between sheets of parchment paper to desired thickness. In a non-stick skillet, over medium heat, cook tortillas, 2 to 3 minutes, turning once, until lightly browned on each side. Let cool then store sealed.

SWEET ENDINGS

DARK CHOCOLATE MINI COCONUT CUPS

Cacao is a beneficial superfood that contains a wide spectrum of minerals and phytonutrients. This recipe calls for two of the world's healthiest fats, coconut oil and ghee. Ghee is rich in butyric acid which suppresses inflammation in the gut and coconut oil is famous for its anti-viral, anti-bacterial, anti-fungal, anti-oxidant and immune-stimulating properties. You can most definitely enjoy this treat without any guilt and actually improve your health while indulging.

2 tbsp Ghee, page 265 (30 mL)
2 tbsp extra-virgin coconut oil (30 mL)
4 tbsp dark cocoa powder (60 mL)
Pinch Celtic® sea salt
$^1/_8$ tsp liquid vanilla stevia (0.5 mL)
  OR 2 tbsp equivalent (30 mL)
$1^1/_2$ tbsp finely shredded coconut, (22 mL)
  (unsweetened)

Yield: 8 mini-cups
1 cup (250 mL) per serving
77 calories
0.5 g protein
7.9 g fat
1.1 g fiber
0.6 g net carbs

In small glass dish, melt together Ghee, page 265 and coconut oil in the microwave for 30 seconds. Gently mix in dark cocoa powder 1 tbsp (15 mL) at a time. Add a pinch of sea salt and liquid vanilla stevia, OR equivalent and mix. Spoon evenly into paper-lined, mini-muffin tins.

Add heaping $^1/_2$ tsp (2 mL) shredded coconut in the center of each mini-muffin cup. Freeze until hard then transfer to sealed container. Store in freezer.

~~Bits & Bites~~
Food addiction is a real issue. The "just this once" mentality is the best way to keep the addiction alive. The only way a sober alcoholic loses his or her sobriety is by taking that first sip of alcohol. It's no different with trigger foods and food addictions. The short-term satisfaction of a spoonful of ice cream, a bite of pizza or a piece of cake is not worth the pain, frustration and discouragement of gaining back the weight once lost.

Vanessa Romero

DEATH BY DARK CHOCOLATE PUDDING

The first death by chocolate occurred in the 17th Century in Mexico. The people were so addicted to chocolate that they refused to adhere to a chocolate ban that forbade them to eat it during church services. The Bishop who passed the law was later found dead due to poison being mixed into his daily cup of chocolate.

1 envelope unflavored gelatin (7.5 g)
$^1/_4$ cup cold water (60 mL)
$^1/_3$ cup boiling water (75 mL)
$^3/_4$ cup granulated erythritol (175 mL)
$^3/_8$ tsp stevia extract powder, (1.5 mL)
  OR $^1/_2$ cup equivalent (125 mL)
$^2/_3$ cup dark cocoa powder (150 mL)
2 cups canned coconut milk (500 mL)
2 tsp vanilla extract (10 mL)

Yield: 8 servings
1 serving
127 calories
2.2 g protein
10.6 g fat
2.6 g fiber
4.3 g net carbs

Sprinkle gelatin over cold water in small bowl, mix with spoon and let stand 2 minutes. Add boiling water and stir until gelatin is completely dissolved. Set aside.

Powder erythritol with stevia, OR equivalent by pulsing in a coffee grinder until it resembles powdered sugar. In large bowl, combine powdered erythritol-stevia mixture and cocoa powder; add coconut milk and vanilla extract. With electric mixer, beat on medium until well combined. Pour in gelatin mixture and beat until well blended.

Spoon into eight dessert dishes and refrigerate at least 30 minutes. Garnish with berries and top with Dairy-Free Whipped Cream, page 263.

~~Bits and Bites~~
Eggs also offer high protein content, as well as iron, zinc, folate, vitamins A, B, D and E, choline, lutein, and zeaxanthin — nutrients that benefit your immune system, heart and eye health — even lower your risk of cancer.

270

GINGERBREAD MEN WITH DAIRY-FREE ALMOND CREAM CHEESE FROSTING

No Christmas cookie platter is complete without gingerbread men. These are made extra special by frosting with a dairy-free version of cream cheese made from almonds. The work involved in rolling and cutting out the cookies is worth it to enjoy this seasonal classic.

Gingerbread:
1 cup unblanched almond flour (250 mL)
$^1/_2$ cup coconut flour (125 mL)
$^1/_2$ cup granulated erythritol (125 mL)
1 tsp aluminum-free baking powder (5 mL)
1 tsp baking soda (5 mL)
1 tsp cinnamon (5 mL)
$^1/_2$ tsp ginger (2 mL)
$^1/_2$ tsp guar gum powder (2 mL)
$^1/_4$ tsp ground cloves (1 mL)
$^1/_4$ tsp Celtic® sea salt (1 mL)
$^1/_8$ tsp stevia extract powder (0.5 mL), OR $2^1/_2$ tbsp equivalent (37 mL)
3 large eggs, room temp
$^1/_3$ cup extra-virgin coconut oil, melted (75 mL)
1 tbsp blackstrap molasses (15 mL)
2 tsp grated orange peel (10 mL)
1 tsp vanilla extract (5 mL)

Dairy-Free Cream Cheese Frosting:
1 recipe Dairy-Free Almond Cream Cheese, page 264
$^1/_4$ cup powdered erythritol (60 mL)
2 tbsp extra-virgin coconut oil (30 mL)
1 tsp vanilla extract (5 mL)
$^1/_{16}$ tsp stevia extract powder (0.25 mL), OR $1^1/_4$ tbsp equivalent (19 mL)

Yield: 28 cookies
1 cookie with frosting
92 calories
3 g protein
8 g fat
2 g fiber
1.5 g net carbs

Gingerbread: In medium bowl, sift together almond flour, coconut flour, erythritol, baking powder, baking soda, cinnamon, ginger, guar gum, cloves, salt, and stevia, OR equivalent. Set aside. In small bowl, whisk together eggs, coconut oil, molasses, orange peel and vanilla extract. Add wet to dry and with a spoon mix well. With your hands form dough into a large ball and chill for 30 to 45 minutes covered. Roll out dough between two pieces of parchment paper and cut into desired shapes. With a spatula, transfer cutouts onto a parchment-lined baking sheet. Bake at 350°F (180°C) for 12 minutes or until lightly brown.

Dairy-Free Cream Cheese Frosting: In medium bowl, with electric beaters, mix together Dairy-Free Almond Cream Cheese, page 264, erythritol, coconut oil, vanilla, and stevia, OR equivalent and fill a piping bag. With a small star tip, decorate as desired.

271

EASY DAIRY-FREE REFRIGERATOR FUDGE

For portion control and easy serving, use mini-muffin cups lined with pretty, festive papers to make this fudge. These are best right out of the refrigerator and will soften at room temperature.

$1/2$ cup granulated erythritol (125 mL)
$1/4$ tsp stevia extract powder, (1 mL)
 OR $1/3$ cup equivalent (75 mL)
$3/4$ cup canned coconut milk (175 mL)
8 oz unsweetened chocolate, chopped (250 g)
1 tsp vanilla extract (5 mL)
$1/4$ cup chopped walnuts (60 mL)

Yield: 24 servings
1 piece
50.6 calories
0.8 g protein
4.5 g fat
0.7 g fiber
1.1 g net carbs

Place erythritol and stevia, OR equivalent in coffee grinder and pulse until powdered fine. In small saucepan over medium low heat, gently warm coconut milk and then add chopped chocolate. Whisk until melted and smooth. Add in vanilla extract and powdered sweetener and then finally nuts. Line mini-muffin tin with festive paper and divide fudge into 24 pieces. Refrigerate overnight or until firm.

MACAROONS

Coconut, which contains immune-boosting medium-chain fatty acids, has long been thought to have special healing powers. For example, in Thailand, where coconut appears in virtually every dish in the national cuisine, cancer rates are the lowest of the fifty countries surveyed by the National Cancer Institute.

4 large egg whites
$1/8$ tsp Celtic® sea salt (0.5 mL)
$1/2$ cup granulated erythritol (125 mL)
$1/8$ tsp stevia extract powder, OR (0.5 mL)
2$1/2$ tbsp equivalent (37 mL)
8 oz finely shredded coconut, (250 g)
 (unsweetened)

Yield: 40 macaroons
1 cookie
40.6 calories
0.7 g protein
3.7 g fat
0.7 g fiber
0.7 g net carbs

In clean, large stainless steel bowl, whip egg whites and salt with electric beaters until stiff peaks start to form. Add in erythritol and stevia, OR equivalent and continue to beat until really stiff. With a rubber spatula, gently fold in coconut. Using a small cookie scoop, drop cookies on parchment lined cookie sheets. Bake at 350°F (180°C) for 15 minutes. Outside should be golden and inside slightly soft. Let macaroons completely cool on rack and then store covered.

272

PUMPKIN BARS WITH CREAM CHEESE FROSTING

Pumpkins are a squash-like, low-carb fruit adored by many. Most people associate pumpkin with pie. However, there's a whole host of other uses for this orange-fleshed fruit and my personal favorite are these pumpkin bars with a topping made from Dairy-Free Almond Cream Cheese, page 264.

Pumpkin Bars:
2 cups almond flour (500 mL)
$^3/_4$ cup granulated erythritol (175 mL)
2 tsp cinnamon (10 mL)
2 tsp aluminum-free baking powder (10 mL)
1 tsp baking soda (5 mL)
$^1/_2$ tsp salt (2 mL)
$^1/_2$ tsp ground ginger (2 mL)
$^3/_8$ tsp stevia extract powder, OR (1.5 mL)
  $^1/_2$ cup equivalent (125 mL)
$^1/_4$ tsp ground cloves (1 mL)
15 oz can 100% real pumpkin (425 g)
1 cup extra-light olive oil (250 mL)
4 large eggs

Dairy-Free Cream Cheese Frosting:
6 tbsp granulated erythritol* (90 mL)
$^1/_4$ tsp stevia extract powder (1 mL), OR $^1/_3$ cup equivalent (75 mL)
1 recipe Dairy-Free Almond Cream Cheese, page 264
$^1/_4$ cup Ghee, page 265 (60 mL)
1 tsp vanilla extract (5 mL)

> **Yield:** 24 servings
> 1 bar
> 233.1 calories
> 5.4 g protein
> 22 g fat
> 2.9 g fiber
> **2.3 g net carbs**

Pumpkin Bars: In large mixing bowl, sift together almond flour, erythritol, cinnamon, baking powder, baking soda, salt, ginger, stevia, OR equivalent and cloves. In smaller bowl whisk together pumpkin, oil and eggs. Add wet ingredients to dry ingredients and mix together well. Pour into 9 x 13-inch (23 x 33 cm) greased glass pan. Bake at 350°F (180°C) for 35 minutes or until toothpick inserted in center comes out clean. Let cool completely on wire rack before frosting.

Dairy-Free Cream Cheese Frosting: In coffee grinder, powder together erythritol and stevia, OR equivalent. In medium bowl, with electric beaters on medium, beat together Dairy-Free Almond Cream Cheese, page 264 and Ghee, page 265 and then add sweetener mixture and vanilla. Beat until smooth.

Helpful Hint: *Using commercially-powdered erythritol will yield superior results without as much recrystallization in the frosting.

273

LOW-CARB FRIENDS
APPETIZERS AND BEVERAGES

JALAPENO SHRIMP CEVICHE BOATS

These colorful, crisp and fun ceviche boats are sure to be a hit at your next event.
*(Submitted by **Tamara Jones**. Find more of her recipes at*
http://www.lowcarblayla.blogspot.com/)

12 large jalapeno peppers
$^1/_2$ lb raw shrimp, (250 g)
  peeled and deveined
3 limes, juiced
2 plum tomatoes, diced
1 Haas avocado, diced
$^1/_2$ onion, diced
1 celery rib, diced
$^1/_4$ bunch cilantro, chopped
$^1/_4$ tsp salt (1 mL)
$^1/_8$ tsp pepper (0.5 mL)

Yield: 6 servings
1 serving (4 boats)
96.5 calories
5.4 g protein
5.5 g fat
4.7 g net carbs

Halve the peppers lengthwise and remove the stems and seeds. Leave a few seeds if you would like to keep the heat. Wear gloves when handling peppers!

Meanwhile, coarsely chop raw shrimp. Place in a medium non-reactive bowl (glass) with lime juice, tomatoes, avocado, onion, celery, cilantro, salt and pepper. Marinade until shrimp turn opaque (approximately 1 hour), stirring on occasion. Once shrimp has "cooked", spoon ceviche mixture into each jalapeno pepper half. Serve immediately.

~~Bits & Bites~~
A 2010 Heartwire report states that people on on a low-carbohydrate diet have higher HDL cholesterol levels than those following a low-fat diet. HDL or the "good" cholesterol, carries the LDL cholesterol through the bloodstream to the liver, where the liver removes it from the body. The National Heart, Lung and Blood Institute states that the higher your HDL cholesterol level, the lower your risk of ever developing heart disease, since LDL cholesterol tends to build up along the walls of one's arteries, thus restricting crucial blood flow to the heart.

ROASTED ONION BACON JALAPENO DIP

Caramelizing onions in the crockpot makes this dish very easy. (Submitted by **Susie T. Gibbs.** *You can find her blog at:* **http://fluffychixcook.blogspot.com)**

6 medium bacon slices (130 g)
1 large red onion
1 large white onion
2 large shallots
3 cloves garlic
1 large jalapeno pepper, fresh
1 large serrano pepper, fresh
1 tbsp bacon grease (15 mL)
$^1/_2$ tsp kosher salt (2 mL)
$^1/_2$ tsp black pepper (2 mL)
$^1/_4$ tsp dried thyme (1 mL)
1 tbsp balsamic vinegar (15 mL)
1 tbsp Worcestershire Sauce (15 mL)
$1^1/_2$ cups Greek yogurt (375 mL)
$1^1/_2$ cups sour cream (375 mL)
$^1/_4$ cup mayonnaise (60 mL)
$^1/_4$ tsp Apple Cider Vinegar, (1 mL)
  (Bragg® Unfiltered ACV preferred)

Yield: 4 cups (1 L)	
1 serving	
138 calories	
3 g protein	
13 g fat	
4.2 g net carbs	

In nonstick skillet, sauté bacon until brown. Drain and reserve bacon. Cool and chop bacon. Seal and refrigerate until ready to add to dip. Reserve 1 tbsp (15 mL) bacon grease for use in cooking vegetables.

Wash veggies and peel outer layers of tough skin from onions, shallots, and garlic. Coarsely chop onions, shallots, garlic and jalapenos. Don't bother seeding the jalapenos. Toss vegetables with bacon grease and season with salt, pepper and thyme. Add balsamic vinegar and Worcestershire Sauce.

In crock-pot turned to high cook vegetables for 4 hours or until tender and falling apart. Onions should be caramelized at that point.

Allow onions to come to room temperature. Combine vegetables and bacon with Greek yogurt, sour cream and mayonnaise. Taste for seasoning and add salt and pepper if necessary. If dip tastes too sweet, add apple cider vinegar $^1/_4$ tsp (1 mL) at a time or you can add a few drops of lemon juice.

BAVARIAN CHEESE SPREAD (OBATZDA)

Obatzda is a Bavarian cheese delicacy, made by blending a combination of soft cheeses, butter, and seasonings. The result is a delectable concoction which is traditionally spread on bread or pretzels and is just as wonderful on vegetables or a low-carb cracker! (Submitted by **Birgit Kerr***. Her blog is at* ***http://birgitkerr.blogspot.com/)***

1 medium-sized, white onion (100 g)
7 oz soft Brie cheese or camembert (210 g)
$3^1/_2$ oz cream cheese, softened (105 g)
$1^1/_2$ oz butter, softened (45 g)
1 tsp paprika (5 mL)
Salt and pepper, to taste
Garnish (optional):
1 tbsp chopped chives (15 mL)

Yield: 4 servings
1 serving
337 calories
12 g protein
30.8 g fat
3 g net carbs

Very finely chop a medium-sized onion and set aside.

Trim the rind off the Brie cheese, unless your chosen Brie has a very soft rind, then you can skip this step. Place the soft part of the Brie in a bowl and soften it further by mashing it with a fork. Add the finely chopped onions, the softened cream cheese, butter and paprika and continue to mash and mix with a fork. Once you have a smooth spread, add salt and pepper to taste.

Cover the bowl and refrigerate a minimum of 1 hour so all the flavors can develop. Chilling overnight would be even better, even though not necessary!

Garnish: Place the cheese spread in an attractive serving dish and sprinkle with chopped chives and another sprinkling of paprika.

Helpful Hints: Traditionally this spread is prepared with all butter. In this take on the traditional recipe, I lighten things up a little, but lose none of the flavor!

The kind of brie you choose for this spread very much determines the "strength" of flavor in this spread. The more aged the brie or camembert, the stronger the flavor.

~~Bits & Bites~~

A meat fast for 3 days can be just as effective as the Fat Fast. On a meat fast you can have 2 hard boiled eggs a day and make sure you have a variety of meats. You can fry in olive oil and use mayonnaise and mustard. That's it! These protocols are sure to break a stall, however, for people who lose weight very quickly these sorts of quick weight loss tactics can be dangerous as too much water weight loss can cause a serious electrolyte imbalance.

GUACAMOLE CON ZUCCHINI

*Can be used as a topping for tacos, rolled up in a ham slice or as a dip for veggies. It's a great way to use up that zucchini because you won't be able to taste the flavor of the zucchini. No one will ever know! Submitted by **Sandra Rodriquez**. Visit her Facebook page, **Sandy's Simple Recipes and More** at: http://www.facebook.com/SandysSimpleRecipes)*

1 large zucchini, diced (375 g)
1 large avocado, diced or mashed (250 g)
$1/4$ cup cilantro, chopped (60 mL)
1 small roma tomato, diced
3 green onions, chopped, OR
  $1/4$ cup chopped onion (60 mL)
$1/4$ tsp salt (1 mL)
1 tbsp mayonnaise (15 mL)

Yield: 2 cups (500 mL)
$1/4$ cup (60 mL) per serving
62.5 calories
1.2 g protein
5.3 g fat
1.8 g net carbs

In covered casserole dish, cook zucchini in microwave oven until tender, about 4 to 5 minutes. Drain in a strainer over a bowl to remove moisture. Meanwhile in medium bowl, mash the avocado and mix in chopped cilantro, tomato and green onions, OR chopped onion. Add the cooked drained zucchini and salt to taste. Blend in mayonnaise. Serve with pork rinds or veggie sticks.

CRAB CAKES

*You won't even miss the breadcrumbs in this induction-friendly crab cake recipe. (Submitted by **Tiki Byrd**. Her blog is at: http://lowcarbtiki.blogspot.com)*

12 oz lump crab meat, picked over (375 g)
  to remove shells and cartilage
2 tbsp dried parsley (30 mL)
1 tbsp golden flaxseed meal (15 mL)
1 tbsp mayonnaise (15 mL)
1 tsp Old Bay® seasoning (5 mL)
1 tsp mustard (5 mL)
1 egg
Garlic powder, to taste
Salt, and pepper, to taste

Yield: 4 crab cakes
1 crab cake
127.5 calories
19.1 g protein
5.2 g fat
0.6 g net carbs

In medium bowl, combine crab meat, parsley, flaxseed meal, mayonnaise, Old Bay® seasoning, mustard egg, garlic powder, salt and pepper to taste. Form into cakes. Heat oil in large skillet, over medium high heat. Fry the crab cakes on both sides until lightly browned.

CHAR'S MOCHACCINO FRAPPE

This sugar-free frappe is the perfect mix of chocolate and coffee. (Submitted by Char ('Charski') Cunningham. You can find more of her recipes at: http://lowcarb4life.proboards.com)

8 fl.oz unsweetened non-dairy milk, (250 mL)
  (chocolate almond or soy milk)
$^1/_3$ cup whey protein powder, (75 mL)
  (vanilla, chocolate, or plain)
2 fl. oz heavy cream (60 mL)
1 fl. oz Da Vinci® Sugar-Free Syrup, (30 mL)
  (chocolate flavor)
1 tbsp instant coffee powder (15 mL)
1 tsp dark cocoa powder (5 mL)
1 tsp guar gum, OR xanthan gum, OR (5 mL)
  glucomannan powder
1 tsp liquid stevia, OR (5 mL)
  1 cup equivalent (250 mL)
8 to 10 ice cubes

Yield: 2, 12 fl. oz servings
12 fl. oz (375 mL) serving
173.5 calories
7.45 g protein
13.4 g fat
4.1 g net carbs

In blender, blend non-dairy milk, whey protein powder, heavy cream, Da Vinci® Sugar-Free chocolate syrup, coffee powder, dark cocoa powder, guar gum, OR xanthan gum, OR glucomannan powder and stevia, OR equivalent until all the powders are dissolved and then add the ice cubes, blending until smooth

Helpful Hints: Adjust sweetness to your preference and you can also make variations by using different flavors of sugar-free syrup and/or protein powders.

CAROLYN'S LOW-CARB MILK

Carolyn Follmer created this unique and convenient recipe. It mimics a commercial low-carb milk product called Hood® Calorie Countdown milk.

1 to 2 tbsp heavy whipping cream (15-30 mL)
  (depending on how creamy you like it)
$1^1/_3$ tbsp skim milk powder (20 mL)
1 cup cold water (250 mL)
$^1/_8$ tsp SPLENDA® Granular, (0.5 mL)
  (optional)
Sprinkle of salt

Yield: 1 cup (250 mL)
1 tbsp/2 tbsp heavy cream
65.0/110.0 calories
2.0/2.0 g protein
5.0/10.0 g fat
3.0/3.0 g net carbs

In container with lid, combine whipping cream and skim milk powder. Using a whisk, stir in cold water gradually. Add SPLENDA® Granular, if using and salt. Replace lid and shake really well to combine. Refrigerate.

SALADS AND SOUPS

CHICKEN ALMOND WITH PEACHES AND CREAM
SALAD

Summer can be a wonderful time with a bounty of good fruits and veggies. Take it easy on yourself and get a roasted chicken from the store. (Submitted by **Barbara (Barbo) Goldstein**. *You can find more of her recipes at Barbo's Low Carb Kitchen:* ***http://barboslowcarbkitchen.proboards.com/index.cgi)***

Salad:
$^1/_2$ chicken breast, chopped
1 chicken thigh, chopped
2 small (or 1 medium) peaches,
  peeled and cut into small pieces
Celery hearts, sliced thin on diagonal
Handful of almonds, roughly chopped

Cream Cheese Dressing:
2 tbsp cream cheese, softened (30 mL)
$^1/_4$ cup sour cream (60 mL)
Squeeze of lemon juice
Sweetener, to taste
$^1/_8$ tsp salt, OR to taste (0.5 mL)

Yield: 3 servings
1 serving
236.3 calories
18.0 g protein
14.4 g fat
7.2 g net carbs

Salad: In large bowl, combine chicken, peaches, celery hearts and almonds. Chill.

Cream Cheese Dressing: In small bowl, combine softened cream cheese, sour cream, squeeze of lemon juice, sweetener and salt, to taste. Mix all of the ingredients together well, pour the dressing over the salad mixture and toss. Serve on a bed of lettuce.

~~Bits & Bites~~
You don't have to count calories or even carbs on a low-carb diet, but it does not mean that the calories and carbs don't count. Let your own hunger guide you and eat when hungry. If you eat for all sorts of other reasons, chances are you will not lose weight and if you are still a little bit hungry at the end of the day, chances are you will lose weight!

OLD TIME SHRIMP SALAD WITH THOUSAND ISLAND DRESSING

This cold and crisp salad with chilled shrimp dates back to the 1950's.
*(Submitted by **Barbara (Barbo) Goldstein**. You can find more of her recipes at*
Barbo's Low Carb Kitchen:
http://barboslowcarbkitchen.proboards.com/index.cgi)

Thousand Island Dressing:
1 cup mayonnaise (250 mL)
$^1/_4$ cup sugar-free ketchup (60 mL)
Chopped dill pickles, to taste
$^1/_8$ tsp salt, OR to taste (0.5 mL)
$^1/_8$ tsp pepper, OR to taste (0.5 mL)
Salad:
Iceberg lettuce, chilled
Shrimp, cooked and chilled
Sliced radishes (optional)
Boiled egg slices (optional)
Olives (optional)

Yield: $1^1/_4$ cups Dressing
2 tbsp (30 mL) per serving
162.5 calories
0.0 g protein
19.2 g fat
0.5 g net carbs

Thousand Island Dressing: In medium bowl, mix together mayonnaise, sugar-free ketchup, dill pickles, salt and pepper. Taste and if necessary add lemon juice to add more tang or ketchup for more sweetness. Chill well.

Salad: In large bowl, toss the cold lettuce with the dressing. Add the lettuce to serving bowls; add the shrimp, and any other accompaniments. Serve with toasted, low-carb English Muffins, page 87, *Low-Carbing Among Friends, Volume-2* and Iced Tea.

~~Bits & Bites~~

If you think you cannot lose weight, then chances are almost certain that you will not lose weight. A big part of losing weight is keeping daily in your mind thoughts of success and not entertaining negative thoughts. Keeping a journal is a great way to remain accountable.

BEEFY MUSHROOM SOUP

*I was eating some leftover soup one day and for some reason it reminded me of Campbell's® Golden Mushroom Soup, which inspired me to come up with this version. (Submitted by **Linda Sue Genaw**. Find this recipe with a photo at:*
http://www.genaw.com/lowcarb/beefy_mushroom_soup.html)

2 lbs ground beef (0.9 kg)
16 oz fresh mushrooms, sliced (500 g)
2.5 oz onion, chopped (75 g)
1 clove garlic, minced
15 oz can pumpkin (425 g)
14 fl oz can beef broth (414 mL)
  OR 2 cups homemade beef broth (500 mL)
2 cups chicken broth (500 mL)
1 tsp beef bouillon granules (5 mL)
1 tsp salt, OR to taste (5 mL)
$^1/_4$ tsp pepper (1 mL)
$^1/_2$ cup heavy cream (125 mL)
$^1/_2$ cup dry white wine, OR water (125 mL)

Yield: 8 cups
1 cup serving
302 calories
23 g protein
19 g fat
4 g net carbs

In a 6 to 8-quart (6 to 8 L) pot, brown the ground beef along with the mushrooms, onion and garlic; drain the fat. Add the pumpkin to the ground beef mixture; blend well and then add the broth {if using canned broth add water to equal 2 cups (500 mL)} and bouillon. Season with salt and pepper.

Cover and simmer 20 to 30 minutes. Add the cream and wine, OR water; simmer 10 to 15 minutes longer. Adjust the seasoning, if needed.

Helpful Hints: It seems to make a difference what brand of pumpkin you use. The second time I made this, I used a store brand of pumpkin and the soup didn't turn out nearly as thick. I stirred in about $^1/_2$ tsp (2 mL) of xanthan gum to get the right consistency. I suspect that the cheaper brand of pumpkin had more water in it than Libby's®.

~~Bits & Bites~~
When approaching a low-carb diet, don't expect an instant fix, especially if you only have 10 lbs to lose. Some people will lose weight extremely fast, especially if it is their first time low-carbing. My experience is that the body remembers and for many people the second and third time low-carbing is not quite as easy and the pounds don't simply drop off. Persevere each meal and each day and you will see results. If you don't see results, it may be time to get your thyroid function checked or take probiotics for suspected Candida.

BREAKFASTS

EGG-TILLAS

*Here is an easy recipe to make a breakfast tortilla with a variety of fillings such as ham, cheese and green onions, for example. This recipe has been contributed by **Dottie**, a longtime administrator of **Lowcarbfriends.com**, where you can find more of her lovely recipes.*

2 large eggs
1$^1/_3$ tbsp coconut flour (20 mL)
2 to 3 tbsp water (30 to 45 mL)
$^1/_8$ tsp salt (0.5 mL)
$^1/_4$ cup chopped, cooked spinach, (60 mL)
  drained (optional)
Coconut oil, OR butter

> *Yield:* 2 Egg-tillas
> 1 egg-tilla
> 94.5 calories
> 6.9 g protein
> 5.5 g fat
> ***1.9 g net carbs***

Beat the eggs until smooth and add coconut flour, 1 tbsp (15 mL) water and salt. Beat until smooth and add the spinach, if using, and more water if necessary to get a thick but spreadable batter.

Heat an 8-inch (20 cm) skillet over medium heat and add coconut oil, OR butter. Pour half the batter into the skillet and spread out as evenly as possible. Cook about 2 minutes until it can flip easily and finish cooking. Place on rack to cool so that air can circulate all around it. Repeat with remaining batter.

Helpful Hints: **To refrigerate:** Place the egg-tilla on a piece of wax paper that is positioned on a paper towel. Gently roll it up. Repeat with remaining egg-tilla and place them in a container or baggie and refrigerate. Before using after refrigeration, allow to come to room temperature for 15 minutes to prevent cracking when unrolling it. These are sturdier after a day of refrigeration.

~~Bits & Bites~~
Acetyl L Carnitine can help mobilize fat and break a stall.

MEXICAN BREAKFAST

*Here's a little secret....This meal might look like it is time consuming but it's not...it's as fast as cooking an omelet. The key to making this meal quick is either having fresh hamburger meat or thawed hamburger meat in the fridge ready to be used. (Submitted by **Carol Lovett**. Find more of her recipes at **http://ditchthewheat.com**)*

$^1/_2$ small onion, chopped
2 tbsp or more chopped green pepper (30 mL)
2 tbsp or more chopped red pepper (30 mL)
Olive oil, OR preferred fat
$^1/_2$ cup raw ground beef (125 mL)
$^1/_8$ tsp salt (0.5 mL)
$^1/_8$ tsp pepper (0.5 mL)
$^1/_4$ cup salsa, (60 mL)
  mild, medium or spicy
1 large egg

Yield: 1 serving
1 serving
353 calories
28.5 g protein
20.9 g fat
6.6 g net carbs

In a large frying pan, sauté the chopped onions, green and red peppers in olive oil, OR preferred fat.

Add the ground beef and season with salt and pepper. Continue stirring until the beef is no longer pink. Add the salsa. Stir to evenly coat the beef and sautéed vegetables.

In the same frying pan or another frying pan, fry your egg to your liking and season with salt and pepper.

Serve immediately.

~~Bits & Bites~~

With regard to oats and insulin spikes – remember if the Gluten-Free Bake mix was purely oat flour, it would be a problem, but since the oat flour is a small amount diluted in a large amount of almond flour and a bit of coconut flour, the glycemic load (which is more important than glycemic index) is a lot lower, and, therefore, the insulin response would be a lot lower. It is still a "your mileage may vary thing", but I have several friends who also have diabetes and they love the bake mix.

MAIN COURSES AND SIDES

PIZZA-STUFFED CHICKEN

*This simple recipe is fun to make, the kids will love it and it is elegant enough to serve to company. Everyone loves pizza and everyone will love pizza-stuffed chicken. (Submitted by **Tamara Jones**. Her blog is at http://www.lowcarblayla.blogspot.com/)*

4 boneless, skinless chicken breasts
32 pepperoni slices
4 oz shredded Mozzarella cheese, (125 g) divided
$^1/_2$ cup no-sugar-added pasta sauce, (125 mL) divided
$^1/_4$ cup mayonnaise, divided (60 mL)
2 oz finely crushed pork rinds (60 g)
1 oz shredded Parmesan cheese (30 g)
1 tsp dried Italian seasoning blend (5 mL)

Yield: 4 servings
1 serving
428.0 calories
46.25 g protein
25.5 g fat
3.8 g net carbs

Preheat oven to 375°F (190°C). Butterfly chicken breasts. Place 6 pepperoni slices on each breast. Place 1 oz (30 g) Mozzarella cheese over pepperoni slices. Spoon 1 tbsp (15 mL) of no-sugar-added pasta sauce over Mozzarella cheese.

Carefully roll up each breast and place in a casserole dish, folded side down and spaced to make sure the breasts do not touch.

Place 1 tbsp (15 mL) of mayonnaise over each breast, spreading to cover as much of the breast as possible. In a separate small bowl, mix the crushed pork rinds, shredded Parmesan cheese and Italian seasoning blend together.

Push/mash the breading mixture into the mayonnaise, covering as much of each breast as possible. Bake uncovered at 375°F (190°C) for 40 minutes. Plate chicken and spoon 1 tbsp (15 mL) of no-sugar-added pasta sauce over each breast.

~~Bits & Bites~~

There are several different approaches to low-carb diets out there and it's important to find what suits your particular needs and lifestyle. Most people think of Atkins when they think of low-carbing and it is the most popular approach out there, however, even Atkins can be adapted to the individual. Some people doing Atkins actually eat 100 grams of carbohydrate a day (lots of good eating!), but that is still considered low-carb compared to the 300 to 400 grams or more of carbohydrate per day that many people consume.

SLOW COOKER FAJITAS

*These slow cooker fajitas are easy to prepare and make a delicious meal. This recipe comes from **Christine F**. Her blog is at **http://www.lowcarbcrock.com/**)*

2 lbs beef stewing meat (0.9 kg)
2 medium red peppers, sliced in thin wedges
1 medium green pepper, sliced in thin wedges
1 small yellow onion, chopped
$^1/_4$ cup tomato paste (60 mL)
1 tbsp chili powder (15 mL)
2 cloves garlic, chopped
2 tsp Better Than Bouillon® (10 mL)
  Beef Base
$^1/_2$ tsp olive oil (2 mL)
$^1/_2$ tsp oregano (2 mL)
$^1/_2$ tsp salt (2 mL)
$^1/_3$ tsp pepper, OR to taste (1.7 mL)

Yield: 5 servings
1 cup (250 mL) per serving
389 calories
33 g protein
21 g fat
2 g fiber
7 g net carbs

In slow cooker, stir together beef stewing meat, red peppers, green pepper, onion, tomato paste, chili powder, garlic, Better Than Bouillon® Beef Base, olive oil, oregano, salt and pepper.

Cover and cook for 8 hours on LOW or 4 hours on HIGH or until your fajita meat is pull-apart tender.

Drain the liquid from the meat and veggies.

Serve as is, over shredded lettuce, or on low-carb tortillas with sour cream and avocado.

Helpful Hints: There is no need to pre-brown any of the ingredients; just mix them together in your slow cooker and you're ready to go.

Although chili powder is used in this recipe, the resulting tender fajita meat is very mild and suitable for most tastes.

1

ZUCCHINI LASAGNA

*This is a tasty dish that is especially good to make when all the excess zucchini is overwhelming us! Delicious when served with a green salad and English Muffins (Vol. 2, page 87) toasted with butter and minced garlic. (Submitted by **Cathy Lawrence**.)*

1 tbsp olive oil (15 mL)
1 lb ground beef (0.45 kg)
$^1/_3$ cup chopped onion (75 mL)
15 oz can tomato sauce (425 g)
1 tsp oregano (5 mL)
$^1/_2$ tsp basil (2 mL)
$^1/_2$ tsp Italian seasoning (2 mL)
$^1/_2$ tsp black pepper (2 mL)
$^1/_4$ to $^1/_2$ tsp red pepper flakes (1-2 mL)
1 cup cottage cheese (250 mL)
$2^1/_2$ cups shredded Mozzarella cheese, divided (625 mL)
$^1/_4$ cup Parmesan cheese (60 mL)
1 large egg, beaten
2 tbsp fresh parsley (30 mL)
$1^1/_2$ tsp garlic powder (7 mL)
2 medium zucchini, sliced lengthwise (750 g)

Yield:	12 servings
1 serving	
206.4 calories	
16.4 g protein	
13.7 g fat	
1.1 g fiber	
4.7 g net carbs	

In skillet, heat oil over medium high heat. Brown the ground beef and onion until beef is cooked and onion is tender. Drain fat if needed. Add tomato sauce, oregano, basil, Italian seasoning, black pepper and red pepper flakes. Bring to a boil, reduce heat and simmer 10 to 20 minutes, stirring occasionally.

In medium bowl, combine cottage cheese, $^1/_2$ cup (125 mL) Mozzarella cheese, Parmesan cheese, and egg. Add parsley and garlic powder. Set aside.

Slice zucchini lengthwise. Spray 9 x 13-inch (23 x 33 cm) casserole dish with nonstick cooking spray. Layer half the zucchini, spread with the cheese mixture and half of the meat. Layer remaining zucchini, 1 cup (250 mL) Mozzarella, remaining meat and 1 cup (250 mL) Mozzarella. Sprinkle with Parmesan cheese, if desired.

Bake at 350°F (180°C) for 45 minutes or until zucchini is tender.

LIVER AND ONIONS IN GRAVY

*When it comes to liver, you either love it or hate it. This liver is tender with gravy that is smooth and delicious. The cream cheese not only thickens the gravy, but gives it a great taste. Top it off with onions grilled just the way you like them. What a wonderful feast for liver lovers. Submitted by **Joyce Vennum**.*

1 medium onion; sliced, separated into rings
2 tbsp butter (30 mL)
1 lb beef liver, rinsed (0.45 kg)
$1^1/_2$ cups water (375 mL)
$^1/_2$ teaspoon salt (2 mL)
$^1/_8$ teaspoon pepper (0.5 mL)
4 oz cream cheese (125 g)

Yield: 4 servings
1 serving
199.5 calories
8.5 g protein
16.7 g fat
4.2 g net carbs

In a skillet, fry the onions in the butter until they are grilled the way you like them. Remove the onions and set aside.

Add the liver to the skillet and brown over medium heat. Pour water in medium bowl and stir the salt and pepper into the water, and then pour it down the side of the skillet. Cover, bring to a boil, reduce heat and simmer for 30 minutes.

Remove the liver, bring the liquid in the pan to a boil and stir in the cream cheese. Cook and stir until the cream cheese is melted and the gravy is thickened. Remove from heat. Return the liver to the skillet and spoon gravy on top. Sprinkle on the grilled onions.

Helpful Hints: Calf liver will be tenderer and better tasting than beef liver, but both taste great.

When simmering food for an extended period of time, use a pan or skillet with a tight-fitting lid and there will be less chance that all of the liquid will evaporate and less chance of the food burning.

GYROS

Gyro means "to turn" in Greek. These get their name from the vertical rotisserie where these are usually cooked but this is made in your own oven. Thinly-sliced lamb gyros wrapped in lettuce leaves instead of the traditional pita bread will satisfy those cravings for Mediterranean food. You won't even miss the pita! Serve with Tzaziki, page 296. (Submitted by **Kelly Schumann.** *Her blog is at:* **http://happytexans.blogspot.com**).

1 medium onion, chopped coarsely	**Yield:** 6 servings
2 pounds ground lamb (0.9 kg)	1 serving
1 tbsp minced fresh garlic (15 mL)	446.1 calories
1 tbsp dried marjoram (15 mL)	25.2 g protein
1 tbsp dried ground rosemary (15 mL)	35.4 g fat
2 tsp salt (10 mL)	0.2 g fiber
$^{1}/_{2}$ tsp ground black pepper (5 mL)	**0.5 g net carbs**

Preheat the oven to 325°F (160 °C).

In a food processor, process the onion for 10 to 15 seconds and then pour into a kitchen towel. Gather up the ends of the towel and squeeze until almost all of the juice is removed. Discard juice.

Return the onion to the food processor and add the lamb, garlic, marjoram, rosemary, salt, and pepper and process until it is a fine paste, approximately 1 minute. Stop the processor as needed to scrape down sides of bowl.

Place the mixture into a loaf pan, making sure to press into the sides of the pan. Place the loaf pan into a water bath and bake for 60 to 75 minutes or until the mixture reaches 165°F (74°C) to 170°F (77°C). Remove from the oven and drain off any fat. Place the loaf pan on a cooling rack and place a brick wrapped in aluminum foil directly on the surface of the meat and let set for 15 to 20 minutes, until the internal temperature reaches 175°F (79°C).

To serve, slice and wrap in lettuce leaves with tomato and Tzaziki, page 296. I also like to slice the meat and sauté in a little oil. Or use the meat in salads for a delicious gyro salad. Also wonderful sprinkled with Feta cheese.

DIJON THYME PORK CHOPS

*Pan-fried pork chops topped with a Dijon thyme pan gravy is perfect for a busy weeknight meal. (Submitted by: **Karen Sorenson**. Find more of her recipes at: http://lconeday.blogspot.com)*

1 tbsp oil (15 mL)
2 lbs thickly cut pork chops (0.9 kg)
$^1/_2$ tsp salt (2 mL)
$^1/_2$ tsp pepper (2 mL)
$1^1/_2$ cups chicken broth, divided (375 mL)
2 garlic cloves, minced
1 tbsp fresh thyme (15 mL)
1 tbsp Dijon mustard (15 mL)

Yield: 5 pork chops
1 serving
295 calories
37.9 g protein
14.4 g fat
1.1 g net carbs

Heat 1 tbsp (15 mL) of oil in a large skillet over medium high heat. Season the pork chops with salt and pepper. Sear the pork chops for 4 to 5 minutes on each side.

Add 1 cup (250 mL) of broth to deglaze the pan. Reduce heat to medium and add garlic and thyme. Cover the pan loosely and cook for 5 minutes or until the pork chops are cooked through. Remove the pork chops and add the remaining broth and the Dijon mustard. Cook for another 2 to 3 minutes or until the sauce reduces and thickens. Spoon the pan gravy over the pork chops and serve.

~~Bits & Bites~~
Many people wrongly assume that a low-carb diet means a high-protein diet when in actual fat it is rather a high-fat diet, adequate-protein diet. The fat in a low-carb diet is key to satiation and contrary to years of indoctrination, fat is not the enemy, instead refined carbohydrates and too many carbohydrates in the diet are the enemy.

POOR MAN'S PHILLY CHEESE STEAK STUFFED PEPPERS

The Philly cheese steak-stuffed peppers cure the craving for a cheese steak without a bunch of unnecessary carbs and bread. (Submitted by Susie T. Gibbs. You can find her blog at: http://fluffychixcook.blogspot.com)

Meat:
1¹/₂ lbs ground chuck (0.68 kg)
1 tbsp Worcestershire Sauce (15 mL)
1 tbsp freeze-dried parsely (15 mL)
1 tsp kosher, OR sea salt (5 mL)
¹/₂ tsp black pepper (2 mL)
¹/₂ tsp granulated garlic powder (2 mL)
¹/₄ tsp red pepper flakes (1 mL)

Veggies:
1 tbsp beef fat, drained from cooking beef (15 mL)
¹/₂ lb mushrooms, chopped (250 g)
4 oz onion, chopped (125 g)
1 large red bell pepper, chopped (125 g)
1 clove garlic, chopped (5 mL)
¹/₂ tsp kosher salt (2 mL)
¹/₂ tsp black pepper (2 mL)
¹/₄ tsp dried thyme (1 mL)

Philly Cheese Steak Cheese Sauce, OR see below*:
2 oz cream cheese, softened (60 g)
¹/₂ cup cream, heavy (125 mL)
¹/₂ cup water (125 mL)
2 tbsp Dry Vermouth, OR dry white wine (30 mL)
1 cup shredded Provolone Cheese (250 mL)
³/₄ cup shredded Sharp Cheddar Cheese (175 mL)
¹/₄ cup Parmesan Cheese, grated (60 mL)
¹/₄ tsp kosher salt (1 mL)
¹/₄ tsp black pepper (1 mL)
¹/₈ tsp dry mustard powder, (0.5 mL)
 (optional)

Cheese Steak-Stuffed Peppers – 6 Pepper Halves Yield:
3 large green bell peppers
1 recipe prepared meat
1 recipe prepared vegetables
1¹/₂ cups Philly Cheese Steak Cheese Sauce (375 mL)
4 sprays Vegetable Oil Spray

Yield: 6 pepper halves
1 pepper half per serving
514 calories
29 g protein
40 g fat
7 g net carbs

Meat: Into nonstick skillet, crumble ground meat. Add Worcestershire sauce, parsley, kosher, OR sea salt, black pepper, garlic powder and red pepper flakes and cook until meat is browned and almost cooked through. Remove from heat and reserve meat. Pour off all but 1 tbsp (15 mL) of meat drippings.

Veggies: In pan and to reserved beef fat from cooking the meat, add chopped mushrooms, onion, red bell pepper, garlic, kosher salt, black pepper and thyme. Sauté over high heat until veggies are tender and starting to brown. Remove pan from heat and reserve vegetables. Add reserved meat back to the pan and combine with the veggies.

Philly Cheese Steak Cheese Sauce: In small bowl, microwave cream cheese for 30 to 45 seconds to soften. Add cream cheese to medium-sized saucepan and slowly add cream, water and Vermouth, OR dry white wine. Stir cream cheese with a whisk as you add the liquid to avoid forming lumps. Heat contents over medium heat. Bring sauce to a slow simmer and allow sauce to thicken.

Reduce heat to low or turn off burner completely. Add grated Provolone, Cheddar, Parmesan cheeses, salt, pepper and mustard powder, if using and stir into sauce with large spatula. Stir until all cheese is melted and sauce is well combined and warm throughout. Adjust seasonings for salt and pepper. If sauce is too thick, add a bit more water or cream. If sauce is too thin, remove from heat for a few minutes and see if it thickens up as it cools in temperature. If sauce doesn't thicken, add a bit more cheese, about $^1/_8$ cup (30 mL), at a time. Sauce should be the consistency of thick queso. Do not boil this sauce or heat it too quickly once the grated cheese has been added or the sauce will separate and curdle.

Poor Man's Philly Cheese Steak-Stuffed Pepper Assembly: Preheat oven to 450°F (230°C). Wash and dry green bell peppers. Split peppers lengthwise and remove the seeds. Spray split pepper halves with olive oil spray and place on foil-lined cookie sheet. Roast bell pepper halves cut side down for about 20 minutes or until starting to brown a bit and peppers have softened. You don't want them mushy, just soft to the point of a knife or fork. Divide up the meat-and-veggie mixture into 6 portions. Stuff each half pepper with $^1/_6$ of the meat-andveggie filling. It's fine if it spills over the top. *Top with $^1/_4$ cup (60 mL) of cheese sauce and return to oven, OR if you prefer, top with your favorite sliced or shredded cheese. Make it easy on yourself! Bake the stuffed peppers for 20 minutes until cheese is bubbly and meat is done to your preference. If you prefer, you can also finish the pepper under the broiler instead of baking them. Broil for 3 to 5 minutes on the top rack of the oven until cheese starts to brown and peppers are hot.

HERBED PORK TENDERLOIN

Pork tenderloin marinated in an herb marinade that is easy to throw together. The tenderloin is seared and then roasted until juicy and tender. (Submitted by **Karen Sorenson***. Her blog is at:* ***http://lconeday.blogspot.com)***

10 fresh basil leaves
2 sprigs fresh thyme
2 sprigs fresh rosemary
2 sprigs fresh oregano
3 cloves garlic
Juice of 1 lemon
$^1/_4$ cup extra-virgin olive oil (60 mL)
1 tsp Dijon mustard (5 mL)
$^1/_2$ tsp salt (2 mL)
$^1/_2$ tsp black pepper (2 mL)
2 lbs pork tenderloin (0.9 kg)
Oil for searing

> **Yield:** 5 servings
> 1 serving
> 349 calories
> 37.5 g protein
> 20.7 g fat
> *1.5 g net carbs*

In a mini-food chopper, place the basil, thyme, rosemary, oregano, and garlic. Process until finely chopped. Add lemon juice, olive oil, Dijon mustard, salt and pepper. Rub the pork tenderloin with the herb mixture and let it marinate for 15 to 20 minutes.

Preheat oven to 400°F (200°C). Right before the pork is done marinating, heat 1 to 2 tbsp (15 to 30 mL) oil in a skillet over medium high heat. Remove the pork from the marinade and sear for 3 to 4 minutes per side. Place the pork in a baking dish and bake for 10 to 20 minutes, or until cooked through with an internal temperature of at least 145°F (63°C).

~~Bits & Bites~~
Hair and skin changes may occur when a person does not eat enough protein. Hair may become fine and brittle and may even lose some of its color. Hair loss can result. Delayed wound healing is common and skin can undergo changes in pigmentation, and the individual may develop dermatitis or pressure ulcers. Typically low-carb diets provide plenty of protein. If one is vegetarian and following a low-carb diet, it is important to make sure one gets enough protein and to supplement with iron, zinc and the B vitamins and especially B-12 or permanent nerve damage can result.

MUSHROOM STROGANOFF

*The earthiness of the browned mushrooms in this recipe adds a great depth and the creamy sauce coats the zucchini "noodles" very well to make for a very comforting dish. (Submitted by **Darryl Reid**. Find more of his recipes at* ***http://lowcarbboy.com/***)

8 oz cremini mushrooms (250 g)
3 tbsp butter (45 mL)
$^1/_8$ tsp salt (0.5 mL)
1 small onion, sliced
1 clove garlic, sliced
$1^1/_2$ cups beef stock (375 mL)
$^1/_3$ cup sour cream (75 mL)
2 tbsp cream cheese (30 mL)
Salt and pepper to taste
2 zucchini, sliced into ribbons
1 tbsp parsley (15 mL)

Yield: 4 servings
1 serving
168.0 calories
4.1 g protein
14.1 g fat
1.8 g fiber
6.1 g net carbs

In skillet, fry mushrooms in butter for 5 to 7 minutes until browned. Add a pinch of salt after 3 to 4 minutes. Add sliced onions and garlic and cook for another 4 to 6 minutes or until onions are soft.

Deglaze the pan with beef stock. Simmer for 5 minutes until liquid is reduced by half.

Remove from heat and add in sour cream and cream cheese. The consistency of the sauce can be adjusted by reducing further to thicken or adding water to thin it out. Adjust seasoning with salt and pepper to taste.

Use a vegetable peeler to get the ribbons from the zucchini. The zucchini ribbons can be served raw or fried briefly in butter (nutritional information is for raw zucchini). Serve sauce over zucchini "noodles" and garnish with parsley.

~~Bits & Bites~~
Just some benefits of low-carbing are appetite suppression or lack of hunger, improvement of diabetes symptoms, elevated mood and increased energy levels, joint and muscle improvement, and disappearance of yeast infections, heartburn and bloating.

EGGPLANT BAKE

*Eggplant and ground beef combine to create a delicious, Italian-style casserole dish. (Submitted by **Tiki Byrd**. Her blog is at: **http://lowcarbtiki.blogspot.com**)*

1 lb ground beef (0.45 kg)	***Yield:*** 4 servings
Seasoning to taste	1 serving
1 large eggplant	526.8 calories
1¹/₂ cups tomato basil sauce (375 mL)	39.9 g protein
(low-carb)	36.5 g fat
5 to 6 slices Sharp Provolone cheese	***4.7 g net carbs***
3 slices Sharp Cheddar Cheese	
Italian Seasoning, to taste	

Preheat oven to 350°F (180°C). Brown the ground beef, seasoning to taste and drain. Trim and cut the eggplant into chunks. In an oven-safe dish, mix ground beef, eggplant, and sauce. Top with Provolone cheese and sprinkle with Italian seasoning to taste. Bake 20 to 25 minutes or until cheese has browned slightly.

COCONUT RICE

*Coconut rice is a tasty side dish or used as a bed for curry dishes. This recipe is contributed by **Barbara Goldstein**. Find more of her recipes on her board:*
http://barboslowcarbkitchen.proboards.com/index.cgi

1 medium head cauliflower	***Yield:*** 4 servings
13.5 fl oz coconut milk (400 mL)	1 serving
Salt and pepper, to taste	221.5 calories
	4.6 g protein
	20.7 g fat
	7.2 g net carbs

Wash cauliflower and cut into florets. Place in blender (Barbo uses a Vita-Mix® or use a food processor grater assembly) with water to barely cover. Put on full throttle for about 1-2-3 OFF. Drain well and press down with paper towels to remove excess moisture.

In large nonstick skillet, place cauli-rice, coconut milk and season with salt and pepper to taste. Let it simmer slowly until it is like a rice dish. Use a slotted spoon to transfer the cauli-rice to a dinner plate. Cover with curry and top with coconut, crushed peanuts, green onions or sugar-free chutney (See Smokey Mountain Meatballs, page 120, for an easy chutney recipe made in a jiffy starting with sugar-free apricot or peach jam).

ZUCCHINI FRITTERS

These fritters are great with breakfast by themselves or topped with a fried or poached egg (instead of a muffin) for a creative eggs benedict-type dish. Or they could also be used as a side dish in another meal or snack.
(Submitted by Ivonne Carlo)

2 medium (or one large) zucchinis
2 large eggs
3 tbsp finely cut red onion, OR (45 mL)
  dehydrated red onion
1 tsp baking powder (5 mL)
$^1/_2$ tsp salt (2 mL)
$^1/_4$ tsp pepper, OR to taste (1 mL)
6-10 tbsp Gluten-Free Bake Mix, (90-150 mL)
  page 140
Coconut oil (preferable for a crispier fritter), OR butter to fry

Yield: 6 fritters
1 fritter
110.5 calories
6.1 g protein
6.7 g fat
5.3 g net carbs

Cut the ends off of the zucchinis and using a cheese grater, shred into fine pieces. Once shredded, place in a strainer and absorb any excess water with some paper towels. Apply pressure to remove as much water as possible.

In medium bowl, whip eggs. Add zucchini, onion, baking powder, salt, pepper and Gluten-Free Bake Mix 1, page 140. Mix together well while preheating coconut oil, OR butter in a frying pan. Add by spoonfuls (spoon depends on the size you want your fritters) into hot oil (medium heat) and fry on both sides until browned and crispy.

~~Bits & Bites~~
In the absence of carbohydrates the body will burn fat for energy. Therefore, limiting carbohydrates encourages your body to burn fat and helps you maintain a lower body weight.

MISCELLANEOUS

TZAZIKI

*This is a delicious Mediterranean sauce used on everything from Gyros, page 288 to dolmas (stuffed grape leaves). It's also great as a dip for vegetables. While most versions use yogurt, this one is dairy free. (Submitted by **Kelly Schumann**. Her blog is at **http://happytexans.blogspot.com/**)*

1 large cucumber, peeled, seeded, and finely chopped
1 tsp salt (5 mL)
1 cup mayonnaise (250 mL)
2 cloves garlic, crushed
1 tbsp fresh mint, finely chopped (15 mL)
1 tbsp fresh parsley, finely chopped (15 mL)
1 tbsp lemon juice (15 mL)
$^1/_4$ tsp pepper (1 mL)
$^1/_4$ tsp cayenne pepper (1 mL)

Yield: 32 servings
1 tbsp (15 mL) per serving
46.7 calories
13.8 g protein
5 g fat
0.1 g fiber
0.2 g net carbs

In colander, place chopped cucumber and sprinkle with salt. Let stand in a colander for an hour. In large bowl, combine mayonnaise, garlic, mint, parsley, lemon juice, pepper and cayenne pepper. Stir in cucumber.

~~Bits & Bites~~
Having this series of wonderful cookbooks in one's low-carb arsenal is sure to help reduce boredom with one's diet. Boredom can derail the best of intentions when one is hungry and craving something particularly tasty.

BREADS, MUFFINS AND MORE

BARBO'S ONION-RYE BREAD

*This recipe is the perfect low-carb substitute. The unique way of slicing the bread yields sandwich-size slices suitable for a Rueben sandwich. (Submitted by **Barbara (Barbo) Goldstein**. You can find more of her recipes at Barbo's Low Carb Kitchen: **http://barboslowcarbkitchen.proboards.com/index.cgi**)*

$2^1/_3$ cups unblanced almond flour (575 mL)
1 tbsp caraway seeds (15 mL)
1 tsp organic onion powder (5 mL)
$^1/_4$ tsp salt (1 mL)
$^1/_4$ cup water (60 mL)
$^1/_4$ cup peanut oil, OR light olive oil (60 mL)
3 extra large eggs
1 tbsp molasses (15 mL)
1 tbsp PLUS $^1/_4$ tsp white vinegar (16 mL)
$^3/_4$ tsp baking soda (3 mL)

Yield: 10 slices
1 slice serving
229.2 calories
7.81 g protein
20.2 g fat
4.6 g net carbs

Preheat oven to 350°F (180°C). Grease an 8 x 4 x 3-inch (1.5 L) nonstick loaf pan (if pan is old, line with parchment paper (first spray pan with nonstick cooking spray) or foil and spray with nonstick cooking spray. In food processor, combine almond flour, caraway seeds, onion powder and salt; process 30 seconds. Add the water and peanut oil. Process about 1 minute. You will have thick batter.

Add the eggs and molasses. Process well, and let batter emulsify. Give it some time and you will be able to see it become a thicker batter. You may want to stop the machine and use a spatula to come up from the bottom and stir a bit. Then proceed. Add the white vinegar and baking soda. Process about 60 seconds.

Pour into your prepared pan and bake 35 to 40 minutes. Cool on rack. When completely cool and at room temperature, turn it out and cut it in half. Next, stand the bread up and cut each half into 5 slices. You will have 10 bread-sized slices in total. Refrigerate and enjoy.

Helpful Hint: I just wanted to add that this recipe has been thoroughly tested on lowcarbfriends.com by friends over there and people raved about it! It has a dense, firm texture.

PUMPKIN SPICE NUT BREAD

*This sweet bread combines pumpkin and nuts to make a versatile low-carb substitute. (Submitted by **Char ('Charski') Cunningham**. You can find more of her recipes at: **http://lowcarb4life.proboards.com**)*

Vegetable oil spray for pan
2 tbsp gluten-free oat bran for pan (30 mL)
$2^1/_2$ cups blanched almond flour (625 mL)
1 cup granulated erythritol (250 mL)
1 tsp stevia, OR (5 mL)
 1 cup equivalent (250 mL)
$1^1/_2$ tsp baking powder (7 mL)
$1^1/_2$ tsp sugar-free pumpkin pie spice (7 mL)
1 tsp guar gum, OR (5 mL)
 xanthan gum, OR glucomannan powder
$^1/_4$ tsp sea salt (1 mL)
$^3/_4$ cup pecans, broken into small pieces (175 mL)
7 extra-large eggs
15 oz can (about $1^1/_2$ cups (375 mL) pure pumpkin (425 g)
$1^1/_2$ tsp pure vanilla extract (7 mL)

Yield: 12 slices
1 slice
243.4 calories
10.4 g protein
19.7 g fat
5.7 g net carbs

Preheat oven to 350°F (180°C). Spray a 9 x 5 x 3-inch (2 L) loaf pan heavily with cooking spray, and then line the bottom with a piece of waxed paper. Spray lightly again and sprinkle in the raw oat bran, tilting the pan to coat bottom and sides. This helps prevent sticking. In large bowl, whisk together blanched almond flour, erythritol, stevia, OR equivalent, baking powder, pumpkin pie spice, guar gum, OR xanthan gum, OR glucomannan powder and salt. Stir pecans into dry ingredients.

In large bowl, beat the eggs and then whisk in the pumpkin and vanilla. Add the dry ingredients to the wet in 3 increments, stirring just until blended each time (don't beat!). Spoon the batter into the prepared pan. Bake in preheated oven until golden brown and a toothpick comes out clean, about $1^1/_2$ hours. Let cool on rack 5 to 10 minutes, then run a table knife, dull edge towards you so as not to cut into the bread, around the edges to loosen. Invert onto cooling rack, carefully remove waxed paper if using, and allow to cool completely. Wrap in foil and stash in fridge overnight to let the flavors blend and mellow.

Helpful Hints: You can let it cool completely in the pan, but I find this makes the bottom a bit soggy. It's good served with plain cream cheese or frosted with sweetened cream cheese, butter, and vanilla. This can also be made in a Bundt pan, baked at 350°F (180°C) about 45 minutes, and as muffins, baked at 375°F (190°C) for 12 to 15 minutes (check with tooth pick before removing from oven) – it is my *most requested* baked pumpkin item, no matter what shape it takes!

MAPLE PECAN MUFFINS

*This muffin screams fall flavors. It is a light muffin with hints of cinnamon and vanilla brought together with the flavor of maple syrup. The amount of maple syrup in this recipe is about 1 tsp (5 mL) per muffin. It adds a subtle sweetness. (Submitted by **Carol Lovett**. Find more of her recipes at* ***http://ditchthewheat.com***)

Muffin:
2 large eggs, separated
2 tbsp extra-virgin coconut oil (30 mL)
1 tbsp maple syrup (15 mL)
1 tsp vanilla extract (5 mL)
$^1/_2$ tsp cinnamon (2 mL)
$^1/_8$ tsp salt (0.5 mL)
2 tbsp coconut flour, sifted (30 mL)
$^1/_4$ tsp baking powder (1 mL)
Maple Pecan Topping:
$^1/_8$ cup pecans, chopped (30 mL)
$^1/_2$ tsp maple syrup (2 mL)
$^1/_2$ tsp cinnamon (2 mL)

Yield: 3 servings
1 muffin
206.7 calories
5.6 g protein
16.7 g fat
7.1 g net carbs

Muffin: Preheat oven to 350°F (180°C). Separate the egg whites from the egg yolks and place in two mixing bowls. Whip the egg whites to stiff peaks.

In a separate bowl, mix the egg yolks with the coconut oil, maple syrup, vanilla extract, cinnamon, and salt.

Sift the coconut flour and add to the egg yolk mixture. Add the baking powder. Mix the egg yolk mixture until smooth.

Slowly add the egg yolk mixture to the egg whites. Mix until well combined.

Pour the mixture into muffin liners. Fill to the top.

Maple Pecan Topping: In a small bowl, combine the pecans, maple syrup and cinnamon. Sprinkle on the muffins.

Bake 18 minutes or until tops are firm to the touch.

FROSTED CAKE DONUTS

*These delicious donuts are light and airy. The glycerin makes them moist and the cream cheese frosting with a hint of lemon is the crowning glory. (Submitted by **Joyce Vennum**).*

6 tbsp pork rinds, (90 mL)
{approx. $^1/_2$ oz (15 g)}
$^3/_4$ cup almond flour (175 mL)
8 packets SPLENDA®
$^3/_4$ tsp baking soda (3 mL)
3 large eggs
2 tbsp pancake syrup (30 mL)
 (Da Vinci® or Walden Farms®)
2 tsp food-grade glycerin* (10 mL)
1 tsp vanilla extract (5 mL)
$^1/_4$ cup butter (60 mL)
Cream Cheese Frosting:
4 oz cream cheese, room temperature (125 g)
$^1/_4$ cup butter, room temperature (60 mL)
4 packets sweetener of choice
$^1/_2$ tsp lemon extract (2 mL)
3 tbsp heavy cream (45 mL)

Yield: 10 servings
1 serving
223.4 calories
5.4 g protein
20.8 g fat
0.4 g net carbs

Preheat oven to 350°F (180°C). Oil the donut pans.

Place the ground pork rinds in a food processor and grind into flour. Pour into a small bowl and stir in the almond flour, SPLENDA® and baking soda. In another small bowl, use a fork or wire whisk to beat together the eggs, pancake syrup, glycerin and vanilla until well blended.

In a microwave-safe bowl, melt butter in microwave on high about 30 seconds. Add half of the dry ingredients into the butter and stir until smooth, and then the other half. Stir half of the butter mixture into the egg mixture until smooth, then the other half. Equally divide the batter into 10 wells of the donut pans. Bake 8 to 10 minutes until lightly browned. Remove from pan immediately. Let cool before frosting. Keep refrigerated.

Cream Cheese Frosting: In medium bowl, beat cream cheese, butter, sweetener of choice and lemon extract with a fork until well blended. Stir in the heavy cream until smooth.

Helpful Hints: These can be baked in an electric donut maker or a mini-donut baking pan, just be sure to adjust the baking time. *Food grade glycerin can be purchased in the cake decorating aisle at most hobby/craft stores.

CREAM CHEESE DANISH

This pastry filled with cream cheese is the perfect way to start off your morning.
(Submitted by Anita Kinsella.)

$^1/_4$ cup Gluten Free Bake Mix 1, (60 mL)
  page 140
1 tsp baking powder (5 mL)
$^1/_4$ tsp xanthan gum (1 mL)
2 tbsp SPLENDA® Granular (30 mL)
2 tbsp brown sugar substitute (30 mL)
2 large eggs
$^1/_2$ cup shredded mild Cheddar, OR (125 mL)
  Mozzarella cheese
2 tbsp cooking oil (30 mL)
1 tbsp Da Vinci® Sugar Free Vanilla Syrup (15 mL)
$^1/_4$ cup chopped nuts (60 mL)
$1^1/_2$ tsp vanilla extract (7 mL)
Cream Cheese Filling:
$^1/_4$ cup cream cheese, softened (60 mL)
2 tbsp SPLENDA® Granular, OR equivalent liquid sucralose (30 mL)
1 tsp butter (5 mL)
$^1/_4$ tsp vanilla extract (1 mL)
Sliced almonds or chopped pecans (optional)
Frosting (optional):
2 tbsp powdered erythritol (30 mL)
1 tsp melted butter (5 mL)
Liquid sucralose to equal 2 tbsp SPLENDA® Granular (30 mL)

Yield: 4 large Danishes
1 Danish
222 calories
6.6 g protein
20.4 g fat
6.6 g net carbs

Preheat oven to 350°F (180°C). In medium bowl, mix together Gluten-Free Bake Mix 1, page 140, baking powder, xanthan gum, SPLENDA® Granular and brown sugar substitute. In a separate bowl, mix together eggs, Cheddar, OR Mozzarella cheese, oil, Da Vinci® Sugar Free Syrup, nuts and vanilla extract. Add the wet ingredients to the dry ingredients and combine well. Drop the batter onto a baking sheet in 4 even mounds.

Cream Cheese Filling: In small bowl, combine the cream cheese, SPLENDA® Granular, OR liquid sucralose, butter and vanilla extract. Drop a dollop of the cheese filling in the center of each Danish. Sprinkle with sliced almonds or pecans, if using. Bake 12 to 14 minutes or until light golden brown on top.

Frosting (optional): Combine powdered erythritol, melted butter and liquid sucralose, OR SPLENDA® Granular. Add the frosting to a plastic sandwich baggie, snip off the corner and squeeze lines of frosting over the top.

SWEET ENDINGS

BARBO'S PECAN PUMPKIN PIE

*We love this pie. It's so pretty with the pecans all around and in the center I make a big flower. You get the crunch and the pie is quite big, standing firm and tall. (Submitted by **Barbara (Barbo) Goldstein**. You can find more of her recipes at Barbo's Low Carb Kitchen:*
http://barboslowcarbkitchen.proboards.com/index.cgi)

29 oz can pumpkin (822 g)
Liquid sucralose to equal $1^1/_4$ cups (300 mL)
 SPLENDA® Granular
$^1/_4$ cup erythritol (60 mL)
1 cup heavy cream (250 mL)
5 extra-large eggs
$^1/_4$ cup brown sugar substitute (60 mL)
2 tbsp vanilla extract (30 mL)
2 tsp cinnamon (10 mL)
$^1/_4$ to $^1/_2$ tsp salt (1 to 2 mL)
$^1/_4$ tsp nutmeg (1 mL)
$^1/_4$ tsp cloves (1 mL)
$^1/_4$ tsp allspice (1 mL)
$^1/_4$ tsp ginger (1 mL)
$^3/_4$ cup pecans (175 mL)

Yield: 10 servings
1 serving
200.4 calories
5.2 g protein
15.8 g fat
7.8 g net carbs

Preheat oven to 350°F (180°C). Spray a large, 10-inch (25 cm) deep dish pie pan with nonstick cooking spray. In food processor, combine pumpkin, liquid sucralose, OR SPLENDA® Granular, erythritol, heavy cream, eggs, brown sugar substitute, vanilla extract, cinnamon, salt, nutmeg, cloves, allspice and ginger. Process until smooth.

Pour into prepared pie pan. Place pie pan in large roaster pan with 4 cups (1 L) of hot water. Bake 30 minutes. Remove and garnish pie with pecans. Bake another 30 minutes or until a knife inserted in center comes out clean. Remove to rack to cool completely. If desired, garnish the top with freshly ground cinnamon. Chill thoroughly and serve with whipped cream.

Helpful Hints: This pie slices very well, but make sure it is thoroughly chilled. You will not miss the crust as the pecans provide the "crunch".

LOW-CARB DECADENT MOCHA CHEESECAKE

"Decadent" doesn't begin to describe this recipe. It's full-blown sinful! But!
The great part is that it has no sugar alcohols, so the carb count you see is real!
I have to limit this recipe to twice a year – my hubby's birthday and Christmas;
otherwise, I am sure we'd eat it three times a day, every day. (Submitted by
Georgene Harkness.) *Her website is* ***http://georgeneharkness.com/***.

Crust:
2 cups pecans (500 mL)
1 tbsp SPLENDA® Granular (15 mL)
1 tbsp cocoa powder (15 mL)
3 tbsp butter, melted (45 mL)
Filling:
16 oz regular cream cheese, softened (500 g)
1 cup heavy cream (250 mL)
1 cup SPLENDA® Granular (250 mL)
1 tbsp freeze-dried coffee crystals (15 mL)
1 tsp vanilla extract (5 mL)
3 eggs
8 oz unsweetened baking chocolate (250 g)
$^1/_4$ cup butter (60 mL)
Topping:
12 oz sour cream (375 g)
3 tbsp SPLENDA® Granular (45 mL)
1 tsp vanilla extract (5 mL)

Yield: 16 servings
1 serving
400 calories
7 g protein
39.9 g fat
6 g net carbs

Crust: Preheat oven to 350°F (180°C). In bowl of food processor, combine pecans, SPLENDA® Granular, cocoa and butter. Process until pecans are finely chopped and all ingredients are combined (this will be somewhat wet). Press mixture into bottom of 10-inch (25 cm) pie pan (using plastic wrap to cover nut mixture will keep it from sticking to your fingers). Set aside.

Filling: In same bowl of food processor (no need to clean the bowl), combine cream cheese, cream, SPLENDA® Granular, coffee crystals, vanilla and 1 egg. Process until well blended, scraping down bowl. Add the next two eggs one at a time, scraping down the bowl. In microwave-safe bowl, combine chocolate and butter. Heat in microwave at medium power until melted. Add mixture to food processor. Process 1 minute. Taste and adjust sweetness. Pour mixture into pie pan, spreading evenly. Bake in preheated oven 1 hour, checking carefully after 50 minutes. Do not allow top to burn.

Topping: In medium bowl, mix sour cream, SPLENDA® Granular and vanilla. Spread over cheesecake, making sure to cover completely to crust. Return cheesecake to the oven for 5 minutes. Remove, cool, and chill overnight.

MOCK RICE PUDDING

This is my good friend Nancy's recipe and it's a favorite in our house. I usually double the recipe and make it in a larger casserole dish. (Submitted by Linda Sue Genaw. Find this recipe with a picture at http://www.genaw.com/lowcarb/mock_rice_pudding.html)

3 eggs
1 cup heavy cream (250 mL)
$^3/_4$ cup SPLENDA® Granular, (175 mL)
 OR equivalent liquid sucralose
2 tsp vanilla extract (10 mL)
$^1/_2$ tsp blackstrap molasses, optional (2 mL)
$^1/_2$ tsp cinnamon (2 mL)
1 cup full-fat cottage cheese (250 mL)

Yield: 4 servings
1 serving
340 calories
12 g protein
28 g fat
9 g net carbs

In a medium bowl, whisk together well eggs, cream, SPLENDA® Granular, OR liquid sucralose equivalent, vanilla extract, blackstrap molasses and cinnamon. Stir in cottage cheese. Pour into greased $1^1/_2$-quart ($1^1/_2$ L) casserole dish and bake at 350°F (180°C) 60 to 75 minutes until top is nicely browned and a knife inserted into the center comes out clean. Gently stir the mixture after 40 minutes of cooking so that the cottage cheese does not settle on the bottom. Serve warm or cold.

Helpful Hints: I do recommend gently stirring the outside cooked parts into the center about halfway through the baking time. You may need to add 5 to 10 minutes to the baking time. I like this best cold but it's still very nice warm.

~~Bits & Bites~~
Caffeine in large amounts can stimulate the release of insulin, give a temporary lift in energy followed by hunger, fatigue and slower weight loss for some folks. Other folks, however, can handle caffeine in moderate amounts and still lose weight quite easily.

CATHY'S RASPBERRY ICE CREAM

*I saw this recipe made on TV with regular sugar and strawberries and it looked so good and so easy, I just had to low-carb it! (Submitted by **Cathy Lawrence**.)*

12 oz raspberries (375 g)
$^1/_4$ cup SPLENDA® Granular (60 mL)
$^1/_4$ cup white Diabetisweet® (60 mL)
$^1/_4$ cup erythritol (60 mL)
1 tsp fresh lemon juice (5 mL)
1 tsp fresh lemon zest (5 mL)
$^1/_4$ tsp Lorann® raspberry oil (1 mL)
$^1/_8$ tsp salt (0.5 mL)
1 cup half and half (250 mL)
1 cup heavy cream (250 mL)
$1^1/_2$ tbsp food-grade glycerin (22 mL)

Yield: 6 servings
1 serving
237.1 calories
2.7 g protein
22.3 g fat
7.1 g net carbs

In medium bowl, mash the raspberries with SPLENDA® Granular, Diabetisweet®, erythritol, lemon juice, lemon zest, raspberry oil and salt. Let sit 10 to 15 minutes.

In food processor, put half of raspberry mixture and process with the half and half and cream until smooth. Return this mixture to bowl with remaining mashed raspberries. Mix together and add glycerin; mix again. Put into a covered container in refrigerator 4 to 6 hours or overnight.

Process in an ice cream machine. Soft serve and ready to eat right away or put into containers and freeze. This ice cream *does remain scoopable* and is delicious!

~~Bits & Bites~~
To maintain a significant weight loss, it will be necessary to exercise. Many people who have lost significant weight, keep it off by running or walking significant distances regularly.

INDEX

A

ALMOND BUTTER CR CHS FROST 151
ALMOND BUTTER CUPS 154
ALMOND CHOCOLATE BUNDT CAKE 156
ALMOND CRUST 229
ALMOND CRUST 241
ALMOND FLOUR FRENCH TOAST 199
ALMOND JOY TART 229
ALMOND PARM ZUCCHINI CRISPS 167
ALMOND PIE CRUST 90
ALMOND SESAME CRACKERS 139
ANY FLAVOR SAUCE/FROSTING 131
ASIAN DIPPING SAUCE 257
ASIAN LETTUCE WRAPS 183
ASIAN MARINADE 188
ASPARAGUS RIBBONS PARM VINAI 71
AVOCADO FETA SALSA 186
AVOCADO FRIES 83
AWESOME BROCCOLI CASSEROLE 46

APPETIZERS & BEVERAGES
APPETIZERS
CHIPS
GARLIC AND HERB NUT THINS 192
KALE CHIPS 65
PARMESAN ALMOND CHIPS 66
DIPS
AVOCADO FETA SALSA 186
CAPER & ARTICHOKE TARTAR 187
CARAMELIZED ONION BACON 166
CHORIZO QUESO DIP 162
GUACAMOLE CON ZUCCHINI 277
HOT SHRIMP & ARTICHOKE DIP 161
PEANUT BUTTER COOKIE DOUGH 97
ROASTED ONION BAC JALAPENO 275
ROASTED RED PEPPER AIOLI 187
ROASTED RED PEPPR SPIN ARTICH 163
TZAZIKI 296
MISCELLANEOUS
CHIPOTLE LIME COCKTAIL NUTS 191
BAVARIAN CHEESE SPREAD 276
BEDIVILED EGGS 21
HOT VOCADO 22
PECAN CHEESE RING 98

MEAT
BUFFALO BLUE CHICK MEATBALLS 164
CHICKEN LIVER PATE 63
COCKTAIL FRANKS 247
SESAME HAM ROLL 98
SRIRACHA HOT WINGS 190
SEAFOOD
CAJUN TRINITY CRAB CAKES 165
CRAB CAKES 277
JALAPENO SHRIMP CEVICHE 274
SMOKED SALMON AND WASABI 191
VEGGIES
ALMOND PARM ZUCCHINI CRISPS 167
AVOCADO FRIES 83
EGGPLANT BRUSCHETTA 99
FRIED PICKLES 20
HAZELNUT BRUSCHETTA 246
HERB ROASTED OLIVES 62
JALAPENO SHRIMP CEVICHE 274
STUFFED MUSHROOMS 67
BEVERAGES
CAROLYN'S LOW-CARB MILK 278
CHAR'S MOCHACCINO FRAPPE 278
CINNAMON TEA 100
CRANBERRY MARGARITA 249
LIME RICKY 68
LIMEADE 67
MATCHA GREEN TEA SMOOTHIE 192
MOCHA COFFEE COOLER 248
ROSE LASSI 69
SALTY LASSI WITH MINT 70
SPARKLING CRANBERRY JUICE 249
STRAWBERRY LIMEADE 100

B

BACON DONUTS 26
BACON LEEK SOUFFLE 78
BACON, GRUYERE & MUSHROOM 196
BACON-WRAPPED CHICKEN 27
BAKED ALM PARMESAN SWAI 116
BAKED CHICKEN WITH TOPPING 115
BAKED FENNEL IN CREAM 84
BANANA FLIP 58
BANANA NUT BREAD 52
BARBECUE BAKE 39
BARBECUE SAUCE 121
BARBO'S ONION-RYE BREAD 297
BARBO'S PECAN PUMPKIN PIE 302
BASIC ALMOND FLOUR BREAD 216

BREADS, MUFFINS & MORE

BAKE MIXES

BISCUITS

BREADS (SAVORY)

BREADS (SWEET)

CRACKERS

DONUTS

MISCELLANEOUS

MUFFINS & COFFEE CAKE

SCONES

TORTILLAS

BREAKFASTS

BACON

BREADS

CEREALS

CREPES AND PANCAKES

EGGS

Index

CRANBERRY RAISINS 128
CRANBERRY SAUCE 247
CRANBERRY UPSIDE DOWN CAKE 245
CREAM CHEESE DANISH 301
CREAM CHEESE DRESSING 279
CREAM CHEESE DRIZZLE 133
CREAM CHEESE FROSTING 300
CREAMY ITALIAN DRESSING 127
CREAMY STRAWBERRY PIE 94
CREAMY WHITE FREEZER FUDGE 160
CRÈME FRAICHE 132
CREPES WITH PEACH CUSTARD 111
CRISP-BRAISED DUCK LEGS 81
CRUMB TOPPING 146
CRUMB TOPPING 220
CRUNCHY TURKEY MEATBALLS 257

D

DAIRY-FREE ALM CREAM CHEESE 264
DAIRY-FREE CR CHS FROSTING 271
DAIRY-FREE FRIDGE FUDGE 272
DAIRY-FREE RANCH DRESSING 266
DAIRY-FREE SOUR CREAM 266
DAIRY-FREE WHIPPED CREAM 263
DARK CHOC MINI COCONUT CUPS 269
DEATH BY DARK CHOC PUDDING 270
DECADENT COCOA BROWNIES 155
DENVER MUFFINS 25
DEVONSHIRE CREAM & STRAWBER 92
DIJON THYME PORK CHOPS 289
DOUBLE CHOC ZUCCHINI MUFFIN 267

E

EARL GREY PANNA COTTA 242
EASY BREAKFAST BISCUIT 268
EGGPLANT BAKE 294
EGGPLANT BRUSCHETTA 99
EGGPLANT, TOMATO & ONION 126
EGG-TILLAS 282

F

FALL PUMPKIN SOUP 106
FAUX POTATO AND ONION SOUP 104
FENNEL WALNUT CHICKEN SALAD 193
FLAX BREAD 51
FRENCH OMELET 109

FRIED PICKLES 20
FROSTED CAKE DONUTS 300
FROZEN CAPPUCCINO MOUSSE 240
FROZEN CHOC ECSTASY CHSCK 152
FRUIT COCKTAIL CHEESECAKE 150
FUDGEY PRUNE CHIP SPICE BARS 159

G

GARAM MASALA 89
GARLIC AND HERB NUT THINS 192
GARLIC MASHED FAUXTATOES 262
GHEE 265
GINGER WALNUT PEAR MUFFINS 221
GINGERBREAD MEN COOKIES 271
GOLDEN FLAX WALNUT MUFFINS 219
GRAHAM CRACKER-LIKE CRUST 152
GRANOLA AND GRANOLA BARS 108
GRASSHOPPER BARS 231
GREEK SALAD 169
GREEK SHRIMP FETA, CAULI-RIC 208
GREEN CHILI SAUCE 201
GUACAMOLE CON ZUCCHINI 277
GYROS 288

H

HALIBUT SUPREME 180
HAZELNUT BRUSCHETTA 246
HAZELNUT CHOC BUNDT CAKE 156
HERB ROASTED OLIVES 62
HERBED PORK TENDERLOIN 292
HOLUBETS CABBAGE ROLLS 43
HOMEMADE CHOC HAZELNUT SPR 214
HONEY MUSTARD CHICKEN 32
HONEY MUSTARD SALAD DRESS 47
HONEY ROASTED BBQ SAUCE 119
HOT SHRIMP & ARTICHOKE DIP 161
HOT VOCADO 22

I

ITALIAN CHOPPED SALAD 169
ITALIAN MEATBALLS 177

J

JALAPENO & CHEDDAR HAMBURG 207
JALAPENO SHRIMP CEVICHE 274

Index

MAIN COURSES AND SIDES
MAIN COURSES

BEEF

BARBECUE BAKE 39
BIG MAC PIE 32
BEEF STROGANOFF PATTIES 178
BUFFALO CRACK SLAW 34
CHILI RUBBED STEAKS 202
HOLUBETS CABBAGE ROLLS 43
ITALIAN MEATBALLS 177
JALAPENO & CHEDDAR HAMBURG 207
LIVER AND ONIONS IN GRAVY 287
PHILLY CHS STEAK-STUF PEPPERS 290
PIZZA BURGER 29
PIZZA QUICHE 35
REUBEN CASSEROLE 37
SHEPHERD'S PIE 204
SLOPPY JOE STUFFED RED PEPPERS 82
SLOW COOKER FAJITAS 285
SMOKEY MOUNTAIN MEATBALLS 120
ZUCCHINI LASAGNA 286

FISH & SHELLFISH

BAKED ALM PARMESAN SWAI 116
CADDY GANTY 80
GREEK SHRIMP FETA, CAULI-RIC 208
HALIBUT SUPREME 180
OVEN-BAKED SALMON 258
SEA BASS IN GARLIC BUTTER 114
SOUR CR SMOTHERED CHICKEN 181
TUNA CAKES 41
TUNA GREEN BEAN CASSEROLE 184
SPICY SHRIMP 121

LAMB

GYROS 288
SHEPHERD'S PIE 204
SKILLET LAMB, CABBAGE, TOM 256

MISCELLANEOUS

MUSHROOM SPINACH TORTA 209
MUSHROOM STROGANOFF 293
PASTA CARBONARA 30

PORK

COFFEE-SPICED TENDERLOIN 206

Index

Index

*FOR AN ONLINE SEARCHABLE INDEX, GO TO AMONGFRIENDS.US AND CHOOSE THE ADDENDUM BUTTON.